D0789720

,E

the sex revolts

the sex revolts

gender, rebellion, and rock'n'roll

DISCARD

Simon Reynolds and Joy Press

Harvard University Press
Cambridge, Massachusetts

Copyright © 1995 by Joy Press and Simon Reynolds
All rights reserved
Printed in the United States of America
First published in the United Kingdom in 1994 by Serpent's Tail.
Second printing, 1996

First Harvard University Press paperback edition, 1996

Library of Congress Cataloging-in-Publication Data

Reynolds, Simon, 1963–
The sex revolts : gender, rebellion, and rock 'n' roll / by Simon
Reynolds and Joy Press
p. cm.
Includes bibliographical references and index.
ISBN 0-674-80272-1 (cloth)
ISBN 0-674-80273-X (pbk.)
1. Feminism and music. 2. Rock music—History and criticism.
3. Women rock musicians. 4. Music and society. I. Press, Joy,
1966– . II. Title.
ML82.R53 1995
781.66′082—dc20   94-30683
MN

To our parents

contents

acknowledgements

We'd like to thank the following people who were willing to raid their shelves for records or old articles, traded ideas, brainstormed over titles, dispensed practical advice, or read early versions of this book: Simon Frith, Jon Savage, Michael Krumper, Craig Marks, Dana Gross, Sue Patel, David Stubbs, Dana Dickey, Mark Sinker, Mike McGonigal, Susan Masters, Barney Hoskyns, Mat Smith, Keith Riches, Mike Rubin, Lisa Mendelsund, Jon Selzer, Pat Blashill, Jones, Erik Davis, Ian Penman, Caren Myers, Jessica Maynard, Burhan Tufail, Dominica D'Arcangelo, Alyssa Katz. Thanks also to Pete Ayrton, Tony Peake, Ira Silverberg, Lindsay Waters and Alison Kent.

introduction

When we started working on this project, we knew there was a book to be written, but we weren't sure exactly what it was. Telling people about our subject – gender and rock – elicited such intense and diverse responses we were even more convinced and confused. It was as though we'd confronted our friends with a Rorschach inkblot: everyone saw something different. Some women proffered examples of songs that they loved, but whose lyrics unsettled them; many men tended to assume that this was to be a book about that old chestnut, 'women in rock' (as if male artists were somehow exempt from the category of 'gender'). Others were defensive or even derisive at the mere mention of the word 'misogyny'.

Clearly, everyone felt that something was *at stake* in an investigation of rock'n'roll 'through the lens of gender'. Rock offers an imaginative space in which you can reaffirm your sexual identity, or stretch and sometimes escape its limits altogether. Suzanne Moore calls this imaginative activity 'gender tourism'. This might mean venturing where the grass seems greener, taking a walk on the wild side, enjoying a cheap holiday in other people's misery, or simply leaving your everyday self behind. Shy women can glimpse ferocity in the Stones or Sex Pistols; emotionally armoured men can toy with androgyny, while male wimps can 'play soldiers', taking vicarious pleasure in warrior masculinity or megalomaniac fantasies.

The Sex Revolts began as a critique of misogyny in rock, gradually evolved into a survey of images of femininity in the rock imagination, and finally solidified in its present state: a kind of psychoanalysis of rebellion (male and female). In the first section, Rebel Misogynies, we explore ways in which the male rebel has dramatised himself *against* the 'feminine'. These include the born-to-run impulse (Rolling Stones, Iggy Pop), the soldier or warrior who takes refuge in the camaraderie of brotherhood-in-arms (the Clash, Public Enemy), and self-aggrandising fantasies of man-machine omnipotence (heavy metal, techno) and of kingship (the Doors, Nick Cave, gangsta rap).

The second section, Into the Mystic, examines idealised images of women and femininity in male rock – the endless expressions of a longing to *come home*, to return to the womb, that often take the form of cosmic/oceanic mysticism or worship of Mother Nature. This tradition – the psyche-delic mother's boy – includes the Byrds, Van Morrison, Pink Floyd, Can, Brian Eno, My Bloody Valentine, et al.

In the third section, Lift Up Your Skirt and Speak, we trace some of the ways in which female artists have struggled to imagine and create a specifically female rebel-lion. Since this involves defining themselves against conventional notions of femininity, female rebels find themselves grappling with slippery contradictions. We concentrate on the strategies that seem most telling: masquer-ade/mystique (Kate Bush, Siouxsie, Annie Lennox, Grace Jones), demystification of conventional femininity (Slits, Raincoats, Riot Grrrl), the tomboyish mimicry of male rebellion (Joan Jett, L7), the 'confessional' mode (Janis Joplin, Lydia Lunch, Hole), and artists who embrace con-tradiction and revel in flux (Patti Smith, Throwing Muses, Mary Margaret O'Hara).

Why have we so starkly separated the men from the women, and the 'real men' from the mother's boys? Because it seemed the best way to bring out the patterns and con-nections that stretch across different eras. When it comes to gender difference, we share Gilles Deleuze and Felix

Guattari's suspicious but pragmatic attitude towards 'all the dualisms that are the enemy, an entirely necessary enemy, the furniture we are forever rearranging'. From dualism to duo-ism. . . the intrinsic problems involved in two people writing as a single voice. Our male-female partnership has been both an advantage and a constraint; we've been able to correct each other's biases and blindspots, but we've also found it difficult to write directly about our individually gendered experience. At times, we've been tempted to shatter this neuter, univocal 'we' and open the text up to internal dissension. (We even toyed with using two type-faces, but ultimately shied away from this gambit as Derrida-esque whimsy.)

Because we leapfrog across time and space to sketch major threads, themes, lineages, traits, metaphors and obsessions, this book is necessarily far from comprehensive. We ignore many major figures, and spotlight some marginal artists, because they take certain tendencies to the furthest limit, and so reveal more. Earlier books about 'gender and rock' mostly concerned themselves with women's struggle against chauvinism in the music industry or with the more routine forms of sexism (as in heavy metal and gangsta rap). These blatant kinds of misogyny are, we feel, self-explanatory, so we've focused instead on what isn't so obvious: the misogynist subtext, the secret complicity in patriarchal values, that often lurks beneath the apparently subversive and libertarian. We're intrigued by the way that what sounds and feels like 'freedom' – the music of the Rolling Stones, the Stooges, Sex Pistols, for instance – can conceal the seeds of domination.

Iggy Pop once said of the women in his life: 'However close they come I'll always pull the rug from under them. That's where my music is made.' This is rock'n'roll *in excelsis*; this male ferocity, resentment, virulence, is the ESSENCE. Part of our goal in writing this book was to discover whether it's possible to imagine a rock'n'roll that *isn't* fuelled by this violent fervour to cut loose.

The Sex Revolts is not an attempt to bring these rock

rebels up before the sexual politics tribunal – it's more like an interrogation than a trial. For what it's worth, nearly all of the artists covered in the book are ones we like. Some of the 'worst offenders' – the Stones, the Stooges, Nick Cave, etc. – are among our all-time favourites. Our argument is simply that these artists' very exhilaration is inseparable from their entrenchment in 'unsound' gender politics. What makes these rebels so powerful is the psycho-sexual dynamic of breaking away.

Of course it is possible to get off on rock's energies without 'agreeing' with its anti-women impetus or even being consciously aware of it. For years, women have managed to find release in what – in the cold, dispassionate light of analysis – would seem clearly oppressive to them (e.g. Led Zeppelin, Guns N'Roses). It's a bit like being thrilled by a missile's flight while ignoring both its fuel (misogyny) and its target (you!). Or gasping at the Pyramids and blithely forgetting the immense suffering of the slaves who erected them.

If you choose to venture along the path of critical awareness, though, and start to dissect rock's psychosexual underpinnings, you quickly arrive in an interesting interzone of double allegiances – torn between the conflicting criteria of rock fandom and feminism, aesthetics and ethics. Ellen Willis captured this ambivalence in her essay 'Beginning to See the Light', in which she grappled with the apparent paradox that she, as a feminist, could be far more excited by the Sex Pistols' anti-abortion tirade 'Bodies' than by the wholesome positivity of most 'women's music'. 'Music that boldly and aggressively laid out what the singer wanted, loved, hated – as good rock-and-roll did – challenged me to do the same, and so, even when the content was antiwoman, antisexual, in a sense antihuman, the form encouraged my struggle for liberation. Similarly, timid music made me feel timid, whatever its ostensible politics.'

This paradox informed our thinking from the start, even before we opened Willis's book to find it spelled out so succinctly. And we certainly haven't resolved the aesthetics v. ethics, rapture v. responsibility dilemma, just consented to an uneasy truce. At times, we wondered whether we'd ever be able to listen innocently to the Stones or the Stooges again. While it hasn't interfered with our pleasure, we do notice that our easy sense of abandon is ever so slightly checked, our listening shadowed by what we've unearthed. Don't say we didn't warn you.

rebel misogynies

angry young men:
precursors and prototypes for rock rebellion

*'One is still bound to the mother. All one's rebellion was but dust
in the eye, the frantic attempt to conceal this bondage....."Forever
outside! Sitting on the doorstep of the mother's womb."'*
Henry Miller (on Arthur Rimbaud)

Rebels come in all shapes and sizes. Some are goaded into
revolt by the constraints of their specific social environment. There are the perennial rebels without cause (like
Marlon Brando's biker in *The Wild One*, who, when asked
what he was rebelling against, retorted 'what have you
got?'). And there are rebels who look for causes to validate
their insurrectionary temperament. What, if anything,
unites these boys, these men? Precisely their masculinity.

That is, after all, what springs to mind when we think of
The Rebel. Our argument is that, whatever the ostensible
pretext or context, a large part of the psychological impetus
of any rebellion is an urge to separate from the mother.
Male rebellion is a re-enactment of the primal break that
constitutes the male ego: the separation of infant from the
maternal realm, the exile from paradise. The rebel re-
enacts the process of individuation in endless and diverse
rites of severance, continually flees domesticity. Inevitably,
this flight is alloyed with regret, and often – as in the
music of the Rolling Stones and Jimi Hendrix – leads on to
a quest for a new home; unrest subsides and comes to re-
berth in a mystical or idealised maternal idyll. As
Nietzsche put it: 'to build a new sanctuary the old sanctu-

ary must be first destroyed.'

So the rebel may simultaneously worship an abstract femininity (a home away from home) while ferociously despising and fearing real-life women. He can long for the womb and for an idealised mother-lover, while shunning or abusing the flesh-and-blood women in his vicinity. In the rebel imagination, women figure as both victims and agents of castrating conformity. Women represent everything the rebel is not (passivity, inhibition) and everything that threatens to shackle him (domesticity, social norms). This ambivalence towards the feminine domain is the defining mark of all the classic instances of rock rebellion, from the Stones through the Doors, Led Zeppelin, the Stooges, to the Sex Pistols, Guns N'Roses and Nirvana.

Jean-Paul Sartre's distinction between the rebel and the revolutionary is useful here. For him, the rebel is secretly complicit with the Order he revolts against. His goal is not to create a new and better system; he only wants to break the rules. In contrast the revolutionary is constructive, aims to replace an unfair system with a new, better system, and is therefore self-disciplined and self-sacrificing. Because of his irresponsibility, the rebel has access to the ecstasy of dissipation and living in the now; the revolutionary enjoys the satisfaction of merging his identity with the collective, long-term project of improvement whose fulfilment lies in the future. We take it as read that rock is not a revolutionary art, that its insubordination and ego tantrums are complicit with or bound within the terms of capitalism and patriarchy.

For the most part, the rebel's main grievance is that a particular patriarchal system doesn't let his virility flourish freely, but instead offers a life of mediocrity. He languishes as a cog in the machine, while dreaming of a life fit for heroes. Meanwhile, women have been left stranded between the status quo of patriarchy, and the alternative *filiarchy* of the rebels, the rock'n'roll brotherhood of Prodigal Sons. Here, too often women's only scope for self-fulfilment is as the muse, moll, and groupie: hangers-on admiringly watching the male rebels' derring-do.

'We are victims of a matriarchy here, my friends.'
Harding, psychiatric ward inmate in Ken Kesey's *One Flew Over the Cuckoo's Nest* (1962)

Rock'n'roll rebellion emerged at roughly the same time as post-war 'mom-ism', a fashionable critique which singled out the mother as the cause of a hefty proportion of America's ills. The term 'mom-ism' was coined by Philip Wylie in *Generation of Vipers* (1942), a virulently misogynistic tirade against the degeneration of American culture at the hands of 'the destroying mother'. Wylie argued that America was being engulfed by materialism and shallow popular culture, which he associated with women. Soap opera, fashion, TV, radio, sentimental pop songs, Hollywood, department stores: these 'degraded' forms of mass culture, designed to appeal to feminine sensibilities, were undermining the virility of American culture. 'The radio is mom's final tool, for it stamps everyone who listens with the matriarchal brand,' ranted Wylie apocalyptically (a few years later, he would have said 'the television'). Wylie railed against the mass media's tyranny of 'matriarchal sentimentality, goo, slop, hidden cruelty', seeing in it 'the foreshadow of national death'.

Analysing Wylie's rabid discourse, Jacqueline Rose notes how 'the dangers of femininity and the dangers of mass culture stand in the most intimate and isomorphic relationship to each other'. This association of popular culture with women was standard fare in criticism in the '40s and '50s, as in Dwight MacDonald's 1953 essay 'A Theory of Mass Culture', which claimed that 'staying power is the essential virtue of one who would hold his own against the spreading ooze of Mass Culture'. Ironically, such gender-based snobbery reappeared later *within* pop culture, in the form of the rock v. pop distinction. Here the correct response (male connoisseurship, discerning and discriminating) is opposed to degraded feminine fan-worship (superficial, hysterical, idolatrous, at once fickle and blindly loyal). The negative association of femininity and popular culture has a long history. Andreas Huyssen traces it back to Flaubert's *Madame Bovary*, in which one of the fathers of modernism ('an aesthetic based on the uncompromising repudiation of what Emma Bovary loved to read') presented an unflattering portrait of a woman addled by Romantic fiction. The reflex endures. Public Enemy's 'She Watch Channel Zero' (from 1988's *It Takes A Nation of Millions to Hold Us Back*) blames black mothers for gawping at soaps and counselling shows like Oprah Winfrey and neglecting their duty (rearing strong black warriors). On the title track of his 1993 album *Home Invasion*, gangsta rapper Ice T's animosity towards White America is aimed specifically at 'yo moms!' (perhaps because of the matronly public image of the rock censorship lobby PMRC). The threat that Ice wields with such relish is his influence on white kids, who grow up wanting to be black and street-wise and to throw off the stultifying thrall of mom's white-bread values.

In post-war America, fear of mom-ism linked up with anxieties about Communism and the democratisation of culture. Like the cod-Freudianism from which it was ultimately derived, anti-momism filtered down into popular culture itself: it became a way of attributing blame for the bland conformism of '50s America. Wives and mothers were administrators (rather than, as would seem to be obvious, the principal victims) of domesticity, enslaving their husbands in the 9 to 5 regime of breadwinning. Mothers were also to blame for delinquency and crime because they brought up their sons badly, smothered them with love. In a curious double bind, women were regarded both as architects of the conventional life (with all its limits and shackles on male wildness), and as its most visibly crushed victims: both castrators and castrated.

This sub-Freudian analysis percolated throughout mass culture in the '50s and '60s, via movies like *How to Murder Your Wife* and *Psycho*. In the latter, Norman Bates – having murdered his mother when she threatened to shatter their near-incestuous intimacy by remarrying – interiorises her personality out of guilt. This phantom-Mom is similarly jealous whenever Norman finds a woman attractive, and each time forces Norman to eliminate her rival. More relevant to rock'n'roll is the rampant anti-momism of *Rebel Without a Cause*. Right at the start, in a scene in which the drunk and disorderly Dean has a heart-to-heart with a sympathetic police officer, the film establishes that the teenager's delinquency is caused by a domineering mother and a weak father. In fact, Dean's home has *two* castrating mothers (his maternal grandmother lives with them). Dean wails: 'They eat [Dad] alive. . . they make mush out of him, just mush', adding 'if he had the guts to knock Mum cold once, then she'd be happy and stop picking on him'. His character's agony is the absence of a strong paternal/masculine principle with which to identify, leaving him vulnerable to the monstrous regiment of womankind.

John Osborne's *Look Back in Anger* had a role similar to *Rebel Without a Cause* for a generation of malcontents in Britain. On the surface, the play is a vitriolic response to Britain's post-Imperial decline, to the inertia of the '50s, in which the reconstruction hopes born during the Second World War turned sour and a Conservative government attempted to patch up an inglorious version of the pre-war social order. This was how the play was received by admirers and detractors alike. But *Look Back in Anger*'s real psychosexual subtext is strikingly close to *Rebel Without a Cause*: the absence of a strong patriarchal principle with which to identify, the anguish of young men in a world of derelict, impotent fathers, and above all a venomous fear and loathing of females, representatives of an all-pervading mediocrity.

The play's anti-hero, Jimmy Porter, lost his father when

he was young. (In real life, Osborne's beloved father died when he was ten years old, leaving him prey to a detested, domineering mother.) Porter's virulent monologues are directed at his impassive, upper-class wife Alison, who cowers stoically behind her ironing board. Jimmy likes Alison's father, empathising with this desiccated relic of Britain's imperial glory, who, like the socialist Jimmy, has no role in the post-war order. Alison's mother, however, is a terrifying matron, a threatening incarnation of social snobbery, petty materialism and prudish propriety. Alison and her mother merge as a phantasmic threat to Jimmy's masculinity. One of the most striking passages in *Look Back in Anger* has Jimmy imagining being sucked into Alison's entropic womb: 'Me, buried alive down there, and going mad, smothered in that peaceful coil. . . She'll go on sleeping and devouring until there's nothing left of me.'

Porter is suffering from demobilisation blues. He dreams of a 'burning virility of mind and spirit', but is smothered in the damp claustrophobia of cold war England. Jimmy Porter's angst is that there's no channel for his manhood, no scope for heroism; he's literally a rebel without a (political) cause. All the energies galvanised by the war have petered out, the idealism of the immediate post-war period (with its massive shift towards the Left) has curdled. Porter's rage has nowhere to go. His marriage to Alison (against her family's strenuous resistance) was a last gasp, a kind of guerrilla attack against the upper class who had conspired to stay in power. But Porter's is an empty victory. Mired in low-rent domesticity, all he can do is fester in his own bile. Abusing his wife is the only way he can feel like a man, the only terrain left for his class warfare.

The rebel discourse of the '50s is haunted by the figure of the matriarch as the chief organiser of conformism and mediocrity. Poet Ted Hughes described the mainstream English literary tradition as a 'suffocating maternal octopus'. Alice Jardine has identified a matricidal tradition of twentieth-century American writers like Norman Mailer,

Henry Miller and William Burroughs, in whose work the mother figures as an 'almost always evil, cancerous, viscous, chaotic, uncontrollable, essentially monstrous phallic power'. Particularly in Burroughs's fiction, adds Robin Lydenberg, 'the mother, as defined by conventional notions of sexual difference and family structure, is a necessary instrument in a larger system of patriarchal power which seeks to dominate the individual from his earliest moment of life.'

Rock in the '60s was founded on just such an opposition between rebel masculinity and Woman as conformism incarnate. Rebellious women found themselves caught in a double bind, as Ellen Willis noted in an essay on Bob Dylan: 'At the time I did not question the idea that women were guardians of the oppressive conventional values: I only thought of myself as an exception. I was not possessive; I understood men's need to go on the road because I was, spiritually speaking, on the road myself. That, at least, was my fantasy; the realities of my life were somewhat more ambiguous.'

Jack Kerouac's *On the Road* (1957) – arguably the seminal text for rock rebellion – propounds a very gender-specific quest for self-discovery. The story concerns two young men, Dean Moriarty and Sal Paradise (based on Neal Cassady and Kerouac himself) who embark on a spiritual odyssey that, while dependent on female support and funding, pushes women to the margins of the text. It is women (in particular Sal's aunt) who continually subsidise their wanderings. On one of their jaunts, they pick up a hitchhiker who promises to repay them by borrowing money off his aunt. 'Yes!' yells Moriarty gleefully, 'we've all got aunts.' Then there is the long line of long-suffering girlfriends, like Galatea, who foots the bill for one adventure with her savings. When she runs out of cash, they give her the slip. There's a huge disproportion between the amount of quoted speech uttered by men and by women in *On the Road*. Women are a sort of vaporous presence in the background. They prepare meals, sew socks, listen respectfully, and are usually quoted verbatim (rather than in reported speech) only when protesting or bitching. The beatniks combined this cavalier attitude to womankind with a mystical longing to fuse with some kind of cosmic Natural Essence. (Kerouac is said to have once made a hole in the ground and fucked it in an attempt to have congress with Mother Earth.) If the beatniks abandoned any domestic set-up as soon as it got too comfy, it was because they were searching for some grander kind of home, a blissful merger with an Eternal Feminine. The holy grail they searched for was *satori*, which Norman O. Brown defines as 'the experience of the unborn'. As Kerouac wrote: 'The only thing that we yearn for in our living days, that makes us sigh and groan and undergo sweet nauseas of all kinds, is the remembrance of some lost bliss that was probably experienced in the womb and can only be reproduced (though we hate to admit it) in death.'

In a standard misogynist sleight of attitude (later typical of hippie rock), Dean Moriarty can profess to worship Woman while actually treating the real women in his life like shit. He digs all the 'gone chicks' – 'oh, I love, love, love women! I think women are wonderful!' – while abandoning his lovers as soon as he gets restless. When he leaves Camille with one kid and another on the way in order to go off on another adventure with Paradise, neither man can understand why she gets so darn upset.

But Kerouac's alter ego (and doubtless Kerouac himself) can't totally escape the reproaches of his conscience. Later in the novel, down-and-out and so hungry he's having visions, Sal hallucinates a woman in the street as his mother and himself as the prodigal son 'returning from gaol to haunt her honest labors in the hashery. . . "No" that woman seemed to say with that terrified glance, "don't come back and plague your honest, hard-working mother. You are no longer a son to me."' Shortly after this terrifying vision, Paradise has an experience of nirvana: '[I] flew into the holy void of uncreated emptiness, the potent and inconceivable radiancies shining in bright Mind Essence, innumerable lotus-lands falling open in the magic mothswarm of heaven.' The morning after this encounter with the Eternal Feminine, Paradise is nevertheless back to his usual tricks, sponging $100 off a rich girl he's slept with in order to subsidise another trip.

According to Kerouac biographer Dennis McNally, 'One of the central myths of Jack's life was of Dostoevski's wife and her unflagging support of her husband, of the duty of the untalented to support the creative artist.' And so the one constant woman in his life was his mother, *memère*, source of unconditional love; eventually, having renounced his beatnik ways, he returned to live out the rest of his days with her.

The beats were trying to re-open the American frontier, the closing of which in the 1890s was so traumatic for American identity. This 'new frontier' of the 1950s was a psychic terrain, but like its geographical antecedent, it was a terrain in which rugged, manly individualism flourished. Women were simply absent, a symbol of the home that was left behind. In his essay 'The White Negro' (1957), Norman Mailer defined hip anti-conformism in traditional American terms: 'One is a frontiersman in the Wild West of American nightlife, or else a Square cell, trapped in the totalitarian tissues of American society, doomed willy-nilly to conform if one is to succeed.' In order to escape and find a truly virile life, one must 'divorce oneself from society'; Mailer's language typically links matrimony with emasculation. Around the same time, *Playboy* was offering a sort of square counterpart to the beat lifestyle, with its fantasy of the swinger: suave and sophisticated, but, like the beatnik, a confirmed bachelor determined to avoid settling down.

The pursuit of altered states of consciousness in the

1960s was an extension of the beats' new frontier into the realm of inner space. In a familiar pattern, Timothy Leary, prophet of LSD, grew up idolising an absent father, Captain Tote Leary, who had abandoned the family. His father was restless, tempestuous, a drunkard and debtor who was continually in flight from domesticity. 'During the thirteen years we lived together he never stunted me with expectations...' reminisced Leary Jr, fondly. 'Dad remained for me a model of the loner, a disdainer of the conventional way.'

His mother, Abigail, was left holding the baby and the brunt of Tim Leary's contempt. A pious Catholic and a middle-class wanna-be with an inbred suspicion of 'all things joyous, frivolous or newfangled', she was saddled with the responsibility of bringing him up, rather than the glamour of total abdication of responsibility. In return, Leary strove to emulate all the most obnoxious qualities of his father's side of the family. This familiar dialectic between male adventurism and female conformism, male wildness and female domestication, foreshadows Leary's discourse of heroic odyssey into the acid maelstrom. Leary espoused LSD as a way of de-familiarising the world: beneath this project lurked his desire, derived from his dad, to escape the family. The point of the acid trip was to shatter one's sense of being at home in the world, to rip up the map and disorientate the bearings that made life comfortable and habitual. Only after surviving these turbulent white water rapids of consciousness could you make it through to the lagoon of serenity wherein your shattered ego merged with the cosmos. It's Nietzsche again: 'To build a new sanctuary the old sanctuary must be first destroyed.'

Ken Kesey is the bridge that connects Norman Mailer's vision of American suburbia as a concentration camp of mediocrity with Leary's flight into the psychedelic wilderness. In *One Flew Over the Cuckoo's Nest* (1962), Kesey drew on his experience as a psychiatric aide in a hospital to present the asylum as a microcosm of '50s America. The novel's hero, R.P. McMurphy, pretends to have psycho-pathic tendencies in order to escape the rigours of the prison farm. One of his original crimes was sex with an under-age girl, and he's unrepentant. The exuberant McMurphy galvanises his fellow patients – crushed, castrated men unable to cope with the demands and hypocrisies of subur-ban matriarchy – to buck against the system.

There are two kinds of women in *One Flew Over the Cuckoo's Nest*: whores and matrons (the latter being both repressed and oppressive). McMurphy's hooker gal-friends are dumb, pretty, compliant. The frigid matriarchs include the controlling wives and mothers who don't appear but who, it is hinted, are originally responsible for breaking the inmates' spirits, and uptight dominatrixes like Nurse Ratched, who rules the ward with her rigid schedule of activ-ities, pacifying muzak and regular doses of tranquillisers.

Ratched's name sounds phallic, violent and staccato, like the ratchet, a cutting instrument. At one point, McMurphy struggles to convince a fellow inmate that Nurse Ratched is a monstrous tyrant 'peckin' at' every man's 'everlovin' balls... that nurse ain't some kinda monstrous chicken, buddy, what she is is a ball-cutter. I've seen a thousand of 'em... all over the country and in the homes – people who try to make you weak so they can get you to toe the line.' America is ruled by a conspiracy of moms. In fact, Ratched is a friend of the mother of one ward inmate, Billy, a 31-year-old man driven to a breakdown by his mom's posses-sive prudishness. When McMurphy gets one of his loose girlfriends to help Billy lose his virginity, Ratched disco-vers them *in flagrante* and threatens to tell his mother. Billy is unmanned again, and commits suicide; in revenge, McMurphy tries to strangle Ratched, but fails, and ends up a lobotomised zombie.

Kesey went on to form the Merry Pranksters, whose membership included that old rogue Neal Cassady. Roaming the USA in a gaudily painted bus, they intro-duced people to the psychic wilderness of the acid trip. In his LSD history *Storming Heaven*, Jay Stevens compares the machismo of Kesey's acid-evangelism (are you man enough to handle the Acid Test?) with Leary's mellow mysticism. One of Kesey's pals, the LSD-mass-manufacturer Augustus Owsley III, apparently taunted his friends to 'take two and really cut loose into the cosmos'. Part and parcel of the Pranksters' reinvocation of rugged, frontier masculinity was their eulogisation of the Hell's Angels. The Angels were admired for their virile non-conformism, but in fact offered a distorted mirror image of straight America's notions of proper gender relations (they were misogynist, jingoistic and anti-Communist). In October 1965, a gang of Angels beat up some anti-war protesters in Berkeley. Shortly after, their leader Sonny Barger sent a communiqué to Lyndon Johnson, in which he offered the Angels' services in Vietnam: 'We feel that a crack group of trained gorillas [*sic*] would demoralize the Viet Cong and advance the cause of freedom. We are available for training and duty immediately.' Despite this, the bikers became icons of untrammelled freedom for many in the counterculture (the Rolling Stones, Grateful Dead, Steppenwolf).

While the Angels' bloodlust clashed with the hippies' peace-and-love passivity, it struck a strange chord with the mindframe of the more confrontational elements in the late '60s counterculture. Yippie warrior and neo-Marxist Jerry Rubin told the *New York Times*: 'Young kids want to be heroes. They have an incredible energy and they want to live creative, exciting lives. That's what America tells you to do.... The history you learn is hero-oriented: Columbus, George Washington, Paul Revere, the pioneers, the cowboys. America's promise has been "live a heroic life". But then, when it comes time to make good on its promise, it can't. It turns around and says, "oh, you can get good grades, and then get a degree, then get a job in a corporation, and buy a ranch house and be a good consumer." But kids aren't satisfied with that. They want to be heroes. And if America denies them an opportunity for heroism, they're going to create their own.'

Tom Wolfe saw the Merry Pranksters as a 'true mystic brotherhood – only in poor old Formica polyethylene 1960s America...' The beatniks, the Merry Pranksters, Leary's Politics of Ecstasy, the psychodrama of *One Flew Over the Cuckoo's Nest*, all fit perfectly with the mythological model created by Robert Bly in his '90s bestseller *Iron John*. Bly, a poet, co-founder of the Men's Movement, and wilderness-worshipper, believes that Western society's problems stem from the absence of male role models and rites of initiation for adolescent boys, and from a consequent over-mothering of boys, who grow up emasculated, 'soft males'. Bly calls for a reawakening of the Wild Man within. His ideas are really just a myth-laden rewrite of Wylie's mom-ism: he even blames male teenage delinquency, insubordination and misogyny on the mother, since these are symptoms of the boy's attempts to break away from the cocoon of mother-love. Rock music (and particularly its most obstreperously macho and tribalistic genres like rap and metal) provide surrogate forms of ritual initiation for adolescent males: the charismatic singer is the modern equivalent of the mentor or shaman.

Bly's Iron John legend is too complicated to go into here, but at its heart lies a psychological matrix similar to the Oedipus myth. In both cases, an adolescent upstart is sepa-rated/separates himself from home and mother, disappears into the wilderness, then returns to displace the King/ Father and enjoy union with a Mother-figure, the Queen. (In the Oedipus story, the King and Queen are literally his father and mother.) These myths, blueprints for male rebellion, are psychodramas of incest: an incest that is initially avoided (by fleeing from the smothering bosom) and then returned to, symbolically, in the conquest of the Queen. Incest signifies more than just a longing for the mother. It's an impossible desire for total satisfaction, supreme phallic prestige; a desire that surfaces in rock's most ferocious demands, from Jim Morrison's insatiable *cri de coeur* 'we want the world and we want it NOW' to the implacable rage of Johnny Rotten's 'I wanna be anarchy'. The Doors actually had an explicitly Oedipal anthem in 'The End', and there was a latent theme of incest-cum-matricide in the Sex Pistols. Before he met the Pistols, svengali Malcolm McLaren wrote songs for an imaginary rock group who would spearhead a teen revolution. For one song, 'Too Fast To Live, Too Young To Die', McLaren envisioned 'the singer looking like Hitler, those gestures, arms, shapes, etc, and talking about his mum in incestuous phrases'.

boys keep swinging

Incest in rock figures as both an ultimate metaphor of transgression AND as a claustrophobic, castrating, de-individuating thrall (the stifling domesticity of mother's love). Brian Jones of the Rolling Stones was a supreme example of this conflict; he flitted between effeminate passivity and vicious brutalisation of women. In 1967, when Jones appealed a harsh sentence for drug offences, the court-appointed psychiatrist described him as oscillating between 'phallic and sadistic sexuality' and 'gross passive dependency needs'. The shrink attributed this to 'Oedipal fixations.... Part of his confusion would seem to be the very strong resentment he experiences towards his dominant and controlling mother.' Hence Jones's mix of 'soft male' and obnoxious teen throwing off his mum's shackles.

More than the rest of the band, Brian Jones was the incarnation of the Rolling Stones' mixture of effete dandyism and cruel machismo. He gaily indulged his 'feminine side' through a camp persona and foppish unisex clothing, and occasionally took this identification to the point of female impersonation. According to Anita Pallenberg, during one LSD trip, she and Jones swapped sexual roles (she dressed him up as French chanteuse Françoise Hardy). Yet Jones subjected the real women in his life to violent tantrums and abandoned them with illegitimate offspring. Mick Jagger's image also conflated thuggish virility and effeminacy. 'What really upsets people is that I'm a man and not a woman,' the singer mused. 'I don't do anything more than a lot of girl dancers, but they're accepted because it's a man's world...' The Stones usurped the female 'privileges' of self-adornment and narcissism, while belittling real-life women for just such frivolousness.

At other times, the Stones' cross-dressing had a more derisive, parodic purpose, as with the drag outfits they wore for the cover of the single 'Have You Seen Your Mother, Baby, Standing In The Shadow'. Keith Richards dressed as an air stewardess, Jones was a tarty auxiliary in the RAF, Mick Jagger and Bill Wyman were wizened old biddies, and Charlie Watts was a rich old madam in a fur coat. The Stones' transvestism endured right through to the late '70s twilight album *Some Girls*, whose cover featured the band's faces framed by female wigs. On the back, sardonic, potted biographies – Wyman's spinster 'lacks only one attribute to be the perfect wife – she just doesn't like men', Jagger's career girl sacrifices love for her profession, and so on – have each pseudo-woman ending up alone, without a man: clearly, for the Stones, the ultimate indignity.

Back in the '60s, androgyny was just another weapon in the band's armoury of threats to society's norms. What was conventional in real women became subversive when assumed by men. As paragons of the Dionysian tradition in rock'n'roll, it was no coincidence that the Stones were drawn to femininity. In *Androgyny*, June Singer wrote of the original Greek god, Dionysus: 'He is treated and educated like a girl and he grows up to be effeminate. Unable to differentiate feminine from masculine functioning in himself, he scarcely knows who he is. Like an eternal youth, he wanders over the world, changing shape, going mad, drinking himself into insensibility, living the abandonment of total nature, and like nature, experiencing the cycles of death and rebirth.'

The Stones' fusion of swaggering machismo and self-preening androgyny as a kind of all-encompassing narcissism has endured as a staple of rebel rock: from '60s freakbeat (groups like John's Children) through Lou Reed, David Bowie, the New York Dolls, to Prince, Hanoi Rocks, the Manic Street Preachers and Suede. Punk was too deeply into uglification to play with androgyny, but its very name had an effeminate connotation. In the sixteenth century, punk meant a female prostitute or strumpet; over the centuries, its meaning had evolved to signify the young male 'wife' of a sodomite, in hobo terminology, and, in prison slang, a young, pretty, passive boy who gets fucked by the other convicts. Once again, rebel rock converted the word for an emasculated, contemptible piece of human trash into a positive term of deliquency.

In her essay 'Baudelaire, or Infinity, Perfume and Punk', Julia Kristeva argues that dandyism is an identification with the mother's despised position in the patriarchal order. The dandy's obsession with the 'trivial' business of style is a revolt against the proper model of masculinity that is upheld by the father, and is an attempt to emulate the mother. Kristeva's mention of punk in this context is suggestive: punk style, being conscious, concerted self-defilement rather than prettification, is an inverted form of dandyism. Both dandyism and punk flaunt their inferiority and marginalisation, turn emasculation into style.

But the Stones' dandyism wasn't so much an embrace of the underdog position as an aspiration to overlord status. It was a decadent refusal of the decent, upright, desexualised masculinity promoted in the '50s, in favour of the aristocratic self-indulgence of the playboy. This slippery but virile image was also shared by Jimi Hendrix, and later by his heir, Prince: potent savages in regal finery. Throughout its history, rock has flitted between effete narcissism and rugged scruffiness. But none of these archetypes – neither the Cavalier nor the Roundhead, mod nor rocker – has offered much for women. Rock's great paradox is that it has successively revolted against established notions of manliness while remaining misogynistic. David Bowie's anthem 'Boys Keep Swinging' (from 1979's *Lodger*) was intended as a mockery of male bonding. In the video, Bowie undercuts the lyrics' raucous camaraderie by cross-dressing as a variety of female personas. The idea was that underneath all the machismo, 'the lads' are just latent homosexuals. But the song's subversive wit was undercut by an even deeper irony: it's a male privilege to 'swing', to experiment with female glamour, and adopt 'optional female subjectivities', as Suzanne Moore put it. Female cross-dressing doesn't come across as mischief or transgression. Boys putting on eyeliner provides a frisson, but girls boycotting the kohl pencil is merely dowdy.

she's hit:
songs of fear and loathing

*'What you're is saying is that. . . there's the beautiful dreamy type
and the vicious bitch type. There are also one or two others, but,
yeah, you're right. . . there are two kinds of girls [in my songs]. . .
only I never thought about it before. Ah, I see, I'm not integrating
them properly.'*
Mick Jagger interview, *Rolling Stone*, 1978

It's as simple as this: if you don't like the Rolling Stones,
you don't like rock'n'roll. The Stones are the quintessence
of rock – and they're also one of the most misogynistic
groups ever. Their very name, taken from urban blues pioneer Muddy Waters's song 'Rollin' Stone', contains the notion
of flight – from domesticity, emotional commitment, intimacy, *ties*. The image of the Stones as marauding sexual
nomads was assiduously cultivated by their original manager Andrew Loog Oldham, who fed the press copy like:
'They look like boys any self-respecting mum would lock in
the bathroom. But the Rolling Stones – five tough young
London-based music makers with door-step mouths, pallid
cheeks, and unkempt hair – are not worried what mums
think.' Another slogan Oldham gave *Melody Maker* became
the famous headline, 'Would You Let Your Daughter Go
With A Rolling Stone?'. The Stones' anti-charisma was
inextricably bound up with the notion of an uncouth under-
class preying on the most precious property of the respectable classes: their daughters' bodies.

Where the Beatles' appeal was that they were 'nice
boys', the Stones' ruffian image seduced (some) girls with
the prospect that they would be treated roughly, without

respect. The Beatles/Stones dichotomy solidified the split between pop and rock: between groomed stars and scruffy outsiders, romance and raw sexuality, courtship and brutish ravishment. Of course, the Beatles were always held in rock critical esteem, and the Stones had great pop success with teenyboppers, but they helped enshrine the idea that pop panders to 'girly' sensibilities (pretty boy image, harmony'n'melody, sentimental lyrics) while rock is made by and for tough boys.

The threat and appeal of the Rolling Stones was that they were untamed. In 'Under My Thumb' (from 1966's *Aftermath*), Jagger rejects the domestication of monogamy, while boasting of having domesticated a once proud, independent girl. He measures his own wildness against the inverted mirror image of her docility; he's turned her into all that he despises and rejects. 'Out Of Time' and 'Yesterday's Papers' portray girls as disposable, obsolete goods. It's not enough for the swaggering Jagger to rub his discarded girlfriend's nose in the fact that he doesn't want her any more; he wants her to know that nobody else will either.

'Have You Seen Your Mother, Baby, Standing In The Shadow' (1966) is one of the Stones' most hateful songs. It's also one of the most perplexing and apocalyptic records of the '60s – especially in combination with Peter Whitehead's promo film, which juxtaposed images of riots during the band's live performances with scenes of the Stones preparing for the photo shoot for the single's cover, in which the Stones appeared in drag as various grotesque caricatures of female stereotypes.

Only that most unabashedly phallocratic of rock critics, Nick Tosches, has come close to pinning down the malign magic of 'Have You Seen Your Mother, Baby'. Reminiscing about his teenage love of the band, he writes that he and his gang were struck by 'the surly notion of throwing at the face of the neurotic, castaway girlfriend the image of her mother, and sneering, in afterbreath, at the girl's pregnancy.... swathed and speeding, we prowled with the windows shut against the black coldness, looking for feminine throats in the shadows, where there were none, listening to that, smiling terribly, and feeling, with something like orgasm, our existences contract beatifically into that terrible smiling.'

Domination and contempt are not the only emotions in the Stones' songs, of course: elsewhere there's the pallid devotion of 'Lady Jane' or the mawkish idealisation of 'Ruby Tuesday', a tribute to a free-spirited groupie. In a 1978 *Rolling Stone* interview, Jonathan Cott suggested to Jagger that there was a split in his songs. Girls are either denigrated for being dominating, malicious or treacherous ('Tumbling Dice', 'Sitting On A Fence', 'Let It Loose'); used up and discarded ('Out Of Time', 'Please Go Home', 'All Sold Out', 'Congratulations'); or else they're idealised as elusive, mystical sprites ('Ruby Tuesday', 'Child Of the Moon') – to which Jagger concurred, reluctantly. Cott continues: 'The song "Some Girls" seems to be about what happens when hundreds of idealized Twenties girls try to eat you up, destroy you – taking your money and your clothes and giving you babies you don't want.' Jagger replies: 'I had a dream like that last night, incidentally, but there were dogs as well as girls in it.'

mannish boys and stupid girls

The Stones, along with mid-'60s contemporaries like the Pretty Things and the Animals, took the masculine self-aggrandisement of the blues and exaggerated it. The paradigmatic source was Bo Diddley's 'I'm a Man'. For the black American, this assertion had a racial dimension: it was an affirmation of full manhood in the face of a white supremacist society that called him 'boy'. This dimension was necessarily lost when the music was taken over by white British adolescents. Pride became arrogance; the music of underdogs became the soundtrack of would-be overlords raising themselves up by stomping down women. The British blues persona was the 'Mannish Boy' (the title of Muddy Waters's own version of 'I'm a Man', and later the band name of David Bowie's early blues group, the Manish Boys); that's to say, a sexually precocious teenage boy eager to prove himself by adopting an almost parodic machismo.

The mannish boy's self-assertion became – with the amphetamine-wired mod groups and their freakbeat descendents – a kind of megalomaniac/paranoiac delirium. A good example is the John's Children song 'Just What You Want, Just What You'll Get' (1966), with its combination of fey petulance and brutal military beat, its psychotic lyrics and terror of intimacy. His girl knows how to please him, but he suspects that she's luring him into a tender trap. The chorus trembles with virulence: 'Don't think I don't know just what you want / EVERYTHING!! / Don't think I don't know just what you'll get / NOTHING!!!' It's because the girl is so seductive that's she's so terrifying: violent repudiation becomes a matter of survival for this fragile man-child on the brink of being engulfed in a sexual maelstrom.

In the US, the Stones, the Kinks and the Yardbirds inspired a more straightforwardly masculine horde of imi-tators with the garage punk bands, who amplified the sexual aggression of the blues with simultaneously exhila-rating and comical results. The most famous garage groups – the Count Five, the Seeds, the Standells, ? and the Mysterians, the Castaways – hit the charts. But often the most extreme groups (in terms of musical primitivism and misogynist vitriol) were the obscure, unsuccessful punks, whose songs were subsequently gathered up on '80s compi-lations like the *Pebbles*, *Mindrocker* and *Back from the Grave* series.

As with many rock subgenres, a dynamic set in where, in order to up the formal stakes and beat the competition, the extremity of expression rapidly escalates until self-parody ensues. The Tree's 'No Good Woman', for instance, is a preposterous torrent of abuse aimed at an unfaithful, ungrateful girl. The protagonist bought his girl a Cadillac, yet she's been mistreating him 'for 69 years'. You have to wonder why he bothers, as the accusations and put-downs mount: 'you're ugly and you're fat and you've got no teeth'. Another standard scenario is the put-down of the frigid, stuck-up 'Miss High and Mighty' who won't give the singer satisfaction, as in the Litter's 'Action Woman'. On both sides of the Atlantic, 'rich bitch' songs combined class antagonism with sexual resentment. The Stones' '19th Nervous Breakdown' (1966) taunts a neurotic debutante with the image of her neglectful mother and industrial baron father, while John's Children's 'Desdemona' beseeches a repressed upper-class girl to drop her drawers and get hip to the revolution: 'lift up your skirt and fly'. In British mod and US garage punk, the eternal double standard of 'if you don't you're a drag, if you do you're a slut' meant that girls were either two-faced whores or frigid bores. The male protagonists of these songs are untamed, feral delinquents, dormant volcanoes of pent-up testosterone, and/or victims of feminine wiles. Obviously mod and garage were intimately bound up with the virginity blues of frustrated male youth.

American garage punk and British R&B evolved into heavy rock, and then heavy metal. At each stage, the blues form was progressively more bastardised, its machismo exaggerated. The blues' cocksure strut turned to phallocratic overkill; Muddy Waters's 'You Need Love' (1963) becomes, as Charles Shaar Murray put it, the 'thermonuclear gang rape' of Led Zeppelin's 'Whole Lotta Love' (1969). But garage punk and British mod were also the origins of punk rock. Punk, in fact, was a sort of asexual relative of metal: cock-rock, with the cock replaced by a sort of generalised castration-paranoia (society's to blame). Musically, punk suppressed the remnants of R&B's syncopation that endured in heavy metal, and turned rock into a martial beat for those at war with the status quo. But the vicious vehemence of punk was ultimately derived from the hyper-macho, misogynist white blues of the '60s. The Sex Pistols learned their first lessons in defiance and contempt by playing crude versions of mod put-down songs like 'Stepping Stone' and 'Don't Give Me No Lip Child'. They learned how to express their rejection of society from songs about rejecting women. Occasionally the Pistols returned to source, as on the brilliant B-side 'Satellite', a caustic diatribe against a female hanger-on and scenester who looks like a 'fat pink baked bean'.

devil woman

John's Children's 'Smashed Blocked' (1966) anticipates one of heavy metal's standard themes: woman as bewitching, spell-binding, a spinner of illusions. The singer's lovesick whisper is engulfed in a nauseous whirlpool of psychedelic sound, his mind reels on a carousel of confusion: 'Where is the love I thought I'd found?'. Love is disorientation, debility and paralysis. Led Zeppelin's 'Dazed and Confused' (from the 1969 debut LP) is the definitive take on this scenario. Doomladen glissandos of blues guitar and a scabrous, burdened bassline conjure a sepulchre of sound for Robert Plant's languishing moans and tortured shrieks. Plant is prostrated on 'the killing floor', a standard blues metaphor that originally referred to an abattoir. His mind is poisoned and befogged by the noxious fumes of her feminine miasma. He's at death's door, flaccid and enfeebled, until he and the music rally for one last attempt to claw their way out of this aural slough of despond. But to no avail: the riff-mania subsides again into a dank decay, with Plant emitting his final death-rattle moans and whimpers.

The devil-in-disguise motif recurs in 'Black Dog' (from Led Zeppelin's untitled fourth LP, 1971). Plant is wracked with desire, shivering and shuddering like he's going through cold turkey; the turgid, gruelling riff incarnates sex as agony and toil. Once again, Plant is laid low, financially and emotionally ('Black Dog' is a classic metaphor for nameless Evil or depression), and he can only pray that she and her soulless kind will stay away.

Fleetwood Mac wrote a number of classic songs about a phantasmic *femme fatale*, most notably 'Black Magic Woman' (as famously covered by Santana) and 'Gold Dust Woman' (from 1977's *Rumours*). The latter's misogyny is barely mitigated by the fact that a woman, Stevie Nicks, sings the lyrics. Nicks is a passive narrator, observing the man's torment, at once gloating and solicitous. The deadly 'Gold Dust Woman' is precious but elusive, slipping through the man's fingers. A forever-receding mirage, she shatters the poor sap's life and 'illusions of love'. Musically, the song is a stealthy, ominous blues, with an astonishing slow fade, in which cadaverous wails and shrieks from a high-pitched male voice seem to disappear into a quagmire of sound. Haunted by this woman-spectre, the man has become a ghost of his former self.

model of perfection

Roxy Music were even more bedevilled by the gap between ideal and reality. An artschool band influenced by Warhol and Pop Art, Roxy used the language of commerce and advertising to rewrite the madonna/whore complex in postmodern terms. Their first three albums are set in a fantasised jet-set high life, a surface-deep world where authentic love is impossible. 'Femininity' here has nothing to do with an essential psychological or biological reality, and everything to do with accoutrements and cosmetics. Roxy women are the sum of the products they use, and are treated like commodities. In 'Ladytron' (from the 1972 eponymous debut album), Ferry's 'lounge lizard' persona is involved in a futile quest for an impossible ideal woman, whose intimidating perfection inspires him to imagine his revenge in advance: he promises to 'use you, confuse you, then lose you', but she'll never suspect him. It's the classic notion of the male sexual predator who enjoys the chase more than the capture, but translated into consumerism's logic of planned obsolescence and 'purchase of the moment'. 'Beauty Queen' (from 1973's *For Your Pleasure*) is about the doomed love affair between Ferry and a starlet, both of whom are obsessed with surfaces, and who share only 'an ideal of beauty'. For Ferry's character, love is consummated in the gaze: she makes his 'starry eyes shiver'. Connection is impossible in this world of voyeurism and exhibitionism, and so the solipsistic would-be lovers part, remaining a mystery to each other.

In 'Editions of You', Ferry's looking for a 'Remake/Remodel' (to quote another Roxy song-title) of the girl that broke his heart: a classic torch song trope – 'they only remind me of you' – is rendered in the language of mass production. 'In Every Dream Home A Heartache' makes the leap from woman-as-replaceable-commodity to commodity-as-woman, with the tale of a man destroyed by his obsession with an inflatable woman. The blow-up bimbo can't, of course, reciprocate his love, and her pristine surface is impenetrable. His yearning for flawlessness and total control ultimately dehumanises him. In the end, the playboy is enslaved to the object that was meant to be his ideal plaything. He must now serve her. As the 'affair' intensifies, he gets 'further from heaven' and nearer the living hell of schizophrenia. He's punished for his own superficiality, ending up in thrall to the unresponsive, shiny surface of his 'disposable darling'.

On the third album, *Stranded* (1974), 'Mother Of Pearl' plays on the idea of a girl as a precious gem, but quickly collapses into the realisation that polished surfaces can hide rough-cut origins. Ferry's search for love in a 'looking glass world' curdles into cynicism. By the end, the girl is 'so-so semi-precious': when Ferry's character declares that he wouldn't exchange her for any other girl, the sarcasm behind the word 'trade' is acrid. The illusion of uniqueness is replaced by the realisation that on the sexual market, everyone is interchangeable.

ladykillers

Sometimes there's a more savage solution to the fissure between appearance and actuality that haunted Roxy Music: murder, the elimination of the fickle, fleshy reality whose changeability threatens to shatter the illusion on which the lover depends. Conflicted feelings of love and hate achieve explosive release.

Edgar Allan Poe wrote, 'The death of a beautiful woman is, unquestionably, the most poetical topic in the world.' It's also very much a rock'n'roll topic. The traditional song 'Hey Joe' (much covered in the '60s, most famously by Jimi Hendrix) is a classic example; the killing of an unfaithful woman propels the hero outside the law, turns him into a fugitive. A wife-killer who *doesn't* get away is the protagonist of 'Long Time Man', by the '60s folk-blues singer Tim Rose (who also did a brilliant version of 'Hey Joe'). Serving a life sentence, the jailed man is tormented by regret for an impulse killing whose motive he can't even remember. The emphasis is not on the woman's death but on the ruined dignity and agonised conscience of the singer. In fact, the song skips the act itself in the transition from his grabbing a gun to her dying murmur that she loves him. Murder becomes a way for this man to exteriorise his intense feelings, which can't be expressed in any other form. Unable to bleed emotionally, he must make her bleed, literally.

In *The Lust to Kill: A Feminist Investigation of Sexual Murder*, Deborah Cameron and Elizabeth Frazer suggest that 'an existentialist account of sex murderers' might reveal them to be 'the ultimate rebels, the ultimate actors-out of eroticism in its purest form'. In the passionate crime, the woman's body becomes literally the *raw* material of the hero's narrative. Murder is the final expression of his passion, the proof and testament of love. It's a form of absolute possession, a terrible sanguinary intimacy.

In rock, the most powerful exploration of these ideas (because almost pathologically obsessive) comes from the post-punk icon Nick Cave (who, incidentally, has covered both 'Hey Joe' and 'Long Time Man', as well as John Lee Hooker's 'I'm Gonna Kill That Woman'). 'I've always enjoyed writing songs about dead women,' Cave admitted in a 1986 *Melody Maker* interview. 'It's something that crops up that still holds some mystery, even to me.' In Cave's first group the Birthday Party and as a solo artist, the murder of a beloved girl becomes a way of petrifying for eternity the madonna image and eradicating the whore ('whorishness' here perhaps signifying everything connected with a woman's sexual autonomy, with the looming possibility that she might leave him for another). Murdered, the flawed, all-too-human woman can't threaten to shatter his fetishised image of her. He controls her mortality and her immortality (she remains as a freeze-frame ideal in what Barthes calls the lover's Image-Repertoire, the set of consecrated images that he cherishes in his mind's eye). finally, murder *distinguishes* the lover, renders him larger than life, heroic and historic.

Ironically, Cave seems to have felt his way through to the girl-murder theme via an acute, inflamed sense of womankind's vulnerability. The opening track on the Birthday Party's 1982 album *Junkyard*, 'She's Hit', is a blues lament for all the murdered girls of the world. Moaning imagery of mutilated murder victims and 'bleeding' skirts, Cave seems to be deeply troubled by women's propensity to revert to the level of meat, to 'woman-pie'. For Cave, woman seems to have an intimate relationship with death, perhaps because of her procreative role. Beneath his grief lurks a strange resentment, a sense of betrayal that might be transcribed as 'never love a woman, not even your mother, because she'll die on you'. Elsewhere on *Junkyard*, that sense of betrayal becomes literal in 'Six Inch Gold Blade', where the protagonist takes bloody revenge on an unfaithful lover whom he's caught *in flagrante*, by knifing her through the head: 'She: lying through her teeth', her lover underneath her, still inside her. The song reels with hallucinatory imagery that conflates carnality and carnage, copulation and stabbing.

On the first Nick Cave and the Bad Seeds' LP *From Her To Eternity* (1984), the title track is a febrile tale of emotional voyeurism. Upstairs, a girl paces and weeps, her tears dripping through the floorboards and into the protagonist's mouth. Obsessed with saving and healing her wounds, he climbs into her room and reads her diaries. But he quickly goes from feeling tender to wanting to rend her, as an irresistible logic takes hold: he wants to possess her, but to have her would mean that he'd no longer desire her, so he decides that 'lil girl' simply has 'to go!'. Addicted to his own unrequited love, he fastens on murder as a means to make her permanently his, yet eternally out of reach.

After the gynocide-free *The Firstborn Is Dead* (1985), *Your Funeral...My Trial* (1986) returned to Cave's grisly norm with a vengeance. The inside sleeve illustrations include an engraving of a whore examining her swollen vagina with a hand-mirror, while the title track is a delirious excavation of the madonna/whore complex, full of imagery of Virgin Marys luring him into sin, 'crooked bitches (mongers of pain)' and 'the bells' of 'whoredom' tolling his doom. The title, *Your Funeral...My Trial*, encapsulates the process at work in Rose's 'Long Time Man' (covered by Cave on this album): the woman's death elevates the man, makes him tower above the nobodies who would like to follow their darkest desires but are too domesticated. Because he refuses limits, society punishes and destroys him. 'The Mercy Seat', centrepiece of 1988's *Tender Prey*, is another grandiose ballad sung by a murderer on Death Row. While the legal system weighs up and measures truth, his passion speaks louder than mealy-mouthed ver-biage. A close-up of a wedding ring on the hand that com-mitted the murder as a shackle 'collaring' his 'rebel blood' hints darkly that his victim was a woman.

Rationalising his fascination in an interview around the time of 'The Mercy Seat', Cave proposed a kind of ethics of violence. Defining himself against 'a certain numbness in the world today', he proclaimed his belief in the nobility of the *crime passionnel* as opposed to 'sadism, or violence through greed'. Cave's Romanticism is in stark contrast with the macabre obsessions of US hardcore or the endless carnage of death-metal groups like Slayer. In hardcore band Big Black's 'Kerosene' (from *Atomizer*, 1986), the song's narrator is driven by the boredom and claustropho-bia of his small town to seek ultimate release. He combines the town's two forms of amusement (blowing things up and fucking the town slut) into a single blast of catharsis. Whereas Cave's baroque imagery ennobles passionate murder, the deadpan nihilism of 'Kerosene' emphasises lowly desperation.

A parallel to this contrast between Nick Cave and Big Black can be found in the movie *River's Edge*, which cen-tres around the impulse killing of a girl by her boyfriend John, and the misguided attempts by the boy's friends to cover up the crime. The gang's leader persuades John to go into hiding with a character called Feck, a crippled, decrepit ex-biker who's been on the run for years after killing his own girlfriend. The encounter between Feck and John becomes a dialogue between two different ethics of murder, two kinds of fucked-up masculinity. Feck is a relic from a more romantic era (the '60s) when outlaws ran loose in the countercultural wilderness; like a Nick Cave charac-ter, his crime is the result of a tragic excess of desire. Whereas John is very '80s, very Big Black: his violence is as contextless, random and unmotivated as the hardcore punk and thrash-metal he and his male buddies listen to. Feck killed his girl because he loved her, John because she was 'talking shit', and because he 'wanted to show the world who's boss'. He mourns not the dead girl but the loss of the ecstatic moment of murder: 'I felt so REAL. I felt so fucking ALIVE.' For an instant, life was as intense as TV's hyper-real realm of quick-cut editing and gratuitous ultra-violence. Feck's moral and aesthetic disgust for John's murder-without-narrative or 'soul' is the most telling moment in the film. Moved to pity, he eventually shoots John to put him out of his misery.

In fact, the death of motivation haunts *River's Edge*. An ex-hippy teacher nostalgically eulogises the achievements of his generation (stopping the Vietnam War) and talks about how there was 'meaning in the madness'. But he's disappointed by a pupil's response that 'wasting pigs is radical'. The meaning of 'radical' has shrunk to meaning 'intense' or 'cool'. The '60s sense of generational unity has contracted to an amoral gang loyalty, or worse, to John's solipsistic code of survivalism (he prizes his ability to 'waste the other guy, even if I get wasted – because I might as well keep my pride').

John's behaviour conforms to the model of psychopathology proposed by Margaret Mahler. Here, the psychopath is 'not-fully-born', has never been completely extricated from the infant-mother symbiosis of the first two years of life. Possessing only a fragile, precarious ego, the 'not-fully-born' man can only cope with the flood of instinctual drives from within, or over-intense stimuli from without, by aggressive defence mechanisms. He's impelled to *ward off* any threats from outside, and killing makes his brittle sense of self stronger and more real.

Where late twentieth-century impulse-killing is a form of self-preservation against engulfment, in the Romantic imagination, murder is to love what orgasm is to sex: a supreme moment of possession, a release of tension, an explosive overflow of spiritual largesse. The idea that death – whether via a suicide pact or amorous murder – is the pinnacle of transgressive eroticism runs from the Marquis de Sade through the Romantic poets, to Genet, Bataille, Mishima, Miller, Marguerite Duras's *Moderato Cantabile*; a similar lineage runs through rock from the Doors' 'Light My Fire' (with its love as funeral pyre metaphor) and 'The End', through the Stooges to Nick Cave. On Stooges' songs like 'I Wanna Be Your Dog', 'Loose' and 'Search and Destroy', Iggy Pop's sexuality is predatory verging on militaristic, its goal mutually assured destruction. In 'Death Trip', love is close combat: Iggy croons the threat/promise 'come be my enemy'.

Nick Cave takes Iggy's aggression and recasts it in more poetic, late Romantic imagery. The Birthday Party's 'Zoo Music Girl' fuses the language of devotion and devastation: one minute, he's kneeling to kiss her skirt's hem, the next he's murdering 'her dress 'til it hurts'. In 'Hard On For Love', from *Your Funeral...My Trial*, Cave is a robber ransacking the female body's 'altar of love'. He imagines his phallus as God's 'sceptre', venturing into the perilous, dark and dank domain of the female, which he compares to the valley of death. Like Iggy's 'Death Trip', sex is a missile attack, a kamikaze raid: Cave's aim is 'to hit this miss'. The thrust and spasm of murder is like a ghastly parody of the orgasmic embrace. In the annihilating release of sex-murder, the object of love/hate is simultaneously possessed and purged: peace is finally achieved by putting her out of his misery.

careers in misogyny:
the stranglers and malcolm mclaren

'I like dominating women. That doesn't necessarily mean I think they should be dominated. I just get off on it. I think everybody does.'
Hugh Cornwell of the Stranglers, 1977

In the official history of rock, punk is regarded as a liberating time for women, a moment in which the limits of permissible representations of femininity were expanded and exploded. Women were free to uglify themselves, to escape the *chanteuse* role to which they were generally limited and pick up guitars and drumsticks, to shriek rather than coo in dulcet tones, to deal with hitherto taboo topics. All this is true, but... Punk had learned the art of defiance from '60s mod and garage bands whose songs aggressively targeted women; it redirected the riffs and accusatory machismo at society or at a despised, anonymous 'you' (either a crushed conformist or an oppressor). But inevitably, punk's roots in the masculinism of '60s rock were bound to resurface. At times, the misogyny was even more virulent than in the '60s, because punk's general nihilism and 'we hate everybody' attitude encouraged a no-holds-barred assault on liberal values (including feminism) and common decency. This chapter focuses on the careers-in-misogyny of two prominent players in punk rock, one central and hugely influential (Malcolm McLaren) and the other peripheral but hugely successful (the Stranglers).

The Stranglers were peripheral because they were never hip, and musically they were more 'advanced' and more wilfully eccentric than the straight-and-narrow rabble-rousing rage with which punk came to be synonymous. At the same time, the Stranglers were the most commercially successful 'punk' group (with the possible exception of the Sex Pistols). The Stranglers' first two albums each sold a quarter of a million copies; they had more UK Top Ten hits than any other 'punk' group. For many people they were the acceptable face of punk.

Yet the Stranglers were one of the most misogynist groups in rock history, exceeding even the Stones in their sheer nastiness. The band's very name was a threat, being a murder technique associated with the slaughter of women. The debut album, *Rattus Norvegicus* (1977), kicked off with 'Sometimes', a song about beating up a girlfriend. Singer/guitarist Hugh Cornwell told the *NME* that it was inspired by 'a personal experience when there was a breakdown of communication between me and a girl and I ended up hitting her. Cause there were no words I could use to describe how I felt.' Cornwell explained that '"Sometimes" is a song about a bloke hitting a woman as a protest against her behaviour. Put her back down under his domination. I think a lot of men like to dominate women. A lot of women like to be dominated. . . .I think subservient women are a bit pitiful.'

Then there was 'London Lady', a vicious put-down of a female scenester who's scorned for her fading looks and her 'vampiric' tendency to hang around rock stars. Bassist/vocalist Jean-Jacques Burnel defended the song on the grounds that 'that's no way for a chick to be. . . . We were drawing lots on who was going to screw this female column writer, and someone said, "but it'd be like chucking a sausage up the Mersey Tunnel". [The song's] just about some chicks in a very small scene.' Then there was 'Peaches', the Stranglers' first big hit, with Cornwell impersonating a lecherous beach prowler whose idea of women's liberation is girls taking off their bikini tops. Most sinister of all was 'Ugly', in which Burnel imagines strangling a girl after sex, because he's offended by her hideous acne; the song ends with the thuggish chant 'MUSCLE POWER'. Of course, the British music press were quick to criticise the Stranglers for their sexism. This didn't stop them from becoming extremely popular. The Stranglers' appeal was based in their combination of traditional hard rock menace with a smidgen of punky nihilism. Their baroque, organ-draped sound had the same relationship to the Doors as a hangover has to a bout of drunkenness. It was suffused by a poignant, gruff melancholy which was part and parcel of the Stranglers' aura of lone ranger masculinity – a sort of 'I'll soldier on alone in this bereft and fallen world' stance that was crystallised in the 1980 single 'Who Wants the World'. (Their mascot was the rat, sewer survivalist who thrives in a world turned shitty.) Bilious rebels without a cause, the Stranglers seemed to be mourning something – perhaps, like Jimmy Porter, the absence of great causes, the lost possibilities for heroism.

All this was brought into focus with the title track of their second album *No More Heroes* (1977), an elegy for a lost breed of 'warriors' like Leon Trotsky. Sexism reared its ugly head again on 'School M'am' (an overwrought fantasy whose main thrust seemed to be that menopausal women were obsolete) and on 'Bring On the Nubiles', a sex-anthem whose chorus summons a faceless plurality of passively fuckable girls. More than misogyny, *No More Heroes* bristles with an extreme homosociality as the Stranglers imagine themselves the leaders of a belligerent brotherhood of moody but magnificent malcontents. 'Dagenham Dave' is a tribute to a die-hard Stranglers fan whose passion was so extreme that when he was displaced in the Stranglers' affections by a gang of working-class toughs called the Finchley Boys, he committed suicide by jumping into the Thames River. The song notes, in passing, that Dave had no real need for chicks. 'He thought so much of us that he even went so far, at one point, as to offer his wife to us, for, er, our use,' Hugh Cornwell fondly recalled, years later in a 1983 *Trouser Press* feature. Meanwhile,

'English Towns', as Julie Burchill and Tony Parsons noted in *The Boy Looked at Johnny*, seemed to think that finding no love in a thousand girls and doing alright with the boys was no cause for concern.

In the Stranglers' 1977/8 interviews, J.J. Burnel emerged as the member whose obsessions and life story were most revealing. A martial arts adept, Burnel took up karate at school in an attempt to discipline his inner being and control his temper. At school, he ran a neo-Nazi magazine called *The Gubernator* (Latin for helmsman) and joined the far-Right British League of Youth. Burnel went from fascism to the fast lane, becoming infatuated with the Hell's Angels (because 'they glorify individuality and freedom, but individuality within the pack' he explained later) and even joined a gang of surrogate Angels. In 1977, he was still a fan, expressing admiration for a chapter of Angels in Amsterdam: '[They] live in their own exclusive community in Amsterdam and they don't have to worry about working for a living because all their women ARE ON THE GAME! They're able to devote all their time to their bikes. It's great, they've created a totally new society.' Utopia or what?

Other Burnel heroes included London East End mobsters the Kray Twins (often sentimentalised because of their code of honour and paternalistic care for their local community) and the Japanese writer and proto-fascist Yukio Mishima, whose ideas about warrior masculinity were very similar to Robert Bly's. Burnel vigorously defended Mishima from accusations of 'being right-wing and a latent homosexual, just because he had a private army of young men and he took great pride in his body, he didn't like his body getting old.... It was a very erotic, narcissistic thing...like being on stage.... I love the feel of the guitar in my hand'. Mishima inspired the song 'Death and Night and Blood' (from 1979's *Black and White*), written from the point of view of a prowling sex-murderer or rapist. In the nasty chorus, Burnel's alter ego warns a sexy girl not to bend over because 'your brain's exposed', revealing 'rotten thoughts, yeeucch!'. Burnel explained: 'That's a chorus about women and it's very much a part of Yukio... he was a homosexual – in the best possible warrior way, like the Spartans, the Samurai, and Alexander the Great's guard. It was an integral part of their warriorhood, of being very close to fellow warriors. It has to be like that, because you don't take women to war with you.'

For the Stranglers, the significance of punk was that music had gotten hard again after years of limp soft-rock. 'In 1977 rock has become very much a gladiatorial sport,' commented Burnel approvingly. Females were too weak to participate in this men-only activity: 'their bodies decline so quickly. . . by the time they're forty they're soft and flabby, whereas you see handsome men at forty'. Women's place in the scheme of things can be best judged by sampling some of the Stranglers' sniggering humour. On the Women's Movement: 'I like women to move when I'm on top of them.' Or their comment about an incident in Lansing, Michigan, where their appearance was greeted by a demonstration by forty feminists: 'So we tried to kidnap one and kinda manhandled her into the coach whilst being fought off by these women with their big placards and banners. There was a big fracas and she got away, unfortunately. . . but I bet she was really excited and turned on by it.'

The Stranglers' blatant chauvinism and malice was pretty exceptional by the general standards of punk, and was effectively pilloried by the press. The Stranglers were easy to marginalise as a retrogressive throwback, given the traditionalism of their music. More pernicious, and largely ignored, was a strain of sexism peddled by Malcolm McLaren, who, as manager and propagandist of the Sex Pistols, was one of punk's principal ideologues. To echo an infamous quote of the '60s black civil rights campaigner

Stokely Carmichael, McLaren seemed to think 'the only position for women [in the movement] is prone'.

Compare the wildly inventive scams and schemes he dreamed up for the Sex Pistols to his proposed ideas for the all-female group the Slits (McLaren was offered the chance to manage them shortly after Rotten left the Pistols in early 1978). Talking to *Melody Maker*'s Michael Watts in the summer of 1979, he revealed that Chris Blackwell of Island Records offered him a hundred thousand pounds to take on the Slits and make a film with them (with a soundtrack produced by Eurodisco pioneer Giorgio Moroder).

According to Watts, 'McLaren worked out a plot which bears the unmistakable influence of Russ Meyer [the American porn director who was involved in the original unfinished Pistols movie, *Who Killed Bambi?*]. They would be four girls, sent to Mexico by a cheap London cabaret agency, who discover that in effect they have been sold into slavery. Their adventures would be sensational. McLaren still gets excited as he outlines his idea: "The girls, you see, believe in the whole fabulous thing of a rock'n'roll group going to Mexico and making an experience for themselves. But what I wanted to prove was that when they arrived in Mexico, the only thing that the Mexicans wanted to see was their ass and fanny; they would end up strip-tease dancers, totally fed-up and worried and being fucked from one end of Mexico to the other. finally they are married to certain forces in Mexico and become fabulous disco stars."' Clearly McLaren was unable to conceive of a female rebellion or outrage equivalent to what he'd wreaked with the Sex Pistols. He never even considered the Slits as *agents*, only as pawns. Whereas he vicariously identified with the Pistols, McLaren's plans for the Slits were purely exploitative.

After the collapse of the Russ Meyer/*Who Killed Bambi?* project, McLaren began collaborating with Julian Temple on the script for the movie that evolved into *The Great Rock'n'Roll Swindle*. According to Temple, interviewed in

New Music News in 1979, the early version of this script involved guitarist Steve Jones 'going to all these Jewish princesses' homes in Stanmore [where he keeps] seeing these naked girls who invite him to this party, and there'd be a kind of orgy because these girls wanted all these rock stars to come all over them in their suburban drawing room, they wanted Robert Plant to wank all over them ... it did have all the lessons, it was a Swindle, but it was another story, much more anti-feminist'. The idea that it was both cool and subversive for the Pistols' story to have an anti-feminist edge passed by without comment from the interviewer or elucidation from Temple. *The Great Rock'n' Roll Swindle*, when it finally appeared in a much-bowdlerised, de-fanged form, was not devoid of misogyny. There's a scene in which a character based on the music journalist Caroline Coon upbraids Steve Jones for his sexism, only to have ants crawl over her face in an echo/rip-off of Buñuel's *Un Chien Andalou*.

Another peculiar aspect of McLaren's ideology was the concept of incest as a metaphor for cultural stagnation or entropy. Interviewed in *New Music News*, McLaren provocatively declares that buying the Pistols' records was never the point of punk. The interviewer suggests that playing the records was the only way that a 'sixteen-year-old kid in his room with nowhere to go' could feel involved.

MC: 'That's sad, that's really sad. I would prefer him to play nothing. Kick the TV in, smash his mother screw his mother.

NMN: Speaking of fucking one's mother, what happened to *Who Killed Bambi?*, we heard rumours of an incest scene.

MC: Yes, there was, and I think it's the best scene ... for me the wonderful thing was, you know, Russ Meyer, the epitome of American fascism, and y'know, the woman with the big tits ... meets the Sex Pistols and I thought that was very funny. And the scene where Sid [Vicious] fucks his mother, in the midst of it all, was equally funny and, in a way, very moving. I'm very much of the opinion that England ... is a very incestuous country and it's very much a part of its culture. It was especially great 'cos it was written like he'd been doing it for years, it was no big deal. His mother was a hippie, and she was also a heroin addict ....

Julian Temple, a McLaren protégé who later usurped the director's chair for *Swindle*, also parroted the party line: 'I think England is obscene in its stagnant kind of culture; the whole cultural feeling is morbid and incestuous.' A key scene that made it into the final version was one in which Sid Vicious sings 'My Way', and then, at the climax, guns down his audience, including his mother.

Clearly, at some subconscious level, McLaren saw punk as violence aimed at a suffocating, (s)mothering culture. So when Sid Vicious stabbed and killed Nancy Spungen, he was literalising the matricidal content of punk, returning it to source. Spungen was a mother-surrogate, smothering Vicious, turning him against his 'mates', hooking him on heroin, feeding his weaknesses (or so many in the Pistols' camp charged). Vicious's deadly deed re-awakened McLaren's flagging interest in the Pistols, and he rushed off to New York to work on the case for the defence. He saw Spungen's death as a springboard for launching Vicious as a global megastar. There were plans for Vicious to record, while on bail, an album of favourites like 'White Christmas' and 'Mac the Knife' (tasteless or what?). Meanwhile, others in the Pistols' milieu were quick to aim the blame at Vicious's mother, Mrs Anne Beverley, in true anti-momism style. Pistols couturier and McLaren's lover, Vivienne Westwood, accused Mrs Beverley of over-indulging her son. 'Whenever Sid got into trouble she always supported lies to get him off, and then they both ended up believing the lies, or pretending to each other that they did .... taking heroin in front of his mum was like, "look mother, I'm dicing with death. What are you going to do about it?" '

McLaren's dream of turning the killer into a superstar

was an uncanny echo of an earlier scam of his, back when he was just a boutique owner. The idea was to turn 'the Cambridge Rapist into a Pop Star. . . . I thought when they catch this guy, they'd put it on the front pages and proclaim him a terror to our society and make him a scapegoat. So I thought, great, why don't I associate him with Brian Epstein and the Beatles. So I took this mask that he wore and put it on a T-shirt and put "Cambridge Rapist" over it in Pop Star letters and at the bottom put a small picture of Brian Epstein and then wrote a few words about him [not committing] suicide but [dying] of S&M,' he told *New Music News*. McLaren saw his obnoxious T-shirt as a gift to bored fifteen-year-old teenagers – though presumably not to the female ones who really were under daily threat from the Cambridge Rapist. 'I think those ideas really invigorated kids, y'know, they saw them as slightly shocking and that's all that was important . . . to annoy a few people, because they felt so lethargic.'

In the event, Sid died of an overdose; McLaren lost control of what was left of the Pistols, and, disillusioned, went off to make porn movies in Paris. A year or so later, he re-emerged with a new concept, more nakedly anti-woman than ever and with clear links to the aborted Slits project: Bow Wow Wow. This group was fronted by a four-teen-year-old Anglo-Burmese schoolgirl called Annabella Lwin who he claimed he discovered in a London dry cleaner's. Bow Wow Wow would be a vehicle for him to expound a new post punk ethos of 'nouveau savagery', which combined cassette piracy, Burundi rhythms, swashbuckling clothes and tribal style. Another part of the package was underage sex, which included a magazine called *Chicken*. McLaren envisaged it as 'a junior *Playboy* . . . for the primitive boy and girl'.

But before the magazine ever got off the ground, its editor Fred Vermorel resigned. According to *NME*, he alleged that Annabella had been pressured by McLaren to be photographed nude for the magazine, and that McLaren was introducing a pornographic element into the proceedings, effectively turning what was supposed to be a sort of sexy *Smash Hits* into 'a magazine for adults that features kids as objects'. 'Chicken', for those in the know, is slang for underage boys or paedophile jailbait. Later Annabella was prevailed upon to shed her Vivienne Westwood togs for an album cover shot that recreated Manet's once-controversial painting, 'Le Déjeuner Sur L'Herbe'. In five years, McLaren had gone from being a neo-Situationist *agent provocateur* to dirty old man.

born to run:
wanderlust, wilderness and the cult of speed

'*No great man in history ever aspired to get married.*'
Robert Lindner (author of *Rebel Without A Cause:*
The Hypnoanalysis of A Criminal Psychopath)

The rebel is always running away from home. He defines himself against domesticity and dreads being house-trained; home is precisely where adventures don't happen. Heroic life is only possible when the rebel has made the break, distanced himself from what Robert Bly calls the 'force-field' of women.

In interviews, Bly expounds the theory that a generation of young men – 'soft males' – have grown up confused and unhappy because women have sapped their energy, and need a resurrection of male initiation rites to induct them 'completely into the instinctive male world'. Bly had been a peace activist and self-confessed female-identified man in the '60s. But he explains that recently 'I began to think of my father...not as someone who had deprived me of love and attention or companionship, but as someone who had himself been deprived, by his mother or by the culture.' Rather like the Charles Atlas wimp who tires of getting sand kicked in his face, Bly took up theoretical arms.

In his mythomanic tract *Iron John*, Bly converts the ideas of Carl Jung and Joseph Campbell (author of *The Hero With A Thousand Faces*) into a sort of spiritual work-out. He argues that men must reawaken the Wild Man or warrior spirit within. Bly co-founded the Men's Movement, whose activities include men-only consciousness-raising weekends held in the wilderness. Away from women, men were able to get back in touch with their lost virility and commune with the spirits of their negligent fathers. In Bly's view, men's problems stem from identifying too strongly with women, and in particular, their mothers. In mythopoeic terms, they must spurn the Great Mother, and identify with the Serpent.

Robert Bly's schtick is very Jim Morrison; it's easy to imagine the rocker-turned-aspiring-poet, if he hadn't drowned in the bath, becoming a grizzled, big-bellied bard very like Bly. In fact, the Doors' drummer John Densmore is now a disciple of the Men's Movement. In his memoir *Riders on the Storm*, Densmore writes fondly that 'as long as there's young people, they can look to Jim to help them cut the umbilical cord'. One of Morrison's most mythological works, the epic song-cycle 'The Celebration of the Lizard' (from *Absolutely Live*) concerns the psychedelic odyssey of a young man. Significantly, it starts immediately after the death of his mother, which seems to free him existentially. Later in the song-cycle, he wakes up in a motel room, with a shiny, sweat-drenched reptile in his bed: Bly's serpent, symbol of the lost phallus. The death of the mother (Morrison had stressed the fact that her freshly buried body was rotting) seems intimately connected with the boy's access to manhood. By the end of the song-cycle, Morrison's protagonist is a fully fledged Lizard King; in one of his most portentous, preposterous, but mesmerisingly impressive flights of fancy, Jim addresses the audience as though they're a nomadic tribe and he's their prince.

Nomadism, estrangement and flight were constant themes in Morrison's work (one of the most intense sections of 'Celebration of the Lizard' is a panicky, paranoiac ditty simply titled 'Run'). 'Our music is like someone not quite at home,' Morrison said. The Doors' version of psychedelic experience was about disorientation ('Strange Days'), not blissful communion with the cosmos. Morrison actively sought out this feeling of disorientation, driven by Baudelaire's 'Great Malady – horror of one's home'.

Morrison owned nothing and lived nowhere; he lived like a bum and by all accounts stank like one too. Women constituted his 'Soul Kitchen', a nourishing hearth that provided a brief resting-place before he hit the road again.

Domesticity was the enemy, a death of the spirit, in much of British pop culture in the '60s, from social realist films like *A Kind of Loving* and *Saturday Night, Sunday Morning* (where bloodyminded young jack-the-lads are lured into marriage and mired in mediocrity despite all their intentions to the contrary), to songs like the Who's 'A Legal Matter'. Here, marriage makes the protagonist feel like his mind and will are succumbing to the 'household fog' of furnishings, baby's clothes and wedding arrangements. But through the miracle of divorce, he escapes in the nick of time. Like the social realist anti-heroes, he's caught in the trap of working all day for a boss, only to pay it all back to the missus.

The archetypal Stones anthem '(I Can't Get No) Satisfaction' (1965) was a protest against a society which denied young men the possibility of an untamed, virile existence. 'Satisfaction' was a crucial, loaded term in the lexicon of mid-'60s desire, evoking both sexual release and some kind of authentic grandeur of being. And it was the prospect of 'satisfaction' that lured the wild boys into the cage of matrimony. The Stones bounced back with songs like 'Jumping Jack Flash' (1968), the triumphant, strutting story of a boy who's risen above the forces that corral his exuberance – in particular the nagging hag who raised him and chastised him with a strap. The fear of the hag, of the girlfriend metamorphosing into the mother, comes through in 'Have You Seen Your Mother, Baby, Standing In The Shadow' while 'Mother's Little Helper', a sneery song about middle-aged housewives who depend on tranquillisers, identifies women as the enfeebled victims of suburbia.

One of the most striking songs of the '60s to deal with

the mother as a malign, counter-revolutionary force is John's Children's 'Sarah Crazy Child' (1967). Sarah is a wild girl-child who suddenly loses her innocence and savage free spirit. One verse she's 'devouring all her street' with her pagan energy, the next she's turned thirteen and has 'forgotten how to dream'. Her brother is similarly untamed, but neither are able to escape a lugubrious fate that's somehow connected to their 'broken dusty mother' with her melted-wax face. Their craziness is crushed by stifling conformity: 'soullessly they submitted to the guillotine of their home'.

this is not a love song

As part of its all-out assault on the illusions of conventionality, punk also repudiated domesticity as a quicksand of comfort which blunted one's 'edge'. It rejected the love song, and by implication love, as escapist and sentimental. Johnny Rotten (John Lydon) dismissed sex with squeamish indifference as 'two minutes of squelching'. In Public Image Limited's 'Fodderstompf' (from the 1978 self-titled debut LP) he impersonated an emotionally needy parent (almost certainly a mother) as a high-pitched amoeba-like creature whimpering that they – the clingy, over-protective parents – 'only wanted to be loved'. For Lydon, this is weak: emotional bonds are really sucking wounds that vampirishly extract your will-power and pull you into a dank quagmire of sentimental, invertebrate goo. Later in PiL's career came the sexual-intercourse-as-black-hole scenario of 'Track 8', with its imagery of erupting fat, looming tunnels, and sardonic parroting of phrases like 'total commitment'; the anti-security and comfort diatribe of 'Home Is Where the Heart Is'; the self-explanatory 'This Is Not A Love Song'. For John Lydon, love is a distraction from the vital business of hate and rage and disgust. Even later on in his career – married and happy to talk in interviews of the joys of mature love –

he was unable to deal with sentimental themes in his music, which remained at the level of bilious diatribe. A similar idea resurfaced in Gang of Four's 'Love Like Anthrax' (from *Entertainment*, 1979). With the key image of the lovesick victim as 'a beetle on its back', this bunch of neo-Marxists seemed to regard love as a disabling, paralysing force that diverted energy from the righteous business of political analysis and activism. The track has two vocalists. One sings, lamenting his lovelorn addiction; the other speaks in a dry monotone, dissecting the way love is privileged in pop. It's as though Gang of Four regard love as the twentieth century's equivalent to religion, Marx's 'opiate of the people'.

Of course, it wasn't just male punk groups that pissed on ideas of emotional commitment, as can be seen by all-girl group the Slits' gleefully sarcastic 'Love Und Romance'. Gang of Four's anti-love stance was inspired by radical feminism's critique of romance, marriage and the family. But whereas women questioning romantic love is a break with the norm (female singer-songwriters' subject matter usually being confined to affairs of the heart), male rockers rejecting commitment unfortunately chimes with a long tradition in rock. Punk's anti-love stance has endured: in the sleevenotes of *Atomizer* (1986) Big Black saluted all the groups 'who don't write love songs' (which recalls the Italian Futurist declaration that painters should abandon the female nude) while Nirvana's multi-million selling *Nevermind* (1992) contains two songs, 'Breed' and 'In Bloom', that are riddled with the fear of reproduction and emotional stagnation. 'Breed', commented singer Kurt Cobain, was about 'Middle America. Marrying at age eighteen, getting pregnant, stuck with a baby – and not wanting it'. (Ironically, Cobain was married and a dad within a year.) As for punk-metal brutes Guns N'Roses, even their tenderest song, 'Sweet Child O' Mine' (*Appetite for Destruction*, 1987) is riddled with ambivalence about love. At first Axl Rose waxes lyrical about his girl as a womb-like sanctuary from an intolerable world. But towards the end, the music turns from idyllic to rampant as Rose runs up against the impasse of happiness: 'Where do we go now?' It's almost as though the cocoon has gotten too cosy, and Axl's thinking, 'time to make a break'.

Even that most unmanly and housebound of anti-rebels, Morrissey, has made attacks on the holy institution of matrimony. The Smiths' 'William It Was Really Nothing' (1984) is addressed to a male friend and possibly unrequited paramour of Morrissey's who is on the verge of abandoning their life of intensity for the ignominy of marriage to a plump girl who doesn't 'care about anything'. William is betraying their spiritual, high-minded relationship for the conventional rewards of comfort, materialism and readily available sex.

Generally, in songs and interviews Morrissey comes over as the paradigm of the mother's boy. But in one song, 'The Queen Is Dead' (title track of the Smiths' 1986 album), Morrissey appears to be grasping for some way to make a break. 'The Queen Is Dead' is a complex allegory of England's decline. It is consciously intended as a sequel to the Sex Pistols' anti-Royalist anthem 'God Save the Queen', which lambasted the Jubilee celebrations of 1977 as regressive nostalgia for a lost British glory. Unconsciously, 'The Queen Is Dead' also seems to hark back to Malcolm McLaren's vision of English culture as incestuous, claustrophobic and moribund. One verse is addressed to Prince Charles, jestingly asking if he's never wanted to appear on the front pages of the tabloid newspapers wearing his mother's bridal clothes. This peculiar identification with the Prince of Wales can be perhaps explained as the recognition of something in common between Morrissey – the ascetic recluse whose life has never begun – and Charles, the increasingly pathetic figure who's never been allowed his birthright. As Julian Barnes put it: 'What is his role as he waits in limbo, knowing that he can become what he was born for only by the death of his mother?'

Charles is an emasculated, eccentric and risible figure because his domineering matron of a mother won't step down. Similarly Morrissey declares of himself: 'When you're tied to your mother's apron/no one talks about castration'. England's stagnation seems intimately connected to this state of matriarchy, which condemns the sons to the stasis of arrested development and eternal adolescence. Morrissey knows the umbilical cord must be severed, yet he's fixated nostalgically on both his youth and the mythical glory of an earlier England. The title 'The Queen Is Dead' refers both to the rule of matriarchy and Morrissey's own neurasthenia and non-life. In another song on the album, 'I Know It's Over', Morrissey calls out to his mother, wailing that he can 'feel the soil' covering his body: he's being buried alive.

At other points in his oeuvre, love and successful relationships appear to Morrissey as rose-tinted glasses that blur one's view of the void. 'In a way, I believe all those things like love, sex, sharing a life with somebody, are actually quite vague,' he's said. 'Being only with yourself can be much more intense.' To maintain such clear vision, he's dedicated himself to a life of keeping satisfaction at arm's length: 'I don't want anything to interfere with this state of dissatisfaction.'

runnin' scared

'If I'm free it's 'cause I'm always running.'
Jimi Hendrix

Why are rock rebels so restless? Immobility is threatening; movement in itself defines them as 'free men'. These men are continually re-making the break by making a break for it. Commitment and closeness quickly become enclosure.

For the beatniks, constant mobility re-affirmed possibi- lity. The beat ethos filtered into rock via Bob Dylan. According to Philip Saville, 'Dylan was *going out on the road*. That was the main reason, I think, why he had such an impact. . . You had this whole new generation of middle- class young people who used Dylan as a role model of rebel- lion against parental constraint.' His songs often concerned lone rangers making solitary journeys. In 'Hurricane', a man finds paradise riding the horse trails, but the danger of jail, where society turns a free man into a mouse, always looms. These heroic odysseys often begin with a man leaving a woman ('Don't Think Twice', 'Going Going Gone', 'We Better Talk This Over', 'Isis'). As Paul Hodson wrote in his essay, 'Bob Dylan's Stories About Men', 'Dylan had con- tested many aspects of the dominant culture, but not its preferred styles of masculinity.' Women are still bookends to men's journeys of self-discovery.

Elsewhere, Dylan identified with outlaws and itinerants. 'Ballad of Donald White' was about a killer who killed because, said Dylan, 'he couldn't find no room in his life. Now they killed him cause he couldn't find no room in life. They killed him and when they did I lost some of my room in life.' Dylan liked to portray himself in a similar light: he made out that he was an orphan from New Mexico who'd spent a lot of time on the road, when in fact he was from a middle-class Jewish family from Minnesota.

A contemporary of Dylan's who really brought out the machismo inherent in the lone ranger posture was the folk- blues singer Tim Rose. For him, going your own way was the only response to a world where you're either a vassal or a renegade. In his sleevenotes for Rose's 1968 debut album *Morning Dew*, David Rubinson is more than a little in awe of the singer's prodigious masculinity. 'Tim Rose hits you in the belly. . . . He is a man, and he is his own man. His songs are about his loneliness in a world of neuters. . . . He must be swallowed whole – progressively detailed analyses. . . serve only to uncover the further depths of this man's masculinity. . . . And if you choke, and cannot consume – don't be polite – for the last thing Tim would ever do would be to apologise for sticking in your craw.' Fascinating imagery – particularly the bit about choking on Rose's enormous manhood!

In song, Rose's personas ranged from the emotionally armoured man-fortress who's a law unto himself ('I'm Gonna Be Strong', 'I Gotta Do Things My Way', in which he resists a woman who tries to mould him like clay) to the wife-killers of 'Hey Joe' and 'Long Time Man'. The great appeal of Rose's songs and tough-guy persona is the way he makes poignantly vivid the painful cost of such a lone ranger existence, as in 'Where Was I?', the lament of an emotionally constipated man who mourns having kept his feelings inside all his life and missing his chance for tenderness.

Dylan's neo-beatnik romanticism birthed a tradition in rock that includes Bruce Springsteen's paeans to (auto) mobility ('Blinded by the Light', 'Born to Run', 'Thunder Road' *ad nauseam*), which present small-town life as a claustrophobic death-trap. Tom Petty is another inheritor of the Dylan posture. In 'Freefallin' (from 1989's *Full Moon Fever*), his girlfriend is the quintessence of sugar-and-spice-and-all-things-nice, but he callously breaks her heart anyway, because he's a 'bad boy' with the itch of restlessness in his soul. The video for the song contrasts the squeaky-clean niceness of the girl's '50s-style garden party with the Petty character runnin' wild with a pack of subcultural boys and girls in the funkier streets of LA. 'Freefallin' is, for Petty, a sublime state of suspension, a cutting loose from the sterility of the 'woman's world' of shopping malls and suburbia. The song harks back to Chuck Berry's prototypical rock'n'roll motor anthem 'No Particular Place to Go' and links up Berry's freeway freedom with a modern form of going nowhere fast, skateboarding (which figures in the video as a symbol of free-fall).

Other songs by Tom Petty, solo and with the

Heartbreakers (and what a suggestive band name!) – like 'King's Highway', 'Into the Great Wide Open' and 'Learning to Fly' – obsessively reiterate this fantasy of motion as a means of transcending mundanity. 'Into the Great Wide Open' is intended as a satire on certain cliched notions of rebellion – a wry, avuncular comment from the experienced Petty on the tantrums of Guns N'Roses and their ilk. But in the video, the punky puppet Johnny Rebel (played by Johnny Depp) really comes a cropper when his female manager (Faye Dunaway), having been spurned, casts a malign spell on his career, and when, even more bizarrely, his starlet wife gets pregnant and has a baby. Those darn women! In the end, Depp leaves his wife and home on the back of a motorbike driven by his roadie, played by Petty: two generations of rebels riding off into the sunset together.

no expectations

For the sexual nomad, anywhere he lays his hat is home. It's a classic persona – from early rock'n'roll (the hit'n'run lover of Dion's 'The Wanderer'), through mid-'60s R&B (the Pretty Things' 'Roadrunner' and 'Don't Bring Me Down', which boasts 'don't want a home') to heavy metal (Led Zeppelin's 'Ramble On', whose hero is forever bidding farewell and heading off in search of an impossible ideal woman). He's kinetic, won't be tied down to any one chick or place.

The Rolling Stones enshrined this stance in their restless name and with songs like 'No Expectations' (from *Beggars Banquet*, 1968), the blues of a wandering cocksman. Also on that album, the Stones seized on a Biblical prototype of the footloose rebel in 'Prodigal Son'. As Simon Frith points out, the appeal of the legend is that the Prodigal Son is rewarded and beloved by Father far more than the boy who stayed at home and behaved: his return is greeted with the killing of the fatted calf. The Prodigal

Son's sin is that he rejects the 'constant behavioural calculus' and 'moral accounting' of settled existence, makes up his life as he goes along, lives for Now. To be prodigal is to be extravagant, to squander time, to refuse to worry about consequences and other inhibitions inherent in maturity.

But living without laws, on call to desire twenty-four hours a day, is a dangerous way to live. The revolt against the reality principle (which enforces deferment of gratification) opens up an existential void in which desire can turn demonic. The ultimate rebel turns out to be the psychopath. On 1969's *Let It Bleed*, the Stones' sexual nomad has turned into a sinister predator, the roaming sex-murderer of 'Midnight Rambler' who doesn't just break away from home-life, he breaks *into* homes. *Let It Bleed* was the first time the Stones acknowledged that the counter-culture's push to shake off all moral constraints had gone too far. Once they mocked, in 'Mother's Little Helper', the desperate middle-aged housewives who run 'to the shelter' of tranquillisers; now, in 'Gimme Shelter', it's they who are retreating from the world, who yearn for sanctuary. Once the Stones were menacing, their prowling machismo pregnant with the subliminal promise of rape; now they warn us of the ever-present threat of 'rape and mu-u-urdah'. 'You Can't Always Get What You Want' is their acquiescence to limits, their abandonment of abandon and declaration that they've had their fill of insatiability.

The road-and-world-weary homecoming of 'Moonlight Mile' (*Sticky Fingers*, 1970) leads on to 1972's *Exile on Main Street*, where the Rolling Stones are really starting to gather some moss. The travelling minstrel of 'No Expectations' and the rebel-nomad of 'Prodigal Son' are replaced by a more derelict cast of tattered vagabonds, hobos, gamblers, transients and desperados, all footsore on the road to nowhere. The strutting braggadocio of the early Stones becomes the ragged, burnt-out decrepitude of 'Torn and Frayed', the longing for salvation of 'Let It Loose', 'Loving Cup' and 'Shine A Light', and at best, the battered resilience of 'Soul Survivor'.

But after this 'low' point – their most affecting, unmacho album – the Stones gradually recovered their mean streak, even exceeding their past misogyny with the S/M advertising campaign for *Black and Blue* (a bruised and bound blonde declared 'I'm Black and Blue from the Rolling Stones and I love it'). As late as 1978's *Some Girls*, Jagger was still espousing a life free of ties. 'Beast of Burden' cloaks a shying away from commitment in terms of generosity: Jagger says he doesn't want a drudge to nursemaid him, but what he really wants is sex without emotional bonds.

Iggy Pop was another archetypal rock rebel obsessed with mobility and scared of emotional stagnation. 'I never want to be stuck with peas and potatoes, and some hag with gook falling off her face, nagging, and me taking it,' he said in an 1979 interview with the *NME*. 'I tell you all the bitches – all these women – want me now because they can sense that strength in me, and they want it so-o bad. But they're not gonna get me uh huh – only on my terms, and my terms are simply phoning 'em up, telling them to be at such and such a place and such and such a time, in good physical condition, to be fucked and then leave, goddamnit. Because I've got more important things to do, and I cannot, and will not, have my time wasted.' Beyond mere sexual nomadism, Iggy had organised a sort of home delivery sex system. In the Stooges' 'Scene of the Crime', Iggy tells of an affair with an older woman in the suburbs: she gave him money, love, head, but now she's getting old, ugly and slow-witted, so he's gonna abandon her. 'I Gotta Right', meanwhile, is a declaration of independence, which can only be upheld by exercising his right to move on 'any old time' he likes.

The Stooges' raw proto-punk is regarded as the antithesis of Lynyrd Skynyrd's sprawling Southern boogie. In fact, their street tough swagger was almost identical, bar the accent. Skynyrd's 'Freebird' is a simultaneously stalwart and sorrowful statement of autonomy, with singer Ronnie Van Zandt bidding farewell to his woman and taking full blame for his incorrigibly restless nature, to the accompaniment of a poignant slide guitar figure that has all the pathos of a detumescent penis slipping out after sex. After the verses, the freebird's flight above the mundane is conjured by a long solo, whose agonised lyricism, swashbuckling derring-do and endlessly escalating crescendos make it a Dixie cousin to Television's 'Marquee Moon'. In his lyrics, Van Zandt vacillated between 'comin' home' and running scared of settled life. 'On the Hunt' recognises a kindred spirit in a groupie who's also looking for sexual kicks without commitment, and therefore deserves his respect instead of traditional rock chauvinist contempt.

wild in the wilderness

Lynyrd Skynyrd's stagnant but febrile boogie perfectly caught the downered vibe of the counterculture's aftermath, the sense of contracted possibilities. The band also had something in common with the Outlaw movement in country and western (trailblazed by artists like Waylon Jennings and Willie Nelson), which rejected the rhinestone MOR-isation of country. Like early '70s rock, the Outlaw movement mourned the closing of the frontier: for rock, what was lost was the existential wilderness opened up in the '60s; for country, it was the Wild West. And where rock romanticised the biker, country romanticised the trucker as a twentieth-century cowboy. Both were throwbacks to a grander age.

Post-war, demobilised soldiers who couldn't face settling down to peacetime mediocrity often became truckers or bikers. Both were a sort of lumpen version of the beatnik: 'travelling but never arriving', popping pep-pills to keep going, leaving the women behind. The beatniks' optimism and wanderlust also came out of the exuberance of the post-war period, a momentum that peaked in the '60s and then ebbed in the '70s. Actor Dennis Hopper's career marks out the trajectory of this spirit – from the hippie road-wanderer Billy in *Easy Rider* to the psychotic drug fiend of *Blue Velvet* to the crippled, house-bound biker Feck in *River's Edge*. In the latter films, the directors (David Lynch and Tim Hunter respectively) were clearly playing on Hopper's aura as the rebel outsider – an iconic status derived from *Easy Rider*. This 1969 movie was really just a psychedelic era update of the Western; at one point Billy jokes that he and his cohort Captain America (Peter Fonda) are 'out here in the wilderness, fighting cowboys and Indians'. *Easy Rider* reimagines the frontier as a state of mind as much as a geographical zone; its argument is that the counterculture has more to do with the 'true' spirit of America (rugged individualism, pioneer adventurism) than do all the flag-waving conformists and corporate men who regard themselves as patriotic citizens and see hippies as un-American.

Just as in the real historical pioneer era, women are extremely marginal figures in *Easy Rider*. Early in their journey from Los Angeles across the desolate southwest, the biker heroes stop to rest at a farmer's place; they're impressed by his settled self-sufficiency, complete with silent, baby-machine wife. It's clear that they respect him because he's 'his own man'. Later, the duo stop off at a hippie commune, where middle-class drop-outs are trying to grow their own food and reinvent the pioneer ideal. Just like at the good ol' boy's farm, the commune women are largely occupied with cooking and looking after the kids.

When they get to New Orleans, Billy and Captain America stop off at a whorehouse, but seem uninterested in such base activities as sex; instead, they take two hookers with them on an acid trip. At the height of the trip, Captain America can be found hugging a statue, weeping 'you're such a fool, mother, and I hate you so much', which obscurely hints at some kind of anti-momist impetus driving his wanderlust. Finally, the duo hit the road again, not knowing that they're heading towards their deaths. The movie may have kicked off with the revved-up anticipation of Steppenwolf's 'Born To Be Wild', but by the end, the devil-may-care optimism has become road-weary defeatism, evoked by Roger McGuinn's version of Bob Dylan's 'It's Alright Ma, I'm Only Bleeding'.

With its influences – *On the Road*, Dylan, Ken Kesey's romanticisation of the Hell's Angels – *Easy Rider* could hardly fail to have a misogynist subtext. Ellen Willis saw the movie as another symptom of the male-supremacist nature of the counterculture. 'Some heroes of the counterculture [she cites John Sinclair, the jailed Michigan activist, MC5 manager and White Panther supremo, as a classic example] equate rebellion with the assertion of their maleness, become obnoxiously aggressive, arrogant and violent, and espouse a version of utopia in which women are reduced to faceless instruments of their sexual fantasies.' But the hippie idea of resurrecting the pioneer spirit was fraught with problems for women from the start. As Peter N. Carroll and David W. Noble note in *The Free and the Unfree: A New History of the United States*, 'frontiers were the domain of soldiers, of the strongest young men'; survival in that domain demanded a soldierly mentality. Part of the appeal of the frontier is that it's a woman-free zone, or at least one where women's role is limited to bandaging wounds, keeping the pot warm, and waiting for the men to return from their adventures.

Around the same time as *Easy Rider*, Sam Peckinpah was making movies like *Pat Garrett and Billy the Kid* and *The Wild Bunch* – elegies for the lost Wild West that echo many of the counterculture's themes about the betrayal of an original American frontier spirit. Peckinpah saw the Wild West as governed by a 'natural justice': might was right, the quickest draw won. Peckinpah grew up as a cowboy and hunter, went to military school, then fought with the Marines. His personality certainly conformed to the soldierly model that thrived in the frontier zone: he was paranoid and always kept a gun by his bedside; he was a workaholic who feared inactivity would drain away his masculine life-essence (James Coburn described him as 'afraid he would dissipate' if he stopped working).

A Peckinpah film was a men-only desert of battle-forged camaraderie, where pent-up emotion finds release in orgasmic carnage. Peckinpah's lone ranger ethos resonates throughout rock culture, from the Eagles' *Desperado* album to Los Lobos' *How Will the Wolf Survive?* to the outright corn of Jon Bon Jovi's *Blaze of Glory*. Heavy metal has often been a home for Peckinpah-style survivalism. On their self-titled 1991 album, war-obsessed Metallica wrote a hymn to the wilderness in 'Of Wolf and Man', while in 'Wherever I May Roam' singer James Hetfield describes the open road as his bride, and growls 'off the beaten track, I reign'. Then there's Ted Nugent, the doyen of Libertarian Right metal, with songs and albums like 'Fist Fightin' Son of A Gun' and *Weekend Warriors* (1978). Nugent combines heavy metal's sexual predator stance with a quite literal obsession with hunting: he even publishes his own bow-hunting magazine in order to propagandise for the mystical relationship of 'mutual respect' between hunter and prey.

after the goldrush

Although it began with high hopes ('lookin' for adventure', as Steppenwolf sing it), *Easy Rider* is gradually shadowed by a vague foreboding feeling that the counterculture 'blew it' (as one of the bikers concludes). If *Easy Rider* has an unofficial sequel, it's *Two Lane Blacktop*, in which James Taylor plays a near-catatonic driver who roams the US highway system competing in drag races, but only to win enough money to keep moving down the road to nowhere.

The film ends with the celluloid catching fire, as Taylor accelerates blindly forward in yet another race, symbolising post-counterculture burn-out.

As this sense that the moment had passed deepened, Neil Young captured the vibe with albums like *Everybody Knows This Is Nowhere* (1969) and *After the Goldrush* (1970). The latter was situated in the aftermath of the two great traumas of American history: the foreclosing of the geographical frontier in the late nineteenth century and the psychic wilderness opened in the late 1960s. Neil Young and Crazy Horse became rock's counterpart to Peckinpah's gang of grizzly, aged outlaws in *The Wild Bunch*: renegade survivors of a nobler age, extinguished by the railroad companies in the 1890s and by the systematisation of the record industry in the 1970s. Right through to the '90s, Young's songs replayed the same old themes: the longing for open space free of settlements and sell-outs, where you could be your own man.

Back in the era of post-goldrush *tristesse*, with the '60s fading but its after-image still haunting the collective mind's eye, Bruce Springsteen emerged: not the future of rock'n'roll so much as a reinvocation of its past glory and continued dogged survival (if we all kept the faith). Initially, he appeared to be a kind of small-town Dylan, with bilious irony replaced by open-hearted populism. Like the itinerant Dylan persona, Springsteen's alter egos were invariably 'Born To Run'. In 'Lost In the Flood' (from 1973's *Greetings from Ashbury Park N.J*) he's a lone wolf with 'bound for glory' painted on the side of his Chevy, who rides headlong into a hurricane and disappears. Cars and speed are the heroic way out of the claustrophobic confines of small-town mediocrity. In 'Thunder Road' (*Born to Run*, 1975) his girl's looking for a saviour but he can only offer his car; Heaven lies somewhere at the end of the highway.

The freedom to just up and move somewhere else has always had a special utopian resonance in American culture. But the root meaning of utopia is 'no-place': the search for the dream can take you out of nowheresville only to strand you on the 'going nowhere' of the road. In 'Born to Run', the small town is a 'death trap', yet Springsteen knows that his flight is foredoomed: the road is littered with 'broken heroes'. In this masculine last-ditch break for freedom, women are offered the passenger seat; Springsteen suggestively invites his girl to wrap her legs around his throbbing machine.

born to go: the motorik beat

'Movement is always to be preferred to inaction. In motion a man has a chance... his instincts are quick... he can make a little better nervous system, make it a little more possible to go again, to go faster next time...'
Norman Mailer, 'The White Negro: Superficial Reflections on the Hipster', 1957

The idea of rock as an odyssey or flight gradually sublimated itself into a desire for pure *speed* – velocity itself as the guarantor of freedom. To be in motion is to be neither here nor there, to inhabit flux. The beats perceived the onrush and saturation of stimuli as a way of breaking down psychic defences and opening the soul to oceanic fusion with the world. Steppenwolf's 'Born to be Wild' is the classic rock'n'roll expression of this headlong drive. The road-warrior thrusts forward ('explode into space') but is enfolded in the world's 'love embrace': he's both penetrator and penetrated. The poet Lord Byron believed that mobility encouraged a 'feminised' receptivity in men, 'an excessive susceptibility of immediate impressions' that allows for a kind of psychic wholeness or androgyny.

In Camille Paglia's *Sexual Personae*, Byron comes off as a psychic surfer, whose breezy, fluid style incarnated a desire to never get bogged down or domesticated. And she sees a connection between this Byronic skimming and the

American 'born to run' sensibility: 'Driving is the American Sublime, for which there is no perfect parallel in Europe.' Certainly, it's true that American rock'n'roll pioneered auto anthems with Chuck Berry's 'No Particular Place to Go' and then the Beach Boys' sun-kissed odes to surfing and driving. But arguably the aesthetic really flowered in Europe with the *motorik* sound – bands like Kraftwerk and Neu! whose music simulated the steady pulsating rhythm of vehicular motion.

The dawn of *motorik* was probably the Doors' 'LA Woman', with its regular-as-carburettor beat and swirly images of Los Angeles as urban wilderness. Jim Morrison imagines the city as a lonely woman, as the love of his life, and he's so entranced by his vision he gets an erection ('Mr Mojo risin''). Jonathan Richman and the Modern Lovers' 'Roadrunner' is a proto-punk paean to the neon beauty of the modern world, a serenade to the highway, described as 'my girlfriend'. Then there was Hawkwind, who gave the Steppenwolf biker pose a cosmic twist on space rock(et) mantras like 'Silver Machine' and 'Born To Go'.

The German bands Kraftwerk and Neu! took this rhapsodic exaltation of motion to its highest pitch (appropriately enough, since the Third Reich actually invented the freeway). It's also true, as Lester Bangs noted, that the Germans invented speed, i.e. metamphetamine, 'which of all accessible tools has brought human beings within the closest twitch of machinehood'. Kraftwerk's 'Autobahn' (1974), which flattened out the steady beat of 'LA Woman' and 'Roadrunner' even further into a perfect, uninflected regularity, was a hymn to the ease and nonchalance of driving. This was a state of grace, of being at home in the world, that depended on being *between homes*, never stationary. Kraftwerk were fond of the Velvet Underground and the Stooges (who'd both played trance rock mantras and ingested a ton of speed), but their biggest rock influence was the Beach Boys. The latter represented the Apollonian rather than Dionysian side of rock: serene, sun-worshipping, classically proportioned, contemplative.

The Apollonian tendency in art – towards clarity of form, contour, elegance – is a flight from the murk and goo of the Dionysian, animalistic side of humanity. Among Kraftwerk's early '70s 'Krautrock' contemporaries, Neu! took this Apollonian tendency the furthest. Their music was pure *motorik*: regular-as-clockwork, unsyncopated beats, with nary a trace of boogie grit or raunch, and an iridescent, transcendental guitar sound. This mostly instrumental rock conjured a sense of frictionless forward movement into a realm of ever-widening wonderment. Neu!'s name evoked a sense of rebirth. Their music's fleetness, airiness and sun-blessed radiance banished the shadowy murk of 'the dark side' of the psyche and soared, Icarus-like, for the heart of the sun. While Neu! songs mostly evoked motion or ascension, 'Leb' Wohl' (from *Neu! 75*) looked to the ocean for its image of beatific plenitude, with gasped, awe-struck vocals and nonchalant whistling set amidst lapping waves, and music that for once summons up a sense of coming to rest rather than propulsion. After this seaside idyll, the album revs up with the spangly blur of 'Hero', whose glorybound protagonist hurtles headlong into the void. Immobility and speed are the two poles of the quest for nirvana.

the new speed freaks

In the early '90s, speed made a comeback with British youth desperate to exempt themselves from an increasingly oppressive reality. This was the subculture called 'ardkore, or hardcore techno (a brutal *motorik* dance music, distantly descended from Kraftwerk). As rave culture's drug of choice, Ecstasy, became progressively more adulterated with amphetamine, or usurped by bogus E tablets concocted from speed and LSD, the music's beats-per-minute rate accelerated. House had been about 120 bpm; 'ardkore reached speeds of 140, 150, 160 bpm, and beyond. In the process, a new speed-freak subculture was spawned that combined the euphoria of raving with the manic rage of punk.

Amphetamine promotes sexless concentration, single-minded focus; in overdose, it can cause temporary psychosis. From the highly combustible narcissism of mod and Northern Soul, to the grandiosity and paranoia of punk (Johnny Rotten sang, in the Pistols' 'Seventeen', of how speed was 'all I need', how it made him vacantly self-sufficient), amphetamine-spiked rock has had a solipsistic, megalomaniac aura. The Jesus and Mary Chain's 'The Living End' captured the psychopathic element to speed: the self-worshipping motorbike rider declares 'there's nothing else but me'. In their book about amphetamine abuse, *The Speed Culture*, Lester Grinspoon and Peter Hedblom cite the case of a needle-using speed-freak who talked of his chronic habit as 'a love affair' and referred to himself as 'we'. In a later chapter, we'll connect this 'royal we' to the 'royal nirvana' (Paul Virilio) provided by drugs like heroin and speed. Suffice it to say that if disconnection 'is the genius of patriarchy', as Robin Morgan claims, then speed is the ultimate patriarchal drug.

Hardcore techno sometimes reaches an apoplectic intensity that's pure punk. The cyber-Wagner bombast of Human Resource's 'The Dominator' is topped with a psychotic rap that climaxes with 'There is no other/I wanna kiss myself'. 'Ardkore's frenzy offers a kind of autistic bliss. The music surges blindly, its acceleration-to-nowhere captured in the intransitive catchphrases chanted by MCs: 'let's go', ''ere we go', 'rush!', 'buzzing', ''ardkore's firing'. Like a rollercoaster, the music is a test of ego against ultra-intense sensation, taking the individual through panic (in the original Greek meaning, a transport of ecstasy-beyond-terror) to the brink of blackout.

Paul Virilio, the great theorist of speed, writes of velocity's effect as a 'perpetually repeated hijacking of the subject from any spatial-temporal context'. You're gone, totally out of it. You can trace a line from the beat novelist John Clellon Holmes's Go, through Marlon Brando's biker in *The Wild One* (who declares 'we don't go anywhere, we just go'), through to techno whizzkid Moby's dancefloor hit 'Go'. From the beatnik odyssey to the ballistic rush of beats-per-minute culture, the destination is nirvana.

In the subcultural politics of rave culture, the rise of 'ardkore was perceived as a swing towards a more masculine aesthetic (harder, faster, noisier, brutal, anti-melodic). For some it was a degeneration from the polymorphous sensuality of earlier rave music, with the scene being invaded by hordes of rowdy, working-class nutters. 'Ardkore was denounced as 'the new heavy metal'. But the sublimity of pure speed is as much a longing for ego dissolution as a hyper-masculine assertion of self. The urge to surge and the urge to merge fuse in a raging oceanic feeling. In 'ardkore's chaotic swirl, you become an androgyne.

In the '60s, the word 'raver' was used to describe hysterical/nymphomaniac teenage groupies. Rave music induces a hysteric-isation of the male body. Rave culture is all about clitoris-envy. Where the multi-orgasmic '70s disco of Donna Summer's 'Love To Love You Baby' once provoked male lust, techno's sped-up, euphoric female vocals conjure a hyper-real rapture that (male) ravers *identify* with and *aspire* to. And here, they're taking their cue from gay culture, where the men always identified with the disco diva's ecstasy. Gay eroticism has filtered, via house and techno, into the body-consciousness of straight, working-class boys, and finds a perfect fit with their homosocial laddishness. Rave culture, like its speed-freak ancestors mod and Northern Soul, is remarkable for its asexuality; dancers frug and twirl for the self-pleasuring, narcissistic bliss of it, not to attract a potential mate. This 'androgyny' may really be a subconscious attempt to usurp female potencies and pleasures, in order to dispense with real women altogether. In Holland, there's an ultra-fast counterpart to UK 'ardkore called gabberhouse – gabber meaning 'mate, lad, yobbo' – where tracks reach a suicidal 200 bpm. One of the biggest gabber hits was by a band called Sperminator, simply titled: 'No Woman Allowed'.

brothers in arms:
combat rock and other stories for boys

The frontier, the road, the wilderness: the rebel's realm is a world without women. Another men-only zone is the battlefield. In *Male Fantasies*, Klaus Theweleit psychoanalyses the warrior mentality, revealing the 'soldier male' to be someone who uses the fraternity of combat to escape Robert Bly's 'force-field' of women. Theweleit focuses on the Freikorps, a right-wing militia formed by veterans of the First World War who banded together to put down working-class uprisings amid the chaos that followed Germany's defeat. These soldiers felt there was an intimate connection between the humiliation of the German Reich by the Allies and their own feelings of emasculation following demobilisation. The end of the war meant, for them, an ignominious return to the mediocrity of bourgeois life, to domesticity – the world of women. They yearned for a new, potent father figure to follow, and eventually found one in Hitler. But in the meantime, civil war – attacking the 'enemy within', the German proletariat – allowed the soldier males to sustain their dream of a heroic life.

It might seem a long leap from the proto-fascist Freikorps to the left-wing rabble-rousing punk anthems of the Clash. Yet the Clash's songs ache with a lust for glory and are riddled with highly charged militaristic imagery. All the Clash's role models are young, masculine, and in some sense at war – sometimes literally, as with the Sandinista guerillas or the Baader Meinhof terrorists, sometimes symbolically, as renegades repudiating a failed and fatally compromised society. Their oeuvre is a veritable feast of rebel iconography, from the classic American outsiders (James Dean, Montgomery Clift, Marlon Brando, Robert De Niro's vigilante in *Taxi Driver*, the Western gunslingers of *The Magnificent Seven*) to the Jamaican rude boy hoodlums of *The Harder They Come* and the Rastafarian 'exiles on Main Street' of roots reggae.

Along with their desperate search for heroic role models, the Clash's worldview was homosocial in the extreme. It's not that their songs are misogynist, but rather that they seem to have nothing to say to, about, or for women. You can count on one hand the number of songs in their immense oeuvre that are addressed to or even passingly refer to a woman, while there are endless anthems exhorting (the) 'boys' to action. The real object of the Clash's ardour is the bliss of boyish camaraderie, the potency of a strength-in-numbers that falls midway between the teenage gang and a military formation. A 1954 'dream letter' from the beat novelist John Clellon Holmes to Allen Ginsberg captures the Clash's spirit decades before they existed. 'The social organisation which is most true of itself to the artist is the boy gang' – to which Ginsberg added, 'not society's perfum'd marriage'. Perhaps it was a recognition of this shared homosocial sensibility that led Ginsberg to write and recite some poetry for the track 'Ghetto Defendant' on the Clash's *Combat Rock*.

From very early on the Clash were paired with the Sex Pistols, each representing one side of punk's soul. The Clash were punk's super-ego: socially committed (if seldom explicitly politically affiliated), idealistic and generally more life-affirming. The Sex Pistols were punk's id: unbridled negativity, oscillating between rage and self-abuse, ultimately tending towards solipsism and self-destruction. The Clash were about bonding, about creating a sense of 'we', a unity of disaffection. The Sex Pistols were about breaking bonds; their art was a theatre of tyranny and abjection. As such the Pistols could at least acknowledge the existence of sexuality, if only in terms of horror and disgust ('Bodies', 'Submission'). The Clash's music is amongst the most chaste rock'n'roll ever created: hoarsely hollered insurrectionary anthems, carried by martial, unsyncopated rhythms.

'We had group discussions,' recalled singer Joe Strummer, 'Bernie [Rhodes, the Clash's manager] would say "An issue, an issue. Don't write about love, write about what's affecting you, what's important."' One of the few songs about a relationship with a girl, Mick Jones's 'I'm So Bored With You' was misheard by Joe Strummer as 'I'm So Bored With the USA', and so he wrote an anti-American lyric for it. You couldn't ask for a more dramatic example of the way punk learned the art of rejection from mod put-down songs, and metamorphosised misogyny into militancy. The only song on their debut album *The Clash* (1977) that even acknowledged sexuality was 'Protex Blue', which was about the soullessness of depersonalised sexual encounters.

The Clash's real subject matter was frustration, bore-dom and the lust for action. In 'London's Burning' the metropolis is ablaze with ennui. 'Career Opportunities' rages against spirit-nullifying employment, while '48 Hours' concerned the 'weekender' lifestyle, with its fruit-less quest for kicks and Monday forever looming ahead like a 'jail on wheels'. This sort of grim social realism – imagery of tower blocks and dole queues – was an innovation and a radical break with rock'n'roll tradition. But the emotional framework behind the Clash – bored boys breaking loose and letting rip – was actually as traditional as they come.

Compare *The Clash* to an album released less than a year earlier, Thin Lizzy's *Jailbreak*. The Irish hard rockers presented a more or less identical mix of renegade mythos and mid-'70s fear of totalitarianism, except that they wrapped it up in science-fiction imagery and laid it on top of a marginally more traditional sound (Hendrix-tinged raunch'n'roll) than the Clash's garageland stomp. *Jailbreak* was a sort of concept album, set in a computer-controlled dystopian future, about a revolt against the evil Overmaster. The sleevenotes describe a band of prisoners (i.e. Thin Lizzy) who start off a jail riot and escape. Then they record and broadcast 'selected material' that inspires 'a following who eventually took to the streets in what was to become the Final War'. With songs like 'Warriors', 'Fight or Fall' and 'Cowboy Song', frontman Phil Lynott ran through the same gamut of rebel male archetypes that the Clash would impersonate on later albums, while the hit single 'The Boys Are Back in Town' was an anthem that Allen Ginsberg would doubtless have heartily endorsed.

In the year punk broke, Thin Lizzy were briefly in critical favour: 'The Boys Are Back in Town' topped the *NME*'s critics' poll for 1976. As punk became the new orthodoxy in 1977, Lizzy were discredited, owing to their sentimental romanticism and swaggering chauvinism. But the fundamental similarity between the laddishness of hard rock and punk was underlined when, post-Pistols, guitarist Steve Jones and drummer Paul Cook started hanging out with Phil Lynott, and briefly formed a sideline group called the Greedy Basstards. As for the Clash, despite their declaration of 1976 as rock's Year Zero, it was always clear that they were deeply embedded in rock'n'roll tradition (even if no one at the time saw the Thin Lizzy connection). Inevitably, despite 'I'm So Bored With the USA' their music and imagery turned more American as their energies felt the pull of the US market. Within four years they were supporting geriatric rebels the Who at huge arena shows in the States. Eventually, the Clash's place in the rock pantheon was sealed when *Rolling Stone* critics voted *London Calling* the greatest album of the '80s.

white riot

If society was a prison, the Clash proposed not a jailbreak but a riot. 'White Riot' was inspired by the Notting Hill

Carnival riots of August 1976, where black British youth, goaded by police persecution, exploded in the most serious outbreak of civil disorder in the UK since 1958. The Clash both identified with and envied the rioters, calling for white youth to stage a revolt of their own. It was the latest instalment in a long tradition (including Norman Mailer's 'The White Negro' and the late '60s organisation the White Panthers) of white radicals looking to blacks for a model of rebel masculinity. Both the punks and the West Indian rastas and rude boys felt like exiles and outcasts, but unlike the latter, punks had no spiritual homeland in Africa of which to dream.

The Clash's early brand of crude rabble-rousing eventually devolved into Oi, the late '70s/early '80s movement dedicated to the proposition 'punk's not dead!'. Playing up the proletarianism which artschool band the Clash affected, the Oi bands were ferociously working class but politically ambiguous. Some were aligned with the far Right, some were far Left; there are a few cases of bands switching allegiance from neo-Nazi to Trotskyite almost overnight. For the most part, Oi bands stayed stuck at a pre-political level, protesting the conditions of their everyday life while maintaining a ferocious pride in working-class culture. But the far Right Oi bands, like Skrewdriver, did literalise the meaning of 'White Riot' (which some had misconstrued at the time as a fascist anthem, owing to punk's cloudy political allegiances). The militancy of the Left is sometimes hard to distinguish from the belligerence of the Right; similar hormonal energies fuel both. In the early '90s there was a resurgence of 'Hate Rock', with the rise of white supremacist punk bands in America and Europe (particularly in Germany and Eastern Europe). The very fact that the skinhead look was appropriated by both far Right and far Left groups indicated a similar mindset and body politics: both Left and Right were disciplinarian and dogmatic, both, as Simon Frith pointed out, referred to their enemies (each other!) as vermin and scum, both were equally contemptuous of effete, middle-class, arty decadence.

street fighting men

All this is some distance from the romanticism of the Clash. Yet part of the band's appeal was that they were clearly fighters. After an initial, artschool influenced phase (clothes daubed with slogans or Jackson Pollock splashes), the Clash's image mixed military clothing with the quiffs and leather of the traditional American rock rebel. They used war-torn Belfast to make striking images for stage backdrops and cover art; many songs had wartime settings and martial imagery. On the first album, '1977' imagined machine guns being fired in upper-class Knightsbridge. During the period when the media panic about punk was at its height and gigs were regularly cancelled by local authorities, Bernie Rhodes fantasised about responding to one particular banning by driving up the motorway to the doors of the town council in a tank!

By the second album, *Give 'Em Enough Rope* (1978), the Clash had elevated themselves to leaders of a ragged army of followers, mobilising as Britain itself was seemingly being torn apart by labour disputes, political strife and economic collapse. The album included songs like 'English Civil War' and 'Tommy Gun', and on a poster inside the sleeve the Clash could be found posing in front of a world map, with zones of confrontation or atrocity marked out country by country. On *London Calling* (1979), 'Spanish Bombs' waxed nostalgic for the righteous opportunities for heroism offered by the Spanish Civil War, while 'Death or Glory' was a raucous lament for the compromise that eventually crushes every rebel: domesticity. From small-time gangsters to rock'n'rollers, they all wash up 'making payments on a sofa or a girl'. The title track of *London Calling* was styled as a stream of consciousness radio broadcast, set against an apocalyptic backdrop of social collapse; its title echoed the BBC's propaganda broadcasts of World War Two, while the chorus was a wake-up-and-take-sides alarm call to the 'zombies' of Britain's cultural sleep. The Clash would revive this metaphor a couple of years later with the single 'This Is Radio Clash', another wartime broadcast from a pirate satellite, with the group dispensing 'aural ammunition'. The quasi-rap lyrics look ahead to the panoramic paranoid visions of Public Enemy, who saw rap as 'black folks' equivalent to CNN', the American twenty-four hour news channel.

1980's *Sandinista* paid homage, in its title, to the left-wing guerrillas who'd seized power in Nicaragua, having finally overthrown a corrupt, American-puppet government. The title of the next album, *Combat Rock* (1982), was their most blatant and clumsy attempt yet to define the Clash as music for fighters, not lovers. The hit single it spawned, 'Rock The Casbah', imagined an Islamic ruler ordering his bombers to attack a building in which rock music is being played: a jokey scenario, but there might have been a tinge of envy, too, a sense that it would be exciting to live in a society where to play or even listen to rock'n'roll was a crime against the state. Something tangible to fight against – the rebel's dream!

Amidst all the militaristic imagery, you could also find anti-war songs. Like 'The Call Up' (*Sandinista*), a ghostly, dub-inflected mirage of a song inspired by the then-recent introduction of new American draft regulations, or the haunted, harrowing 'Straight to Hell' (*Combat Rock*), an around-the-world-at-war-in-five-verses guided tour of hell-zones where boy-soldiers had languished. Like any great rock'n'roll band, the Clash were deeply confused, a tangle of contradictions. One minute they were itching to fight, if the cause was noble; the next, they were recoiling from the carnage and the wrecked souls.

One thing was clear: the Clash had the temperament of warriors. As Lenny Kaye put it in 'Americlash', his homage to the band that accompanied the 1991 CD retrospective *Clash on Broadway*: 'Every good insurrection needs a cause, or at least that's how the Clash saw it. The music's mythic structure was grand enough to create a soundtrack for any identikit, a call to arms both spiritual and militant, depending on which way the cultural winds sheared.... It hardly matters what triggers the confrontation.' Kaye seems to have instinctively grasped the fact that the urge to rebel came first, the search for a suitable cause followed.

The borders between the Clash's anti-establishment militancy and for-Queen-and-Country militarism could get pretty blurry at times, though. During the recording of *Give 'Em Enough Rope*, the band grew bored doing countless takes for producer Sandy Pearlman. So Dave Mingay, the director of the Clash movie *Rude Boy*, went to the Imperial War Museum and borrowed films of the Second World War. A large screen was erected at the back of the studio and films like *The Defence of Stalingrad, The Battle of the Bulge* and *El Alamein* were shown between takes. 'We had jet bombers diving all over the studio while we were sitting around or playing,' remembered Paul Simenon. Perhaps, like Jimmy Porter in *Look Back in Anger*, the Clash's real lament was that they longed for a Britain that was truly Great, a country that deserved their pride and fervour, a country worth dying for.

Just as Porter directed his ire at the docile figure of his wife, forever dutifully tending the ironing board, the Clash also seemed to regard the housewife as the antithesis of the renegade derring-do to which they aspired. One of their most touching songs, 'Lost in the Supermarket', offers an empathetic portrait of a crushed figure of indeterminate gender (either a downtrodden housewife or a male nonentity) whose only experience of the world is neglect and narrow horizons. S/he wasn't 'born so much as... fell out', and grows up a timorous, wee cowering beastie, corralled by suburban hedges too high to see over. Frail, dejected, s/he can only find succour in commodities and junk culture. As with so much rebel rock, it's shopping, an activity associated with femininity, that seems to symbolise, for the Clash, this sad figure's castration.

generation terrorists

'We ourselves were dynamite... planted beneath the vast edifices of a materialist Ice Age... we ourselves were "explosive"; layer upon layer of our being burned and annihilated those massed obstructions.'
Friedrick Wilhelm Heinz, Freikorps officer

Punk came from the same milieu of lower middle-class/upper working-class disaffection as the Angry Young Men (or indeed the Freikorps), and shared many of the same longings: a desire to distance themselves from a society felt to be irretrievably corrupt, a hankering for the lost possibilities of heroism. Peacetime society offered no scope for explosive release, only the drudgery of clerical or bureaucratic life, of book-keeping and time-keeping.

But there are other reasons why the military looms so large in the rock imagination. In *Teenage Wasteland* Donna Gaines examines the American subculture of 'burn-outs', shaggy-haired malcontents who live for heavy metal and get wasted on drink and drugs. 'For those shipwrecked in the dead-end towns of suburbia, the recruiting station looms as an island of possibility.' Forming a rock band or joining the Army are often the only alternatives to a service sector job or unemployment. Like rock'n'roll, the military offers a life of adventure, the chance to live like a man rather than a minion.

Manic Street Preachers grew up in a small town in Wales just as claustrophobic as the burn-outs' nowheresvilles. When they emerged in 1990, the Manics had the early Clash's look (clothing covered with vague apocalyptic slogans), a similarly rough-and-ready take on classic American rock'n'roll, and the same desire to come over as class warriors /media terrorists. Reminiscing for the *Clash on Broadway* retrospective, Joe Strummer explained that 'Tommy Gun' had been about 'the ego of terrorists. It suddenly struck me that they must read their press clippings, like rock stars or actors and actresses do.' This was Manic Street Preachers all over: they existed to make an impact in the press, deliberately seeking controversy and making enemies by attacking other bands. They scoured the music papers for references to themselves, and later attested that they knew every review they'd ever received by heart.

The group's very name was a gesture of repudiation directed at a music scene they defined themselves against. The ruling Brit-pop aesthetic in 1991 was the dazed-and-confused androgyny of 'dreampop' bands (Lush, My Bloody Valentine, Slowdive), whose songs largely concerned the rapture of love or forlorn feelings of being adrift in a cruel world. Every element of the Manics' name jarred with this 'feminised' aesthetic: 'manic' was their amphetamine-spiked renunciation of dreampop's sleepiness; 'street' signified a return to the urban spaces of punk as opposed to inner space – a zone of revolution rather than reverie; 'preacher' announced the Manics' intention to 'tell it like it is', as opposed to the hazy apolitical ambiguities of the dreampop aesthetic. Preachers and demagogues tend to be men, and the subtext of the Manics' discontent with rock in 1991 was that it was way too girly.

The title of their debut album, *Generation Terrorists* (1992), was a reproach and a wake-up call to their own 'useless generation'. Their creed was similar to Sergei Nechaev's 1869 tract 'Catechism of a Revolutionist' which proclaimed the revolutionary to be a doomed man, with no spare energy for sentimentality, romanticism or rapture. He was 'an implacable enemy of this world, and if he continues to live in it, this is only to destroy it more effectively. . . . All the tender and effeminate emotions of kinship, friendship, love and gratitude. . . must be stilled in him by

a cold and singleminded passion'. And so Manics' bassist/
lyricist Richie Edwards argued that 'once you fall in love or
get your girlfriend pregnant. . . you've got no chance, you've
got responsibilities. There's no way you can ever do anything. Once you're reduced to a couple, alone together. . .
with your TV set, you're cut off.' It was as though the band
dreaded the spectre of amorous comfort as something that
would mute and melt their tunnel-visionary zeal.

Instead, the Manics preferred the 'sexless' intensity of
amphetamine, which fuelled their fervour and allowed
them to bone up on political theory without being distracted
by the body. They revived punk's ethics of drug use, favour-
ing speed (because it boosts ego, IQ and will) and denouncing drugs like marijuana, LSD and Ecstasy that promote
contemplation or empathy. As the post-Manics, neo-punk
band These Animal Men put it: 'Amphetamine culture is
like. . . you know when old guys say "What we need is a
good war."? It gets everything moving again.'

The Manics' trip was the rock rebel fix of self-worship/
self-hatred, the glamour of alienation (being fucked up,
fucking other people off). But the Manics' biggest buzz of
all came from using the language of the manifesto, from
decreeing and denouncing. The manifesto is the supreme
genre of phallocratic discourse; incisive and categorical, it's
the antithesis of poetry, of language that aspires to the
condition of music. Manic Street Preachers' lyrics were
therefore anti-musical, a cut-and-paste assemblage of slogans. Women have seldom issued stern manifestos (with
the exception of Valerie Solanas and her Society For
Cutting Up Men), traditionally avoiding polarised stances
or categorical utterances and leaving the pulpit or soapbox
to preacher men.

On the album, 'Stay Beautiful' was a homage to youth as
the supreme existential state, with its (male) camaraderie,
its sense of total possibility and total waste. For the Manics,
staying beautiful meant dying young or at the very least,
ending your rock career before senility and disgrace. In *The*

Hero With A Thousand Faces, Joseph Campbell had declared: 'The hero of yesterday becomes the tyrant of tomorrow, unless he crucifies himself today.' The Manics pre-planned their martyrdom. They would replay the Sex Pistols' story, including Johnny Rotten's heroic manoeuvre of destroying the band before it became a grotesque money-spinning caricature of itself. The Manics' masterplan was a kamikaze mission in which they'd become the world's biggest rock band, only to autodestruct after releasing one huge-selling album. They wanted to become myth, frozen for ever as an ultimate gesture of repudiation. But the Manics inevitably reneged on their suicide pact, and continued slogging towards middling success by the tried-and-tested route – hard gigging and releasing singles in numerous editions. Like career soldiers, they signed on for another tour of duty.

rebel without a pause

The two contemporary bands that the Manics admired were arguably the most masculinist role models available in the early '90s: Public Enemy (stern, puritanical, rigidly doctrinaire, ideologically patriarchal) and Guns N'Roses (rampant, pelvis-as-weapon renegades). The Manics' greatest affinity with Public Enemy was the media terrorist's love of perusing their press clips. Over the years, Public Enemy's albums became riddled with sampled soundbites from the media controversy they'd incited. And they had their own symbol of martyrdom: their logo was a silhouette of the black revolutionary between the marksman's sights.

Public Enemy pioneered 'conscious' or 'righteous' rap; they took the pre-political rage of 'gangsta' rap and gave it political articulation, just as the Black Panthers had tried to mobilise the delinquency of young black street hoods. Even more than the Clash, Public Enemy wished to turn the teenage male gang into an army. Black gangs are organised on military lines; righteous rap hoped to transform this absurd-but-deadly patriotism for gang 'colours' (Crips, Bloods, etc.) into black nationalism. Why wage war on each other when you can unite against the real enemy?

Where gangsta rap mostly speaks as a tyrannical 'I', righteous rap is about a totalitarian 'We'. Public Enemy tried to represent a collective consciousness/conscience – one that could see further than the short-term, quick-killing vision of the gangsta. Evangelising for the elevation of the black race, Chuck D, Public Enemy's frontman, rapped with the weighty cadences of a preacher. Gangsta rap's raging erections were replaced by rectitude, its misogyny became militancy. Since Public Enemy saw themselves as paramilitaries at war with white supremacist society, they had little time for women. Gangsta rap denigrates women as treacherous bitches and ball-breakers; righteous rap marginalises them as non-combatants. Later, after being criticised for the chauvinist aspects of the Public Enemy worldview, Chuck D attempted to include women in his programme. On *Fear of A Black Planet*, 'Revolutionary Generation' envisaged the female role in the struggle as breeding and rearing good soldiers. The band also brought in a female auxiliary, Sistah Souljah, to make public appearances and declaim the odd slogan on record.

None of this is to deny the very good reasons that Public Enemy had, as young African-Americans, to wish to educate, agitate and organise in order to 'Fight the Power'. Much more than the Clash, Public Enemy's quasi-military rhetoric and imagery was a response to real oppression. But you have to wonder whether part of the appeal of combat rock and righteous rap is the way it elevates the camaraderie of the teenage gang to a higher realm, gives it the dignity of political gravity. In the case of the Clash, Manic Street Preachers and Public Enemy, waging a 'just war' allows not just flight from the company of women, but a 'legitimate excuse' to ignore them as a subject matter and as a presence in the world.

holy war

A sense of loss is intrinsic to the human condition. Acquiring language and ego brings to an end the pre-Oedipal phase of infancy, in which the infant is unaware of any difference between itself and its mother. For the infant, this blissful symbiosis is the *entire universe*: enfolding, benign, free of alienation. In a way of which we can scarcely conceive, the infant feels godlike, invulnerable, totally secure. The longing to recover this state of wholeness – what Jacques Lacan provocatively calls 'the phallus' – underscores much of human activity, from mysticism to drug addiction to ideological faith.

This lost phallic potency can be identified with the father or with the mother. The combat rockers identify it with the former, with patriarchal values: utopia lies somewhere in the future, as a goal to fight for, march towards. Another strain of rock – the mystical, psychedelic tradition that concerns this book's second section – is female-identified: utopia lies somewhere in the past (a lost golden age, childhood, the pre-linguistic realm of dreams, the unconscious).

A variation on the combat stance of the Clash & Co. is *crusading rock*. U2 is the quintessential example, corresponding to an archetype that Robert Bly calls the 'eternal boy'. Like the warrior, the eternal boy is attempting to escape the force-field of women. But instead of going to war, he attempts to rise above the earth-bound and mundane into a stratospheric realm of pure spirituality. Georges Bataille called this impulse 'Icarian revolt', after Icarus, the mythological figure who built wings for himself and tried to reach the sun.

The Icarus complex pops up all the time in rock, if you know where to look. In the '60s, the Byrds fused folk with Indian ragas to create a radiant, celestial sound on songs like 'Eight Miles High' and albums like *Younger Than Yesterday*. Pink Floyd's cosmic rock ('Astronomy Domine',

'Set the Controls for the Heart of the Sun') abandoned the earthiness of the blues for the blue yonder. In the mid '80s, Hüsker Dü disappeared in a blinding blizzard of droning distortion, while REM combined Byrdsian folk-rock with vague imagery of rebirth for the American spirit.

U2 are unique, however, in that they've brought an explicit moral aspect to this guitar transcendentalism. In Bly's terms, U2 looked to redeem a world gone to ruin thanks to the dereliction of political fathers. Like combat rock, the crusading impulse provides an escape from the banal doldrums of domesticity. Like the Clash, U2 made their appeal to *the boys*; in a different but equivalent way, they were just as fixated as the Clash and Manic Street Preachers on the adolescent boy as the pinnacle of being: pure, idealistic and ready for self-sacrifice.

Although they were inspired into being by punk, musically U2 were influenced not by the ramalama buzzsaw drone of English bands but by Television, the least punkoid, most psychedelic of the New York scene groups. Television rarefied rock of its blues traces, sublimating sexual tension into plangent friction. Lyrically, their subject matter was the sublime (their songs had vague, mystical titles like 'Elevation', 'The Fire', 'The Dream's Dream', 'Glory' and 'Carried Away'). When they emerged in the early '80s, U2 were steeped in Television's innovatory blues-lessness. Like the latter's Tom Verlaine, U2 guitarist the Edge developed a style that was a frictionless slipstream of chimes and effects-laden tones, rather than riff or powerchord propelled. The rhythm section was unsyncopated, sometimes martial, but always adamantly refused to appeal to the hips. Until very late in their career, U2's rhythms were inert, marking time while the Edge and Bono soared and swooped, never distracting the listeners' attention downwards to the body. Bono's voice beseeched and implored, 'soul' purified of every last trace of R&B carnality.

On the 1980 debut album *Boy*, U2's themes – wide-eyed

innocence, a sense of wonder – are abstract but relatively small-scale (at least compared with the grandiosity that ensued). The image on the cover of the album crystallised their spirit: a barechested boy, perhaps seven or eight years old, with golden hair and dazzling eyes. The cover and the song 'Stories for Boys' spelled out rather literally what had been abstract in the Television album title *Adventure*: a quest for grail or glory, a desire for something to be devout about.

U2's Christianity got more explicit on the next album, *October* (1981), which featured devotional songs like 'Gloria' and 'Rejoice'. The original rock'n'roll 'Gloria' (by Van Morrison's first band, Them) was a lust-crazed paean to a woman. U2's 'Gloria' (their own composition) was pure ascesis, a psalmic anthem that directly beseeched and exalted the Lord. Bono offered his services, his body and soul, as a pilgrim-warrior for God. Their third album *War* (1983) announced U2 as crusaders (the title indicated both their pacifism and their readiness to fight for righteousness). In 'New Year's Day', the chosen few gather, 'eyes aloft', waiting to be filled with a born-again spirit. U2 imagined a spiritual awakening, a chance for rock to 'begin again'. Musically, the Edge's playing was at its most celestially Caucasian. The video was set in a snowbound zone of great altitude, blindingly white.

'Eyes aloft': U2's secret was that, more than any other band, their music appealed to the eyes rather than ears. Producers Brian Eno and Daniel Lanois further developed this visual/visionary aspect of their sound on the next two albums, *The Unforgettable Fire* (1984) and *The Joshua Tree* (1987). The inventor of ambient music, Eno was obsessed with evoking a sense of place through sound. For U2, Eno and Lanois developed a panoramic sound that downplayed the kinetic aspects of rock (dynamics, rhythmic heat) in favour of the cinematic. This was perfect both for the Edge's aerial playing and for exploiting the compact disc's scope for wispy detail. The resulting music invited the listener to 'gaze' into the far distance. Meanwhile, both albums saw Bono's lyrics growing more specifically political, albeit tackling issues with which no 'right-thinking' person could take issue. 'Pride (In the Name of Love)', for instance, was a tribute to Martin Luther King; like Gandhi, King was a paradigm of the towering visionary inspired by his religious convictions to fight against earthly wrongs, the model of the Christian soldier.

For the young warrior, ardour for lofty abstractions and cosmic intangibles is a way of sublimating sexuality; male-bonding is purged of homoeroticism because passion is projected outwards on to a distant goal or vision. It was very apparent, at the height of U2's success in 1987, that their missionary spirit involved a similar evasion of sexuality and gender. Everything about U2 – from their lyrics to Bono's bellow to the Edge's ionospheric guitar – was 'uplifting', veering towards the sun and away from seething male hormones and sticky female secretions. It was remarkable, for a band with five albums under their belt, that not a single U2 song dealt with desire or love – unless it was universal rather than flesh-and-blood.

On *Rattle and Hum* (1988), U2 plummeted, like Icarus, into the mud of the blues, the very delta swamp that had birthed rock'n'roll and whose grit U2 had so successfully turned to ether. The album was an attempt to re-root the band in American country and R&B traditions, to return to the primal source. Appropriately, the first single from the album signposted their change of course: 'Desire' was their first song about sex. Inevitably, it was a failure: abstract and schematic, it signalled a desire to deal with desire, rather than actually evoking any kind of carnal cravings.

Three years after the manifesto came the genuine mess. On 1991's *Achtung Baby*, U2 demolished their persona, their distinctive sound, and their reputation as chaste and pompously pious. They went out of their way to absorb ideas from underground rock, defacing their sound with industrial clangour and funking up the previously inert rhythm section. Their 'Zoo TV' tour attempted to replicate the chaos of media overload; in one fell swoop, U2 went from pre-modern missionaries to late twentieth-century post-modernists. Videos were doused with sleaze; Bono changed his image from the rugged pioneer/Inca mountain-guide look circa *The Joshua Tree*, to a wasted, pallid, leather-clad, chain-smoking rock reptile sporting sun-glasses after dark. With *Achtung Baby*, U2 reinvented themselves with a fervour that rivalled the chameleonic metamorphoses of Bowie or Siouxsie Sioux.

It worked remarkably well, and nowhere better than on the song and video 'Mysterious Ways'. Here, U2 ditched the Onward Christian Soldiers image, and became acolytes of a female Deity: from sky-god to earth-cult. Bono mocked U2's earlier transcendentalism with lyrics that slyly linked 'kissing the sky' with kneeling to perform cunnilingus. 'Tryin' to Throw Your Arms Around the World' was Bono's auto-critique of the grandiosity of his former saviour pos-ture. The album as a whole announced a shift from the airy absolutes of U2 discourse to the intimacy and proximity of sexual love in the here-and-now. There were more instances of 'she' and 'her' in the lyrics of a single song on *Achtung Baby* than in the rest of the U2 oeuvre put together.

'Mysterious Ways' is the great proclamation of intent, a shift from being male-identified to female-envying. The song simultaneously divinises a woman and feminises God. As such, it recalls Talking Heads' 'The Great Curve' (off the Eno-produced *Remain in Light*), a gynocentric funk mantra whose lyrics link the turning of the world's axis with the swivelling of a woman's hips. (The video for 'Mysterious Ways' filched this idea by cheesily featuring a belly-dancer gyrating in front of an immense full moon). Musically, 'Mysterious Ways' incarnates U2's shift from dazzling open spaces to dark moist interiors. Instead of Eno/Lanois's ambient horizons and the Edge's raunchless radiance, U2 churn up a thick, viscid funk-rock. The model is no longer Television but Sly Stone; the music sounds like it's constructed not from painstaking layering of sound but something close to jamming in real-time; listener response takes the form not of the classic U2 'chesty surge' but grinding hips.

The video brilliantly matched this new U2. Set in a labyrinthine Middle Eastern city, the procession of images are distorted like in a hall of mirrors. One's field of vision seems to curve, buckle, undulate, fold in on itself. Where once the lofty gaze was privileged in U2, now it's as though the male eye is intoxicated and disorientated by the miasmic fumes of femininity. 'Mysterious Ways' is a heady hymn of fealty to Woman and to Nature. (Of course, you could argue that U2 only replaced one mystification with another, what Theweleit calls 'oppression through exaltation'.) U2's aesthetic – for so long retarded at the level of pre-pubescent idealism – finally confronts sexuality, that scary zone over which their music took flight. Coming down to earth with a lubricious squelch, *Boy* becomes man.

flirting with the void:
abjection in rock

'It is a soft, yielding action, a moist and feminine sucking. . . .
Slime is. . . sickly-sweet feminine revenge. . . . The obscenity of the
feminine sex is that of everything which gapes open.'
Jean-Paul Sartre, *Being and Nothingness*

The adolescent idealism of combat and crusading rock is an
attempt to transcend the biological reality of adolescence:
hormonal turmoil, unfamiliar and insistent urges, unsettling bodily changes. Icarus rock's ascent into a sublime
higher realm (political righteousness, spiritual abstractions) is a flight from the base animalism of the human
condition, an attempt to soar over the dank, dark realm of
abjection.

'Abject' is Julia Kristeva's term for viscous fluids (mother's milk, semen, vaginal secretions, menstruation, saliva,
mucus, excrement, urine, pus) that blur the border
between me and not-me, inside and out. They're neither
liquid nor solid but *sullied*: slime that must be expelled, not
just to upkeep the clean and proper body, but in order to
maintain a strong ego. Substances are abject when they
hark back to what Kristeva calls 'maternal horror', that
fuzzy state from which the infant's precarious sense of self
gradually emerges.

In *Sexual Personae*, Camille Paglia writes about
humans' 'evolutionary revulsion from slime', stemming
from its echo of the 'miasmic swamp' of the womb. She
believes that Western art and literature oscillate between
evading Mother Nature's fluidity and confronting her terrible power as a means of ritual exorcism. Examples of the

latter range from the mythological figure of Charybdis (a perilous whirlpool), to Jonathan Swift's squeamishness in 'The Lady's Dressing Room' ('should I the Queen Of Love refuse/because she rose from stinking ooze?') to Edgar Allan Poe's tales of Gothic horror like 'Descent into the Maelstrom' and Coleridge's 'The Ancient Mariner' (in which, Paglia writes, 'the open sea turns to a rotting sepulchre. . . [a] daemonic womb').

Sartre also felt a deep ambivalence about the fluid and the feminine, as Margery L. Collins and Christine Pierce demonstrate in their essay 'Holes and Slime: Sexism in Sartre's Psychoanalysis'. In *Being And Nothingness*, the philosopher recoils from slime as horrifying, leech-like, soft and clinging, and, write Collins and Pierce, 'regardless of its docility, threatening'. In the sexual act, the phallus is 'endangered' by the vagina. Sartre described woman's sex as 'a voracious mouth which devours the penis. . . . The amorous act is the castration of the man, but this is above all because sex is a hole'. But according to Freudian psychoanalyst Sandor Ferenczi, the male sexual urge is impelled by a drive to return to the uterine void that Sartre feared. For Ferenczi, mankind's oceanic mysticism is simply a sublimation of this atavistic hankering for the womb.

Drowning in 'the sea of love' is Man's deepest desire and his darkest fear. And so abject fluids inspire bliss as much as instil dread, because they evoke the lost incestuous paradise of infancy. The incest prohibition creates identity by bringing to an end the symbiosis of baby and mother. Incest looms as both a terrifying, identity-shattering regression and as a consummation devoutly to be wished. Dionysus, the god of ego-dissolution and intoxication, is the archetypal rebel, chafing against the incest taboo; he is identified with liquids (blood, sap, wine, milk, semen). Dionysian art melts form and line, courts chaos and disorientation. Similarly, the Dionysian tradition in rock is all about a flirtation with the abject. It's about literally living on the edge: teetering on the brink of oblivion, the swamp of primal formlessness. Whenever the vital masculine thrust of Dionysus begins to flag – that's when the threat of the mire gapes.

The abject began looming in rock when the insurrectionary energy of the late '60s started to flag, and rock turned *heavy*. After the high, the comedown. On the first side of *The Stooges* (1969), the incendiary teen revolt of '1969' and the lust-for-abasement of 'I Wanna Be Your Dog' dwindle into the lapidary lassitude of 'We Will Fall', a ten-minute mantra that equates nirvana with numbness. Iggy Pop's nihilistic aggression curdles into void-worship. The song is a rock mausoleum marbled with Indian raga drones that hark back to the Doors' 'The End'. But where Jim Morrison imagined cataclysm as a prelude to some kind of spiritual rebirth (à la T.S. Eliot's 'The Wasteland'), 'We Will Fall' is terminal, the triumph of death drive over eros, a return to the womb-tomb.

The Stooges' second album *Funhouse* (1970) follows a similar trajectory. The first side is structured like the male sexual adventure, from predatorial ('Down on the Streets') through violent intercourse ('Loose') to explosive release ('TV Eye') to dwindling, tingling aftermath ('Dirt'). Here, Iggy Pop sounds spent. On the flip, 'Funhouse' imagines the excess of sex, drugs and rock'n'roll as a primal playpen: for far too long, he suggests, 'we've been separated', but now let's rollick in the primordial ooze. The music's a turgid torrent of brackish guitars, thickened further by a freeform saxophone that wails and brays like a newborn. (Iggy Pop has long included infantile gestures like thumb-sucking and scratch-and-sniffing his crotch in his stage repertoire.)

The Stooges' revelling in animalism evolved into punk's sexual revulsion. Punk style incorporated elements from sado-masochism and fetishism, perversions which replace carnal intimacy with elaborately codified rituals that keep flesh and fluids at arms' length. Generally, punk professed indifference to sexuality. But beneath the professions of ennui (Rotten's 'yawn! just another squelch session') lurked a fear of engulfment. One of the Sex Pistols' greatest songs, 'Submission', is all about drowning in the ocean of love. The brilliant pun of the title links submission (as in sexual bondage) with a submarine mission into the mysterious depths of female sexuality. For Rotten, (the) woman was literally unfathomable, a bottomless chasm which threatened his identity. The music is the Sex Pistols at their most sinister, a murky, ponderous churn veined with eerie backing chants and sub-aquatic echoes that sound like dolphin chatter or sonar. By the end, Rotten acquiesces to his fate, as her 'undercurrents' drag him down to doom, and he screams a dread-full affirmation of love: 'wanna drown!!'.

The metaphor of 'Submission' may have been borrowed, consciously or not, from John Cale's 'Momamma Scuba' (off 1974's *Fear*). But Rotten really made something of the scenario, because he clearly *felt* it in the depths of his heart. A similar sexual squeamishness recurred in his post-Pistols career, most notably in the Public image Limited song 'Track 8' (from 1981's *Flowers of Romance*), which described an unsatisfactory sexual encounter with ripe imagery of erupting fat and yawning tunnels.

pretty girls make graves

'At the climactic moment of erotic surrender, as the active, pulsating, masculine erection subsides in conjunction with the more passive (feminine) ejaculatory spasms and inner pelvic expansions and contractions, the male yearns to give himself up to his passive, receptive, feminine-baby wishes. However, a man who dreads these sensations and wishes will quickly extricate himself. . . . To such a man, erection is life; ejaculation and detumescence, death.'
Louise Kaplan, *Female Perversions*

Something very similar to what Kaplan describes above – the terror of amorous engulfment, and the defensive fantasy of an endless, invincible erection – takes place in the Stooges' 'Ann', one of their greatest and most perturbing songs, and a prototype for the Pistols' 'Submission'. Iggy feels like he's adrift in the 'swimming pool' of his girl's dilated pupils. The reverie is blissful, but he also feels weak, despondent; the girl has broken his 'will'. There's a parallel scene in Sartre's *No Exit*, where Garcia rejects Estelle's seduction: 'I won't let myself get bogged in your eyes. You're soft and slimy. Ugh! Like an octopus. . . like a quagmire'. 'Ann' is a ballad, Iggy singing like a stoned Sinatra through a narcotic haze of guitar. Suddenly he reaches the dilemma faced by the Freikorps soldier when confronted by a threatening throng, as described by Theweleit: 'to swoon or to kill'. The croon suddenly turns to a feral snarl, and the woozy 'I love you' abruptly shifts from amorous passivity to an active verb, as Iggy adds the war-cry 'RIGHT NOW'. The song suddenly ignites, as the limp(id) guitar rigidifies into a riff, erect and rampaging, blazing with menace. Love's idyll is shattered as phallic desire rears its ugly head.

Rock is full of songs that recoil from the 'abyss' of female sexuality. From John's Children's 'Smashed Blocked' to the Eyes' 'You're Too Much', '60s freakbeat was a giddy mix of urgent lust and terror of being sexually devoured. In 'You're Too Much', the girl is too fast, too ardent, for him to handle. She belongs to a younger, wilder generation, and he's 'starved of my relaxation' – a strange turnabout considering how another Eyes' song, 'My Degeneration', replayed the more typical '60s scenario of a boy sneering at a girl for being too prudish, frigid and un-cool to satisfy. By the end of 'You're Too Much', the singer's voice is overwhelmed by a deluge of sound, as the irradiated guitars flare up, a beautiful and terrible sexual apocalypse that dazzles your ears.

A decade and a half later, the Smiths' 'Pretty Girls Make Graves' (from 1984's self-titled debut) offered a similar candid admission of male feebleness in the face of female voraciousness. Morrissey may have borrowed the phrase 'Pretty Girls Make Graves' from Jack Kerouac (it was one of his favourite sayings), but in the song, it's less about a dread of settling down, more about a terror of being sexually devoured. Morrissey wants a platonic, highminded, spiritual relationship, but the girl wants his body. In a witty inversion of rock rebellion's studly stance, it's Morrissey who's the wilting wallflower, and the woman who's the impatient, sexually precocious ruffian. She goes off with the first dumb-but-virile bloke to present himself, leaving Morrissey bitter. Could it be that the 'grave' that pretty girls make isn't just a tomb for man's shattered romantic illusions, but rather the 'death' of 'ejaculation and detumescence' that, according to Louise Kaplan, inspires male sexual dread?

bodies

One of the most ferocious confrontations with the realm of 'maternal horror' in rock'n'roll is the Sex Pistols' 'Bodies' (from *Never Mind the Bollocks*, 1977). It remains one of the Pistols' most threatening and incoherent songs. At the time, the right-on British music press were at a loss to reconcile the song's apparent anti-abortion stance with their idea of punk's proper political orientation. The song's rage and disgust places 'Bodies' right there on the edge of the human condition, along with 'Belsen Was A Gas'. Like 'Belsen', it's a turgid churn, rock'n'roll devolving into a black hole – a black hole that's somehow come alive and gone on the offensive. Rotten howls the Catholic blues: he revolts (as in the stomach revolting) against the bestiality of human existence and the horror of flesh and blood.

'Bodies' couldn't be more graphic, Rotten practically gargling the imagery of gurgling discharges. Rotten's persona in the song is split between the father who won't face his responsibility and the foetus shrieking 'mummy, I'm not an animal'. The girl, Pauline, is little better than an animal. That she works in a factory seems to emphasise the mechanical nature of female biology, churning out life automatically. The foetus is aborted in a toilet, reminding us that we enter the world between the faecal and urinary tracts. In 'Bodies', female biology and nature enslave man.

This link between the dehumanising, machine-like quality of abjection and the totalitarian nature of industrial life was developed further by Throbbing Gristle, who pioneered the post-punk genre of 'industrial' music. Throbbing Gristle were all about 'confronting all assumptions', testing the outer limits of their audiences' tolerance. The music mirrored a world of unremitting ugliness, dehumanisation, and brutalism. They degraded and mutilated sound, reaching nether limits that even now have yet to be under-passed. Throbbing Gristle trailblazed the gamut of industrial obsessions: serial killers, conspiracy theories, subliminal mind-control, etc. Above all, they coined the industrial attitude, a drive to peel back reality's epidermis and expose the visceral mess behind everyday facades. Woman was the privileged victim, in Gristle's oeuvre, of all this vivisection. 'Slugbait' was a corny tale of a 'wicked boy' who pulls a foetus out of a seven months' pregnant mother and chews its head off (a later version of the same song features a taped confession by a girlchild-murderer). 'Hamburger Lady' goes into grisly forensic detail about a real-life burns victim. There's even a song called 'We Hate You (Little Girls)'. The name Throbbing Gristle managed to combine phallic innuendo with a sense of the abject nature of fleshly existence, a reminder that being alive means being subject to involuntary processes (excretion, reproduction, decay, death) and the everpresent possibility of violence.

Throbbing Gristle evolved out of the radical art group COUM Transmissions. Like Gristle, the main thrust of COUM's taboo-busting confrontationalism involved highlighting the grossness of the female body and sexuality.

Their *tour de force* was a 1976 exhibition at London's Institute of Contemporary Arts entitled 'Pornography'. Porn magazines were framed and dated as though works of art; each featured COUM member Cosey Fanny Tutte, whose art had involved her working as a porn model. Other installations included a cast of Venus De Milo with a used tampon on each arm, an Art Deco clock with its insides removed and replaced by a month of used tampons, and a work that illustrated the cycles of life with a box of maggots turning into flies, along with another month's worth of used tampons. For menstruation-obsessed COUM, female reproduction clearly signified 'the grim truth', an abyss in which the lofty pretensions of high art foundered. Female abjection was turned into a male weapon of outrage – with great success, since the 'Pornography' exhibition inspired aghast headlines in the British press and even debate in Parliament.

woman-pie

The Birthday Party took punk's sexual horror in a different direction, back through the Stooges, the Doors, rockabilly and blues, to reconnect with the febrile visions of late-Romantic poets like Rimbaud, Baudelaire and Lautréamont. Nick Cave's writing in the Birthday Party (and later as a solo artist) is the fullest, most hideously voluptuous flowering of the abject in rock. On their eponymous debut (1980) and its sequel, *Prayers on Fire* (1981), the Birthday Party play a music of dis-ease, nausea and discomfort. In 'King Ink', Cave's alter ego – the classic swaggering anti-hero of rebel lore – feels as though he's 'a bug swimming in a soup-bowl'. Throughout his songs, Cave experiences melancholy as drowning, ennui as viscosity. In *Prayers on Fire*, the eye is jaundiced, the nostril's aghast; the lyrics are a psychedelic malaise of squalid imagery, teeming with dull hues, slimy textures, foul odours, which are matched by the febrile but lugubrious jazz-punk music.

On the next album, *Junkyard* (1982), and subsequent EPs, abjection is more voraciously purulent. 'She's Hit' is a blues lament for women's vulnerability, bemoaning the way they're prone to liquefy into 'woman-pie' at the hands of man. In 'Deep in the Woods' (from the *Bad Seed* EP), worms carve patterns into the beloved's murdered body, and women's special propensity for dying means that only fools fall in love. Cave's imagery often conflates putrefaction and perfection. 'Mutiny in Heaven' (from the *Mutiny* EP) peeks into an infested, verminous, garbage-strewn heaven that recalls Lautréamont's vision in his 1868 novel *Maldoror* of a derelict kingdom presided over by a corrupt and senile deity who sits on a throne of excrement and boils human beings in blood in order to gorge his depraved appetite for flesh.

The Cramps provided a cartoon version of the Birthday Party's sex'n'horror schtick. Rockabilly fundamentalists, the Cramps were dedicated to resurrecting the 'true spirit' of primordial rock'n'roll: the uncontrollable urges and pent-up libido of the '50s rebel male. In the puritanical South, sex was sinful and real dirty; the Cramps added a B-movie schlock twist to the idea of rock'n'roll as the devil's music. With songs like 'What's Inside A Girl', 'Smell of Female', 'Her Love Rubbed Off' *ad nauseam*, they proclaimed themselves born-again Swamp Things who just loved to wallow in the 'Googoomuck' of female secretions. Even their name testified to their icky-yucky fascination for female biology, being American slang for menstrual pains.

By the mid '80s, both the industrial genre and the Birthday Party school of grotesquerie had begun to influence American post-hardcore bands. With groups like Butthole Surfers, Big Black, Scratch Acid and Killdozer, the abject surfaced in a fixation on the limit-experiences that reduce humans to meat – from serial murder and psychotic violence to car-crashes and other bizarre forms of maiming and mangling. Butthole Surfers performed in front of forensic and autopsy films, images of car-crashes and sex-change operations. Big Black's 'Cables' imagined visiting a slaughterhouse for amusement.

Scratch Acid seemed particularly obsessed with everything that threatened not just one's mental composure but the composition of the human form. On albums like their self-titled debut and *Just Keep Eating* (both 1986), the songs teem with imagery of decay and disintegration, while the music is pure halitosis: it seems to reek of death. 'Holes' is the blues of a man who's realised his life is just a brief interval between popping out of one hole (the vagina) and plopping back into another (the grave). 'Spit A Kiss' imagines becoming 'a breeding ground for flies'. With Scratch Acid and their kindred spirits, there seemed to be an intimate connection between the fear of decay and disintegration and the impulse to kill women. Because of their proximity to the processes of birth, women seem to have a threatening power that can be dissipated only by dismembering them. This defuses the danger momentarily, and reaffirms the man's mastery and wholeness.

But there is also a mystical element to this fascination with the body's interior: to confront abjection is to apprehend the ultimate, *raw* truth of human existence. The British band Godflesh captured this idea of transcendence-through-abasement in their very name. Songs like 'Spine Nerve Shatter' imagined being pulped and mulched into a primal goo as a kind of annihilating ecstacy. Godflesh were a bridge between the avant-garde/post-hardcore scene and a subgenre of heavy metal called 'grindcore'. These groups developed thrash metal into a remorseless threshing machine, an aural abattoir of hacking riffs and flagellating drum rolls. Any sense of organic musical flow was brutally ruptured by tempo changes and gear shifts, while the grisly lyrics were morbidly fixated on threats to the organic integrity of the body.

Carcass, a group who deliberately took grindcore's carnographic tendencies beyond self-parody, reached the dizzy limit with song titles like 'Excoriating Abdominal Emanation' and 'Crepitating Bowel Erosion'. The *Reek of Putrefaction* LP featured a montage of vivisected human remains on its cover, while *Symphonies of Sickness* was decorated with a human head with its skin peeled off. Carcass's music was as surgical as the lyrics, a staccato battery of incisions and perforations. Grindcore's fascination with the gruesome is a testament both to the threat and the almost voluptuous allure posed by the abject. Skin Chamber, for instance, describe 'emasculation' as a 'blessing': to be dismembered and mutilated is to be returned to the undifferentiated gloop of the womb.

dam that river

A crucial part of child-rearing has always been teaching kids to 'police' their bodily fluids (mucus, saliva, urine, excreta, tears, vomit), and to think of the body's interior as a reservoir of vile gook. In *Male Fantasies*, Klaus Theweleit suggests that for the Freikorp soldier males, who underwent a particularly stringent child-rearing regime, the struggle to maintain a 'clean and proper body' was intimately linked to the fight to uphold the German Reich. In the soldier males' writing, one idea – that the Communist working class was dragging Germany into the cesspit – undergoes endless variations (mire, morass, abyss, sewer, dungheap, etc.). For the proto-fascist soldier males, the masses were literally revolting! And so the post-First World War civil war was fought on two fronts – the larger body politic and the micro-politics of the individual body – and the goal was to dam up the threatening deluge of gooey emotion.

Of course, child-rearing practices have loosened up a lot since the First World War. Even so, it's remarkable how thoroughly rock'n'roll is imbued with squeamishness about bodily fluids. There are even a couple of rock songs about dams bursting – one of the central phobic metaphors of the proto-fascist imagination. The most famous is 'When the Levee Breaks' by Led Zeppelin, a band whose hyper-phallic bombast and Viking/Tolkienesque warrior obsessions were attacked by many critics at the time as proto-fascist. The song is an old blues classic which Zeppelin inflated into a *tour de force* of Doomsday boogie. Why Plant and Co identified with the scenario (a real threat to the black farmers who originally heard the song), we can only guess. But women often loom as a demonic threat in Led Zeppelin's songs ('Dazed and Confused', 'Black Dog' et al.). Is 'When the Levee Breaks' a sort of allegory of this fear of feminine engulfment, elevated to a histrionic pitch of cosmic dread?

Two decades later, the burst levee metaphor reappeared in rock with Alice In Chain's 'Dam That River' (from 1992's *Dirt*) – a dank dirge full of sexual foreboding. The most metallic of the Seattle grunge bands, Alice In Chains draw on the moribund, ponderous blues of Black Sabbath and Led Zep. Their riffs sound literally doom laden, like limbs struggling to avoid being sucked down into the slough of despond. The morbid 'Them Bones' claims that we're born into the grave. Alice In Chains seems to share the novelist Louis-Ferdinand Céline's despairing belief that man is nothing but a parcel of 'arrested putrescence'. Abjection looms everywhere in *Dirt*: in the nodded-out paralysis of addiction ('Junkhead', 'Godsmack'), but above all, in the 'slow castration' of love ('Rain When I Die').

castration blues

Fusing punk's belligerence and heavy rock's despair, grunge is the sound of *castration blues*. Instead of boogie's groiny grind, grunge's turgidity embodies the struggle *not to go under*. Nirvana sang of political and existential impotence, of being 'neutered and spayed'. Ann Powers has argued that their success was a desperate attempt by the rock community to resurrect the phallus (a return to hard, masculine, aggressive sound, to rock as a signifier for youth rebellion). But the crucial qualifier is that it was a *failed* attempt, closer to flaunting the scars of castration. When the band wore dresses in the video for 'In Bloom', Nirvana weren't just deflating/mocking grunge's hard rock masculinism, they were bringing out the original meaning of punk: a feminised, sexually passive boy.

Throughout Nirvana's work, there are many hints of a regressive impulse to repudiate manhood and seek refuge in the womb. The cover of *Nevermind* features a baby swimming underwater; in front of him dangles a dollar bill on a fish-hook, luring him to abandon his amniotic paradise for a corrupt world. Nirvana's 1993 follow-up was simply titled *In Utero*; its first single, 'Heart-Shaped Box', oscillates between womb-nostalgia and dread of sexual/emotional engulfment. Cobain begs to be hoisted back to safety with his head in an 'umbilical noose', he longs to be sucked into 'your magnet tar-pit'. The highly charged imagery seems to dramatise Cobain's divided impulses. On one hand, the desire to make a break with the suffocating comfort of domesticity. On the other, an urge to refuse manhood in a world where most manifestations of masculinity are loathsome, a desire to be infantalised and emasculated. The metaphors in 'Heart-Shaped Box' also recall the voluptuous imagery of death in poems by Sylvia Plath and Anne Sexton (Sexton's poem 'Wanting to Die' writes of how failed suicides never 'forget a drug so sweet', of 'an almost unnameable lust'). Cobain's desire to retreat from the world into numbed-out sanctuary passed through heroin addiction, then blossomed into a full-blown death-wish (a surrender to what Freud called the nirvana principle, a tendency in all organic life to revert to the lowest possible level of irritation, to become inanimate). In April 1994, Cobain shot himself dead.

Being female-identified (another song on *In Utero* complains that he 'never had a father') made Cobain even more vulnerable to the lure of abjection. All of which explains why Nirvana struck such a chord with grunge youth, since their agony is precisely the feeling that they have no defence against stagnation. Commentators described Nirvana's constituency as the 'slacker' generation, twentysomethings who were directionless, incapable of personal or political commitment. Similarly, Cobain talked about feeling 'disgusted with my generation's apathy, and with my own apathy and spinelessness'. Nirvana's music quakes with the frustration of the slacker who wants to become vertebrate. But unlike the Clash, Nirvana couldn't shift from dormant to militant because, like most of the American underground, they were sceptical about attempts to politicise rock and marshal it into a movement.

One solution to this impasse was espoused by Henry Rollins. He'd formerly been the singer with Black Flag, the early '80s hardcore band whose cathartic blasts of wounded masculinity on albums like *Damaged* and *My War* were a primary source for Nirvana. As a solo artist, Rollins developed Black Flag's Sabbath-influenced aesthetic into a kind of solipsistic combat rock. A blend of Robert Bly, Yukio Mishima and Travis Bickle (the vigilante in *Taxi Driver*), Rollins disdains solidarity, yet refuses the soft option of being a slacker. With his musclebound physique, close-cropped hair, high-stamina performances, and 'don't fuck with me' aura, he's a one man army on continual red alert.

But what Rollins is really waging war against isn't so much external threats as *abjection*: his own body and soul is the battle zone. Writing eloquently about his almost mystical attitude to working out with weights, the singer revealed that as a teenage boy 'I had no sense of myself. All I was, was a product of all the fear and humiliation I suffered.' Like Cobain, Rollins grew up fatherless, without a male role model. A kind teacher took pity and taught him how to work out; Rollins never looked back. But that precarious sense of selfhood must be constantly maintained if abjection is to be kept at bay. 'Time spent away from the Iron makes my mind degenerate. I wallow in a thick depression. . . . [Iron] never lies to you. . . . Always there like a beacon in the pitch black. . . . my greatest friend'. There's a near-autistic quality to Rollins's bodybuilding (witness the Zen-like tautology of 'there is no better way to fight weakness than with strength') that carries through to his personal code of behaviour (rule number one: 'Do not attach. To anything or anyone.').

On Black Flag's 'Damaged I', Rollins was prostrate, castrated. But with the Rollins Band, he's taut and tense, a lean-and-mean fighting machine. Rollins's music is a kind of tai chi for the soul, inducing an ecstatic state of muscular/mental alertness. Like the classic survivalist or samurai, he's automated his responses through rigorous training, and achieved the sterile grace of the man-machine. He's Sabbath's 'Iron Man', impenetrable, invulnerable, invincible.

are we not men?

Perhaps the most clinical rock'n'roll of all time was created by Devo. Emerging in 1978 from the depths of Ohio, their squeamish fascination for the ickiness of human biology seemed to be part and parcel of punk's disgust with the body. In fact, Devo's morbid obsession predated punk's assault on taboos. Their early '70s material (released posthumously on the compilations *Hardcore Devo* Volumes One and Two) was grotesquerie a-go-go. 'Soo Bawls' was a paean to a cute mongoloid whose toilet water all the guys want to sip. 'Buttered Beauties' imagined the black belles of the title smearing their 'glossy tallow' over the singer. In 'Midget', the protagonist, who has the body of a toddler but the lusts of a grown man, plays under his mother's skirts all day, until his daddy has him put in a home. At this point, Devo were playing a robotic, hygienic version of the raunch and boogie so popular in early '70s America, which the band seemed to have drained of its sexual secretions, only for them to seep out again in the vile lyrics. The album *Are We Not Men? We Are Devo!* (1978) was riddled with an aversion to sexuality and female biology. 'Uncontrollable Urge' expressed desire in terms of involuntary discharges and tics that embarrass the body's owner. 'I Saw My Baby Getting Sloppy' was sex through the jaundiced eyes of Sartre, with singer Mark Mothersbaugh whining that he'd 'missed the hole'. 'Shrivel Up' rubbed the listener's face in the facts of physical deterioration and death, gloatingly reminding you of your mother's inevitable demise. And 'Gut Feeling' was an update of the classic '60s misogynist put-down, rendered in unusually vivid gastric and olfactory imagery.

Accompanying this distasteful but strangely addictive fare was a fully fledged if opaque philosophy called 'de-evolution'. The gist of it was that humanity was in decline, owing to the brain-eroding influence of TV and advertising. Devo's goal was to sever rock'n'roll's residual links with counterculture utopianism and re-make rock as a fully functioning element in a new conformist, totalitarian pop culture. Songs like 'Are We Not Men?' and 'Mongoloid' were anthems of rock's new role in Western civilisation's decline. As a parody, de-evolution was a brilliant prophesy of rock's integration in the '80s, via MTV, advertising and Hollywood tie-ins, with a mainstream leisure culture that was controlled and controlling.

What's most striking now, though, is how old-fashioned Devo's disgust was, so in tune with Judaeo-Christian body-fear. The group's chief theoretician, Jerry Casale, said: 'We base our aesthetic on self-deprecating humour. We have that [Mid-Western] sense. . . of shame about being human.' He explained that rock music is 'exciting because it's filthy – nauseous yet erect.' He argued that 'the '60s were definitely like genital-oriented sex. The '70s became narcissistically oral, and now we're in an anal phase, and like, that has to do with pre-genital sexuality, infancy. Again, just like playing in your own pooh-pooh.'

Underneath Devo's pseudo-futuristic image lurked the most traditional rock'n'roll misogyny. Casale told an interviewer of the time he'd been fired from teaching graphics at a college when a female student stole a book of Mothersbaugh's drawings from him and 'had a rather traumatic experience perusing pictures of Mark Mothersbaugh, in a surgeon's outfit, happily dismembering female bodies'. And why did Devo wear uniforms redolent of laboratory researchers and technocrats? 'We told everyone they were for protection. When you think about it, you're just like a horrible maggot with no crustacean shell over you. . . . If you were the size of an ant you'd be easy to crush. You'd be like a pinchy little blackhead.'

By the time of their commercial breakthrough, Devo had shed guitars for the stainless sterility of synthesizers, and their fear-of-flesh was expressing itself through the S/M imagery of 'Whip It' (sex without risk of contamination). In interviews, they talked of imagining a new, ultra-clean sexuality for the twenty-first century. They were obsessed with the efficiency of Japanese society. But their revulsion from the body, and in particular the liquefacient abjection of the female body, was as ancient as the Old Testament.

wargasm:
metal and machine music

'War is beautiful because it initiates the dreamt-of metalisation of the human body.'
F.T. Marinetti, 'Manifesto on the Ethiopian Colonial War'

For Devo, the uniform was a shell holding in the squishy mess of the body's interior, like armour. The proto-fascist imagination is riddled with an envy of the machine, its invulnerability and impenetrability. Being a good soldier means mechanising your responses, becoming a cog in the killing machine of the army.

Similar longings and loathings throbbed in the writings of the Italian Futurists and the British Vorticists, two early twentieth-century art movements with fascist tendencies. Wyndham Lewis, chief Vorticist theoretician, worshipped machines for their dynamism and hygiene, and recoiled from the 'naked pulsing and moving of the soft inside' of organic life. 'Deadness is the first condition for art,' he declared in the novel *Tarr* (1918). 'The second is the absence of soul, in the human and sentimental sense. . . good art must have no inside.' Good art betrayed no sign of its fluid interior; it was all exteriority, stark lines and sharp contours. For Lewis, the formless goo of biology was a threat to reason and the detached artistic eye.

The Futurists, too, repudiated the curvacious organicism and blurriness of Romantic art. Umberto Boccioni declared: 'Poetry must consist of straight lines and calculus.' F.T. Marinetti's *The Founding and Manifesto of Futurism* (1909) could almost be a manifesto for heavy metal: 'We will glorify war – the world's only hygiene – militarism, patriotism, the destructive gesture of freedom-bringers, beautiful ideas worth dying for, and scorn for woman.' His polemic ends at a bombastic pitch of priapic triumphalism: 'Look at us! We are still untired! Our hearts know no weariness because they are fed with fire, hatred, and speed!. . . Erect on the summit of the world, once again we hurl our defiance at the stars!' Like the speed-crazed punks, the Futurists disdained sleep, languour, gentleness. They wanted to break with nature in a violent gesture of severance, and impose themselves like a monument on the landscape.

For the Futurists, the machine was the embodiment of an anti-natural but self-sufficient potency. They were the first to identify with the car or motorbike as an expression of virility. This emerges as a theme in rock'n'roll very early on – from Chuck Berry's and the Beach Boys' nonchalant cruising anthems to Steppenwolf's 'Born to Be Wild' (which contained the first rock usage of William Burroughs's phrase 'heavy metal'). More suggestive, however, is the case of Kraftwerk, whose first big hit, 'Autobahn', was a twenty-minute-long freeway hymn. One of the first groups to base their entire aesthetic on synthesizers rather than the 'dirtier' electric guitar, Kraftwerk's image was futuristic and technocratic. They were the first full-blown example in rock of the desire to become machine-like (with the possible exception of James Brown's 'Sex Machine').

But where the Futurists and heavy metal bands imagined technology as an expression and a reinforcement of their virility, for Kraftwerk, machines usher in a world where gender is abolished. Their ideal being, the Man-Machine, was a sexless androgyne stripped of its animalism, possessed of a superhuman grace. Rather than an instrument for liberating pagan savagery, technology, in Kraftwerk's songs, makes possible a smoother-functioning, orderly world: compare the turbulence-free transience of 'Autobahn' and the stately progress of 'Trans-Europe Express' with the speed-freak uproar of Motorhead's

'Locomotive' or 'Iron Horse'.

Despite their state-of-the-art technology, Kraftwerk's music is a pastoral symphony: their vision of the future is closer to British 'garden cities' like Milton Keynes and Welwyn than the polluted, mongrelised chaos of the twenty-first-century megalopolis in *Blade Runner*. 'Neon Lights' (from 1978's *The Man-Machine*) is a halcyon vision of this techno-utopia; synths twinkle like the aurora borealis and the song glides smoothly and serenely as though carried on an environmentally-sound mono-rail. 'The Man-Machine' itself is android doo-wop, a multitracked choir of psalmic vocals like the Beach Boys gone cyberdelic. Here, the cyborg is a kind of angel whose clarity of thought is unmuddied by the murky stirrings of emotion or sensuality, and whose body is not composed of plasma, mucus or tissue, but of crystal diodes, platinum, electricity. Kraftwerk want to be 'made of light' (which is how they describe the heavenly city in 'Neon Lights').

Kraftwerk's Apollonian aesthetic had everything to do with post-war German culture. Nazism was the result of the catastrophic intrusion of the abject into politics: segregating and liquidating social 'vermin' (the Jews, homosexuals, Communists) was an attempt to purify the body politic. After this eruption of the id into politics, the post-war reconstruction of Germany involved the removal of passion from political life, resulting in a culture of unnatural restraint and placidity. Germany remade itself as the moral centre of Europe.

Kraftwerk were perfectly attuned to this anti-Dionysian spirit. Their music elevates super-ego over id, calculation over spontaneity, mind over body. Their cyborgs were neuters, and the sole reference to womankind, to the fact of gender, in their entire oeuvre is the condescending portrait of the superficial, manipulative, man-hungry girl in 'The Model', who sells her pulchritude to any available camera, and allows her sexuality to be used to sell consumer products: she's all body and no soul. Kraftwerk's homoerotic image – exaggeratedly neat, anti-rock'n'roll clothing, well-groomed hair, and sometimes lipstick   was part and parcel of their vision of a world without women.

That light-fingered art-rock magpie David Bowie took a leaf out of Kraftwerk's book when formulating his mid-'70s image – the glacial androgyne of *The Man Who Fell to Earth* – only to be ripped off himself by Gary Numan. Numan became a huge teenybopper idol in early '80s Britain with songs that took on much of the same lone ranger pathos that had animated Andy Williams's 'Solitaire' or Neil Diamond's 'I Am I Said', and rendered it in sci-fi terms. He became a sort of cyborg Johnny Ray with an irresistible appeal to legions of teenage girls who wanted to thaw the cold and lonely man-machine. What lent Numan's gauche futurism its conviction was the fact that young Gary seemed genuinely cut-off from human beings. The fantasy of being made of circuitry seemed to be a way of handling the unmanageable emotions of adolescence, of turning insularity into insulation. Hence songs like 'Me! I Disconnect from You' and 'Are Friends Electric?', which examined the interchangeability and disposability of human relationships, and embraced autism as a way of evading the disruptive intimacy of communication. On the other hand, with 'Cars' and his real-life fetish for aeroplanes, Numan, in classic male adolescent fashion, seemed to find machines easier to relate to than people.

Kraftwerk-esque and Numan-oid notions have re-emerged at numerous points in the evolution of electronic dance music, from early '80s electro, through industrial disco, to early '90s techno. Interfacing with machines in order to attain superhuman potency is a fantasy that has perennial resonance for a certain kind of repressed male adolescent. Techno certainly has some things in common with heavy metal: a fetish for technology (music-generating and otherwise) and an obsession with oppressive decibel levels (metal boasted of making the listeners' ears bleed, while techno raves about nosebleed-inducing sub-bass frequencies). Heavy metal and techno have a masculine, 'hardcore' aesthetic, valorising roughness, speed, and impact, testing the listener's capacity to handle the punishment. Thrash metal and hardcore techno magically combine psychotic aggression and autistic masochism (metal's headbanging and techno's twitching, rocking movements have a striking resemblance to autistic behaviour). Engulfed in a tidal wave of metallic noise, overwhelmed by the ultra-tactile on-rush of techno, penetrated to the core by the bass, the listener is enfolded by sound; a hallucinatory return to the lost maternal body.

But it could be that this loss of ego boundaries is not regressive and proto-fascistic, but blissful and utopian. At a rave, overwhelming music and empathy-amplifying drugs like Ecstasy diminish ego and inhibition. Dancers feel connected together as a giant, polymorphously perverse, collective organism; at the same time, their individual bodies seem to interface directly with the sound-system, their nervous systems plugged into the music's circuitry. Raves correspond to Gilles Deleuze and Felix Guattari's concept of the 'desiring machine', a spontaneous assemblage (of people, technology, etc.) that has no exterior goals outside its own continued propagation. Rave culture is 'about' nothing, it's a celebration of celebration. Where fascism is a killing machine, rave is an orgasmatron: a system for generating euphoria and excitement out of nothing, and for no good reason.

kinky machine

Much of rock's fetishisation of technology does seem regressive: machines are used as security blankets or to assert one's strength. In rock'n'roll, phallic totems include cars, motorbikes, guns and, not least, guitars. In rap, they include the turntable, the microphone (often referred to in lyrics as a weapon), and the ghetto blaster. In LL Cool J's 'I

Can't Live Without My Radio' (1985), the adolescent rapper marks out his territory with the din generated by his boom box. Several years later, 'The Booming System' combined car and mobile sound system as the ultimate masculine imposition of self: the marauding B-boy roams the neighbourhood, blasting noise that violates passing pedestrians' ears.

This kind of fetishism figures in other masculinist forms of rock like industrial, techno and heavy metal. Metal's technophile imagery ranges from the bawdy, ballistic sex-metaphors of AC/DC's 'Heatseeker' to the outright S/M perviness of Judas Priest, whose singer Rob Halford used to dress in leather head-to-foot and sometimes made his stage entrance on a roaring Harley Davidson. The biker-metal power trio Motorhead based their entire aesthetic around the idea that true bliss was man and machine conjoined to form a single hyperphallic hybrid. Motorhead took their name from US slang for speed-freak: chronic amphetamine abuse literally motorises your nervous system, causing a syndrome known as 'punding' (tic-like gestures, meaningless and repetitive acts, etc.). Motorhead recorded anthems to propulsion ('Bomber', 'Iron Horse', 'Locomotive'), and blitzkrieg-style destruction ('Overkill', 'Iron Fist'), while songs like 'No Sleep Til Hammersmith' and 'White Line Fever' declared war on slumber with a fanaticism worthy of the Futurists. For Motorhead, rock'n'roll was literally a desiring machine (they called one album 'Orgasmatron'), cranked up with speed, and hungry to explode.

When Motorhead revamped biker rock, they also revived the Hells Angels' flirtation with Nazi imagery. Singer Lemmy Kilmister collects Third Reich memorabilia and admires Hitler as 'the first rockstar. First one to use a lightshow. First one to put on a show. First one to use the radio and aeroplane. . . .' Another link between Hitler and Motorhead: at the height of the war, the Führer was receiving methamphetamine injections up to eight times a day – which explains his paranoid, erratic policy decisions!

raw power

In rock, technology has always been used to unleash sava-gery or to empower flight. But beyond the aspiration to machine-like perfection, beyond the use of machines as phallic props, lies a pure worship of dynamic forces, a desire to become KINETIC ENERGY. In 'Search and Destroy' (from 1973's *Raw Power*), Iggy Pop warned his honey to watch out 'cos he's 'using technology', comparing himself to a guided thermonuclear missile.

Talking later about this period when he was (over)loaded with the artificial energy of drugs, Iggy said: 'I just got caught up in that, and any thoughts – I think they just got suppressed. Rather than become a person singing about subjects, I sort of sublimated the person and I became, if you will, a human electronic tool creating this sort of buzzing, throbbing music which was at the time very timely, but isn't now.' In the Stooges, Iggy Pop was the most extreme example of the quest for a hyper-mascu-line propulsion, in which self-assertion and self-destruction merge. Iggy called that state 'Raw Power'. He became a lightning conductor for Nietzsche's world-will, the human circuit in Patti Smith's famous equation 'art + electricity = rock'n'roll'.

Back in 1957, Norman Mailer had described, in 'The White Negro', how hipsters are engaged in an attempt to 'create a new nervous system for themselves', using drugs and sexual excess and a general overload of stimuli. The hipster's Holy Grail is the 'apocalyptic orgasm'. Plugged into the techno-pagan matrix of rock'n'roll, the rebel wants to get charged with primal electricity. He wants to *burn*, even if that means he'll eventually *burn out*.

*

The pressure of being masculine, of containing the 'woman within', demands some kind of explosive release. For soldiers, combat provides a chance to transcend bodily boundaries (their own and others') in violence. In some of the most masculine forms of rock – thrash metal, grunge – moshing becomes a form of surrogate combat. Slam-dancing and stage-diving offer contact between male bodies that is normally illegitimate; the masochistic pleasure of immersing yourself in the sweat-and-bloodbath of the moshpit is a kind of macho (per)version of oceanic feelings.

Probing soldiers' writings, Klaus Theweleit pinpoints three obsessively reiterated images that seem to offer a way of purging tension and dread. The first is the 'black-out', in which dammed-up sexual and emotional energy is finally released in a giant tidal wave; the body protests and overthrows the ego by *swooning*. The second is the 'bloody miasma': here external threats are liquefied and liquidated. Reducing the enemy to *mush* ensures the soldier's wholeness, while at the same time allowing him contact, through carnage, with the carnal. Finally, there's the 'empty space', the desolate aftermath of battle, devoid of threatening stimuli, and thus reassuringly serene in its death-ly quiet.

In rock, the black-out, the bloody miasma and the empty space all figure in the lyrics of hardcore, thrash metal, grindcore et al. These groups eroticise the imagery of destruction in a manner not unlike the soldier males, who would write poetically about 'the embrace of burning grenades, the crackling kisses of gunfire'. Musically, the bloody miasma and the black-out merge as WARGASM, those moments of crush-endo like a guitar solo's climax or the burst of feedback at the end of the song.

Thrash metal, in particular, dwells voluptuously on images of devastation and explosion. Annihilation looms in the metallic imagination as an ultimate orgasm. In 'Blackened' (. . . *And Justice for All*, 1988), Metallica imagine the charred, post-apocalyptic corpse of Mother Earth in language so vivid and highly charged it's obvious that the song is only ostensibly an anti-nuclear war protest. At a deeper level, the scenario of the murdered Mother – of a planet so cauterised that life, in all its verminous, teeming abjection, will never regenerate – corresponds to Metallica's darkest desires.

rock'n'roll soldiers

'Purely on that level of physical reaction, [warfare] could be reckoned as a Dionysian thing – the experience that takes you out of yourself. . . . Ecstasy. . . . In a panic situation, you don't think, you react.'
Ron Keeley, Radio Birdman

We've already seen how soldiers and rock rebels share a fear of slackening; how the combat rockers yearned for a life of heroism, and resented bourgeois mediocrity. Theweleit described the Freikorps as 'compulsive soldiers who would have been termed delinquents in a civilian context'. Perhaps it's possible to reverse this metaphor, to see someone like Iggy Pop as a compulsive delinquent who would have been termed 'soldier' in a military context.

In fact, there's a submerged but persistent militarism running through Iggy Pop's music. The Stooges saw themselves as a military squadron. 'Heavy involvement while you're in the band was forbidden,' recalled guitarist Ron Asheton in an interview with *Motorbooty* in 1990. 'You're like a soldier: you can have all the casual sex you want on the road, but don't let the girl rule or start changing you.' From the age of ten, Asheton started a collection of Nazi uniforms and memorabilia. 'I didn't like what they stood for, but I liked what they wore.' Sometimes he would wear the stuff onstage with the Stooges – iron crosses, a white SS parade belt. Asheton's dad had been a Marine, and groomed little Ron for the military. When Asheton Sr died, Ron got turned on to rock'n'roll, and later dodged the draft.

But despite the long hair, the sex'n'drugs'n'rock'n'roll, Ron took after his pa in lots of ways: to this day, he's seriously into weaponry, collects guns and is a member of the National Rifle Association. Incredibly, Iggy's father was a military man, too, and seems to have instilled warfaring urges into his wayward son. Iggy's whole aesthetic was based around the quest for black-out and bloody miasma. Though he often hurled himself into combat with the audience, the main target for his aggression was his own body: he rolled around on broken glass, smashed his teeth on the mike, engorged huge amounts of drugs. Nietzsche's maxim in *Beyond Good and Evil* fits perfectly: 'Under conditions of peace the warlike man attacks himself.'

Iggy's delinquency started to express itself in militaristic imagery on the third Stooges' album, *Raw Power*. On 'Search and Destroy', Iggy's a roaming, predatory cheetah with a 'heart full of napalm'. On 'Death Trip' he's a man-missile on a kamikaze quest for the ultimate orgasm; he invites a girl along for the death ride. The rebel ethos of speed and will hurtles headlong into a cosmic dead end. The trouble with 'Raw Power' is that it's 'got no place to go'. Except into the embrace of death, the bride that waits at the end of the night.

The title *Raw Power* evokes a sort of megalomania without object or objective, a mastery without slaves. In a 1979 interview, Iggy described himself as 'a leader who does not want to be followed. I am exactly the man who Friedrich Nietzsche could only write about', i.e. the *ubermensch* or superman. When his interviewer, Nick Kent, suggested that some of his statements verged on the fascistic, Iggy replied: 'It would only be in the sense that I know that what I'm dealing with is in essence a military industrial complex, albeit in a smaller scale, which is what rock'n'roll is right now.' Iggy's latent militarism resurfaced with his 1980 solo album *Soldier*, while his interviews of this period saw him expressing support for Ronald Reagan, pawn of the military industrial complex. 'Loco Mosquito' sees Iggy still buzzing with the negative energy that powered 'Search and Destroy', a primal death-drive that vents itself, in one verse, through hitting his girlfriend. Iggy's hopped up on nervous energy that he can't burn, and bemoans the fact that he's too old to enrol in 'military service'.

Iggy's ballistic/militaristic side was taken to the limit by Radio Birdman. They were a band formed by guitarist Deniz Tek, a Detroit exile who emigrated to Australia in the early '70s, bringing with him an obsession with the Stooges and Motor City combat rockers the MC5. Goaded into revolt by Australia's sun-baked ennui and 'plasticity', Radio Birdman developed a cult of ENERGY, which soon expressed itself in military imagery. Tek defined the band's ethos of disciplined camaraderie: '[It's about] keeping us tight as a unit. . . It's an end in itself.' Birdman named one tour 'Blitzkrieg' and called the gigs 'offensives'; they started wearing black shirts with the band's heraldic symbol on the arms.

In *Radios Appear* (1978), the Birdman's world revolves around cars, guns, but no girls: the hero of 'Non-Stop Girls' declares he 'can't use non-stop girls' 'cos all his love's 'gone to another world'. 'Murder City Nights' celebrates that masculine city, Detroit, the world capital of automobile manufacture and homicide. It's a hymn to perpetual motion: he's 'gotta keep movin' because 'I'm a man'. 'Do the Pop', a homage to Iggy, vowed 'gonna burn alive'. 'Descent into the Maelstrom' linked E.A. Poe's story to 'adrenochrome', a mythical adrenalin-based drug that, said Tek, was sup- posed to be 'like being plugged into a million volt socket'. 'Hit Them Again', an *Apocalypse Now*-style commando- raid, again expresses Birdman's dearest dream of self- immolation: 'let's burn!'.

Livin' Eyes (1981) is a protracted exercise in death-wish- fulfilment. Radio Birdman's lyrics are riddled with equiva- lents of the bloody miasma, the black-out and the empty space. 'Alone in the Endzone', for instance, sets up the nirvanic image of the last man alive in the aftermath of global devastation. It's a thermonuclear fantasy, about a pilot hurtling across burning desert sands with just enough fuel to reach his target.

Deniz Tek, the band's songwriter and spiritual core, quit Birdman and eventually became a flight surgeon in the US Navy. But he, singer Rob Younger and bassist Warwick Gilbert did reunite briefly (along with Ron Asheton of the Stooges and Dennis Thompson of MC5) to form New Race (the name came from an anthem on the debut album, which prophesied that wild youth would mutate into a barbarian master race and rise from the ashes of a ruined civilisation). On their one official release, the live album *The First and the Last* (1982), 'Columbia' imagined space travel as a 'giant step' for this 'new race'. Kicking off with the classic '10-9-8. . .we have ignition' countdown, the song is an erectile projectile veering up to penetrate Mother Night. Space exploration is the ultimate power-and-glory trip, opening up the ultimate virgin frontier – an 'empty space' just waiting to be conquered.

reich'n'roll

'I think I might have been a bloody good Hitler.'
David Bowie, 1976

Critics have been commenting on the resemblance between arena concerts and Nazi rallies since the rise of stadium rock in the early '70s. For disillusioned veterans of the counterculture, the scale and bombast of Led Zeppelin's shows made the group seem virtually fascist. Queen hyped up the Wagnerian pomp and ceremony, and flirted with Nuremberg-like crowd-manipulating dynamics. They were perhaps the first to enshrine metal's triumphalism in stomping anthems like 'We Are the Champions' and 'One Vision'.

Roger Waters of Pink Floyd was sufficiently unnerved by the totalitarian vibe of stadium shows to write the musical epic *The Wall* (1979), whose protagonist, Pink, lives through various character-deforming processes as a child, and emerges as a twisted rock'n'roll Führer who actually incites members of his audience to attack gays and blacks. A rather heavy-handed allegory, but not devoid of a certain latent truth. Like the Führer, the Lead Singer is the incarnation of the audience's desires; he lives out their fantasies of the perfect existence, and shapes them into a unity of alienation or aspiration.

Rock Romanticism is continually on the verge of turning fascistic. In the early '70s, rock underwent a radical shift, ceasing to be a music primarily experienced aurally, becoming increasingly visual and theatrical. Glam rock artists like Roxy Music and David Bowie were part of this shift towards *fascination*: spellbinding the eye rather than ear. Their aesthetic was decadent. And in rock'n'roll just as in history, decadence and fascination lead on to fascism. Roxy Music posed in Nazi uniforms; David Bowie returned from a world tour in 1976 with coke-fuelled Messianic delusions and, wrote Simon Frith, 'the commanding gestures of a would-be leader'.

Bowie's roots in the Dionysian spirit of the late '60s had led him to explore magick; from there, he began to succumb to a fascination with the Nazis' secret streak of Romanticism. In 1993, recalling this murky phase of his life for *Arena*, Bowie confessed that he'd been intrigued by the rumour that the Nazis had actually 'come to England at some point before the War to Glastonbury Tor to try to find the Holy Grail. . . . [They had] this Arthurian need. . . for a mythological link with God.' Bowie's bosom buddy Iggy was also on the same drug-addled wavelength around this time. In 'China Girl' (from 1977's *The Idiot*), Iggy's mind's eye is swimming with 'visions of swastikas' and plans for world-domination.

When it comes to Führer-postures and sturm und drang

spectacle, though, nothing beats heavy metal. The critics who accused Led Zeppelin of proto-fascist tendencies were on to something: 'Immigrant Song' (from 1970's *Led Zeppelin III*) saw the band fantasising about being Viking invaders. Like the Nazis, Led Zep identified with the Nordic overlord race who descended on the agrarian societies of Southern Europe, raping, pillaging, wassailing and generally behaving like rock'n'roll animals. Zep chronicler Stephen Davis describes Zep's songs, in *Hammer of the Gods*, as the modern equivalent of the martial music that, combined with intoxicants, whipped up Viking warriors into a furious, fear-deadened, blood-lusting frenzy.

Led Zeppelin's archetypal anthem was also their most phallic and wargasmic. 'Whole Lotta Love' (from 1969's *Led Zeppelin II*) blurred the line between 'ravish' and 'ravage'. In the war between the sexes, 'Whole Lotta Love' announced imminent invasion. According to Stephen Davis, in Vietnam that year 'Whole Lotta' was literally a war cry. American infantry men and marines 'bolted 8-track stereos onto their tanks and armored personnel carriers and rode into battle playing the song at top volume'. The rampaging riff is brutally simplistic and ballistic, coitus as combat. The middle section – a dizzy whirl of hallucinatory drones and stray guitar shrapnel – is pure black-out. For Led Zeppelin, orgasm is agony. But then! the riff magically re-erects, and rampages on unabated.

Led Zeppelin's vision of sex as conquest was once again uncannily prefigured by the Futurists. *The Futurist Manifesto of Lust* (1913) noted with approval the tradition whereby 'after a battle in which men have died, IT IS NORMAL FOR THE VICTORS, PROVEN IN WAR, TO TURN TO RAPE IN THE CONQUERED LAND, SO THAT LIFE MAY BE RECREATED'. Like the free spirits of the counterculture, the Futurists despised romance and sentimentality as 'histrionics of love' that impeded the full rampaging of (male) desire; they exalted lust as 'a force'. But as heavy metal evolved, it went from Led Zeppelin's sex-as-war to war as sexy in itself.

Bands like Iron Maiden and Metallica regressed to the pre-
pubescent boy's fantasy world, all explosions, invasions and
chaste, girl-free adventures.

The connections between machine-worship, fascism,
Futurism and metal really blossomed with the Young
Gods, the Swiss band whose music offers the ultimate techno-pagan, digital-Dionysian apocalypse. Like cyber-Stooges
for the twenty-first century, the Young Gods use the
sampler to unloose a bombardment of vivisected metal riffs
and classical bombast. Singer Franz Treichler's lyrics
brought out all the militaristic, fascistic tendencies inherent in Romanticism, Nietzsche et al., only to transcend and
transfigure them. The title of their 1989 album *L'Eau
Rouge* – 'red water' – hints that the Gods' ultimate dream
is a cosmic bloody miasma. In 'La Fille de la Morte',
Treichler betrothes himself to Death, 'our queen', recalling
Marinetti's fantasy of 'Death, domesticated. . . making
velvety caressing eyes at me'. Except that the Young Gods
go beyond this puerile fantasy of conquering Death, and
gladly welcome her embrace. The martial drums and
orchestral fanfares of 'Les Enfants' evoke a vague, faintly
disquieting aura of mass rally, but this children's army is
really on a crusade to surrender and sunder the fortress of
'I'. Self-exaltation turns to self-annihilation: the Young
Gods yearn to go out in a blaze of abstract glory.

i am the king:
delusions of grandeur from jim morrison to
gangsta rap

From Elvis's pelvis, through the Stones' cock-y swagger,
Led Zep's penile dementia, right up to the Sex Pistols (just
check out the name) and Guns N'Roses, rock is riddled with
the idea of Phallus Power. The subtext is that in a world of
men castrated by the system, here is a REAL MAN, a rebel
aflame with the 'burning virility' Jimmy Porter craved in
Look Back in Anger. You can trace this tendency all the
way through rock: penetration, self-aggrandisement, violation, acceleration and death-wish are conflated in a single
existential THRUST.

Jim Morrison remains the pinnacle of this phallic delirium. Unabashedly macho rock critic Nick Tosches provides
an uncensored insight into Morrison's magnetism in his
introduction to David Dalton's biography *Mr Mojo Rising*.
Tosches reminisces about the day in June 1968 when he
first heard 'Hello, I Love You': 'What I remember is that
gust of annihilation that in two minutes and fourteen sec-
onds destroyed and delivered us from the utter bullshit
that had been the '60s. We were free again, those of us who
did not stink of patchouli, believe in the family of man, or
eat macrobiotic gruel; those of us who found god. . .through
smack, preferred our sex dirty, and supported our boys in
Vietnam because it meant a surplus of left-behind pussy on
the home front. . . . The whole vast noisome toilet bowl of
love [and] peace. . . was overflowing all over the fucking
place. So. . . . Love was all they needed. Well, that summer,
Morrison delivered it, nasty and impersonal. . . like a cold
hard blue-veined cock right up under the tie-dyed skirts of
benighted sensitivity.'

Even sedate Joan Didion could see that the Doors were starkly different from the lovey-dovey mystics of the Love Generation. In her essay on late '60s California, 'The White Album', the Doors are 'the Norman Mailers of the Top Forty, missionaries of apocalyptic sex' whose 'music insisted that love was sex and sex was death and therein lay salvation'. Sexual congress, for Jim Morrison, was not about anything so prosaic and limited as union with a specific, flesh-and-blood woman. As in D.H. Lawrence, Georges Bataille, and a whole tradition of erotic mystics, coitus was cosmic. 'Light My Fire' linked love and the funeral pyre; light the fuse, demands Morrison, and my rocketship will hurtle us into incandescent fusion with the universe. 'Break on Through' is another allegory of sex as a voyage into a virgin, unknown terrain of the soul, a Mother Night that the exploding male briefly illuminates with his pyrotechnics. Morrison's ideal of spiritual adventurism is clearly modelled on the structure of male orgasm: a headlong hurtle towards ruinous self-expenditure.

If Morrison was a rocket, then his fuel was what Tosches' buddy Richard Meltzer calls 'edge substances'. Chemicals like LSD, peyote, amyl nitrate, dope, alcohol. Even more important, though, were the cultural, the literary toxins/intoxicants: Artaud's Theatre of Cruelty, Blake's 'doors of perception', Céline's 'journey to the end of the night', Rimbaud's 'sacred disorder of the mind'. From these Romantic influences Morrison derived the idea of the artist as a 'broker in madness', an explorer of the frontier territories of the human condition.

Morrison took the phallic model of rebellion (transgression, penetration of the unknown) to the limit. But the ultimate outcome of that stance (the refusal to accept and affirm limits) ultimately leads nowhere. As Albert Goldman put it: 'The flipside of breakthrough is estrangement. Once you've broken away, it's pretty bleak out there. The rebel cuts himself off.' Morrison himself expressed regrets that the Doors had never done 'a song, or a piece of music, that's a pure expression of joy...a feeling of being totally at home'. Instead, he stuck with the 'dark side', and inevitably, his final destination was the grave. Nick Tosches fondly imagines Morrison not stopping even then. 'If only he could have conquered that Lady Death who "makes angels of us all", if only he had hurled her into the dirt the way he fucked the '60s into the dirt, maybe he would still be around.' In Morrison's cosmology, 'death and my cock' were the two poles of his universe, and peace could only come with the triumph of Thanatos over Eros.

With Iggy Pop, Jim Morrison's phallic rebellion is shorn of its Romantic trappings. It emerges as undiluted, nihilistic WILL. Morrison's beatnik propulsion devolves into an aimless ferocity which reaches its apotheosis on the second Stooges' album, *Funhouse*, and especially on 'Loose', with its chorus: 'I stuck it deep inside'. Iggy is a kind of rapist without victim, burning for total connection with reality. The lyric is a distant echo of the time when Kerouac made a hole in the earth and fucked Mother Nature. Later, on the Stooges' *Raw Power*, the Doors' 'Break on Through' becomes 'Penetration': a blind thrust without object or destination. Fifteen years later, Dennis Hopper's decrepit psycho-rebel in *Blue Velvet* yells 'Fuck! I Fuck!' – a hyper-masculine speed-freak hollering into the void.

This state of directionless aggression and unbridled velocity was what Iggy called 'Raw Power' – a deadly rigour of being that is the very heart and soul of punk. There was an appetite for destruction in punk that has as much to do with the darkest recesses of the (male) psyche as with the specific social conditions of England in 1976. It's there in the intransitive 'I destroy' at the close of the Pistols' 'Anarchy in the UK', in the bloodcurdling snarls of 'Bodies', in the random, gratuitous violence of 'No Feelings'. This masculinity-in-extremis reaches its climax in the final insane minute of 'Belsen Was A Gas', as Johnny Rotten runs through the options for the phallic principle: 'be a man, kill someone, kill yourself'. These last febrile lines of the Pistols' sickest, cheapest joke reveal the two possible extremes at the end of the rock rebel's phallic trajectory: world-destruction OR self-destruction, apocalypse OR the implosive apocalypse of heroin addiction.

Earlier, we saw how the Pistols learned the art of vicious-ness and dis-connection from misogynist mod anthems like 'No Lip, Child' and 'Stepping Stone', which they then reapplied to society. The Woman-as-Society metaphor re-emerged in 1987 on the notorious cover of Guns N'Roses' *Appetite for Destruction*. Or at least that was the band's rationale for Robert Williams's painting of the aftermath of a vicious rape, with the dazed victim lying against a fence, half-naked. According to Axl Rose, the rapist (a robot) symbolised the inhuman technological forces brutalising society. The picture's vaguely titillating nature and the title of the album somewhat belied this interpretation. Moreover, rape is the subtext of the album's first track, 'Welcome to the Jungle', a strange song addressed to a girl making her first tentative steps into Los Angeles. Axl taunts her with the city's danger, wielding his vision of chaos like a sexual threat, sneering that he hopes it'll bring her to her knees. Midsong, he makes orgasmic cries and moans, seemingly mimicking the sound of the girl being fucked.

Inspired as much by English punk as by Aerosmith-style raunch, Guns N'Roses played a vicious punk-funk-metal hybrid. What's unusual about G'N'R is how few of their songs are driven by sexual lust. Instead of pent-up testos-terone, its fuels are desperation, paranoia and a desolate craving for sanctuary from an intolerable world. 'Paradise City' cuts between an anthemic chorus, full of homesick yearning for a Edenic town full of beautiful girls, and a marauding riff, glowering with sexual menace. With his violent mood-swings and conflicted feelings about every-thing, Rose's motto could be Bataille's 'I MYSELF AM WAR'. Except that, unlike Johnny Rotten who wanted to *be* anarchy, Rose seeks salvation from his own chaos.

By the time of 1991's *Use Your Illusion I* and *II*, Rose is looking to heal himself, to step out of the headlong death-trip trajectory he'd previously celebrated in 'Nighttrain'. The *Illusion* albums sometimes exude a vibe of aftermath and burn-out redolent of the Stones' druggy *Exile on Main Street*. But mostly they are closer to the urgent delirium of the Pistols' 'Holidays in the Sun': 'too much paranoia', the ultra-vivid scream of a man trying to escape from his rebel persona. Paranoia is sometimes interpreted as a desire to reinforce sexual difference, a fear of castration. Everywhere, Rose feels his masculinity/individuality under threat – from backstabbing, 'ball-breaking' women, record biz puppeteers, devious media scum. Being an individual, a real man, is a struggle against insuperable odds.

One minute, he's a sex pistol cocked and loaded; the next he craves the womb. G'N'R's 'Coma' is a sort of 'Gimme Shelter' for the MTV blank generation. The song sees Axl in several minds about seeking refuge from reality: numb the pain or thrive on its edge? One verse, he's strung-out in a stoned, murky stupor; the next, he's haranguing himself to wake up. This drug-induced oblivion is implicitly amniotic; Rose imagines himself at peace, down by the shore. 'Coma' recalls Hendrix's 'Belly Button Window', where an unborn child peeps out at a war-torn hellworld and decides he's staying where it's safe and warm. But 'Coma' is also based on a true near-death experience during overdose; the track comes complete with gimmicky sound-effects of paramedics zapping Rose back to life. And revealingly, a chorus of 'bitches' shrilly complaining about Rose's faults and misdemeanours hints that it's women that have driven him to this bitter end.

In a suggestive piece in *Details*, novelist Mary Gaitskill writes of her attraction to Axl, whom she likens to the cruel boy-monsters who appalled yet fascinated her in junior high. Rose exudes the same alluring, demon-lover aura: 'the kind of boundless aggression that can easily turn to cruelty... intense and generically fierce – generic because it doesn't have to be directed at anybody or anything in particular.... Axl's high, carnal, glandularly defined voice, is an invitation to step into an electrical stream of pure aggression and step out again.'

Gaitskill's writing gets suggestive in another sense, when she pinpoints Rose's phallic appeal in her description of 'Welcome to the Jungle': 'It's not just his hips. His rapt, mean little face, the whole turgor of his body, suggests a descent into a pit of gorgeous, carnal grossness, a voluptuousness of awful completeness where, yes, "you're gonna die".' But this is no politically unsound rape fantasy; women can identify, says Gaitskill, because 'there is great ferocity latent in women – latent because we still don't fully support or acknowledge it'. In the end she sees Axl Rose not as a male tyrant but as a victim who hurts because he's *hurting*. Around the time of the release of the *Illusion* albums, Rose confessed in a *Rolling Stone* interview to being the victim of child abuse ('my dad fucked me in the ass when I was two'). Whether it's true or not, the abused often grow up to become abusers. And that's Guns N'Roses all over: underdogs turned overlords, terrorists turned tyrants.

the king of rock

Rock is full of kings. Some are self-proclaimed despots (e.g. rappers); others are elevated and crowned by their followers (Elvis). There are variants on the regal theme: the Boss (Springsteen), rap's gangster chic, the shaman, prophet or Messiah (Bono). So why does rock lend itself to the kingly posture? On one level, to be king means simply to be the best at what you do. On another, it's the logical culmination of the self-aggrandisement inherent in showbiz. But in a wider sense, the king represents *total possibility*, the zenith of the imaginable. In the same way, the rock star is the incarnation of his fans' forbidden desires and impossible dreams. When Johnny Rotten compared himself to the Antichrist and declared he wanted to 'be anarchy', he wanted to be a law unto himself. This was the meaning of the Pistols' version of anarchy: not workers' councils and self-criticism tribunals, but the right to be your own tyrant.

Actually, one anarchists' commune in 1850s America practised a doctrine of 'Individual Sovereignty' that was pure Rotten: each person was 'the absolute despot or sovereign' of his life. The concept of *sovereignty* assumes a special significance in the thought of Georges Bataille; it was his term for a supreme state of being. Sovereignty (equivalent to Lacan's 'phallus') is a pinnacle of unalienated, uncastrated wholeness of being. For Bataille, sovereignty is marked by extravagance and excess, as illustrated by societies whose hierarchy was organised around the *squandering* of resources. Examples include Aztec sacrifice and Native American potlatch, a form of ritualised gift-giving in which rank was determined by the ability to waste wealth. The modern equivalent of potlatch is rock stars trashing hotel suites or wasting a fortune getting wasted on drugs. From all this, Bataille concluded that there was a fundamental human drive towards prodigality and 'expenditure-without-return'.

True prodigal sons, rock stars have always styled themselves as dandy playboys, always cultivated an aesthetic of excess. Their values are aristocratic, a rejection of the bourgeois creed of deferred gratification, accumulation, investment. Historically, the aristocracy have been the class most able to devote their lives and resources to extravagance (dandyism, combat, gambling, art, 'perverse' sexuality).

Sovereignty is defined by the consumption of wealth because productivity is always *servile*, according to Bataille. A sovereign existence is one that isn't subordinated to utility, that doesn't involve the employment of the present for the sake of the future. And so the bum or hobo ('king of the road') is as much a sovereign as any monarch, despite his apparent destitution. For the defining mark of the sovereign is that he *is*, rather than *does*. Unlike Sartre's revolutionary (who wants to get rid of hierarchy altogether, and who sacrifices his present to work slavishly for that utopian future), the Rebel just wants to usurp the King's place. He wants it ALL and he wants it NOW.

Rock is crowded with these rebel-kings, upstarts turned monarchs. The archetype was Elvis, but he was unconscious, at least at first, of his myth-hood, innocent of the notion that he embodied his audience's desires. Jim Morrison was the first rock icon to see himself from the start in Messianic terms. An admirer of Presley and Sinatra (rulers in their respective realms) Morrison consciously organised his own coronation, anticipated his own martyrdom.

Morrison proclaimed himself the Lizard King. According to Mick Farren in *The Black Leather Jacket*, Morrison was obsessed with 'the kind of ancient fertility religions that ensured their followers' survival and prosperity by choosing a monarch (usually young, cute, male and virile) who would be sacrificed (usually by young, cute, nubile females) after seven years or some other suitable mystic period.' Morrison recognised a similar process at work in rock'n'roll, and conscientiously aspired towards it. Armed with ideas derived from Nietzsche's *Birth of Tragedy*, the neo-Freudian scholar Norman O. Brown's *Life Against Death* and Kerouac's *On the Road*, Jim Morrison became the first pop deity who stage-managed his own self-deification.

Combining shamanic charisma and regal potency, the persona of the Lizard King symbolised a truly virile existence. This first came to the fore in the mysterious and wonderfully pretentious epic 'The End'. It's an Oedipal psychodrama, with the same latent content as *Hamlet*: the incestuous desire to displace the King/Father, gain possession of the mother's body, and rule supreme. According to

Doors' producer Paul Rothchild, 'kill the father, fuck the mother' was Morrison's catechism. Killing the father meant overthrowing the law, laying waste to the old precepts; fucking the mother meant re-connecting with absolute reality, penetrating to the core. Morrison strove to live like a hobo-king, in the spirit of Neal Cassady, who (according to one of his friends) 'lived right now, right at the moment. . . never planned his life in terms of goals'. Jay Stevens writes that Cassady's life was 'one long *acte gratuit*'.

Iggy Pop took Jim Morrison's persona and turned it into something more ballistic than beatnik. As a solo artist, he wrote his own Oedipal psychodrama equivalent to 'The End' in 'Sister Midnight' (from 1977's *The Idiot*), a nightmare in which he has sex with his mother and is hunted down by his gun-toting father. Although he never explicitly took on regal imagery, Iggy did aspire to be a Nietzschean superman and entertained Führer-fantasies. Iggy is the bridge between the Lizard King and the most king-obsessed rocker ever, Nick Cave.

Cave's regal fantasies began with 'King Ink' on *Prayers on Fire* (1981). Cave's anti-heroic alter ego is the king of bohemia, presiding over a realm of squalor and torpid impotence. On the Birthday Party's next album *Junkyard* (1982), 'Hamlet Pow Pow' turns Shakespeare's Oedipal psychodrama into a cartoon; Hamlet has long been seen as the archetypal male adolescent outsider, and Cave is happy to step into his angst-ridden shoes.

Another kind of ruined king that has haunted Cave's imagination is the pop idol who's seen better days or the rock prophet abandoned by his unworthy flock. He's spoken of his fascination for the late-era Presley, a bloated travesty of his rebel self (Cave's first solo single was a cover of 'In the Ghetto', Presley's last gasp of brilliance before the twilight of his creative life really set in). On his second solo album, *The Firstborn Is Dead*, Cave reappears as 'The Black Crow King'. The album's pastiche ethnological liner notes suggest that the chorus of voices is 'a king surrounded by followers who have learnt to imitate him' – Cave ridiculing and repudiating his Goth cult following? Deserted and preposterous, the Black Crow reigns over 'nothing at all'. This melodramatic posture – the prophet without honour – would be reprised on *Kicking Against the Pricks* with his cover of Johnny Cash's 'The Singer', where a Messianic minstrel rues his abandonment by a fickle, shallow audience who don't understand his vision.

Of course, self-aggrandisement is intrinsic to rebel rock; singers from Johnny Rotten to Morrissey have resorted to the posture of the martyr, the crucified or spurned saviour. Cave seems particularly fond of the delapidated grandeur of the fallen king. The key song here is 'Junkyard'. 'I am the King' intones an obviously wasted Cave amidst a cacophonous turmoil of brackish guitars that at the time (1982) felt like the final self-immolatory throes of rock'n'roll. Once again, Cave's kingdom is in ruins – literally a junkyard. The title is an inspired pun based on Cave's heroin addiction. The junkie feels like a king, omnipotent, cocooned and resplendent in his solipsistic invulnerability (especially if the heroin is cut with the ultimate megalomaniac euphoriant, speed). He thinks he's God, oblivious to the reality of his surroundings. 'Junkyard''s lyrics revolve around violently compacted opposites: king/junkyard, honey/garbage, heavenly body/brutal violation. The crucial line is: 'there's garbage in honey's sack again', which evokes both heroin's wombing nirvana and the horror of mainlining toxins. Cave's voice disappears into a seething quagmire of purulent sound.

The junkie as twentieth-century king? Bataille never considered it, but it's a plausible development of his notion of sovereignty as *sterile splendour*. ('Heroin' comes from the German word 'heroisch', meaning strong, powerful, heroic.) Bataille's final paradox was that the sovereign's last word is 'I am NOTHING'. Heroin addiction is a return to the invulnerable self-sufficiency of the foetus, a total escape from the ignominy of the productive world, the purest form of wasting your life. Robert Bly argues that drug addiction is a perverted expression of the yearning for kingly prestige: 'As Romantics we long for that oceanic feeling we felt in the womb, when we were divine and fed by ambrosia. Addiction amounts to an attempt to escape limitations and stay in the King's Room.'

The heroin high activates pain-and-anxiety killing endorphins in the brain which are similar to those released by orgasm. In rock's definitive smack hymn, the Velvet Underground's 'Heroin', Lou Reed's imagery is uncannily appropriate to the notion of sovereignty. He compares himself to Jesus, sings of trying to reach 'the kingdom', describes the drug as 'my wife' and 'my life'. And he boasts of his indifference to external reality (to the politicians and carnage of dead bodies piling up), of his autistic self-sufficiency (he doesn't need the sweet, silly talk of girls). Heroin is his renunciation of reality, a submission to the death-wish, a near-death experience.

A famous drug fiend who had an enormous influence on rock'n'roll is Aleister Crowley, occultist and magician. In the early twentieth century, Crowley's fantasy of 'erotocomatose lucidity' (orgasm pursued to the point of death) anticipated Jim Morrison's love-as-funeral-pyre. Pharmaceutically indulgent, sexually charismatic and promiscuously polysexual, strongly influenced by Eastern thought and medieval mysticism, Crowley was a rock star before the fact. His magick has been seized upon by many of the most transgressive rock bands (Led Zeppelin, those apocalypticians Killing Joke, the neo-pagan Psychic TV, *ad nauseam*). So it's not surprising that something very akin to sovereignty emerges as a latent theme in his thought.

In his anti-Bible *The Book of the Law*, Crowley decreed 'every man and every woman is a star' and 'do what thou wilt shalt be the whole of the law'. 'Star' suggests pre-eminence, an exorbitant incandescence of being. 'Do what thou wilt shalt be the whole of the law' is the latest version of the secret that the Old Man of the Mountains (Rashid al-din Sinan, leader of the Hashassins) surrendered to his most loyal disciples: 'nothing is true, everything is permitted'. Crowley also proclaimed that his religion was only for 'the kingly men'. Following Nietzsche, he disdained slave-religions like Christianity, Judaism and Islam; Crowley-anity was all about becoming your own god.

free spirits

'Men are all born as saviours and kings.'
Hugo Ball, Dadaist

Crowley's kingly religion can be traced back to the millenarian cults of the Middle Ages. In particular, the Cult of the Free Spirit, which 'cultivated a self-exaltation that often amounted to self-deification', according to historian Norman Cohn. He suggests that drug addiction is inspired by apocalyptic yearnings similar to those of the Medieval Free Spirits: both involve the same fantasy of 'a total emancipation of the individual from society, even from external reality itself – the ideal, if one will, of self-divini-sation'.

Cohn's description of the economic and cultural climate that gave birth to the Free Spirit cult has remarkable parallels with the pre-conditions of the '60s' counterculture. The twelfth century initiated a period of unprecedented prosperity, just as in the post-World War Two West. But this materialism prompted a counter-reaction, in the shape of a new class of voluntary poor who renounced riches in search of spiritual values. These downwardly mobile bohemians formed 'a mobile, restless intelligentsia' who went 'on the road', following the trade routes and preaching a contempt for wordly things.

Like the beats, the Free Spirit brethren divided the world into square and hip, a 'crude in spirit' majority and a 'subtle in spirit' elite who could access the Divine Oneness in this life rather than having to wait until the afterlife. Some cultists went further: they believed they had become God, or surpassed him. Being divine, the Free Spirit adept could sin at will. The result was a rampant, mystical promiscuity, and a shameless parasitism (consume rather than produce, cheat and lie if necessary to fulfil one's wants, and so on. . .). Like hotel-trashing rockers, they showed their contempt for material things by wastrel and wanton behaviour. And like your typical rock god, the Brethren believed that just as animals were created for the use of mankind, so woman had been created for man's pleasure. A final rock parallel: after undergoing a period of asceticism, the Brethren felt free to dress in finery (since wordly comforts were nothing to them); this upset the rigid dress codes of the Middle Ages and made the Free Spirits the first subcultural rebels!

Ironically, the ultimate formulation in rock of this heady brew (self-deification/psychosis/sovereignty/death-wish) is fictional, and the creation of Norman Cohn's son. Nik Cohn's 1975 novel *King Death* is about a contract killer who is turned into the ultimate rock'n'roll megastar by a canny producer who inadvertently sees him plying his deadly trade and is stunned by his grace and finesse. At the height of his fame, the star's fans gladly submit to being his victims on live TV.

King Death is the logical culmination of the complex of ideas at work in rebel rock'n'roll (the quest for sovereignty, the belief, implicit or articulated, that 'do what thou wilt shalt be the whole of the law'). What's amazing is that Cohn wrote this only two years before Sid Vicious realised it: in fantasy (in the video for 'My Way', whose megalomaniac climax sees Vicious machine-gunning his adoring audience), and in brute reality a few months later when he stabbed girlfriend Nancy Spungen to death. Three weeks after his own suicide, Vicious's cover of Eddie Cochran's 'Something Else' became a huge hit in England, selling twice as many copies as the Pistols' biggest single, 'God Save the Queen'. As Jeff Nuttall commented, 'The pop god of the age is a suicidal sex murderer'. Cohn had located a latent potential in rock'n'roll, a fantasy that, sooner or later, would be realised: snuff rock.

There are many more examples of sovereignty in rock and pop. James Brown, the King of Soul, used to have himself crowned onstage. David Bowie's 'Heroes', a song written at the height of his Thin White Duke/coke & heroin phase, imagines being a King 'just for one day'. In 'Sympathy for the Devil', Jagger impersonated the ultimate rebel-monarch, who wanted to depose and usurp the King of Heaven (Satan was the first prodigal son, the first upstart to refuse servility). Then there's the Stones' album *Their Satanic Majesties Request*.

The most powerful expression of sovereignty in recent years has been as a latent theme, never fully articulated, in the music of Jane's Addiction. This Los Angeles art-metal band revived many of Jim Morrison's favourite riffs: Nietzsche's 'beyond good and evil' (rephrased in rock'n'roll idiom in 'Ain't No Right'), derangement of the senses, aristocratic indulgence, perversity and excess, the full shaman trip (an interest in ritual, adornment, and pagan/Christian hybrids like santeria). Musically, Jane's Addiction's deluges of grandeur can only be described as majestic. Lyrically, singer Perry Farrell revelled in feelings of grandiosity with songs like 'Mountain Song' and 'Ocean Size', in which he wished he were as vast as the ocean: an echo, perhaps, of Maldoror's ode to the sea, which he worshipped because of its limitless self-sufficiency, or of poet Pablo Neruda's salutation to the ocean – 'and you lack nothing'.

It's revealing that at the time, two of Farrell's obsessions were heroin and surfing. Both offer a self-exalting rush that's perfectly attuned to the self-deification/self-annihilation complex at work in rebel rock. Both are literally about living on the edge. This idea of the surfer as Nietzschean superman might seem preposterous, since we usually associate the sport with Jan and Dean and the Beach Boys. Then again, when Malcolm McLaren attempted to make it in Hollywood, one of his doomed projects was a film about Nazi surf-punks in California.

Plenty of kings in rock, then, but precious few queens. Aretha Franklin was Queen of Soul, but this title was conferred by others, not self-proclaimed, and she never conducted herself with the hubris of James Brown, her ermine-clad regal counterpart. Patti Smith toyed with the idea of herself as a messiah figure, but then she was one of the most male-identified she-rebels ever, and aspired to be a female Jim Morrison. The kingly model of self-aggrandisement doesn't really seem to appeal to or work for women. In recent years, only rapper Queen Latifah has dared to crown herself, but she's a benign despot, her dignity and composure symbolising her noble African past. Moreover, she's still outnumbered vastly by self-proclaimed rap kings, tyrants and gangstas.

empire in exile

So far, we've talked pretty exclusively about white male rebellion. Of course, from the beats to the '60s rockers, white rebels have learned most of their moves from black culture – a syndrome first pinpointed by Norman Mailer in his 1957 essay 'The White Negro'. When it comes to analysing black rebellion on its own terms, it's impossible to understand 'black machismo' outside of its context (oppression and dis-empowerment). But here we want to highlight the similarities instead of the differences between white and black male rebellion, the tropes and totems that recur across the racial divide.

The King, or his modern day equivalent, the Gangster,

has a special resonance as symbol of supreme virility for black men in the face of a white supremacist society. If you look at the '60s essays of Eldridge Cleaver, Black Panther Minister of Information and a writer who explicitly analysed the (male) African-American experience in terms of emasculation, kingship/sovereignty emerges as a latent theme, as the polar opposite of *castration*.

Cleaver's worldview was phallocentric in the extreme. In his early days of political awakening and cold, smouldering fury, he practised rape as a political tactic, an assault on white men's most jealously guarded property – their women. Cleaver first rehearsed his techniques on black women, an easier target, then moved on to the forbidden domain of white women. For him, rape was 'an insurrectionary act'. Even after disowning this practice (when he realised white women were also oppressed, and that he'd dehumanised them and himself), Cleaver's discourse remained phallocratic. He concurred with Ossie Davis's view of Malcolm X as 'our manhood, our living black manhood... our own black shining Prince'. Echoing the young Marx's dictum 'better that the whole world should be destroyed and perish utterly than that a free man should refrain from one act to which his nature moves him', Cleaver proclaimed 'we shall have our manhood. We shall have it or the earth will be levelled by our attempts to gain it.'

You can find, in Cleaver's writing and in a strain of black music that runs from Hendrix and Miles Davis to modern rap, two closely intertwined tendencies: on the one hand, a longing for some kind of potency, wholeness, sovereign majesty; on the other, an abiding fear of the dissolution of gender boundaries. In a mystic eulogy entitled 'To All Black Women, From All Black Men', Cleaver apologises, as a representative of black masculinity, for his failure to be a warrior-king, which is attributed to slavery's emasculating effect. Despite his protestations of fealty to a pedestallised Black Queen, the real subject of the essay is a lament for his mutilated testicles: 'torrents of blood. . . flow. . . from my crotch'. Cleaver waxes lyrical: 'across the naked abyss of negated masculinity, of four hundred years minus my Balls, we face each other today, my Queen.'

In his sexual cosmology, men and women are radically different, albeit complementary. 'Let. . . your love seize my soul by its core and heal the wound of my Castration, let my convex exile ends its haunted Odyssey in your concave essence which receives that it may give.' Black masculinity's humiliation/mutilation originates in the trauma of being unable to protect his woman from the slave-owner, being forced to listen helplessly to assaults on the 'sacred womb that cradled primal man, the womb that incubated Ethiopia and populated Nubia and gave forth Pharoahs unto Egypt....' In a brilliant sleight of lyricism, banishment from the pre-Oedipal idyll is conflated with exile from the African motherland.

mama said knock you out

In the same essay, Cleaver introduces the notion of African-Americans as a *kingly race* forcibly degraded into servility: 'before we could come up from slavery, we had to be pulled down from our throne'. For Cleaver, boxing is the apotheosis of sovereign virility, and, along with music and entertainment, one of the few avenues through which blacks can achieve a lordly existence. In 'Lazarus, Come Forth', he analyses the Muhammad Ali v. Floyd Patterson contest for the world heavyweight championship as a struggle between two kinds of black masculinity. Ali is an ideological, unbowed black; Patterson (because his name is Caucasian, and his attempt to integrate his neighbourhood led to a humiliating defeat) is reassuring to whites, and thus counter-revolutionary. 'It is a hollow, cruel mockery to crown a man king in the boxing ring and then shove him about outside,' says Cleaver. 'A slave in private life, a king in public – this is the life that every black champion has had to lead – until the coming of Muhammad Ali.'

In its early days, rap was a gladiatorial contest between rival MCs, and to this day it uniquely fuses the superbad flash of the black showbiz tradition with the titanic triumphalism of boxing. Hardly surprising, then, that the most megalomaniac of rappers, LL Cool J, identifies strongly with Mike Tyson. On the inner sleeve of *Bigger and Deffer* (1987) he's dressed as a boxer. In his comeback hit 'Mama Said Knock You Out' (1990), the boxing-ring is the setting for one of his most tyrannical tirades ever, with LL promising to unleash a hurricane of devastation and mayhem. 'I ex-PLODE': LL's rap suggests a psychic structure of volcanically pent-up aggressivity and death-drive that rivals Iggy Pop's persona as a human A-bomb.

What's really intriguing, though, is the question of why it's *Mama* that ordained all this destruction. It's a matriarchal theme brought out in the video, which closes with a grandma figure admonishing the young Cool J for making a racket in the basement (LL was brought up by his grandmother). In a 1992 interview, LL explained that the video was a way of representing 'power. . . . Like balls. . . . The brown gloves are like my balls, doing battle.' Earlier, explaining the rationale for his career, he had said 'I don't do it for the money, I do it for the nuts.'

Miles Davis was another black musical monarch obsessed with boxing. His 1970 album *Jack Johnson* was the soundtrack to William Cayton's documentary about the early twentieth-century black boxing champion. In the sleevenotes, Miles pays tribute to Johnson in terms that recall Cleaver's lionisation of Muhammad Ali: 'Jack Johnson portrayed Freedom. . . . He was a fast-living man, he liked women – lots of them and most of them white. He had flashy cars because that was his thing. . . . And no doubt Whitey felt "no Black man should have all this". But he did and he'd flaunt it.' Framed in a trumped-up 'white slavery' case, Johnson went into exile in Paris, where he'd stroll the boulevards sipping champagne and walking his pet leopard. A regal image echoed on the cover of LL Cool J's *Walking With A Panther* (1989), where LL poses with a black panther at his feet. In his autobiography, Davis reveals that it was the example of Sugar Ray Robinson that gave him the will-power to kick his late '40s/early '50s heroin habit. 'I always loved boxing, but I really loved and respected Sugar Ray, because he was a great fighter with a lot of class and cleaner than a motherfucker. . . . [He] looked like a socialite when you would see him in the papers getting out of limousines with fine women on his arms, sharp as a tack.' Davis copied Robinson's 'arrogant attitude', and even trained as a boxer. 'Ray was cold and he was the best and he was everything I wanted to be in 1954. . . . king of the hill.'

Miles Davis's superbad persona was as close to Sly Stone, Jimi Hendrix, James Brown, or the gangsta rappers as it was to the jazz pantheon. With his voracious appetite for women and drugs (the most regal ones, heroin and cocaine), his flashy clothes and fast cars, he lived like a lord. As Greg Tate put it in his elegy-essay 'Silence, Exile, Cunning: Miles Davis In Memoriam': 'To the aristocratic mind of this East St. Louis scion of a pig farmer/dentist, it naturally followed that if you were playing the baadest music on the face of the earth with the baadest musicians living, then of course you were driving the baadest cars, wearing the baadest vines, and intimate with the most regal of women and celebrated of artists, thinkers, athletes. . . . Miles Davis was a warrior king and we were all enthralled.' Servility of any kind enraged Davis; he railed against the shoddy treatment of black musicians by record companies who were only interested in 'keeping their so-called black stars on the music plantation'.

Davis's music often alluded to the idea of lost (African) powers: hence album titles like *Sorcerer* (1967) and *Dark Magus* (1974), and pieces like 'Pharaoh's Dance' and 'Miles

Runs the Voodoo Down' from 1970's *Bitches Brew*. Jimi Hendrix was thinking along similar lines in 'Voodoo Chile' (from 1968's *Electric Ladyland*). Here, Hendrix is a titanic figure whose birth causes his mother to drop dead from shock. According to Charles Shaar Murray, 'Voodoo Chile' belongs to a 'long, long line of supernatural brag songs. . . in which the singer lays claim to magical and mystical as well as temporal and worldly powers', most notably the 'hoodoo hokum' of Muddy Waters's songs. Above all, 'Voodoo Chile' refers to the legend of Robert Johnson's Faustian contract with the Devil, allegedly made at a crossroads (a voodoo ritual) in return for supernatural blues guitar prowess. In 'Voodoo Chile', West African magic fast-forwards into science-fiction fantasy: rescued by mountain lions and carried off on an eagle's wing to the furthest 'outposts of infinity', superman Jimi can smite a mountain down with the edge of his hand.

Hendrix is not the only black artist to link the recovery of African powers with futuristic or extraterrestrial imagery: he belongs to a continuum that links Sun Ra (who called himself Ambassador for the rulers of the Omniverse, and dressed in the robes of a Nubian king) to George Clinton's Parliament-Funkadelic clan (who futurised the idea of Africa-as-Motherland into an intergalactic Mothership descending to carry blacks home) to Earth Wind and Fire (whose clothes and cover art combined Ancient Egyptian and sci-fi imagery) and the Pharaoh of Electro, Afrika Bambaataa.

the staggerlee syndrome

'Better to reign in hell than serve in heaven.'
Milton, *Paradise Lost*

The pre-eminent model for black sovereignty, however, is neither the boxing champion, the African nobleman nor the extraterrestrial warrior-king, but the gangster, or the folk-loric criminal Staggerlee. The definitive account of Staggerlee is in Greil Marcus's *Mystery Train*. Staggerlee 'is a fantasy of no-limits for a people who live within a labyrinth of limits every day of their lives, and who can transgress them only among themselves'. Breaking all the rules, Staggerlee escapes the fate assigned to blacks (servitude, anonymity, death) by a white society, and wins it all: women, drugs, wealth. Criminality is such a potent metaphor for black pop rebels because it signifies total possibility; the underside of this refusal of restraints is solipsism, psychosis, a Sadeian indifference to others' right to exist.

The core of the legend concerns Staggerlee's shooting of a young man, Billy Lyons, because of a trivial argument, or – in some versions of the story – just to see him die. Marcus sees this murderously elegant sociopath as the prototype for the anti-hero that swaggers through the blues (black and white), from Muddy Waters's Rollin' Stone to Mick Jagger's Midnight Rambler, and as the archetype that connects Robert Johnson, the Black Panthers, Muhammad Ali, Jimi Hendrix, Miles Davis, Sly Stone, and the superfly guys of early '70s blacksploitation movies. Marcus was writing in 1975; today you'd have to add the gangsta rappers, and their Jamaican equivalents – 'ragga' stars (the term comes from 'raggamuffin') like Shabba Ranks, Buju Banton and Mad Cobra, with their sexual braggadocio and flashy image drawn from the style of 'yardies' (hoodlums) or Hollywood gangsters.

Marcus's particular interest, though, was in Sly Stone as a Staggerlee who collided with absolute limits, who discovered that trying to live like a king led to paranoia and delusions of grandeur. Smashing racial boundaries with an image and sound that merged bad-ass funk and hippie freak-out, Sly Stone triumphed in the late '60s with a secular gospel of affirmation, expressed in songs like 'Everybody Is A Star', 'Stand', 'Thank You Falettinmebe

Mice 'Elf Agin'. In 1970, like Staggerlee, Sly had it all. But suddenly, at the height of his fame, the euphoria soured; Sly disappeared into a black hole of drug excess and unreliability. It was from this mire that *There's A Riot Goin' On* emerged in 1971.

Although the title alluded to the bitter racial conflict of the time, *Riot* was really about an interior apocalypse. The utopian hunger that fired Sly's music ultimately had to choose between two options: insurrection or oblivion, explosion or implosion. (Actually, there was a third option: mysticism, redemptive faith. Eldridge Cleaver became a Christian.) *There's A Riot Goin' On*, however, didn't attempt to rise above the limits of (white-controlled) reality, but faced them full on. *Riot* turns the Sly Stone persona inside out, inverts all the life-affirming properties of the Family's music. The sound of *Riot* is deathly dry, drained of all the joy and confidence that once fuelled Sly's fervour.

This is funk-as-prison: locked grooves that incarnate the impasses and dead ends faced by African-Americans. Its totally wired sound has everything to do with the conditions under which it was recorded: a coked-out frightmare, with Sly & Co staying up four nights at a time, the air thick with paranoia, everyone carrying guns. And it shows in Sly's cryptic imagery and unearthly vocals: the sound of a soul in tatters. The disintegrated death throes of 'Thank You for Talkin' To Me Africa' are a glimpse of someone on the threshold of the human condition. A rewrite of 'Thank You Falettinmebe Mice 'Elf Agin', this song turns the original's upful swagger into agonised inertia, the sound of going nowhere slow. In the first song, Sly incarnated total freedom and self-expression; with the rewrite, this is exposed as an act, a persona he can no longer sustain but which his audience expects from him as 'their king'.

The allusion to Africa here and in 'Africa Talks to You (the Asphalt Jungle)' hints that the black struggle to feel at home in America has succumbed to despair. Sly dreams of fleeing to the safe arms of the mother(land). Around this time, a coked-out, paranoid Sly was asked by *Rolling Stone* journalist Timothy Crouse why he didn't make a planned safari to Kenya. 'Can't make all them gigs,' croaked Sly. 'I don't wanna shoot any animals. I wrote a song about Africa because in Africa the animals are animals. The tiger is a tiger, the snake is a snake, you know what the hell he's gonna do. Here in New York, the asphalt jungle, a tiger or a snake may come up looking like, uuuh, you.' In the lost motherland, you can judge a book by the cover; deceit and treachery are impossible.

Forcibly estranged from this African utopia, adrift like an exile on Main Street (but with a racial factor that the Stones, no matter how hard they identified with blackness, never suffered), Sly Stone was homeless, a fugitive. In an interview in 1984, singer Bobby Womack (one of the *Riot* squad) described how Sly liked to keep moving: 'We used to drive around in his motorhome, gettin' high and writing songs and making music. We would ride all up in the hills and he wouldn't never stand still, he'd say, keep drivin'!'

down with the king

Black Panther Bobby Seale wrote that 'Staggerlee is Malcolm X before he became politically conscious.' (Before he became X, Malcolm Little had been a hustler and petty criminal.) The Black Panthers tried to channel the pre-political rage and lust for life displayed by the black street criminal into political activity. Likewise, Public Enemy took rap's solipsistic rage and collectivised it, turning the power-tripping tantrums of the isolated 'I' into the measured policy and resolve of a politicised 'We'. In Public Enemy-style righteous rap, rap's thrust for prestige is elevated into a collective quest for the recovery of racial sovereignty.

In 'The Gangster as Tragic Hero', film critic Robert Warshow declared that 'the gangster always dies because he is an individual'; society cannot tolerate the existence of such an untamed man. But for Public Enemy, the gangster always dies because he is ONLY an individual. In the meantime, his kingly existence is won at the expense of his own people. Just as black-on-black violence is the main cause of death for young African-American males, so rappers are always stomping down their own kind, verbally. For many, the music biz is an alternative to, or step up from, running with a gang or dealing drugs (a lifestyle that involves real, not symbolic, casualties).

Rap's dog-eat-dog ethos changed with the dawn of righteous rap and the Afrocentric Native Tongue posse (Jungle Brothers, Queen Latifah, A Tribe Called Quest), who revived the notion that blacks were kings or nobles in a halcyon Africa before enslavement. Many of the problems in black America have been attributed to a dearth of positive patriarchal figures. In the movie *Boyz N the Hood*, a young man who has strong guidance from his father is contrasted with friends who are brought up by their mother (one is the innocent victim of a gang killing, while his delinquent brother – played by rapper Ice Cube – falls in with gangs and dies a violent death).

Righteous rap is an attempt to fulfil the role of surrogate Good Father, to supercede the Bad Father effect of gangs: witness rappers like X-Clan, Poor Righteous Teachers, KRS-1, who assume the role of preachers, prophets or teachers. Righteous rap videos have even gone so far as to feature lecterns or blackboards, a stark contrast with the truant demeanour of early rap, when the rallying cry was 'let's get stupid'. Just as with Malcolm X, ideology provides a framework of extreme discipline that focuses and contains a rage that might otherwise prove (self-)destructive. Other rappers have made religion their solution. Run DMC were one of the first rap bands to adopt the gangsta posture, proclaiming themselves 'King of Rock'. But when they returned in 1993, after a long spell in the commercial and spiritual wilderness, they declared that they were 'Down With the King': Jesus Christ.

my way:
the cult of the psychopath

'The psychopath is a rebel without a cause, an agitator without a
slogan, a revolutionary without a program; in other words, his
rebelliousness is aimed to achieve goals satisfactory to himself
alone; he is incapable of exertions for the sake of others.'
Robert Lindner, *Rebel Without A Cause – The Hypnoanalysis of A
Criminal Psychopath*

The cult of the criminal as a heroic individual in an anonymous, servile world goes back to the heart of Romanticism.
The murderer, like the artist, privileges aesthetics/desire/id
over ethics/solidarity/super-ego. In the early nineteenth
century, writer Thomas De Quincy equated the sublimity
of psychotic murder with the bliss of opium trance.
Raskolnikov, Dostoevski's anti-hero in *Crime and
Punishment*, believed he belonged to an elite of exceptional
individuals who had the right to transcend the morality
that bound lesser beings, and proved it to himself by killing
a 'worthless' old woman. Raskolnikov would have concurred with Blanchot's dictum that 'the greatest suffering
of others always counts for less than my pleasure'.
   In this century, the notion of the criminal as amoral
superman has intensified, right across the spectrum from
Hollywood and pulp fiction to continental philosophy
(Sartre's 'the criminal kills; he is a poem'). Writing about
the white hipster's identification with the ghetto black in
'The White Negro', Norman Mailer defined the psychopath
as a truly free man: 'in short, whether the life is criminal or
not, the decision is to encourage the psychopath in oneself,
to explore that domain of experience where security is bore-

dom and therefore sickness. . . .' For Mailer, the ghetto black was 'a frontiersman in the Wild West of American night life'. His struggle for a virile existence was a shining example to whites, who were equally emasculated by suburban matriarchy and corporate capitalism.

Mailer's intellectual manoeuvre – transforming the most negative stereotypes of black machismo into an ideal for living – has been updated for the rap era by Timothy Maliqualim Simone. In *About Face: Race in Postmodern America*, he argues that black youth are 'a posse sent ahead to scout uncharted social and psychological domains. The posse may be killed, maimed, or wounded so that the rest of the society can occupy the social terrain that has been scouted. . . . In the same way that the deaths of real cowboys, outlaws, adventurers and soldiers made images of these figures safe for general consumption, elements of the street kid figure are becoming incorporated into the general American character.' In other words, ghetto-exploitation movies like *Menace II Society* and *Trespass* are today's Westerns; young white males learn how to swagger like a 'real man' from gangsta rappers like Dr Dre and Snoop Doggy Dogg, rather than Clint Eastwood. (As it happens, Snoop is a fervent admirer of Clint. . .)

For Mailer, the psychopath was an ideal for living because he was engaged in the creation of 'a new nervous system', freed of the inhibitions and blockages imposed by morality and conditioning that prevented the free flow of 'life-force'. The psychopath's fundamental impulse was 'to try to live the infantile fantasy'. Transgressive acts – drugs, crime, rape, murder – allowed him to 'pass by symbolic substitute through the locks of incest. . . . In thus giving expression to the buried infant in himself, he can. . . free himself to remake a bit of his nervous system.' Mailer was on to something: some psychoanalysts believe that psychopathology is the result of a failure to pass through the Oedipal stage and submit to the reality principle. It's a refusal to abandon the mother's body and accept 'castration' (i.e. lack).

Hence Jim Morrison's anti-Oedipal catechism 'kill the father, fuck the mother'. According to the Doors' producer Paul Rothchild, 'fuck the mother... means get back to the essence, what is reality'. What Morrison demanded in 'The End' was: reject all lawgivers (from the conscience to the State right up to God), accept no limits to desire. But if you don't pass through the Oedipal trauma (with the ensuing abandonment of the infant's delusions of omnipotence) you don't become fully human. Refusing the reality principle leads to psychosis. What the 'edge substances', the extremist art or deranging intoxicants that Morrison indulged in offered was a temporary trip into psychosis. This connected with his equation of the rock idol with the shaman. Shamans, said Morrison, were 'professional hysterics, chosen precisely for their psychotic leaning'.

The Oedipus legend is about the desire to displace the father/king, become king oneself and gain full possession of the mother/queen. Psychosis is the ultimate destination of the quest for phallic sovereignty. In *Bomb Culture*, a seminal work on the mystical longings that connect the beats and the counterculture, Jeff Nuttall wrote: 'Eternity is God. The barrier to God is ego, will and fear. The route to God is insanity, the dissolution of identity through the dissolution of rational relationships. Psychosis has been the common language of art since Rimbaud.'

The beats were very taken with the existentialist notion of the *acte gratuit*: the deed that was spontaneous, unmotivated, unproductive, that transcended and violated means-to-end rationality. The apotheosis of the *acte gratuit* was the impulsive, motiveless murder. One of the Burroughs/Kerouac/Ginsberg circle, Lucien Carr, committed one: he stabbed and killed a lovesick homosexual, David Kammerer, who dogged him for years. And Neal Cassady was described by fellow beat John Clellon Holmes as 'a psychopath in the traditional and most rigorous sense of the term'.

In *The Revolution of Everyday Life*, the Situationist Raoul Vaneigem argued that 'a truly new reality can only be based on the principle of the gift'. He celebrated terrorism as a rejection of 'relationships based on exchange and compromise. . . .' Only the 'purity' of motiveless destruction OR ruinous generosity can transcend bourgeois reality (in which everything has an ulterior motive). For Vaneigem, murder is 'the concave form of the gift'. Talk about *gratuitous violence*! You have to wonder whether Vaneigem would have liked to be on the receiving end of such a 'gift'. Perhaps this is a case of ''tis better to give than receive'.

From Baudelaire's 'oasis of horror in a desert of boredom' to Vaneigem's empathy towards a sixteen-year-old murderer who 'did it because I was bored', cultural radicals have frequently decided that ennui is the ultimate justification for extreme acts. What could be more rock'n'roll, more Iggy Pop, than the terrorist Ulrike Meinhof's account of the 'feeling that your head is exploding.... furious aggression for which there is no outlet.' The rage-to-live so often turns into a will-to-kill. It's 'the poverty of everyday life', as first identified by the Situationists, that incites the delinquent continuum that runs from rock'n'roll and drug addiction to terrorism and psychotic murder. For Jeff Nuttall, it was the same impoverished, entropic culture which spawned both the British bohemians of the '50s and '60s, and the child-murdering lovers Ian Brady and Myra Hindley in 1965. 'Romantics, Symbolists, Dada, Surrealists, Existentialists, Action painters, beat poets and the Royal Shakespeare Company had all applauded de Sade from some aspect or other. To Ian Brady de Sade was a licence to kill children. We had all, at some time, cried "Yes yes" to Blake's "sooner murder an infant in its cradle than nurse an unacted desire". Brady did it.'

By the end of the '60s, another frustrated artist and aspiring rock'n'roller bridged the gap between aesthetics and terrorism. In 'The White Album', Joan Didion noted that no one in Los Angeles was *surprised* by the Manson killings; just as the carnage at Altamont was a realisation of the Stones' devilish advocacy, the Manson murders were the logical culmination of the counterculture's project of throwing off the shackles of conscience and consciousness, the grim flowering of the id's voodoo energies. Writing about Manson and similar psycho-hippie cults in their book *Mindfuckers*, David Felton, Robin Green and David Dalton called the phenomenon 'Acid Fascism': lost souls whose ego-structures had been dismantled by LSD fell prey to father-figure cult leaders like Manson.

With his loopy racist theories, and his retreat to the 'empty space' of the desert, Manson certainly conformed to the paranoid profile of the proto-fascist. Manson talked of paranoia as a form of cosmic awareness; he preached ego-death as enlightenment ('we are all One') and valorised terms like 'empty-headed' and 'mindless'. And all this because his singing career never got off the ground! In fact, the intended target of the murder was Terry Melcher, a record producer who Manson felt had thwarted him. (History repeats: self-proclaimed Christ and cult leader David Koresh once entertained hopes of becoming a rock star, then found a new way to win his fifteen minutes....) Recently, Manson was incorporated into rock history as a precursor of punk when Guns N'Roses covered one of his tunes on their 1993 LP *The Spaghetti Incident?*, along with songs by the Pistols and the Stooges.

'Manson represents a frightening new phenomenon, the acid-ripped street-fighter, erasing the barrier between the two outlaw cultures – the head and the hood,' wrote David Dalton. In Nic Roeg and Donald Cammell's film, *Performance* (1970), the Dionysian rocker and the psychotic gangster are revealed as different facets of the same male rebel archetype: the demon-lover, the son of a gun. Mick Jagger plays Turner, a rock idol turned hermit-king; James Fox is Chas, a sociopathic young hoodlum on the run from his boss. In a key scene, Turner reads aloud a passage in a book about the Hashassin, young warriors who commit murders for their king and are rewarded with access to a paradisical garden full of voluptuous, willing maidens. Both Turner and Chas ply the same trade as the Hashassin, and as each other. Turner, as rebel, commits figurative violence against society's symbolic order; Chas inflicts literal violence. Both are rewarded handsomely. Turner is an androgynous, slippery, decadent dandy; Chas, a stylish sadist, looks as sharp as a mod. Both are victors/victims in the cult of cool, cultivating the fascinating exteriority of persona at the expense of inner life. 'And I'll tell you this, the only performance that makes it, that really makes it, that makes it all the way, is the one that achieves madness,' Turner says. Jagger – with his impersonation in the song 'Midnight Rambler' of a nocturnal girl-murderer, the rock'n'roll sexual nomad with a (knife) twist – wasn't just the obvious choice for the role of Turner, but doubtless its inspiration.

urge to outrage

The cult of cool, of death-mask impassivity and affectlessness, and the rock'n'roll idea of 'reinvention of the self' reached their apotheosis with punk, and above all with a kittenish wimp called John Beverley who transformed himself into a cartoon monster called Sid Vicious.

Vicious's (brilliant) version of 'My Way', the ultimate showbiz anthem of sovereign solipsism, is the breastbeating melodrama of a man who'll 'kneel' for nobody. In the video, the climax of the song sees Vicious shooting the audience (including his mother). Incest and its corollary, a violent repudiation of the maternal body, is, we suggested in Chapter 3, a submerged content of the Sex Pistols' rebellion. *The Great Rock'n'Roll Swindle*'s director Julian Temple declared that 'punk rock was a great electric shock' in the midst of England's 'morbid and incestuous' culture.

The need to zap England out of its dreaming, to shock it alive from its 'living death' of nostalgia and consumerism, warranted all kinds of strategies of outrage. So the punks identified with the demonised figures that had threatened Britain. Like Hitler. ('It was always very much an anti-mums and anti-dads thing,' Siouxsie Sioux said of the punk penchant for the swastika.) And the Moors Murderers. In Derek Jarman's punk movie *Jubilee*, punkette Jordan recites a touching little homage: 'As a child, my heroine was Myra Hindley. Do you remember her? Myra's crimes were, they said, beyond belief. That was because no one had any imagination and they didn't know how to make their desires reality. They were not artists like Myra. I can smile now at the naïveté.' (Later, one of Malcolm McLaren's still-born projects was a band called the Moors Murderers.)

Remember McLaren's 'Cambridge Rapist' T-shirts, which linked this terroriser-of-society with Beatles' manager Brian Epstein? Eventually, McLaren fulfilled his fantasy of turning a criminal into a pop star. Escaped Great Train Robber Ronnie Biggs made it into the Top Ten as guest vocalist on the Pistols' 'No One Is Innocent'. Getting Biggs (and in the movie, 'Martin Bormann', another fugitive criminal) to join the Pistols was McLaren's attempt to spell out the links between anarchism, fascism and crime. All were mortal enemies of bourgeois liberalism; all dreamed of living a life fit for 'warrior males'; all elevated desire over responsibility, aesthetics over ethics. (The Nazis liked to think of themselves as artists.) Anarchism, fascism, crime, all reach their apotheosis in the *psychopath*. After all, what could be more psychotic than the Situationist demand 'take your desires for reality'?

But Biggs was just a 'lovable' London minor villain, who'd gotten away with it and was living the life of Riley in sunny Brazil; when he sang 'Belsen Was A Gas' he imparted barely one tenth of the menace of Johnny Rotten's version. The Biggs manoeuvre smacked of desperation, was risible rather than shocking, and McLaren was left high and dry. Then he lucked out: one of his artists became a real live criminal of infinitely more impressive dimensions: Sid killed Nancy, then OD-ed himself. As a cadaver, Vicious sold more singles than the Pistols at their height. This necrophiliac nadir (Virgin titled a Pistols' collection *Flogging A Dead Horse*) was regarded at the time as the Death of Rock.

Yet rock didn't die and the cult of the psychopath has flourished. In the '80s, punk evolved into hardcore, a genre dedicated to the pursuit of Baudelaire's 'oasis of horror in a desert of boredom'. On both sides of the Atlantic, abduction and murder became a stock narrative for songs, a ritual psychodrama: from Hüsker Dü's 'Diane' through Sonic Youth's Manson-meets-the-Beach-Boys 'Expressway to Yr Skull' (which promised to 'kill the California girls' – symbols of all-American shopping mall mediocrity) to Butthole Surfers' '22 Going 23' (which incorporated a soundbite from a call-in show in which a girl spoke of being raped). Green River, a Seattle proto-grunge band who named themselves after their local serial killer (over forty women slain), later evolved into politically correct Pearl Jam. Meanwhile, UK groups like Therapy? ('Dancing With Manson', 'Innocent X', 'Meat Abstract') turned the cult of the serial killer into cliché. Typically, bands justified their morbid obsessions with the catechism: 'If we didn't write songs about this stuff, we'd probably be doing it ourselves!'

If any group crystallised the noise/horror aesthetic and took it to its limits, it was Big Black. Their songs fetishised atrocities and freakish crimes as a kind of truth: a radical unveiling of the lies that govern social appearance. Big Black's vocalist/guitarist Steve Albini has spoken of his interest in de Sade's view of the world as a power-play between forces of domination and submission. The corrosively brilliant *Atomizer* (1986) contained songs like

'Jordan, Minnesota' (about a town whose population organised a gigantic child-sex network) and 'Kerosene' (in which a bored guy combines his small-town's two major modes of release – blowing things up and sleeping with the town slut – into a single orgiastic self-immolation).

'Fish-Fry' (from 1987's *Songs About Fucking*) is the story of a real-life impulse-murderer. According to the sleevenotes, 'he went to her family's fish fry, took her to the drive-in, porked her, then beat her to death with his boot. It is speculated that he was upset about the ease with which he got into her pants, when she had resisted his brother's attempts earlier.' Throughout Big Black's work there's an ambivalent fascination for those galvanised by their surrender to aberrant instincts; these characters become something close to supermen. At the very least, they're the heroes of these songs, heroes because they act where others censor their desires.

the aesthetic terrorist

Richard Linklater, writer and director of the twentysomething movie *Slacker* (many of whose characters are obsessed with serial killers and assassins) has said that he always feels mass-murderers aren't acting alone, that their exorbitant violence is done somehow on behalf of the rest of us. Linklater's explanation for his generation's fascination with psychopathic or fanatic killers is that, as impotent specks in the sea of mass society, slackers are obsessed with the problem of how an individual can have any effect. In *Slacker*, one of his characters – a middle-aged professor and former '60s radical – expresses fervent admiration for Charles Whitman, a prototypical lone gunman who gunned down citizens of Austin, Texas from the top of Campus Tower in 1966. 'Now there was a man!' he reminisces to an inept burglar he's caught in his apartment, and whom the former radical seems to regard as a kindred spirit. The professor missed Whitman's spectacular feat, because 'my fucking wife – God rest her soul – she had some stupid appointment that day.' Once again, the familiar opposition emerges: orgiastic, phallic freedom v. the female realm of banality and domestication. (In fact, Whitman kicked off his killing spree by murdering his mother and his wife.)

The Killer is a sort of anti-slacker, the envied and admired antithesis of the slacker's inertia. The Killer is a tunnel visionary, singleminded, fanatically focused, and totally vertebrate. The Killer also appeals to the slacker because he stands out from the mediocre mass: he's a star. Inger Lorre of the Nymphs wrote a song called 'The Highway' about the demon-lover allure of Richard Ramirez, a Californian serial killer with a following of teenage girls. Nymphs guitarist Jet Freedom explained: 'Ramirez is like a pop star, he has long hair, he's cute, he's witty, and he could probably go gold if he had a record contract.' Ramirez's nickname, the Night Stalker, even echoes the Stones' 'Midnight Rambler'; in fact, he was obsessed with AC/DC's rip-off of that song, 'Night Prowler'.

The serial killer is a star because he's the ultimate sovereign individual; sovereign because he's wasting the most precious resource, human life, and because his momentary bliss counts for more than another's lifetime of potential. Woman is usually the privileged recipient of this individualism; she's the bloody palette with which this 'artist' wreaks his aesthetic terrorism. At the start of *Slacker*, a woman is run over by a hit-and-run driver. It transpires that the perpetrator was her son, who returns to his bedroom and watches a film loop of himself as a child playing with his mom, projected endlessly on to a screen that's surrounded by a makeshift shrine. Incest/matricide seems to be the psychodrama beneath this unnerving two-minute sequence, but also a latent theme behind the whole movie: slackers need to make a violent break with the suckling bosom of motherlove, get out there and be real men (like the serial killers and assassins). It's unhealthy for a

twentysomething to be still living at home, which is presumably why the son mowed his mom down. Malcolm
McLaren would approve.

Amongst other things, *Slacker* documents the interface
between the post-punk hardcore scene and what's been
called 'Apocalypse Culture'. This was the title of an 1987
compilation of essays published by Amok Press, an organisation dedicated to cataloguing and distributing 'the
extremes of information in print': from autopsy reports to
conspiracy theory to neo-Nazi pamphlets to occult writings.
Amok's general aim is to promote resistance to consensus
and good taste. The editor of *Apocalypse Culture*, Adam
Parfrey, includes his own essay 'Aesthetic Terrorism'. In an
age in which avant-garde gestures are quickly absorbed
and repackaged by the media, Parfrey proclaims that we
must look to the real outsiders for 'aesthetic purity', the
shock of the sublime.

The 'genuine outsiders' hailed by Parfrey include John
Hinckley Jr, the Jodie Foster obsessive who attempted to
kill Ronald Reagan and who also churns out a grisly line in
paedophiliac poesy. But Parfrey's biggest hero is Peter
Sotos, editor and publisher of *Pure* magazine, which 'extols
child torture, murder, and extreme misogyny' and celebrates 'the psychotic outsider such as Ted Bundy, Ian
Brady or John Wayne Gacy'. Prosecuted for possession and
reproduction of child pornography, Sotos is a hero and a
martyr to free expression, according to Parfrey. (Aside from
his magazine, Sotos has performed with the band
Whitehouse, an electro-terrorist unit interested in extreme
sadism.) Parfrey also declares that apart from *Pure*, 'the
most refreshing art or tracts I've seen lately have been
from clinical schizophrenics and racist revolutionaries.
Their avenging monomania powerfully transcends the wan
self-pity and hair-splittings of the status quo.'

Because these forms of extremist art could never become
commercialised or Madison Avenue-d, they somehow

become 'pure': neo-Nazi genocidal venom is, for Parfrey, a distant descendant of anarcho-mystics like the Free Spirits or the Ranters, 'Aesthetic Terrorists of half a millenia ago. . . [who] were burnt at the stake for suggesting the then demonic idea that every human was in some way god-like and should therefore find freedom in the exercise of free will'. In the interview that follows Parfrey's manifesto, Peter Sotos elaborates on his aesthetics of terror: 'I don't find everyone who kills, beats or rapes someone admirable. I'm interested and respectful of those who view and understand their instincts completely and correctly and then go about satisfying them.'

Ian Brady is the consummate murderer as virtuoso ('he fucked and tortured little Lesley Downey every way imaginable before smashing her tiny skull in half') whereas Manson and Ed Gein are incompetent artists who had 'no idea of what they really wanted. . . . It's analogous to fine music – anyone can bash an instrument and make noise but it takes a skilled, intelligent and insightful individual to make music.' Artists in the traditional sense of the word aren't singleminded enough for him; Sotos prefers individuals who bridge the gap between art and life – 'a breed of genius' that includes Hitler, Himmler, Goebbels and Streicher.

Could it be that the urge to outrage is a kind of severance rite, a re-enactment of the original disconnection from the mother's body? The rebel's quest for sovereignty, for god-like independence, ultimately leads to de Sade. According to Susan Suleiman, 'The founding desire behind Sadeian fantasy is the active negation of the mother. The Sadeian hero's anti-naturalism' – his repeated violation of 'natural' laws (incest, infanticide, etc.) – 'goes hand in hand with his hatred of mothers, identified as the "natural" source of life' (and thus of death). The rebel also resents the power of the mother, wishes he was self-created, invulnerable, omnipotent. If you follow the rebel impulse to its logical, if not inevitable, conclusion, you end up here: a place where ascent to wholeness only comes with another being's mutilation and annihilation, where ecstasy means someone else's agony.

part 2

into the mystic

from rebellion to grace:
the psychedelic mother's boy

So what happens to the rebel once he's broken away and asserted his solipsistic majesty? He's done his stint on the road, honed his manifesto, ditched the old homestead, and where has it got him? *Nowhere* – which is the space of total possibility, but also a place that's *uninhabitable*. Which means every rebel has to 'come home' someday. Some rebels make the transition from 'I' to 'we' and affirm something larger than themselves (whether that 'we' takes the form of political community, mystical transcendence, or the amorous couple). Others, electing to remain on the desert island of narcissism, inevitably degenerate into self-parody (Jagger, Rotten, Morrissey). Still others blaze, burn out and fade away: drugs, used to sustain a state of self-exaltation, exact a heavy toll.

This second section focuses on those rebels who tire of the sterility of individualism, and move towards affirming the trans-individual – from insularity to oceanic feelings. Born-to-run nomadism succumbs to a longing to return to the maternal bosom, a sanctuary that can take the form of an idealised woman, or a mystical investment in Mother Nature and the Cosmos. Jimi Hendrix is a prime example. Tired of life in the fast lane, exhausted by the whole 'wild man' adventure, Hendrix's latent mysticism began to blossom, in the last music he recorded before his death, with a devotion to the Eternal Feminine. If he had lived, he would have *gotten jazz* in the way some rock'n'rollers get religion; he looked set to abandon rock for cosmic jazz-fusion symphonies. Before and after his death, many musicians shaped by his influence, from Miles Davis to Can, headed towards such a pan-global fusion of jazz, rock, funk and ethnic music, whose aura was explicitly pantheistic and nature-worshipping.

Of course, the shift from 'I' to 'we' doesn't always take the form of an identification with the 'feminine'. Some rebels identify utopia with the father, or rather an imaginary Good Father (as with groups like the Clash, U2, Public Enemy). This 'we' is fraternal, an army fighting for the Kingdom of Right. But this section is about rock that dreams of a lost unity explicitly identified with the mother. Underneath, say, the pastoralism of the Byrds, the born-again blues of Van Morrison, the oceanic/cosmic flux of Can and Pink Floyd, is a nostalgia (literal meaning: homesickness) for the primal 'we' of the mother-infant dyad. The combat rockers identify with language (especially its most phallic forms – fighting talk, agit-prop, the manifesto). But the mother-fixated groups revolt against words. For them, the lost state of wholeness is not located in the future, but in the pre-linguistic past, the lost paradise of infancy. They want to be babes-in-arms, not brothers-in-arms.

'The rebel is a man who is on the point of accepting or rejecting the sacred. . . . Every question, every word, is an act of rebellion, while in the sacred world, every word is an act of grace. . . . Only two possible worlds can exist for the human mind: the sacred or the world of rebellion. The disappearance of one is equivalent to the appearance of the other.'
Albert Camus, 'The Rebel'

'Meanwhile, down to our nerve cells, everything in us resists paradise.'
E.M. Cioran, *Thinking Against Oneself*

At the dawn of the twentieth century, Henry Adams contrasted The Virgin and The Dynamo as symbols for two incompatible realms of human consciousness. With her divine passivity, the Virgin Mary stood for *sacred mystery*, a force once strong enough to erect cathedrals, but now fading from the world. The electrical dynamo represented the dawning era of *scientific mastery*, in which men could become godlike through harnessing the forces of Nature. A decade or so later, the Futurists exalted the same dynamic forces (electricity, speed) and explicitly identified them with male will-to-power and phallic thrust.

Futurist rhetoric offers another version of Camus's opposition between rebellion and grace, or Adams's mastery/ mystery dichotomy. Rejecting Romanticism's quest for the lost state of grace in Nature's bosom, the Futurists extolled disrespect for Mother Earth – conquest and rape. F.T. Marinetti decried not only 'nostalgia' but 'the picturesque, the imprecise, rusticity, wild solitude': all the things that the mystical tradition in rock celebrates. Ardently urban and secular, the Futurists pitted themselves against the pastoral, poured scorn on the 'holy green silence'; they celebrated sharply defined edges rather than blurred borderlines.

Rock'n'roll throbs with a Futurist exultation in speed, technology, neon and noise. But there is another strain of the rock imagination that isn't madly in love with the modern world, but is instead nostalgic and regressive: psychedelia. Defined in the broadest sense to encompass everything from the Byrds, Pink Floyd, Van Morrison, the Incredible String Band, to Can, Brian Eno, My Bloody Valentine, and ambient house, psychedelia is a resurgence of Romanticism's pastoralism and pantheism. Above all, psychedelia is the quest for a lost state of grace.

back to eden:
innocence, indolence and pastoralism

Its roots may lie in the rural blues of the American South, but in Britain, rock was the sound of the city. Rock was the blues electrified, wired on the hypertension of urban life. In the mid '60s, it was in revolt against nature: rock was 'noise pollution'. It didn't have a lot to do with hedgerows and haystacks, with the peace and quiet of the countryside. Mod was the apotheosis of rock's mid-'60s urbanism. Mod stood for modernist; appropriately, the mods not only embraced but amplified the neuroses of late twentieth-century capitalist life – its obsession with surfaces and commodity fetishism, its rapid turnover of styles and rampant consumerism. Mod lifestyle accentuated the anti-natural rhythm of industrial life, with its strict demarcation between work and leisure. The dead-end drudgery of Monday to Friday 9 to 5 alternated with the explosive release of the mods' sleep-defying, speed-fuelled forty-eight hour weekends. The Easybeats' classic song 'Friday On My Mind' crystallises the vibe of the mid '60s: anticipation, a headlong rush into the future's neon glare.

Pills had everything to do with mod: amphetamine is the urban, twentieth-century drug. In *The Speed Culture*, Lester Grinspoon and Peter Hedblom argue that 'the amphetamine abuser, especially the "speed freak". . . is a gross caricature of many of the pathological, ultimately destructive features of the society that produced him.' If speed is the ultimate conformist drug, it's no wonder that the counterculture fastened on marijuana – a drug that slows things down, promotes contemplation and communion rather than freneticism and competitiveness – in order to facilitate their secession from straight society. Within less than two years, rock's site of fantasy would shift from the city centre to 'getting it together in the country'. Early-to-mid '60s British rock was about the 'mannish boy', about breaking free of the mother's realm, domesticity, good behaviour. Psychedelia, on the other hand, was the culture of the mother's boy, who longed to come to rest in the arms of Mother Nature. Mod's lust for action, its restless craving for kicks and kineticism, was replaced by psychedelia's cult of passivity, indolence and sleep. Amphetamine-induced insomnia (in the '30s, the pharmaceutical had been prescribed as a cure for narcolepsy), gave way to the dreamy dissipation of LSD. Together, all these changes constituted a shift in rock's yin/yang ratio, away from hyper-masculinity to a more feminine orientation.

Mod was a male-dominated subculture: since amphetamines suppressed sexual drives and boosted narcissism, boys dressed to impress other boys; girls were marginal. With psychedelia, ego-dissolution replaced ego-mania. Where speed encouraged a sharp sense of detachment and definition from one's environment, LSD broke down the defences, blurred the borders between self and world. White R&B's violent assertion of manhood gave way to childlike androgyny. Innocence was in, and 'experience' meant something altogether more spiritual than carnal. While mod had looked to the spotless formica future, hippie rock harked back to lost golden ages: hence its love of Edwardiana and medievalism.

Perhaps it's no coincidence that the mods were obsessed with Italian streamlined style, from suits to mopeds. After all, the Italian Futurists despised tranquillity, resisted slumber and worshipped speed. In contrast, psychedelia revived the concerns of Romanticism (Rimbaud's pursuit of synaesthesia through 'a systematic derangement of all the senses') and of Dada (Hugo Ball's sound poetry, which imitated the babbling nonsense and voluptuous echolalia of baby talk). Like these ancestors, psychedelia mistrusted masculine logic, proposed the cultivation of 'feminine' flow and receptivity, and believed that industrial/urban existence was synonymous with living death.

mother nature's sons

'O, Mother, when shall I be blessed by joining your blissful company?'
Quintessence, sleevenotes to *In Blissful Company*, 1969

As the LSD began to kick in, pastoralism erupted amidst mod's urban landscape – literally, with the London park settings of songs like John's Children's 'A Midsummer Night's Scene' and the Small Faces' 'Itchycoo Park'. John's Children's first song, 'Smashed Blocked', had described love's disorientation in the language of amphetamine psychosis ('blocked' being mod slang for being hyped on pills). But by 1967, the band were posing for photos naked in a meadow, their private parts obscured by garlands of flowers. 'A Midsummer Night's Scene' starts with the chant 'petals and flowers' over an ominous heavily distorted bassline, then hurls the listener into a Dionysian whirl of feedback and pagan imagery: glowering heatwave intensity, mad-eyed girls ripping up flowers and dervish-whirling the Rites of Pan.

'A Midsummer Night's Scene' was co-written by Marc Bolan. Prior to his brief stint in John's Children, Bolan was a well-known mod stylist who'd been quoted in *Town* magazine talking about his large collection of expensive suits. By the time he left John's Children, Bolan was a fully fledged flower child with his own acoustic folk-blues band, Tyrannosaurus Rex. On albums like *Prophets, Seers and Sages, The Angels of the Ages* (1968), *My People Were Fair and Had Sky in Their Hair* (1968), *Unicorn* (1969) and *A Beard of Stars* (1970), he sang tall Tolkienesque tales that blended magical mystery, kosmic sci-fi fantasy, and rustic paganism. Bolan was not alone in his faery fancies: 1967 was the year of the man-child minstrel who mixed nursery rhyme artlessness, English whimsy, and fantasies of olden times.

Donovan, all prissy diction, beardless face and curly locks, was a harmless homegrown version of Dylan who quickly became an enduring symbol of the sheer innocuousness of flower power. Songs like 'Mellow Yellow' and 'Jennifer Juniper' took psychedelia's 'hello clouds, hello trees' tendencies to the outer limits of twee, while 'Hurdy Gurdy Man' (1968) evoked the sinister, superstitious side of rustic life. Then there was Steve Winwood, who followed the classic mod-to-hippie trajectory, going from the horny adolescent R&B of the Spencer Davis Group to Traffic, one of the first psychedelic bands to embrace 'getting it together in the country'. Traffic moved into a Berkshire cottage in the summer of '67 to record their debut album *Mr Fantasy*. Their most famous song, 'Hole In My Shoe', combined bucolic bliss with fantastical imagery borrowed from classic children's writers like C.S. Lewis, E. Nesbit and Lewis Carroll; mid-song, a child's voice breathlessly describes being transported on the back of an albatross to a cloud-kingdom 'where happiness reigned' eternally.

When it comes to pastoralism/infantilism, though, the group who did it first and took it furthest were the Incredible String Band. On the cover of their most famous album, *The Hangman's Beautiful Daughter*, the duo of Robin Williamson and Mike Heron nestle amidst the moss-covered trees of an English copse, surrounded by fellow members of their commune, adults and children dressed in raggle-taggle medieval garb. The Incredible String Band's music was as rag-and-bobtail as their clothes, a blend of folk, blues and Indian raga. Albums like *The 5000 Spirits or the Layers of the Onion* (1967), *The Hangman's Beautiful Daughter* (1967), and *Wee Tam* (1968) inhabit a strange and wonderful never-neverland where English folklore and children's fairy-tales mingle with Zen Buddhism.

The Incredible String Band's worldview was pantheistic. In a 1967 interview, Williamson declared: 'Everything is a miracle. It's all magic and we are really here on earth to wonder at all these beautiful things. Our records are no more wonderful or no more magical than a lump of earth.' And so 'Air' is a hymn to – you guessed it – air, Heron marvelling at the intimate way it can penetrate his body and 'kiss my blood'. This mystical pantheism bleeds into a children's storybook anthropomorphism in 'The Hedgehog's Song', where Heron is educated in affairs of the heart by a creature of the field, or in 'Little Cloud', where he befriends a cloud. This genial relationship with Nature takes on an ecological slant in 'Mercy I Cry City', where Heron dreams of 'quiet pastures' where he can escape the city's pollution and hypertension.

What connects the pastoralism, the cult-of-childhood, and the pantheism is a profound nostalgia. In 'Job's Tears', Williamson dreams of returning to an 'old golden land' where worry and loneliness are banished. In the present, this wonderland can only be reached in dreams. The Incredible String Band took psychedelia's cult of slumber further than most, in songs like 'Chinese White' (where Heron sings of laying down to sleep with his arms 'around the rainbow') and 'Nightfall' (in which Williamson longs for the embrace of 'night's daughters'). In 'No Sleep Blues' he's agonised by 'delirium nosleepum'.

Psychedelia's conflation of sleep and innocence was captured in the name of a little-known band, Virgin Sleep. The best of their few recorded songs is the enchanting 'Secret' (1968). Like the Incredible String Band, Virgin Sleep take the anthropomorphism of *Wind in the Willows* and *Winnie the Pooh* and give it a mystical twist. The song offers a new definition of 'hip', in the imagery of A.A. Milne rather than Colin MacInnes: the field mouse, toad and swan know 'what's goin' on', and the place to be isn't the Flamingo nightclub but the woodland glade where the singer takes tea with a teddy bear. The singer hears the 'Secret' whispering through the hedgerows, but he's sworn to silence – he's down with Mother Nature.

Another minor classic of British psychedelia, Tintern Abbey's 'Beeside' (1967), also makes the indolence/innocence connection. Here, it's a creature of the field, a busy bee, who's misguided, and a human who hips him to the true meaning of flower power. Singer David MacTavish contemplates the bee's toil and tells him to mellow out. Like Wordsworth, whose poem gives the band their name, Tintern Abbey believe that indolence feminises man, promoting receptivity and 'wise passiveness'. The state of grace comes when man is de-activated and drowsy, succumbs to what Wordsworth calls 'that serene and blessed mood' in which 'we are laid asleep/In body, and become a living soul'. Tintern Abbey's music recreates Romanticism's primal scene, the bower of bliss – groves and glades 'where the male is captured, seduced and infantilised', according to Camille Paglia, stranded in 'a limbo of lush pleasures but stultifying passivity'. 'Beeside' is all synaesthesia, clouds of phased cymbal scintillating like pollen caught in midsummer sunshine.

The Soft Machine were another British hippie band who proposed indolence as the route to enlightenment in songs like 'Why Are We Sleeping?' (about a man drowning in his dreams) and 'As Long As He Lies Perfectly Still'. 'Heaven on Earth, he'll get there soon', they sing of a beach bum who's waiting for something that's already there: nirvana. And in the Beatles' 'Mother Nature's Son', Paul McCartney blends with the scenery and sings a 'lazy song' in a meadow of daisies. For the hippies, laziness was next to godliness.

younger than yesterday

Unlike the British groups, many Americans went straight from folk to acid rock with no period of urban blues. The Byrds' pastoralism blossomed in their 1967 album *Younger*

Than Yesterday. The title came from Dylan's 'My Back Pages', which the Byrds covered on the album. In the song, the protagonist outgrows his adolescent unrest and relearns the openness and simple wisdom of a child. In 'Mind Gardens', an orchard on a hill is David Crosby's metaphor for the self. In order to protect it from the harsh elements, he walls it in, but his over-zealous fortification blocks out the nourishing sunlight, and the 'Mind Gardens' start to wilt. Just before they perish, he comes to his senses and demolishes the wall, opening himself up to the world. Something similar takes place in the poignant 'Everybody's Been Burned', where emotional scars threaten to harden into an impenetrable psychic epidermis until the hero realises that risking anguish is necessary in order to stay open to rapture. In both songs, the band's music is a rippling, iridescent braid of modal folk and Indian raga chords, a pure evocation of the 'flow' that the Byrds worshipped.

On 1968's *The Notorious Byrd Brothers*, 'Goin' Back' embraces the goalless play of childhood and rejects adulthood as a barren, fun-free zone. Psychedelia is an enervated, unmotivated suspension ('Dolphin Smile', where the singer's 'floating free, aimlessly'), or it's sleep (in 'Draft Morning', the protagonist has to abandon his bed and dreams and wake up to reality – his duty to kill for his country). Throughout, the Byrds' vocals are an effete, susurrating murmur, as distant from the blaring self-assertion of pre-psychedelic rock as is imaginable.

Fantasies of a lost Arcadia pervaded the music of West Coast acid rock. Following the Alice-In-Wonderland-as-psychedelic-prophet analogy in 'White Rabbit', Jefferson Airplane's 'The Ballad Of You and Me and Pooneil' (from *After Bathing at Baxters*, 1967) was a vision of childhood bliss, in which Winnie the Pooh and Fred Neil (one of the band's folk music heroes) were merged as a single playmate. In Moby Grape's 'Lazy Me' (from their 1967 eponymous debut), psychedelia's cult of immobility reaches the brink of terminal entropy (the singer vows he'll 'lay here. . .

decay here'), while the Zen (im)passivity of 'Indifference' verges on a kind of vegetative nihilism. The Grateful Dead's *Aoxomoxoa* (1969) teems with imagery of garden-dreamers. Among the first of the San Francisco groups to leave the city for rural Marin County was Quicksilver Messenger Service, whose name and second album, *Happy Trails* (1969), harked back to a time when America was a virgin wilderness. The cover of *Shady Grove* (1970) depicts a leafy bower dappled with green sunlight, where a nine-teenth-century maiden sits on a knoll, in the company of a squirrel and a frog squatting on a toadstool; on the back sleeve, you can see a horse and buggy, indicating her eco-logically sound means of getting there.

This was the touchstone yearning of the era – finding a path 'back into the garden', as expressed most famously in Joni Mitchell's 'Woodstock'. But unlike the British bands, US psychedelia could tap into the traditional American cult of the wilderness. Lamentations for the loss of the frontier and wide open spaces were squarely in the grain of American culture, from Thomas Jefferson and the anti-urbanism of the late nineteenth-century Populist move-ment to poets like Walt Whitman. The American hippie culture could present their revolt as a return to roots and the true American dream: they were distancing themselves from cold war consumerism because it was a betrayal of the original vision of what America was supposed to be about.

In Britain, psychedelia's pastoralism evolved into folk-rock. The most important folk-rock band were Fairport Convention, who used British folklore as a way of allegorising the impas-ses and struggles of the present, just as the Band did with American history. The lesser lights of UK folk-rock inclu-ded Steeleye Span, Caravan, Tudor Lodge, Renaissance and Dulcimer. They generally looked like hippies gone to (hay)seed, all straggly beards, lank locks riddled with split-ends, moleskin waistcoats, voluminous mock-medieval blouses, a riot of moss-green, peat-brown and hessian hues. Perhaps more generic than most were Forest, whose *The Full Circle* (1970) managed to combine medievalism ('Hawk the Hawker', 'The Midnight Hanging of a Runaway Serf'), visions of heavenly glades ('Bluebell Dance'), odes to mystery girls ('Gypsy Girl & Rambleaway') *and* laments to lost innocence ('Autumn Childhood').

In America, the counterculture's pastoralism survived into the '70s, with the country-tinged soft-rock of Crosby Stills & Nash, the Eagles, and America. Burnt-out hippies found in folk and country music a tenor of desolation and fatalism that fitted well with the aftermath of the '60s. A song that perfectly captures the poignancy of the lost Summer of Love is ex-Byrd Gene Clark's 'Lady of the North' (from *No Other*, 1974). Its setting is the meadow-heaven that was psychedelia's classic backdrop but now is only a tantalising memory. 'The earth was like a pillow', allowing Clark and his sweetheart to drift in dreams. Gravity, anxiety, conflict are all banished. But as the cycle of seasons turns, winter brings this sunkissed idyll to an end. Clark's mournful reverie culminates in some truly transcendental lead guitar: sky-quake peals and tremors, the tears of a cloud.

Neil Young's 'Cortez the Killer' (*Zuma*, 1975) is a blues requiem for the bygone Eden of the late '60s. The song begins with Young imagining Cortez's arrival in the Mexico of the Aztecs, and his conquest and devastation of Montezuma's empire. Then the song abruptly switches from this gilded evocation of a lost pre-Columbian utopia to a more personal lament for a lost lover. 'I know she's living there', sings Young; he knows she still loves him, but he can't find his way back to the paradise they shared and he shattered. Cortez's 'rape' of Montezuma's civilisation becomes an allegory for Young's having wrecked a relationship. In his imagination, the lost kingdom and the lost love intertwine as symbols of the fall from Eden.

agony in the garden

Of all the artists to emerge in the psychedelic era and its aftermath, Van Morrison and Pink Floyd are the most fixated in their nostalgia for Eden. Morrison's *Astral Weeks* was recorded in 1968, and seems to have captured the dawning sense that the moment was already passing. His songs obsessively reiterate Arcadian imagery: 'the barefoot virgin child'; wandering through gardens opalescent with misty rain; quenching a thirsty soul from pure spring water; being draped in 'silence easy'. And just as Morrison's poetry exalts iridescence and fluidity, his voice and music embody these qualities. His scat-soul singing is a brook of babble; the music is a bubbling, winding stream of folk, jazz, blues and soul, all whorls and eddies, scintillation and sunspots under the eyelashes.

The album is a vision, both exultant and tormented, of paradise lost and maybe, just maybe, regained. The first song, 'Astral Weeks', sees Morrison drifting through 'the slipstream' and 'viaducts of your dreams'. He's swimming in dreamtime. He yearns to be anointed with kisses on the eyes, born again. In 'Sweet Thing', Morrison is, like the Byrds, 'younger than yesterday'; he vows that never will he 'grow so old again'. In this heaven-on-earth, nothing needs to be interpreted, meaning is fully present in every word, deceit impossible. Everyone speaks a pure 'Inarticulate Speech of the Heart' (as he titled a later album). In 'Beside You', Morrison aches for the absolute proximity, the alienation-free bliss of pure intimacy, which perhaps is only ever experienced at the mother's breast or in the all-enveloping suspension of the womb. He longs to 'never ever wonder why', to return to that realm where doubt and dread are banished.

M. Mark has written that the 'acknowledgment of unalterable homelessness and the struggle against it' are the essence of Van Morrison's greatest work. But on subsequent albums, as he makes a home sweet home for himself, marrying a flower-child and moving first to Woodstock and then to California, the edge of *Astral Weeks* is gradually softened. 1970's *Moondance* is an altogether mellower affair. 'And It Stoned Me' refers not to dope but the stupefaction of satisfaction, a feeling 'just like going home'. *Tupelo Honey* (1971) is sickly and suffocating in its dozy complacency. On the cover, Morrison has found the heavenly arbour that so haunted his imagination: he's strolling down a leafy bridle path, with his wife Janet Planet beside him riding a white horse. Morrison is starting to look a little chubby on all that home cooking. 'Old Old Woodstock' dwells sentimentally on the image of his wife waiting patiently on the kitchen doorstep, presumably with something nice and hot in the oven. 'I Wanna Roo You' sees the Morrisons cocooned in their snow-bound cottage: while he strums his guitar, she's busy in the kitchen. Snug and smug, they're happy that they 'ain't going nowhere'.

On subsequent albums, Morrison's spiritual concerns resurge; he plunges deeper 'Into the Mystic', looking for some kind of faith that'll allow him to feel at peace everywhere and ransacking the work of mystics, seers and poets for clues. His mid-'70s albums are haunted by a dream of Caledonia, 'an ancient land which sounds like home to him, a land where his ancestors made a brand new start, and where bagpipes gave birth to the blues', as M. Mark put it. Caledonia has the same mythic function in Morrison's cosmology that Zion or Africa has for the Rastafarians, or the 'old, golden land' did for the Incredible String Band: it's a gilded kingdom where alienation is abolished and all men are brothers. On *Saint Dominic's Preview* (1972), 'Gypsy' reconciles homesickness and wanderlust, with the old adage that, for the soul gypsy, anywhere he hangs his hat is home. *Veedon Fleece* (1974) concerns a quest for the holy grail, although no one has ever truly fathomed Morrison's symbolism. In 'You Don't Pull No Punches But You Don't Push the River', Morrison is impatiently waiting to be engulfed in the cosmic stream, returned to his true element. 'Cul De Sac' is more placid, imagining domestic serenity as a backwater from the turmoil of life. These obsessions with revelation, redemption, rebirth and rest continue through Van Morrison's albums to the present. His songs have become more overtly Christian and gospel-tinged in the '80s and '90s with albums like *Avalon Sunset*, *Enlightenment* and *Hymns to the Silence*, and today Morrison communicates little but a plump, spiritually replete serenity.

childhood's end

Pink Floyd were one of the groups that defined psychedelia – musically (with their kaleidoscopic flux of sound) and thematically (through their obsession with 'Childhood's End', their pastoralism). Pink Floyd's singer and original guiding light, Syd Barrett, was the key figure in the shift from the macho frontmen of mid-'60s R&B, to the androgynous Peter Pan figures of psychedelia. Barrett certainly fitted the mother's boy profile. His father died when he was fourteen and thereafter he developed an unusually close relationship with his mother. (Remarkably, Roger Waters, the other key figure in Pink Floyd, lost his father shortly after his birth and also fell under the sway of a 'domineering' mother.) In a 1974 tribute in *NME*, Nick Kent speculated that Barrett's mental instability was related to sinister Oedipal factors. Taking monstrous amounts of LSD pushed Barrett over the edge into a psychotic breakdown; he left Floyd and went back to live with his mum, for ever. . .

All of which may explain the Barrett-era Pink Floyd's idealisation of childhood. Their early single, 'See Emily Play' (1967), is a chaste, rapturous vision of floating on a river for ever; Barrett's fey, nursery-rhyme intonation is a startling break with the manly rasp of white blues. The debut album, *The Piper at the Gates of Dawn* (1967), took its title from the seventh chapter of the classic children's book *The Wind in the Willows*. In 'Matilda Mother', Barrett is a child imploring his mother to read another chapter of his bedtime fairy-tale. The mother's voice turns the 'scribbly lines' into magic, unlocking the door into a mystic wonderland where 'everything shines'. Children become nostalgic at a surprisingly early age: their fantasies of 'the olden days' conceal a yearning to go back to that fantastical no-place from which we've all been banished by the reality-principle. So Barrett renounces realism and longs for fairy-tales. In 'Flaming', Barrett plays the part of a sprite or wood-nymph, an invisible creature with magical powers of teleportation. Elsewhere on the album, there's a dream of pure love untarnished by sexuality in 'Bike', where Barrett, with the boundless generosity of a child, offers to give his sweetheart 'anything, everything', and makes friends with a mouse called Gerald.

By the second album, *A Saucerful of Secrets* (1968), Barrett was already halfway out of the group, but Pink Floyd were still overwhelmingly shaped by his vision. Rick Wright's 'Remember A Day' is pure nostalgia for the halcyon daze of infancy, with its easy spirit of play. In 'See-Saw', a brother and sister frolic happily without a care in the world or a thought for tomorrow. Syd Barrett carried on in this vein midway between twee and psychotic, sickly and sicko, in his erratic solo career. His 1970 albums *The Madcap Laughs* and *Barrett* are full of chaste, childlike love songs, all honey and cream and 'Baby Lemonade'; love here is closer to the toddler's fantasy of owning a sweet-shop than the carnality of adult desire.

Without Barrett, Pink Floyd drifted off into an unproblematic serenity. Control-freak Roger Waters shifted the band's orientation from Barrett's Dionysian intensity towards an Apollonian placidity (all those Icarus-complex songs like 'Set the Controls for the Heart of the Sun' and 'Let There Be More Light'). Once a chaotic flux, the Floyd's sound was now closer to a cathedral: awe-inspiring but orderly. But nostalgia was still the dominant emotion. On *Ummagumma* (1969), 'Grantchester Meadows' returns to the endless Indian summer of childhood. Waters's pallid, pious vocal and meandering acoustic guitar mingle with the sound of larksong, splashing ducks and humming bees. He's in the city, but he's 'basking' in the memory of that 'bygone afternoon' when he lay in the heat-hazy meadow beside a river.

The Floyd's pastoralism blossoms on *Atom Heart Mother* (1970), with its cover image of a cow placidly grazing in a pasture. The title originally came from a newspaper head-line about a pregnant mother who'd been given an atomic-powered pacemaker; drummer Nick Mason explained that the cover explored the connection 'between the cow and. . . the earth mother, the heart of the earth'. The album itself continued this rather pompous symbolism: the whole of the first side was taken up with the 'Atom Heart Mother Suite', a sort of cosmic regression symphony. 'Fat Old Sun' is all heat-baked, opulent indolence, sepia-tinged with regret as the summer afternoon turns to dusk; the lyrics evoke the smell of grass, church bells chiming in the distance, chil-dren's laughter floating on the breeze.

rave 'til mother dawn

The upstarts of punk *reviled* Pink Floyd, officially because of their pompous conceptualism and musical grandiosity, but at a deeper level, because of their bucolic quietude. Punk returned to the moment just before hippie – the urban uptightness of mod. But by the '90s, Pink Floyd's blurry sound and androgynous aura were resurrected by a mini-movement of British neo-psychedelic bands known as 'shoegazers' or 'dreampop'. Slowdive's first single, 'Avalyn', made a girl's name out of the mythical idyllic realm of Avalon, echoing prog-rock's obsession with the olden days of Albion. On the EP, *Holding Our Breath* (1991), pastoral reveries like 'Catch the Breeze' sat next to a cover of Syd Barrett's 'Golden Hair', a late '60s medieval fantasy, with Syd as an entranced courtly lover calling up to a maiden in a tower. Another dreampop band regressed even further back than Barrett's nursery: all the way to the womb. Pale Saints' 'Mother Might' took its title from Swinburne's 'Atalanta In Calydon': 'For there is nothing terribler to men/Than the sweet face of mothers, and the might'. An eerie, morbid hive of unfocused sound, with an anaemic male voice bled dry of will, 'Mother Might' captures the appalling allure of being engulfed and enwombed. 'Baby Maker' mourned the impossibility of never knowing, let alone recovering, 'what you left behind' when you were born.

Pink Floyd's legacy materialised elsewhere in the early '90s, in more improbable circumstances. One of Pink Floyd's earliest London gigs was at an event called the All-Night Rave (the band specialised in performances that went on until sunrise). Later, they recorded the soundtrack to *More*, a movie about drug fiends on the long-time hippie island of Ibiza. In the late '80s, a new psychedelic movement – rave culture – was born in Ibiza, created by British holidaymakers who had such a good time dancing to acid house music while tripping on Ecstasy that they didn't stop when they got back to the UK. Rave culture shares lots of aspects with the Floyd experience: dazzling, psychotropic lightshows, an obsession with three-dimensional sound, and transcendental imagery. Giant, all-night raves held illegally in the English countryside revived the pagan impulses of the counterculture; 1988 and 1989 were celebrated as replays of 1967's original Summer of Love.

By 1990, acid house's brisk pace was mellowing and bands started to make music to accompany and enhance the feeling of 'coming down' as the sun rose. The Beloved's 'The Sun Rising' (with its beatific, madrigal-like female vocal), 808 State's 'Sunrise', Blue Pearl's 'Mother Dawn', the Orb's 'Perpetual Dawn': this music was designed to capture the elegiac euphoria of the all-night rave's end. The genre came to be known variously as New Age house, ambient house or 'chill-out'. That's when the Pink Floyd influence kicked in. Innocence's 'Natural Thing' sampled a curlicue of radiant guitar from Floyd's 'Shine On You Crazy Diamond'; the KLF rushed out an album called *Chill Out* whose cover picture – sheep ruminating in a pasture – was a homage, at once ironic and affectionate, to *Atom Heart Mother*.

Soon the theory emerged that rave culture as a whole, and ambient house in particular, was the expression of a new Gaia-consciousness: ravers were in synch with the biorhythms of Mother Nature. Alex Paterson of the Orb declared that the '90s would be 'a decade of rainforest consciousness, a backlash against the rape of Mother Earth'. The Shamen formulated a vision of rave culture as a revival of 'archaic consciousness'. This was a concept invented by Terence McKenna, a proselytiser for naturally occurring hallucinogens like psilocybin mushrooms and DMT. McKenna believes psychedelic plants can reawaken mankind's sense of connection to the planetary ecosystem and that the resulting revolution in consciousness will help us to outgrow our 'toxic' lifestyles, returning mankind to the symbiosis with nature we once enjoyed.

McKenna was an original hippie who was blown away by the fact that the whole psychedelic project was being rehabilitated by rave culture, not to mention other emergent forms of cyberdelic culture (virtual reality, etc.). Another former hippie turned 'zippie' (a hippie who thinks technology has a friendly, liberating potential) is Fraser Clark, who created *Evolution* magazine in order to evangelise for the techno-pagan promise of rave culture. Clark argues that house music's 120 beats-per-minute is the same as 'the baby's heartbeat in the womb. . . . Imagine twenty-thousand young Westerners dervish-dancing to 120 bpm all night till the sun comes up. You get to feeling you're in the same womb.'

Musically, ambient house harked back to the crystal-clear tranquillity of progressive rockers like Steve Hillage and synth-symphonists Tangerine Dream; to the galactic/ Gaia imagery of jazz-rock fusionists like Weather Report, Return To Forever and Mahavishnu Report. There were obvious links to New Age music, with its sonic simulation of soothing spa waters, or the way its fans used the music to help them recover from the stress-ridden rigours of urban life. Ambient house sacrificed pace for peace. Where faster brands of rave music had a voodoo intensity, ambient house was influenced not by Africa but by the idea of the Pacific as paradise – 'the really motherly, soporific hemisphere', as Paul Oldfield put it. You could trace a line from the Hawaiian guitar on *Atom Heart Mother* and *Meddle* and the mellow blues of Fleetwood Mac's 'Albatross', through early '80s funk-pagans 23 Skidoo's 'Easter Island' and Cocteau Twins' 'Aikea-Guinea', all the way to '90s tracks like 808 State's 'Pacific State' and Future Sound of London's 'Papua New Guinea'.

While the beatific indolence of ambient house endured as a genre, rave music grew more frantic again as the '90s progressed and Ecstasy got cut with amphetamine. But the techno-pagan spirit persisted and evolved. Even in urban dance scenes like the speed-freak subculture 'ardkore, pagan motifs abound (one 'ardkore subgenre is called 'jungle'). Witness the astonishing similarities between the structure of the working-class raver's weekend and the elements that make up the dance rites practised by prehistoric Great Mother Goddess cults (as re-imagined by John Moore in his pamphlet *Anarchy & Ecstasy: Visions of Halcyon Days*). According to Moore, various techniques to disorientate and to weaken defences were practised to make the pagan adept vulnerable to a state of mystic rapture he calls 'bewilderness' – including sleeplessness (all-night raving), fasting (ravers know an empty stomach makes the Ecstasy come on quicker and stronger), and 'enraptured abandonment to a syncopated musical beat'.

Dance, says Moore, erodes inhibitions and psychic/bodily 'rigidities', opening the individual up for 'possession by the sacred wilderness'. The pagan dancers entered 'labyrinthine structures, often caves or underground passages' (not unlike your average nightclub). Here, aided by the contemplation of sacred mandalas (similar to the fractals and kaleidoscopic projections at raves), and by hallucinogens administered by hierophants (dealers!), the adepts are 'deranged into an ecstatic synaesthesia. . . . Both physically and spiritually, they enter the underworld, the womb of Mother Earth'. In the delirium of sacred ecstasy, 'the initiate becomes androgynous, unconcerned with the artificial distinctions of gender. . . . Encountering total saturation, individuals transcend their ego boundaries and their mortality in successive waves of ecstasy'. *Anarchy & Ecstasy* was published just before the rise of rave culture, but could it be that the experience of dancefloor communion that rave offers is actually a faint echo of the lost Edenic rites which Moore mourns and yearns to revive?

skyclad

Ambient music chooses a different route to get to the same feeling of oneness with the Cosmos: not Dionysian freakout, but a gently enfolding sound-bath. Abolishing the gap between foreground and background, ambient aims to unfocus your perceptions, blur all sense of being separate from the music. You can listen attentively or do something else altogether, because ambient is music you live inside.

Ambient music should be considered a descendant of psychedelia because it shares three of its defining attributes. First, it's spatial music: Brian Eno developed echo and reverb in order to create an imaginary 'psycho-acoustic space'. 'I wanted to be situated inside a large field of loosely-knit sound, rather than placed before a tightly organised monolith,' he wrote in the sleevenotes to *On Land* (1982). Like psychedelic/cosmic rock, ambient is wombing. Second and third, ambient tends to be pastoral and fixated on childhood. With *On Land*, Eno was obsessed with recapturing childhood memories of specific places. 'Lizard Point', 'A Clearing', 'Dunwich Beach, Autumn, 1960', 'Unfamiliar Winds (Leeks Hills)', 'Lantern Marsh' all refer to places near where Eno grew up in East Anglia. And like Floyd on 'Grantchester Meadows', Eno used real animal noises (rooks, frogs, insects) as musical elements.

Ambient music has much in common with the most innovatory aspects of house/techno production: it plays with the normal ranking of instruments in the mix, disorientating the listener. And it refuses rock's thrust-and-climax narrative structure in favour of a more 'feminine' economy of pleasure, i.e. plateau after plateau, an endlessly deferred climax.

If one band joins the dots between Pink Floyd-style cosmic rock, ambient, and rave culture, it's the Orb. The group's key member Alex Paterson used to work for E.G., the label that put out Eno's ambient albums; the Orb's debut *Adventures Beyond the Ultraworld* (1990) paid tribute to Pink Floyd with titles like 'Back Side of the Moon' and artwork that spoofed the cover of the Floyd's *Animals*; the Orb's music is the unabashed return of cosmic rock, layering serene washes of synth and spangly guitars over a laidback dance beat. Their sound is an aural counterpart of the visual pun that climaxes *2001: A Space Odyssey*, where an Earth-like planet turns out to be, on closer inspection, a gigantic foetus sky-clad in swirly blue.

The Orb revived many of the psychedelic tropes we saw with the Incredible String Band: infantilism verging on the twee, as in 'Little Fluffy Clouds', which samples Rickie Lee Jones recalling, in an adenoidal coo, how she gasped in wonder as a child at the Arizona skyline; worship of Mother Nature in 'Earth (Gaia)'; a longing for the embrace of eternity in 'Supernova at the End of the Universe'. 'Back

Side of the Moon' is a simulacrum of heaven, all clusters of seraphic harmony, cascades of stardust, shimmery sounds like magic wands working wonders. But the Orb's most beautiful song is the whimsically titled 'A Huge Evergrowing Pulsating Brain That Rules from the Centre of the Ultraworld'. Ever widening ripples of synth conjure a mood of brain-blasted, heart-in-mouth euphoria; in and out of the dazed haze weave church bells, splashing pebbles, choral ascents, jet-plane vapour trails. It's a hive of passivity.

The Orb also explored the links between ambient and dub reggae. Around the same time that Eno was first formulating the idea of ambient, dub reggae pioneers like King Tubby and Lee Perry were also using echo and reverb to conjure a vast 'psycho-acoustic space'. Like ambient and house, dub is based around a decentered soundscape: instruments drop out of the mix for long periods, reappearing as reverb-drenched mirages that loom, then dissipate like mist. Like ambient and house, dub has aspirations to the eternal: mostly instrumental, its meditational air sometimes give it a medieval aura. And, like ambient and house, dub is wombadelic music: its bass penetrates your body, the music floats out to enfold you.

The Orb's music is for stay-at-home ravers, clubbers chilling out after a night of frenzy, and spliff-heads. A mystical appreciation of the divine weed – marijuana, ganja, pot, whatever you care to call it – is *the* common denominator between psychedelia, dub and rave. When high, the listener hears all forms of music with increased fidelity and dimension. But dub reggae, with its echo-drenched spatiality, is *designed* to be enhanced by marijuana. Dope has many properties that work well with 'mystical' music. It decreases the sense of distance between source and listener; it encourages synaesthesia (so that the listener 'sees' the music); it diminishes both memory and future-focused anxiety, so that the listener can be absorbed by the present moment, become 'lost in music'.

With dub, sound becomes incense or fragrance, filling the gaps between listener and speakers. Swathed in this 'holy smoke', the listener sinks into a sacred stupor, achieves the state of grace that is total de-activation. For the Rastafarian, this nirvana is a glimpse of Jah's kingdom of righteousness. Like psychedelia, dub is nostalgic, a music of homesickness and exile: Rastas dream of a return to Zion, the ambrosial, gilded realm that beckons all the lost tribes of the African diaspora. But could it be that this lost utopia is really a subconscious memory of the 'inner ocean' of the womb, where the foetus hears everything refracted, reverberant, *dubbed-up*, via the fleshly amplifier of the mother's body? The post-Orb, 'ambient dub' band Original Rockers suggested as much with the title of their 1993 single 'The Underwater World of Jah Cousteau'.

Although the Orb brought out the links between house, cosmic rock, dub and ambient, it took another group to go all the way and record the first pastoral techno album (seemingly a contradiction in terms, given techno's inorganic, urban, futurist sound). On Ultramarine's *Every Man and Woman Is A Star* (1992), techno is transformed into the sound of tranquillity, solitary communion with Nature. On songs like 'British Summertime' and 'Skyclad', owl hoots, chirping crickets and babbling brooks mingle with acid house bass-squelches and chattering sequencers; cascades of acoustic guitar and dolorous fiddles intertwine with electronic bleeps and undulating rhythm loops. Ultramarine's music is techno infused with the folky-jazzy ambience of Robert Wyatt, Kevin Ayers, Joni Mitchell, and other pre-punk influences like soft-rock (the Eagles, America) and rustic prog-rock (Mike Oldfield's *Hergest Ridge*).

The duo, Paul Hammond and Ian Cooper, came from rural Essex, a part of the English countryside very similar to where Eno grew up, with its desolate estuaries and marshes. And their methodology was similar to Eno's *On*

Land. 'When we write songs, we think in terms of land-scapes', said Hammond. *Every Man and Woman Is A Star* was a soundtrack to an imaginary canoe-trip across the USA. Along with the pastoralism, Ultramarine expounded a Zen philosophy of trance dance. 'Stella' sampled a performance artist theorising about how dance enabled her to shed confining dogmas and fixed ideas, and 'find that emptiness where I can begin again': a sacred expanse in which she was able to connect her innermost self with outermost infinity.

'Intimate immensity' is how the philosopher Gaston Bachelard characterised this sensation – a feeling of oneness with the universe that brings together body and horizon. In the psychedelic imagination, the pastoral, the cosmic and the oceanic merge into a continuum, because they all induce a sense of benign, all-enfolding vastness; a vastness that seems to promise an end to our separateness and the recovery of a lost continuity.

starsailing:
cosmic rock

Because it's the most abstract of arts, music has the capacity to inspire mystical rapture – a sense of the here-and-now that bleeds into infinite expanse. In *Nada Brahma: The World Is Sound*, Joachim-Ernst Berendt explores the idea that music is 'the landscape of consciousness'. He argues that the cutting edge of Western scientific thought confirms the ancient intuitions of Eastern mysticism: that the way the universe works is closer to music than the mechanistic models formulated by Newton. *Nada Brahma* means 'the world is sound'; in Zen Buddhist cosmology, the universe was *sounded* into being. Similarly, quantum physics, chaos theory, et al., suggest that behind the apparent solidity of reality, there's a 'cosmic dance' of wave-forms, vibrations, frequencies, probabilities. Berendt believes that the rules governing reality (from the structure of leaves and crystals, to the distance between the solar system's planets) conform to the laws of musical harmony.

Psychedelic music (defined in the broadest sense) aspires to the amorphous immensity of this 'cosmic dance'. It is music that hints at, reaches out towards, the rushing roar of the Original Sound, the primal OM. You can trace a thread that runs through Indonesian gamelan, Aboriginal didgeridoo music, Indian raga, Tibetan devotional music, Moroccan pipes-of-Pan music as played by the Master Musicians of Jajouka, John Cage, La Monte Young, Terry Riley, the Velvet Underground, the Byrds, Krautrock groups like Can/Faust/Neu/Cluster/Ashra Tempel, Brian Eno, Spacemen 3, My Bloody Valentine, right up to ambient techno artists like the Aphex Twin. What this music shares is a belief that minimal-is-maximal; that simple patterns, repeated, can generate both complexity and immensity. To varying degrees, these artists make drone music, based around overtones and intermediate tones rather than the clear pitch intervals that govern Western classical music. Drone music blurs the gaps between notes to hint at the supra-musical roar of the cosmos breathing.

It's become something of a cliché to use the word mantra to describe songs by wall-of-noise bands from the Velvets to the Valentines. But there's some justification for using this Zen term. Mantras have neither author nor narrative structure: they go nowhere. Psychedelia's secret agenda has always been to help the listener slip the bonds of time, place, self, and escape to a Zen nowhen/nowhere.

These ideas found one route into rock music via the composer and theorist John Cage, who drew on Buddhism and the Christian Gnostic tradition. His ideal music was meditational, encouraging an absentminded receptivity in the listener. 'It is not a question of getting anywhere, of making progress,' wrote Christian Wolff of Cage's music and philosophy, 'or having come from anywhere in particular, of tradition or futurism. There is neither nostalgia nor anticipation.' Through (a)quiescence, the listener lives in the now.

Cage's coterie of avant-garde disciples and allies – La Monte Young, Terry Riley, Steve Reich – developed his techniques: drone-based repetition, gamelan-influenced percussive music, tape manipulation (loops, delay systems), 'random' elements like shortwave radio. And these ideas entered rock through John Cale (who played with La Monte Young prior to the Velvet Underground), Can (whose Irmin Schmidt worked with Young and Terry Riley) and Brian Eno.

Another conduit for Zen ideas into jazz and rock was John Coltrane. Along with Miles Davis, Coltrane reintroduced modal playing into jazz. Modality is a quality shared by folk, blues and Indian music – improvisation based around a scale, mode or single chord (as opposed to Western classical music's continual key changes), resulting in fluid, sliding, droning melodies. In the '60s, Coltrane headed out East, spiritually and musically – an evolution that took him through *India* (1961), *A Love Supreme* (1964) and culminated in his 1965 album *Om*, which took its name from the Buddhist name for the Deity, the Absolute, the first vibration. The album starts and ends with a mass-chant, 'I am OM', in between which Coltrane's band launch into a caterwauling freak-out. It couldn't have been further from Cage's placid music, but the underlying philosophy was similar: the aim was to break down the listener's psychic defences, so that inner chaos merged with the cosmos.

In his 1954 lecture '45' For A Speaker', Cage borrowed an exhortation from an uncredited mystic: 'Cultivate in yourself a grand similarity with the chaos of the surrounding ether: unloose your mind, set your spirit free.' The goal is a return, through music, to the primal 'we' that precedes individuation. Not just to apprehend, but to merge with the Absolute. Sri Chimnoy, guru to jazz-rock fusionist John McLaughlin, said of the latter's *Love, Devotion, Surrender* LP: 'Unfortunately, in the West surrender is misunderstood. We feel that if we surrender to someone, he will then lord it over us. . . . But from the spiritual point of view. . . when the finite enters in the Infinite, it becomes the Infinite all at once. When a tiny drop enters into the ocean, we cannot trace the drop. It becomes the mighty ocean.'

Coltrane's influence percolated into acid rock via the Byrds and Jimi Hendrix. In the Byrds' 'Eight Miles High', folk's modality mingles with the droning fluidity of Indian raga. Coming from folk, bypassing the blues, the Byrds were able to create a sort of non-cock rock, based around a chiming iridescence of jangling chords rather than phallic riffs. Their vocals were mumbled and murmuring, rather than potent and assertive. The Byrds' lyrics embraced Zen principles of selfless surrender as opposed to white blues' aggressive imposition of self upon the environment. '5D' was about opening up to a gently overwhelming, 'loving' universe. 'Ballad of Easy Rider' echoed the wanderlust of the beatniks, and imagined being carried along by the river of life and eventually merging with 'the sea'.

sea of sound

In the mid '60s, rock was all thrust, a violent assertion of sexuality and self directed outwards at the world and the listener. But with psychedelia, rock became oceanic/ stratospheric: a soundscape that surrounded and subsumed the listener. LSD, which expands the spatial qualities of music, coincided with technical advances that allow this spatiality to be enhanced and amplified (stereo, 24 track recording, the studio-as-instrument). Rock lost its hardness, became a medium in which the listener is suspended and *enwombed*.

One of the founding moments in the birth of psychedelia, Jimi Hendrix's 'Purple Haze' (1967), seems to have originated in a fantasy of uterine regression. In the song, sky-kissing Jimi is consumed in a sensual inferno that inspires dread as much as longing, a mixture of love and apocalypse. In *Electric Gypsy*, Harry Shapiro and Caesar Glebbeek reveal that 'Purple Haze' was influenced by Hendrix's interest in the religious beliefs of a Native American tribe, the Hopi. In Hopi cosmology, one of the four phases of creation was Qoyangnuptu, the time of the Dark Purple. An entity called Spider Woman gathered the earth and mixed it with her saliva (the sea), birthing the first world underwater, where light was diffused into a 'purple haze'. For Hendrix, this phrase evoked his childhood method of escaping a troubled, insecure family life. 'Somehow,' write Shapiro and Glebbeek, Jimi would 'find himself floating away, looking down on himself, knowing he wasn't asleep, but drifting through the mists of another dimension, the astral plane, looking for something he could never identify.' The lost tranquillity of the amniotic idyll? Throughout his work, Jimi Hendrix fantasised about escaping earthly alienation, sometimes by ascending into outer space ('Third Stone from the Sun'), sometimes by descending underwater. In '1983...(A Merman I Should Turn to Be)' (from *Electric Ladyland*, 1968), Hendrix seeks asylum from a war-torn world by fleeing to the bottom of the ocean in a magic submarine. Ignoring the sceptics who sneer that it's impossible for a man to live underwater, Hendrix flouts the patriarchal reality-principle that originally banished him from the aquatic Eden of the womb. On this song and its sequel, 'Moon, Turn the Tides...Gently, Gently, Away', Hendrix anticipates dub and ambient music, using studio effects to create an aural version of the Great Barrier Reef: striations of sound like light refracting underwater, riff-clusters that dart and disperse like shoals of tropical fish, twinkle like starfish and dilate like anemones.

The music of the counterculture is full of Neptunian fantasies and water-worship. The Beatles' 'Yellow Submarine' is a nursery-rhyme take on this pre-Oedipal utopia: as in '1983...(A Merman I Should Turn To Be)', a magical sub-aquatic vessel transports us to a realm of limitless plenitude where no one lacks for anything. 'Julia' (from *The Beatles*, 1968) appears to be a song to a siren, an 'ocean-child' whose eyes are like seashells and whose hair is 'floating sky', but is actually an elegy for John Lennon's mother. Donovan waxed aquatic in 'Atlantis' (1968) and 'There Is An Ocean' (1973), the latter being a mystic ode about the 'promised land' that lies within each of us, a realm of heavenly silence we can reach only if 'we deactivate'.

Often oceanic and cosmic imagery are intermingled, gesturing at the same impossible dream: a return to the original home sweet home. Tim Buckley's *Starsailor* (1971) is perhaps the ultimate conflation of ocean and cosmos, homesickness and wanderlust reconciled within a single image. Having started as a folk-rock minstrel, Buckley's songs and singing grew progressively more improvisatory as he absorbed the influence of Coltrane and Miles, and composers like Xenakis, Berio, Cage and Stockhausen. He also fell under the spell of avant-garde singer Cathy Berberian, with her menagerie of 'clucks, gurgles, sighs, yowls, splutters, screams, cries, weeps, wails' (as Lee Underwood, Buckley's friend and lead guitarist, put it). Buckley himself declared: 'The most shocking thing I've ever seen people come up against is dealing with someone who doesn't sing words. If I had my way, words wouldn't mean a thing.' In his struggle to get beyond language, he used his voice as freeform jazz instrument, mad-scatted, gushed glossolalia like a geyser, even sang in Swahili.

Drunk on all these heady avant-garde potions, Buckley produced *Lorca* (1969) and *Starsailor*, one of the most feverishly out-there albums of all time. 'Come Here, Woman' is both a carnal encounter with a real woman and Tantric congress with the Great Mother Goddess. Sex transports them to an intoxicated realm where pain is abolished; the lovers are carried by the tide to 'a coil of peace' (an explicitly uterine image). In *Thalassa, A Theory of Genitality*, Sandor Ferenczi declared that the motive of the male sex drive is 'none other than an attempt. . . to return to the mother's womb'. The mother, in turn, is 'the symbol of and partial substitute for the sea'.

Far more than the words, though, it's Buckley's voice that incarnates his lust for some kind of eroto-mystic apocalypse. On 'Jungle Fire', his voice is volcanic, an eruption of deep-body lava, hurling the stricken ululation 'mama!!!' across the song's horizon like a flaming comet. As with 'Come Here, Woman', the object of his desire for union is at once a flesh-and-blood soul 'mama' and some kind of Ur-Mother. The title track, 'Starsailor', is composed entirely of Buckley's treated and multi-tracked voice; it's a schizophrenic chorale with each voice situated in a soundscape of labyrinthine complexity. Buckley's voice(s) ooze like plasma, coagulating in globules, filaments and tendrils that bifurcate then reconnect, forming a sort of honeycomb of vocal *jouissance* – a grotto of glossolalia. Buckley's eerie vocal polyphony lies somewhere between babytalk, orgasmic moan, and the shattering ecstasies of mystical rapture. Wilhelm Reich believed mysticism was a sublimated longing for orgasm's 'cosmic plasmatic sensations'. Buckley literally sculpted an entire song out of orgasm, taking the ecstatic vocal sounds that appear in most pop only at the climax of a song, and moulding them like clay. 'Starsailor' seems to take place inside the infinite space of orgasm itself, as though we're inside Buckley's body.

the blue you once knew

In their early days, Pink Floyd were influenced by AMM, a Zen-inspired freeform jazz collective who tried to make music as if it was being made for the first time. Floyd took from them the idea of replacing distinct chords with waves of amorphousness. Syd Barrett was one of the first guitarists to use wah-wah, echo-box, feedback and slide guitar to vaporise rock, replacing the riff with radiation.

Pink Floyd's oceanic/cosmic sound was reflected in imagery of beatific blue expanses. The colour blue assumed a special significance in Pink Floyd's imagination right from the start. The opening track of their first album, *The Piper at the Gates of Dawn*, is 'Astronomy Domine', a flux of radiant hues over which an awestruck Barrett babbles about 'the blue you once knew'. This strange, faintly foreboding phrase takes us to the heart of psychedelia.

For Julia Kristeva, colour has the same role in painting that chromaticism (timbre, texture, grain of the voice) has in music. Colour is non-representational, a sheer charge that releases the non-verbal excess, the 'more than can be said', of emotion or libido. In the history of art, the avant-garde has struggled to liberate colour from narrative, representational and figurative constraints: hence the trajectory that runs from Impressionism to Abstract Expressionism and Action Painting. In music, too, the avant-garde has developed the chromatic and spatial aspects at the expense of linear narrative (theme, development, resolution etc.). Psychedelia dramatically expanded rock's chromatic palette and spatiality, at the expense of conventional song structure.

In her essay 'Giotto's Joy', Kristeva looks at the use of the colour blue in Giotto's paintings of the Madonna and Child, where the Virgin Mary is invariably surrounded by a rippling, radiant backdrop of celestial azure. For Kristeva, blue is the colour of pre-Oedipal bliss. The fovea (the eye's central element) takes sixteen months to develop fully. The infant perceives colour, and in particular the blue part of the spectrum, long before it can focus on form and figure. This means that radiant chromatic flux, and above all blue, evokes a time before the fixed 'I'/eye: the blissful, incestuous intimacy of the suckling phase.

In a companion essay, 'Motherhood According to Giovanni Bellini', Kristeva asks: 'How can we verbalize this prelinguistic, unrepresentable memory? Heraclitus' flux, Epicurus' atoms, the whirling dust of cabalic, Arab and Indian mystics, and the stippled drawings of psychedelics – all seem better metaphors than the theories of Being, the logos, and its laws.' Like Giotto, Bellini surrounded his Madonnas with a dazzling field of blue that produces 'a peculiar, serene joy'. Kristeva identifies a similar ecstatic ego-shattering use of colour in modern art, in particular Rothko's luminous blocks of pure colour and Matisse's work. Towards the end of his life, when he abandoned paint for paper cut-outs of pure hues, Matisse's pictures are full of oceanic mysticism: under-seascapes populated by polyps, anemones, and the fronds of subaquatic flora. In 'The Bathers', it's hard to distinguish where the figures of the bathers end and the waves begin.

Pink Floyd's songs combine a fixation on blue expanses

(the ocean, the sky) with obsessively reiterated imagery of maternity and infantile bliss. Despite their reputation as the kings of progressive rock, they were really about regression. The title of *Ummagumma* sounds like babytalk drivel, all echolalia and assonance, while songs like 'A Saucerful of Secrets' take the listener on a cosmic roller-coaster ride akin to the kaleidoscopic time tunnel at the climax of *2001: A Space Odyssey*.

On *Atom Heart Mother*, Pink Floyd composed a regression symphony, the 'Atom Heart Mother Suite'. It begins with 'Father's Shout', pompous mock-classical music: stern and stately horns that comport themselves with the terrible, puffed-up dignity of the patriarchal order, mingled with the thunder of war and the revving of engines. 'Breast Milky' is a glimpse of the lost maternal idyll of nurture and nourishment. It's a poignant blues, all plangent violin, slide guitar, and a female voice, angelic and wordless. The Christian mystics often used imagery of suckling and 'spiritual milk' to describe their experiences. 'Breast Milky' recalls Saint François de Sales' description of the beatific 'orison of quietude', in which 'the soul is like a little child still at the breast'. With 'Mother Fore', the voice becomes a billowing choir, at first soft and tender, then turning eerie and swelling into a cosmic threnody. 'Funky Dung' starts as an ambling, slick blues, then devolves into Dadaist phonetic poetry, all nonsense syllables and gurgles, like babytalk turned to opera. 'Mind Your Throats Please' regresses still further, into total chromatic cacophony. It's as though we've descended from babyhood, through the womb, the ovum, the chromosone and DNA strand, right back to the sub-atomic 'white light' level of consciousness that is the final destination of the LSD trip. Finally, 'Remergence' is the return to reality and distinct, contoured form: the main theme of the suite returns, an aching bluesy guitar figure that mourns the lost utopia, but is resigned to its loss.

Meddle (1971) is also in revolt against the reality-principle. 'A Pillow of Winds', for instance, is an Aeolian lullaby, draped with drooping, gently weeping Hawaiian guitar. Waters and his ladylove drift (off) on 'a cloud of eiderdown', achieve the stratospheric serenity of birds who sleep on the wing. But while the first side of *Meddle* is straightforwardly halcyon, the twenty-four-minute epic 'Echoes' that takes up all of side two is more mournful, less confident that paradise can be regained. An allegory of the counterculture's disintegration and disillusionment, 'Echoes' owes much to Coleridge's 'Ancient Mariner', in which a seafarer is stranded in a stagnant ocean. 'Echoes' was originally entitled 'The Return of the Son of Nothing', and while its elegiac atmosphere obviously stems in part from Waters's feelings about the loss of his father, it also connects to a broader sense of being bereft, disinherited, washed up after the countercultural tide has gone out.

The song suite begins with slowly spreading ripples of keyboard, lachrymose pangs of blues guitar, and a fatigued, faltering rhythm. Waters dwells lovingly, morbidly, on reveries of an oceanic Arcadia, all coral catacombs and coves, before cutting back to his reality of urban alienation, the early '70s sense of being an exile on Main Street. The song grinds to a halt, grows ghostly, as eerily treated guitars wheel and shriek like seagulls, or maybe vultures. Gradually, the song regathers itself after this appalling lull, almost as if Waters is mustering the will to carry on. Reconciled to settling for less, he sings mournfully of how there's no one to sing him 'lullabies' any more. 'Echoes' combines two kinds of nostalgic sorrow – one for the immediate past (the Summer of Love) and the other for wombadelic bliss. The moment has passed when the counterculture looked like it could build a life without alienation, overturn the Oedipal complex en masse. Collective transcendence of the reality-principle has degenerated, with the atomisation of the hippie community, into a life-denying flight from reality. Psychedelia's Eden has contracted to a desert island, barren and insular.

flow motion:
can, eno and oceanic rock

The ultimate cosmic/oceanic rock may well be the work of
the German band, Can. The core of the group – bassist
Holger Czukay, guitarist Michael Karoli, drummer Jaki
Liebezeit, and keyboard player Irmin Schmidt – came from
avant-garde jazz and classical backgrounds. But for all
their schooling in the ideas of Cage, Stockhausen, Coltrane,
La Monte Young et al., the music they made as Can was
among the least forbidding ever. This was free music that
didn't have to ostentatiously signpost its radicalism with
awkward discontinuity and wilful tangents, but instead
freely embraced a structure, a good groove. Can's music is
the alpha and omega of psychedelic dance music. Even
those not influenced by them have unwittingly retraced
trails the Krautrock quartet blazed between 1969 and
1975.

Can were at once progressive *and* regressive, committed
to chromatic complexity *and* rhythmic accessibility.
Virtuosos who believed in the minimal-is-maximal credo,
they stripped their playing of superfluous flash and
avoided bombastic displays of mastery. Czukay declared:
'[Repetition] gives you power. In Japanese music, if you listen to how they restrict themselves. . . they get such a
power out of it. . . It is unbelievable, 'zen' music, it really
knocks you out.' In a 1989 interview, Karoli claimed: 'We
were into the healing powers of music. Not impressing people, but caressing them. . . Certain frequencies have a healing power, or liberate energies. Sometimes music is like
telepathy.'

At their creative peak, Can's *modus operandi* was

'instant composition': they would improvise for hours, then edit down the highlights of their jamming into track-length pieces – much like Miles Davis's approach in the late '60s and early '70s, when he was exploring a similar chaotic jazz/rock/funk/ethnic fusion. Their music's internal organisation was democratic, akin to Weather Report's 'everyone solos and nobody solos' idea. Their vocalists – first Malcolm Mooney, then Damo Suzuki, finally Karoli himself – were treated as another instrument, never placed in the spotlight but just an extra musical element in a soundscape whose decentred mix was the missing link between psychedelia and dub reggae.

In 1980, Andy Gill suggested that 'Can have produced the most successful attempt thus far at making the "Universal music" of Stockhausen's dreams.' Czukay had talked of his search for 'the bass tone of the global sound', and described himself as 'an acoustic landscape painter'. Karoli spoke of studying 'planetary rhythms' and the 'parallels of colours and tones'. Can made the ultimate pan-global, pantheistic music; their music is one long serenade to Mother Nature. Despite the all-male personnel of the band, it is radically 'feminine' music, embodying principles of flow and symbiosis in its structure, texture and aura.

Can's early music, as collected on the albums *Monster Movie* (1969) and *Delay 1968* (finally released in 1981), is like a hybrid of the Velvet Underground and James Brown: locked groove trance rock, compulsive in its spartan, crisp-and-dry way, but a bit sombre and severe, despite Malcolm Mooney's acid-ripped gibberish. What Can needed at this point was moisture, something to lubricate their rather stiff and Teutonic take on rock's groove. As if in recognition of this, *Soundtracks* (1970) features a song called 'Soul Desert', in which vocalist Damo Suzuki gasps a parched and desolate blues as he languishes in a wasteland without woman's love. In 'She Brings the Rain', woman provides life-giving water, making his soul blossom and budding 'magic mushrooms' out of the dead soil.

In between these two hymns to water came 'Mother Sky', Can's counterpart to Pink Floyd's 'Interstellar Overdrive': a fourteen-minute apocalyptic mantra in which an awe-stricken Suzuki raves about how 'madness is too pure like Mother Sky'. The song's title reverses the traditional association of the heavens with the Holy Father. The history of religion can be divided between patriarchal sky-cults and matriarchal societies' earth-cults, between Judaeo-Christian monotheism and pantheism/paganism's panoply of gods. Perhaps with 'Mother Sky', Can were gesturing at Pink Floyd's 'blue you once knew', the halcyon skies that evoke the pre-Oedipal heaven-on-earth.

Can's next album plunged headfirst into the irrational and supernatural, madness and magic. *Tago Mago* (1971), which took its name from a wizard or necromancer, was Can's spookiest, most shamanistic music. On 'Mushroom' and 'Oh Yeah', the rhythm section seethes and roils like a cauldron, an alchemist's alembic. 'Halleluhwah' is nearly nineteen minutes of voodoo polyrhythm churning around a coiled cobra of a funk riff. The soundscape grows progressively more jungle-ish — treefrog chirrups, insectoid drones, strangled bird-cries in every crevice and cranny – finally spiralling skyward as though it has generated its own tornado spout.

Another side-long track, 'Augmn', which took its title from a magick spell of Aleister Crowley's, is an odyssey into the Earth's interior, its huge swathes of dub-like echo simulating the uncanny acoustics of subterranean chambers and corridors. The incantation 'Augmn' rumbles, slow and cavernous, resonating like an Om issuing from the belly of the planet, a sound so deep and wide it's like falling into an abyss. 'Peking O' abandons groove altogether for sheer deliquescence of form, while Suzuki sings of trying to make his way 'back to yesterday'.

Ege Bamyasi (1972) is a slight departure from Can's

liquefacient trajectory. It's the band's most desiccated record, itchy and sharply etched. But 'I'm So Green', with its claim to a newborn child's sensitivity to stimuli, looks ahead to the optimism and openness to oceanic feelings found in Can's prime work: *Future Days* (1973), *Soon Over Babaluma* (1974), and *Landed* (1975). These albums form a kind of Gaia trilogy. The chromatic and spatial innovations that began to bud with *Tago Mago* blossom into kaleidoscopic panoramas that reach out and enfold the listener.

The title track of *Future Days* opens the record, and immediately establishes an aquatic vibe. Eddies of sound rise out of silence, weaving around water-ripples and soft splashes. Ever so slowly, these tremulous sound-vapours condense into a gentle pulsation of rhythm: a bassline as intimate and life-giving as your heartbeat, interlocking with the drums, congas and a wheezing, squeeze-box keyboard riff, in a reciprocal, gently rocking rhythm. Surf laps against a shoreline as a happy-sad violin and Karoli's wistful, fallible voice conjure a mood of anticipatory nostalgia, as though Can are looking back fondly on some golden age yet to come.

'Spray' is all whorls, rip-tides, convection currents, ebbing away to a halcyon stillness. 'Moonshake', with its prehensile polyrhythms, is the first in a series of lunar-fixated songs. Can worship the moon – traditionally associated with the 'dark continent' of femininity and the unconscious, because of the moon's relationship to the ocean's tidal rhythms and the menstrual cycle, and because, in olden days, the mad were 'lunatics', i.e. moonstruck. The sidelong 'Bel Air' could be Can's answer to Pink Floyd's 'Echoes', but this time there's no sense that Eden is irretrievable. Scintillating guitar like light dancing on wavecrests, ocean-breeze synths, lapping surf, recreate a seashore idyll, sun-baked beatitude. The song combines sensations of ascension and immersion, so that you feel like you're swimming in the air or flying underwater; either way, gravity is abolished, leaving a sublime, unburdened nonchalance.

The title of *Soon Over Babaluma*, Can's next album and all-time masterpiece, has the same babytalk assonance of Pink Floyd's *Ummagumma*. Can's titles and lyrics, so voluptuous in the mouth with their slurred, slippery vowel sounds and sibilants, hark back to the oral phase of childhood. Can resisted rock notions of meaningfulness. Karoli declared, 'Meaning can only really lead away from the music. It's the sound of the words that matters more than their meaning. . . . As soon as music creates feelings that can be named by words, it's no longer important to make music.'

So 'Dizzy Dizzy', a love song of sorts, is all nonsense and onomatopoeia. The music is a 'soft machine', a plasma-engine of throbs and pulsions, regular as clockwork but as warm-blooded as a small furry animal. 'Come sta, La Luna' serenades the moon over the tidal sway of a tango rhythm whose gentle erotic urgency is a world away from rock's phallic insistence. Its current carries the listener through a humid, hyper-tactile environment like some teeming, bejewelled rainforest. Then the song seems to plunge several fathoms to another kind of lurid, promiscuous jungle, this time on the ocean bed: Karoli's eerily treated voice hints that a siren or ocean-spirit ('the voice is in the water') has lured him there.

Soon Over Babaluma's second side is taken up by an epic in two parts, 'Chain Reaction' and 'Quantum Physics', that together make up Can's absolute pinnacle. Throughout the Gaia trilogy, Can conjure a sense of benign space, a pulsating mass of sound-tendrils reaching out to caress you like the Sargasso Sea. But on 'Chain Reaction' and 'Quantum Physics', Can go even further. It's as if they recreate in sound the ocean planet of Stanislaw Lem's science-fiction classic *Solaris*: an ocean that's a sentient, telepathic being able to sense its human visitors' deepest longings.

It's been said that architecture is frozen music; 'Chain

Reaction' is *fluid* architecture, an Escher-style lattice of viaducts and waterfalls that defies the laws of geometry and gravity. It ascends and descends between several plateaus: periods of relative calm alternate with turbulence like the agitation of molecules on the brink of the transition from water to gas. Then, just as this undulating soundscape reaches a new pitch of effervescence, it undergoes an abrupt, uncanny change, like one of those freakish substances that can pass straight from gas to solid. 'Chain Reaction' metamorphosises into 'Quantum Physics', an extraordinary piece of music that feels like a glimpse into a realm of infinitely vast or infinitesimally intimate processes.

Can's playing on 'Quantum Physics' is beyond, beneath, between categories like rock, jazz, funk. Czukay's bass and Liebezeit's drums don't interlock as a steady, sustaining pulse, but stitch a percussive/melodic thread; Schmidt's lambent synths wax and wane; Karoli whispers drivel about spinning protons. The instruments seem to follow irregular but mysteriously related orbits around an absent or invisible star. Then there's a moment of harmonic convergence, as they chime together in a glowing chord, which in turn unfurls a plane of marbled light, like sunrays streaking around the moon's circumference in the final minutes of an eclipse.

The title of the piece seems to indicate that Can knew they had confounded the laws of music as utterly as quantum theory undoes the regulations of Newton's clockwork universe. But chaos theory may be a better analogy. Chaos scientists devise non-linear equations in an attempt to map the behaviour of fluids or ultra-sensitive systems like the weather; they use computers to generate images of phenomena whose hidden order can only be perceived by imagining dimensions beyond the four that govern human reality, or even fractions of dimensions. These 'fractal' images, like the famous Mandelbrot Set, are exquisitely beautiful, kaleidoscopic mosaic shapes, offering an infinite variety of details within certain recurring patterns.

Can's music, at its furthest-out, seems to be held together by the musical equivalent of chaos's 'strange attrac-
tors': invisible pivots, located in poly-dimensional space
that organise chaotic phenomena. Can's grooves are 'basins
of attraction', from which the instruments can stray – but
never too far.

Can's later work is more accessible (not that there's anything unfriendly about far-out/far-in tracks like 'Quantum
Physics') and also more literally *affirmative*. Instead of simply creating a spellbinding vision of paradise regained as
they did in *Future Days* and *Babaluma*, they now spell out
their mystical leanings and longings. *Landed* (1975), their
last great album, reiterates the imagery and effects of its
immediate predecessors. 'Vernal Equinox', named after the
day that spring begins, is another Gaia symphony, while
'Red Hot Indians' is a tensile polyrhythmic shuffle that
Karoli calls 'the DNA song'. The lyrics refer to telepathy,
Krishna's cosmic dance, and a mystical materialism in
which everything is connected. The closing thirteen-
minute-long 'Unfinished' actually sounds like DNA soup:
it's a flux of unravelling forms that crystallise into fleeting
focus before dissolving again.

Can pinpointed their guiding principle with the title of
their next album, *Flow Motion* (1976). But by now their
music was relaxing rather than revelatory, less a case of
'only connect', and more of *go with the flow*. The dominant
mood was mellow, as in the easy-going affability of the title
track – leisurely oceanic-reggae, like a sea cow grazing off a
Caribbean coast, basking in the Gulf Stream. *Saw Delight*
(1977) offered more affirmation therapy in 'Don't Say No'.
Its jaunty, 'just let go' nonchalance jarred against punk's
unrest, while its title could almost have been a riposte to
1977's negativism. *Can* (1978) is the band's swan-song. 'All
Gates Open' could almost be Can's manifesto. Karoli's
every proposition is a restatement of psychedelic principles:

the need to abandon psychic defences and surrender to the wonder of the world; music as an allegory of the symbiotic symphony of Nature, a symphony that we all 'blend into'. Can were still singing the same song on their comeback album *Rite Time* (1989), in 'Like A New Child', a slow clockwork groove fringed with dawn-rising synths, over which Malcolm Mooney espouses newborn wonderment. For Can, it's New Year's Day all year long (as the Meat Puppets, another bunch of neo-psychedelic mystics, put it); the Rite Time is always NOW.

flux + mutability

Pantheistic and polymorphous, Can's music opposes barriers and boundaries (musical and generic, psychic and physical). At their peak, Can created the ultimate *anti-fascist* music: healing music that melts rigidities of body and mind, music that is in some sense 'feminine', despite the all-male personnel of the band. Can's music incarnates the notions of philosophers Gilles Deleuze and Felix Guattari – ideals like 'becoming-woman', 'becoming-child' and 'becoming-music'. In their worldview, it's the 'becoming' that is important – the crossing of boundaries, the process of metamorphosis and migration. Stasis is death; flux is life.

Two key terms in their anti-fascist manual, *A Thousand Plateaus: Capitalism and Schizophrenia* are 'arborescent' and 'rhizomatic'. Arborescent structures are tree-like, hierarchical chains of command. Rhizomatic structures are modelled on plants like ferns or weeds, which are connected laterally rather than vertically by a network of bulbs, tubers, stems, in which any point can be connected to any other. For Deleuze and Guattari, arborescent connotes the Law of the Father, the Super-Ego, the State, genitally-fixated adult sexuality, gender-fixed identity. Rhizomatic connotes pre-Oedipal bliss, the Id, anarchy, polymorphous infantile pleasure, androgyny.

Deleuze and Guattari claim that 'musical form, right down to its ruptures and proliferations, is comparable to a weed, a rhizome'; that thought, when truly freed, is not linear and methodical, but promiscuous, proceeding by intuitive leaps and bounds, associations, metaphor and metonymy. But some kinds of music are more rhizomatic than others: the entire project of post-Cage music, jazz improvisation and psychedelia, is to evade and erode the hierarchical narratives of Western music. Can's music fits the rhizomatic model perfectly.

Deleuze and Guattari suggest that 'the fabric of the rhizome is the conjunction, 'and... and... and...' (Can actually named one of their tracks '.........And More'.) Can's extended jam sessions anticipated the 'sampler-delic' aesthetic of today's rave music; techno DJs construct a kinetic cut'n'mix collage that's potentially infinite. Both Can and techno fit Deleuze and Guattari's notion of a 'desiring machine': 'a continuous, self-vibrating region of intensities whose development avoids any orientation towards a culmination point or external end'. In the essay 'How Do You Make Yourself a Body Without Organs?', Deleuze and Guattari connect this deferral of climax to the Zen practice of Tantric sex – the deliberate delaying of orgasm until the body becomes filled with vibrating, luminous energy. The Tantrics believed that this endless plateau of ecstasy was sexual union with the Great Mother Goddess, a kind of cosmic incest.

For Deleuze and Guattari, 'machine' is a neutral term; they resist the Luddite tendencies of Romanticism, with its nostalgia for pre-Industrial intimacy with nature. Instead, they see nature itself as operating like a machine – an attitude that Can shared. Czukay believed 'repetition is like a machine. . . . If you can get aware of the life of a machine then you are definitely a master. . . . [Machines] have a heart and soul – they are living beings'. In their greatest, most Gaia-worshipping music, Can created a vision of Mother Nature as a gigantic, impossibly complex machine, churning out beauty for the sheer splendour of it. We compared 'Quantum Physics' and 'Chain Reaction' to Stanislaw Lem's *Solaris*; this ocean planet is a vast 'plasmatic machine' that amuses itself by generating colossal phenomena midway between the sculptural and the meteorological. Manuel De Landa, a writer who attempts to build theoretical bridges between Deleuze and Guattari and chaos theory, believes that the frontier between order and chaos is where 'magic' happens. This would seem to be true in music, judging by the combination of groove and improvisation, repetition and randomness, in Can, Miles Davis, techno. It's when a (musical) system is 'poised at the edge of chaos', that the most interesting dynamics occur. De Landa argues that if your rules are too restrictive nothing interesting will happen, but if your rules are too loose, nothing interesting will happen either. De Landa also advocates the controlled use of psychedelic drugs as a way of 'liquefying' the mind, opening consciousness to the chaotic truth of nature, the cosmos, and our own bodies and minds. But, echoing Deleuze and Guattari, he warns of the danger of doing so too rapidly: transgressing all boundaries, releasing all brakes, can send the individual sliding into a black hole (fascism, drug addiction, terrorism – all desperate attempts to achieve utopia now).

Avant-garde music, from free jazz to noise rock, often approaches a kind of *aesthetic* 'fascism', with its fixation on extremities of human experience, its sadistic assault on the listener: it breaks too many barriers at once. Deleuze and Guattari believe that avant-garde artists tend to fixate too ferociously on 'the child, the mad, noise', resulting in 'a scribble effacing all lines'. They suggest that what's really crucial is the 'becoming-' prefix – the brink between maturity and innocence, sanity and delirium, melody and dissonance. Instead of the bombastic chaos of free jazz or extremist avant-garde noise, Deleuze and Guattari suggest that minimalism, an almost childish simplicity, is the best way to open up music to the cosmos (or 'chaosmos'). They cite Paul Klee in painting, and La Monte Young in music, as exemplary, but their maxim could equally apply to Can, Eno, the Aphex Twin. This is the psychedelic dream: 'the becoming-child of the musician... the becoming-cosmic of the child'.

another green world

Can were, if not the inventors, then the pre-eminent explorers of oceanic rock, an omni-genre in which psychedelia, funk, jazz improvisation, dub and ambient music meet up. Can's explorations were paralleled by late '60s/early '70s Miles Davis, and by Krautrock contemporaries like Faust, Neu, Amon Duul II, Cluster. Can's descendants include PiL, Talking Heads, A.R. Kane. But the most important figure they influenced – who took oceanic rock to the next stage – was Brian Eno.

Chromaticism, fuzziness and spatiality in music are associated with pre-Oedipal bliss, making a good case for Can as the ultimate *jouissance*-rock. Brian Eno's aesthetic is also based on a vivid palette of timbres and textures, combined with a sense of spatial dimension created in the studio. This combination of colour and space (what Eric Tamm calls 'vertical colour') is for Eno the most innovatory aspect of rock: chromaticism and 3D-spatiality cannot be notated on a conventional score, can only be gestured at by visual, tactile, even olfactory imagery. In his solo albums, Eno plays up these radical, untranscribable elements, gradually abandoning even rock'n'roll's most rudimentary narrative structures, eventually arriving at ambient music's placid, uneventful sound-paintings. Where Can privileged *flow motion*, finding a kind of grace in being captivated by rhythm, Eno's music equates the state of grace with stasis, repose.

In a sense, Eno was rebelling against rebellion. 'Critics can't stand these records,' he said, referring to the puzzled reception of his ambient albums, '. . . because in their search for eternal adolescence they still want it all to be spunky and manic. . . . I'm interested in the idea of feeling like a very young child, but I'm not interested in feeling like a teenager.' Renouncing rock's adolescent kicks and hormonally fuelled (ins)urgency, he looked to experiences and art that put him 'in the position of innocence, that recreate the feeling of innocence in you' – a feeling of blissful bafflement.

Eno's early solo albums are very much part of psychedelia's fall-out. On *Here Come the Warm Jets* (1973) and *Taking Tiger Mountain (by Strategy)* (1974), his persona lies somewhere between Syd Barrett and a crackpot inventor. In these quirked-out, whimsical songs, Eno follows psychedelia's impulse towards nursery rhyme nonsense. In 'Dead Finks Don't Talk', the protagonist suffers from a 'shaky sense of diction'. The lyrics were written using a 'system of syllable rhythm', with Eno making non-verbal sounds that went well with the music, then gradually shaping them into recognisable words. Influenced by automatic writing and the phonetic poetry of Dadaists Hugo Ball, Kurt Schwitters and Richard Huelsenbeck, Eno emphasised the musicality of utterance, rather than sense. With *Here Come the Warm Jets*, even the music was born of nonsense and babytalk: a non-musician, Eno told his instrumentalists what to play using non-verbal noises and body language.

Movement and motion gradually become less and less important in Eno's music. Even before the invention of ambience, Eno becomes fixated on imagery of immobility, indifference, a becalmed beatitude. In *Another Green World* (1975), there's the verdant quiescence of 'In Dark Trees', and 'Golden Hours', where the protagonist wonders how it can be that 'evenings go so slow'. As another day slides away imperceptibly, effete backing vocals seem to be either languishing or revelling in a terminal torpor. 'Becalmed' evokes a sombre serenity: a man waits on the beach for a woman. Although he doesn't know how long he's been waiting – hours, years – he's unconcerned, fatalistic. This is the amnesiac as a model for living.

Before and After Science (1977) is an entire album about treading water. 'Julie With. . .' returns to the 'Ancient Mariner' scenario of Pink Floyd's 'Echoes', its protagonist adrift on a still, empty sea. He and Julie stare into the sky, marvel at its fabulous blueness, and wonder if they've slipped outside time. The music anticipates ambient, all vaporous drones and watercolour washes of sound. Then there's the water-meadow listlessness of 'By This River', and 'Backwater', where a motley crew of castaways have drifted into the still waters at the very edge of time. Eno's limp character has abandoned 'ballistics' for resignation, and seems almost gleeful that there's 'not a sausage to do'. This imagery of unnaturally placid water anticipates the landlocked calm of 'Inland Sea' and 'Slow Water' from *Music for Films*: purely instrumental music, limpid and drained of dynamism.

gathering moss

Eno's characters in *Before and After Science* appear to have haemorrhaged all their willpower and are on the verge of melting into their surroundings. 'Here He Comes' concerns a boy who tries to vanish, floating through the sky to another time. In 'Spider and I', Eno sits with an arachnid, watching the sky and dreaming of being carried away in a ship. This idea of the proximity of boredom to bliss has persisted throughout Eno's work, right up to *Thursday Afternoon*. This 1985 album evoked the inertia of a nondescript weekday afternoon; Eno saw his subdued, contemplative music as a quiet revolt against the 'increasing hysteria and exoticism' of hyperactive '80s pop-videos, so crammed with events and surprises.

Inactivity as the road to nirvana was a psychedelic

touchstone. Eno shared hippie rock's pastoralism, its ecological slant (hence titles like *Another Green World*), and its passivity. Ambient music took psychedelia's torpid tendencies even further, aiming for a kind of vegetative bliss in which 'the body...is identical with environment' (as G. Roheim put it). Ambient's supine immobility infuriated many critics. Of *On Land*, Mark Peel sneered, 'I'll bet plants love it' – an insult that managed to combine the notion that plants respond well to music and that this was music to veg out to. *On Land* (1982) is the most radical of Eno's ambient records: it's all timbre and hardly any pit ches, and narrative development is suspended in favour of a fog of heavily treated instrumental sonorities and found sounds (including insect and animal noises).

Tracks like 'Lantern Marsh' and 'Unfamiliar Wind (Leeks Hill)' suggest terrain draped in mist, with unplaceable sounds reverberating from the distance. A 'landscape' is where a specific terrain seems to bleed into infinity, becomes 'cosmic'. In *The Poetics of Space*, Gaston Bachelard describes this sensation as 'intimate immensity': 'As soon as we become motionless, we are elsewhere; we are dreaming in a world that is immense.... The exterior spectacle helps intimate grandeur unfold.' Bachelard cites the experience of Philip Diole, a deep-sea diver and desert explorer who found a strange equivalence between these ostensibly incompatible expanses. Diole wrote that 'neither in the desert nor on the bottom of the sea does one's spirit remain sealed and indivisible'. Visitors to the parched wilderness of New Mexico and Arizona sometimes remark that far from being desolate and inhuman, the desert is 'just like heaven'.

From *On Land* to *Apollo: Atmospheres and Soundtracks* (which was composed to accompany a film about the moon landings), space is Eno's thing, as opposed to time. He's said that he prefers the Chinese, Zen-tinged idea of time; whereas Westerners face the future with anticipation/anxiety, the Chinese 'look at the past, and the future washes over them.... There's a kind of peacefulness in that attitude that I appreciate. You're standing in one place or treading water in one place, and meanwhile the drift of things is coming past you from behind.' Ambient tries to evoke the Eternal – hence Eno's increasing hostility towards speed and events. Renouncing rock's animal energy, Eno passed through an appreciation of the vegetable and then mineral kingdoms. He even used sticks and stones as musical instruments for *On Land*. French theorist Roger Caillois wrote a mystical appreciation of minerals, crystals and dendrites called 'Stones': in their dispassionate perfection, he glimpsed Eternity, 'the motionless matter of the longest quietude', an escape from the fidgety unrest of human desire. This is the ultimate destination of the quest for nirvana: the deathless grace of the inorganic. And Eno, a rebel against rebellion, completed rock's trajectory: from kicking up a noise to 'the most beautiful sound next to silence'; from rocking (your baby, the boat, the foundations of the law) to cradle-rocking lullabies and petrified passivity.

Eno's project is above all an *emasculation* of rock. The sexual politics of his music have not gone unnoticed. Stephen Demorest noted the way *Another Green World* avoided rock's 'tyrannically thrusting "grooves"'. Lester Bangs, prophet of punk, complained about the album's anaemic enervation: 'Those little pools of sound on the outskirts of silence. . . twilight music perfectly suited to the passivity Eno's approach cultivates'. Eno invented ambient because he wanted to do something that was 'extremely calm and delicate and [that] invites you in rather than pushes itself upon you'. An extremely sexual image, but appropriate – his solo music evolved from the strident 'idiot energy' of Roxy Music's art-rock, to an undulating expanse (the 'sea of seas' that possessed the Romantic imagination). Eno often professed his desire to avoid the bombastic self-expression and self-aggrandising passion that modernist art and rock shared, in favour of something closer to the (traditionally feminine) decorative arts. Ambient is musical decor, tinting the atmosphere, the fulfilment of Erik Satie's dream of a 'furniture music'. It is music of and for enclosed domestic spaces rather than rock's male-dominated streets, wombing rather than wild.

In fact, ambient was conceived by Eno during a period of enforced confinement, disability and dependency when he was hospitalised after being knocked over by a taxi. A friend brought him some eighteenth-century harp music. After she left, he put it on and lay down again, only to realise the stereo was set at an extremely low volume. But instead of struggling up again, he surrendered to a new way of listening. It was music at the threshold of perception, mingling with the sounds of the environment.

Eno had long been a gender tourist. Even before glam-rock stardom in Roxy Music, he'd worn effeminate, flamboyant clothing, and make-up. Asked about his gender politics, he once said: 'The Western version of masculinity opposes rational man against intuitive woman. The part of my being that interests me has always been my intuition.' For his solo albums, he devised techniques for removing his own will from the creative process, using chance and 'Oblique Strategies' (a set of cards with ambiguous advice that could be consulted, like the I Ching, at moments of impasse).

Eno's Gaia-worshipping tendencies flowered in his production of Talking Heads' *Remain In Light* (1980). This pinnacle of the Eno/David Byrne partnership was deeply indebted to Can's sensurround pan-global grooves. 'The Great Curve' linked the Earth's rotation to the swivelling of 'a woman's hips'. 'Once in a Lifetime' was brimming oceanic funk, the sound of Byrne's neurotic protagonist suddenly overwhelmed by the *satori* of here-and-now. In 'Crosseyed and Painless' and 'Houses in Motion', Byrne played the part of Western bourgeois man trapped in schedules and commodity fetishism, longing to get back in synch with natural rhythms. The West's ailment is an excess of yang (masculine reason): it can only learn how to 'stop making sense' by exploring the 'dark continent' (African rhythm, female intuition, yin). Eno is a consummate gender tourist. But the idea of the feminine that he's impelled towards is problematic for real women: passive, immobile, graceful; close to nature; skilled in the healing arts and decorative crafts; non-verbal; linked with childhood, dreamtime and Eternity. If the Rolling Stones' ideal for living was the black bluesman, Eno (always the Stones' antithesis) aspired to be. . . a Chinese peasant woman placidly tilling a paddy field. Getting in touch with his *anima* (Jung's female spirit) meant being inanimate, object-like. As the culmination of the psychedelic tradition, ambient music is about *escaping History*. But women have been excluded from History for so long that this state-of-grace hardly seems liberating.

amniotic asylum

If psychedelia is a culture of mother's boys, Brian Eno fits the mould perfectly. He's a classic 'soft male' who rejects rock's warrior ethos, and with ambient, he replaced desire with pleasure, disruptive noise with music-as-decor. Kevin Ayers and Robert Wyatt of the Soft Machine – who've both collaborated with Eno – are prime examples of this breed of self-indulgent sensualist who defined English art-rock eccentricity of the early '70s, that backwater of meandering experimentalism that followed the turbulent rapids of the late '60s. English psychedelia bred a particular kind of New Man, feminised but not necessarily feminist.

In *Rock Bottom* (1974), Robert Wyatt created one of rock's most astonishing and poignant visions of an undersea paradise. Like ambient, *Rock Bottom* was conceived in a hospital; an intoxicated Wyatt had tumbled from an upstairs window during a wild party at his home and broken his back. The album aches with the anguish of disablement (Wyatt has spent the rest of his life in a wheelchair), while its woozy, refractory sound simulates the effects of heavy anaesthetic. The title, *Rock Bottom*, plays both on the idea of reaching an emotional abyss, and some kind of escape to a subaquatic sanctuary (an environment where Wyatt's mobility and grace could be recovered, in the absence of gravity). The cover depicts a seascape in cross-section: Wyatt's head and torso bob above the surface and he holds a bunch of balloons in his hand, but under the surface we can see that he hasn't got any legs, just tentacles or fronds of seaweed.

The opening 'Sea Song' sees Wyatt serenading his mermaid lover. Their trysts take place with the rising of the full moon, its tidal pull impelling her blood to him: they are both moonstruck lunatics. Then Wyatt spirals up and off into tremulous, bubbling scat, a voluptuous agony of freeform vocal plasma midway between muezzin prayer wail and orgasmic shudders – a carnal polyphony that rivals Tim Buckley's *Starsailor*. In 'A Last Straw', the oceanfloor is 'a home from home'. The oozy, aqueous synths, refractory horns, and imagery of taking refuge inside the mammary gland suggest that the briny deep Wyatt describes is really the 'inner ocean' of the female body.

'Alifib' reaches the nadir of despair, vocally reduced to wracked, barely-there exhalations. This track and its sequel, 'Alife', are wordplays on his wife's name, Alfie: Wyatt, in his abject dependency, has regressed to the condition of a nursling at the breast. He calls her 'my larder': his neediness is oral, a craving for the limitless plenitude of the infantile phase. Sense degenerates into dribbled babytalk, as the music grows ever more sinister and miasmic. He's reached rock bottom, his lowest ebb, and a sax takes over, babbling free form primal scream therapy. But then a woman's voice speaks firmly: 'I'm not your larder'. It's Alfie, putting her foot down, and signalling Wyatt's re-emergence from the foetal position, his coming to terms.

Miles Davis's late '60s/early '70s music – a big influence on Wyatt and Eno – seethed with the dread and lure of oceanic feelings. One half of Davis's soul was pure *punk*: his rage against white society, his coke-fuelled arrogance, his misogyny. But the other half was pure psychedelia, full of mystical yearnings to be drowned in ego-dissolving immensity. *In A Silent Way* (1969) is idyllic: an indolently funky swirlpool of sound as warmly wombing as the Gulf Stream. Herbie Hancock's and Chick Corea's electric piano and keyboards conjure up a cosmic jacuzzi of spume and spindrift, anemone-intricate whorls. 'It's About That Time' makes you feel like a corpuscle in God's bloodstream. But *Bitches Brew* (1970) is far more ambivalent about immersion: it's a jazz-rock counterpart to the Sex Pistols' 'Submission'. The title draws a line connecting the primordial phobic image of the witches' cauldron, the blues tradition of she-devils and spell-binders, and the sticky secretions of the female body. But the real 'bitches brew' is the Id, that cauldron of daemonic drives. Fond of presenting himself as a sorcerer, a dark magus with voodoo powers, Davis is both tempted and terrified of skinny-dipping in this murky, viscid element. Davis surfs and scuba-nauts the raging ocean, flirting with death-by-drowning but evading its embrace.

Elsewhere in Davis's early '70s work, with the titles of the album *Pangaea* (1975) and the track 'Gondwana', he invokes the original supercontinents from which today's continents broke loose: the primordial motherland of all humanity. His music, a fissile tumult of jazz, rock, Eastern music and Stockhausen, is a quest for a 'One World' music. Miles's legacy resurfaced in late '80s rock with the black British duo A.R. Kane. On the 1988 EP *Up Home!*, 'Up' draws a line between Miles's motherland-fixations, George

Clinton's *Mothership Connection*, and Rastafarian reggae's Zion. The song imagines a mother and child ascending a crystal staircase to heaven, and boarding a Black Star Liner (a spaceship, obviously, but its name comes from Marcus Garvey's shipping company, whose ultimate purpose was to transport the victims of the black diaspora back to Africa).

Like Eno, A.R. Kane are non-musicians who use the studio, guitar effects, and dub reggae reverb to create shimmering simulacra of heaven-on-earth. Albums like *69* and *i* combine oceanic imagery ('Spermwhale Trip Over', 'The Sun Falls into the Sea') with pre-Oedipal oral fixations ('The Madonna Is With Child', 'Honeysuckleswallow'). 'Baby Milk Snatcher' is a veiled diatribe against Margaret Thatcher, a terrifying phallic mother who enshrined her aridity in national policy, endeavouring to wean the British population from the Big Mother of the welfare state (whose most famous symbol was free milk for schoolkids). But A.R. Kane's worship of maternity's endless nurture conceals something of a madonna/whore complex. Real women who fail to live up to their high expectations of femininity provoke venomous fury, even murderous fantasies ('Supervixens', 'Insect Love'). The source of this bitter rage is that the beloved's 'failure' to live up to the ideal is an echo, a re-enactment, of the original banishment from paradise.

soft boys:
nostalgia, incest and zen apathy

Eventually, every rebel needs to come home. Domesticity, once so alarming, starts to seem pretty cosy. The idea of woman as sanctuary, as a space where all the action *isn't* (thank God), recurs again and again throughout the late '60s, from the Doors' 'Soul Kitchen' (where Morrison the cosmic beatnik takes a break from breaking-on-through and seeks shelter in a woman's arms) to Love's 'Andmoreagain' (from *Forever Changes*, 1968). Here, Arthur Lee is ravished by a vision of the feminine ideal/idyll, a woman whose name suggests limitless succour. Worn out by the battle of life, lost in a cloud of 'confusions', he longs to shed his 'armour'. Andmoreagain can heal him, reconnect him to solid ground. A similar all-healing woman figures in the Beatles' 'She Said She Said' (*Revolver*, 1966) whose therapeutic powers of understanding are so great she makes the man feel like he's 'never been born': he's returned to the cocooning placidity of the womb.

Jimi Hendrix once said, 'If I'm free, it's cos I'm always running'. Domesticity was a fate to be dreaded: in the exhilarating 'Crosstown Traffic', he's running away from commitment so fast, he runs over his lover, leaves 'tire tracks' all over her back. Throughout Hendrix's work, there's a tension between the craving for unbounded freedom and for female salvation. While songs like 'Voodoo Chile' are grandiose celebrations of phallic potency, elsewhere Hendrix seems to regard masculinity as a state of incompleteness; in 'Stepping Stone' (1969), he sings of searching for this 'other half of me', the woman that will make him whole. A vision of perfect femininity appears before his eyes, an angel who offers him a h(e)aven on earth. In 'May This Be Love' (*Are You Experienced*, 1967), she's called Waterfall, and she makes his 'worries seem very small'. Love here is a secluded bower, with rainbows arcing through the misty spray from the waterfall. 'Little Wing' (from *Axis: Bold As Love* 1967) is a paean to a cloud-walking dreamer with a head full of fairy-tales, whose 'thousand smiles' chase away his blues. Throughout *Axis* and *Electric Ladyland* (1968) the dream woman reappears many times, in 'One Rainy Wish', 'You Got Me Floating', 'Bold As Love', 'Gypsy Eyes'.

On 1971's posthumous album *The Cry of Love*, Hendrix's worldweariness had deepened and his yearning for the ideal woman had blossomed into mysticism. In 'Angel', she descends from heaven and carries him off into the wild blue yonder, while in 'Driftin'', he's sailing across an ocean of 'forgotten teardrops' to her safe harbour. 'Belly Button Window' reinvokes the 'never been born' of the Beatles' 'She Said She Said': Hendrix is an unborn child hesitating to join the turbulent, strife-wracked world which he can see through the navel porthole, and wondering whether he's not better off inside where it's safe and warm. Most mystical of all is 'Hey Baby (The Land Of the New Rising Sun)', a song that was never properly recorded but was intended for a double album to be entitled *First Rays Of the New Rising Sun*. A female saviour arrives offering salvation not just for him but for the whole of humanity. Earlier, Hendrix had spoken of his fantasy of founding 'my own country, an oasis for all the gypsy-minded people', where wanderlust and stability, freedom and domesticity, would be magically reconciled. He dreamed of a world where he could be at home everywhere.

Hendrix was far from alone in feeling such insuperable fatigue: by 1969, many of the counterculture's free spirits were tired of the fast lane. In between the apocalyptic dread of 'Gimme Shelter' (*Let It Bleed*, 1969) and the world-and-roadweary decrepitude of *Exile on Main Street* (1972), the Rolling Stones recorded 'Moonlight Mile' (from 1970's *Sticky Fingers*), one of the most poignant coming-home songs ever. Amidst a silvered, enchanted soundscape that really does seem to be bathed in moonlight, Jagger plays the part of a fugitive or wanderer who's tired of freedom, tired of laying down to sleep with only 'strange, strange skies' for a roof. Nearly home but on his last legs, he longs to warm his bones by the hearth of his woman's love. This shift from woman-as-satisfaction to woman-as-shelter, from the lust for woman's sexual heat to the yearning for woman's consoling warmth, truly signalled the loss of '60s confidence.

Van Morrison often links coming home, spiritual serenity and water. From the slipstreams, viaducts and quenching springs of *Astral Weeks* to *Veedon Fleece*'s 'You Don't Pull No Punches, But You Don't Push the River', water is the very definition of the lost state of grace for Morrison. His search for redemption and a sense of belonging never entirely dispelled the feeling that to be born into this world is to be a fish out of water. Even late in his career, Morrison could record songs like 'Sometimes I Feel Like A Motherless Child' and albums like *Too Long in Exile*.

melancholy's desert island

Then there are those singers whose predicament is far more desolate. It's not just that they share Van Morrison's feelings of being a motherless child and are incapable of following E.M. Forster's dictum 'only connect'. They are, in fact, unable to take solace in oceanic feelings, can't conceive of an imaginary, consoling utopia where lack and loneliness is abolished.

This is the melancholic tradition in rock: castaways marooned on the desert island of individualism. Think of Scott Walker, whose songs are morbidly and brilliantly fixated around feelings of being orphaned and bereft, from his little-boy-lost image in the Walker Brothers to 'Boy Child', the last song on his last pre-retirement album *Scott IV* (1969). The 'Boy Child' is clearly Walker himself, a 'shadow of shadows' forever seeking an idealised, unobtainable Lady, the Mother-Lover who gives but doesn't take.

Think of David Sylvian, almost drowning himself and the listener in the voluptuous melancholy of his voice, forever shedding tears over 'the loss of heaven'. And think of Ian Curtis, stranded in the barren, icy hinterland of Joy Division's music. *Closer* (1980) is a requiem for the impossibility of closeness, proximity, intimacy: 'Isolation' takes as its title a word whose root meaning is *island*, while the ectoplasmic vapour-trails of 'The Eternal' suggests that Death was always destined to be Curtis's bride. (He committed suicide just before *Closer* was released.)

For Kristeva, melancholy is 'the most archaic expression of a non-symbolisable, unnameable narcissistic wound' – in other words, the loss of the mother. To this breed of self-obsessed melancholic, 'sadness is in reality the only object' – a phantasmic object that he cherishes. So think finally of Morrissey, who named himself 'sorrow's native son', and who, asked when he was happiest, replied 'May 21, 1959' – the day before the day he was born. Morrissey, 'castrated' by those invisible threads that attach him to his mother's apron, and thus incapable of any other attachments; Morrissey, with only misery for company, forever licking that 'unnameable narcissistic wound' in the wordless falsetto that climaxes his greatest songs. Morrissey has always insisted on the impossibility of the sexual relation, always argued that 'being only with yourself can be much more intense'. In 'I Am Hated for Loving' (from 1994's *Vauxhall and I*) he sang of still not feeling he belonged anywhere, or to anyone, and declared: 'I am mine'. His refusal of the old maxim that 'no man is an island' seems somehow intimately bound up with his cultural insularity, his belief in a bygone England of the early '60s, uncorrupted by foreign or futuristic influences.

In 1991, Morrissey admitted that he had tried Ecstasy, the 'hug drug' that promotes euphoria, empathy and tactile bonding. Perverse as ever, Morrissey took the drug *on his own*. He described it as the most amazing moment of his life: 'I looked in the mirror and saw someone who was extremely attractive.' The idea of Morrissey taking Ecstasy to bond more closely with himself conforms so closely to the profile of his pathology it's preposterous – beyond self-parody. But more perturbing is the fact that he restaged the primal scene that creates identity: the mirror phase, in which the infant recognises the existence of the Other (usually the Mother). Instead of the Other, Morrissey saw only himself, which is never enough. Failure to pass through the mirror phase properly leads to an inability to form object-relations. And for the melancholic, as we saw, there is no object, only an indefinable sense of lack.

Morrissey's fans have instinctively grasped the idea that their idol is starved of touch, that he never had the caresses that might make him feel *present*. Talking in 1992 about the phenomenon of his fans leaping onstage to kiss and clasp him, Morrissey cast his mind back to infancy. 'If, as a small child, you're in an environment where your own parents don't actually get on, you believe this is a microcosm of the rest of the world – that that is how life is. . . . Even if you can overcome it, it's very debilitating and it stays with you. . . . what happens if you never saw your parents kiss, or you never saw your parents hug each other?' When the interviewer, David Thomas, asks Morrissey whether he thinks he's giving his fans the hugs they don't get anywhere else, the singer retorts: 'I thought they were giving me the hugs that I didn't get anywhere else!' Thomas concedes that it's a mutually beneficial transaction between him and his fans, but even that's not enough for Morrissey's sense of pathos, and he quips, 'Yes, but my need's greater!'

mommy dearest

Morrissey is just one of a lineage of rock (anti-)heroes who allegedly had an unusually charged relationship with their mothers: Jimi Hendrix, Brian Jones, Syd Barrett, Sid Vicious. It seems significant that three of the most epoch-defining rock rebels of all time – Elvis Presley, John Lennon, and Johnny Rotten – had problematic relationships with their mothers (either too close or not close enough).

Lennon's first post-Beatles album, *John Lennon / Plastic Ono Band* (1970), begins with 'Mother', a bitter valediction to a dead mother who never wanted him (and a father who abandoned the family). At this point, John and Yoko were adepts of Dr Arthur Janov's primal scream therapy: in the song's slow fade coda, Lennon beseeches his departed mother and absent father with something midway between a chorus and a sob, a repeated, retching expectoration of rage and regret. (Such cathartic extremity of grief remains unrivalled, apart from John Lydon's muezzin-wail anguish in Public Image Limited's 'Death Disco', in which the ex-Pistol relived, Janov-style, the experience of watching his mother die.) Lennon's album ends as it begins, with the nursery-rhyme 'My Mummy's Dead', the singer still paralysed by a wound that can never be healed.

The original rock'n'roll mother's boy was, however, also the archetypal rebel: Elvis Presley. Elvis's vinyl baptism was a rendition of 'My Happiness', a mawkish 1948 ballad that he covered in Sam Philips's cut-your-own-record booth as a birthday present to mama Gladys Presley. In a 1992 essay in *The Wire*, Hopey Glass provides a revisionist analysis of Presley's 'dcbut'. 'Elvis's mother Gladys is as demonised a power-behind-the-throne as any in rock,' observes Glass, before arguing that this mother's ferocious love, far from retarding Presley's emotional development, was actually the secret source of his potency. 'Did she smother him, leaving him ruinously in emotional hock to her ghost his whole life long, or wasn't it more that her encouragement – her commitment to persuading him that he wasn't just trash – propelled him up and out of his dirt-poor roots?' It was Gladys, a smart woman who had revolted against her respectable background by marrying the sexy ne'er-do-well Vernon, who taught Elvis to be a rebel. And it was only after her death in 1958 that Presley fell under the malign sway of manager Colonel Parker, a truly domineering and manipulative figure who 'castrated' him by diverting his career into MOR.

incesticide

'Incest is, like many other incorrect things, a very poetical circumstance.'
Percy Bysshe Shelley

At its very core, is the meaning of rock *incest*? An incest that is at first renounced, in rebellion's violent gestures of severance and breaking free, but that later reappears as the rebel's ultimate destination. Those 'semiotic' aspects of poetic language that connote the pre-Oedipal – rhythm, intonation, the voluptuousness of utterance – are all intrinsic to rock'n'roll. Throughout its history, rock has oscillated between intelligibility and incoherent excess, between meaning and musicality. After the plainspeaking clarity of '70s singer-songwriters, punk re-asserted the primacy of clamour over coherence. In the '80s, rap revelled in the slurriness of slang; then, as it got more didactic, diction overruled rhythm.

Sonically, rock has spanned a wide spectrum from clarity to fuzziness, Apollonian definition of form to Dionysian chaos. The leading edge in rock has been those bands that have intensified semiotic elements (chromaticism, noise) at the expense of structure (the verse/chorus/middle eight narrative, the 'proper' ranking of instruments in the mix, which usually favours the voice and the lyrics). In fact, the emotionally regressive (that's to say, womb-fixated) seems to go hand in hand with formal progression: both share an impulse to transgress and transcend established limits. In this, rock has imitated the trajectory of modern art, starting with Impressionism, progressing through a succession of assaults on figure and form, culminating in Abstract Expressionism.

Music is better equipped to express these incestuous intensities than art: painters endeavour to abolish the distance that intervenes between the canvas and the contemplative eye, to exceed the frame, but music's defining quality is that it abolishes distance and has no frame. Rock's premium on volume (decibels and cubic) takes music's ability to drown the listener to the limit. It replaces the intermediary with immediacy, interpretation with impact.

Another quality that makes music the supreme art form for expressing regressive, incestuous longings is its ability to induce synaesthesia (confusion of the senses). According to Diane Ackerman, the infant's world is purely synaesthetic: 'Newborns ride on intermingling waves of sight, sound, touch, taste and especially smell.' Just as the infant's visual world is chromatic chaos because eyesight only gradually develops the ability to fix on objects, the baby also has to learn to distinguish between sensory stimuli. Daphne and Charles Maurer claim, in *The World of the Newborn*, that the infant 'hears odors, and sees odors, and feels them too. . . . If we could visit the newborn's world, we would think ourselves inside a hallucinogenic perfumery.'

Late Romantic writers like Baudelaire and Huysmans were obsessed with synaesthesia. Psychedelic music simulates the synaesthetic effects of drugs like LSD: it fills the mind's eye with fantastical, convoluted imagery and kaleidoscopic hues, or caresses the listener's flesh with tactile sensations. Smell is one sense that is seldom invoked, perhaps because the world of odour is as intractable and ineffable as music itself. Nonetheless, in many ways, music has more in common with fragrance than anything else – in its ability to permeate an environment, to pervade and invade the listener's body against his or her will, to reawaken memories. Smell returns us to the pre-Oedipal universe of intimacy and utter proximity, before the infant is able to distinguish between itself and its mother.

Brian Eno uses this link between smell and an inability to *differentiate* to explain his fascination with perfumes: '[It] has a lot to do with this process of courting the edges of unrecognisability, of evoking sensations that don't have names, or of mixing up sensations that don't belong together. . . . You don't have to dabble for very long to begin to realise that the world of smell has no reliable maps, no single language. . . within which we might comprehend it and navigate our way around it.'

Eno compares his own failed attempt to devise a spectrum of smells with the way that the radical, chromatic elements in rock cannot be captured in the language of classical composition: the texture of Jimi Hendrix's guitar sound can't be rendered on a score. Rock works with 'a potentially infinite sonic palette, a palette whose gradations and combinations would never adequately be described, and where the attempt at description must always lag behind the infinities of permutation.' Eno has pursued his obsession with perfume to the point of making his own fragrances, rather like the decadent aristocrat Des Esseintes in Huysmans' novel *Against Nature*, who composes symphonies of scents. Ambient is music as aromatherapy, infusing the home like incense. In fact, Eno's most recent ambient LP is named after an aphrodisiac scent: *Neroli*.

Perhaps the ultimate exponents of music as 'perfumed fog' and as aphrodisiac are My Bloody Valentine (MBV). It's no coincidence that MBV are one of the few contemporary rock bands to impress Eno (he praised their single 'Soon' as 'the vaguest piece of music' ever to be a near-hit in the UK). MBV bridge the gap between acid rock (they've worked with Roger Mayer, maker of effects-pedals for Jimi Hendrix) and ambient. Influenced by the Velvet Underground/Jesus and Mary Chain wall-of-noise school, My Bloody Valentine take rock's form-dissolving impulse to its outermost limit. Their great innovation, 'glide guitar', is a self-devised technique that uses the guitar's tremelo arm to unleash a droning swarm of distortion. In MBV's music, the riff – rock's staccato, thrusting principle – haemorrhages: the riff/phallus fuses with noise/vagina in an undifferentiated blur of lava love.

Loveless, the 1991 sequel to their breakthrough album *Isn't Anything*, is the band's most extreme record. Throughout *Loveless*, you can sense a scarcely imaginable infrarock coming through their songs like a flame burning through a sheet of paper. It's like the music is about to metamorphosise to a higher state that the band themselves can't quite foresee. 'Loomer' isn't rock so much as *magma*, barely conforming to the contours of riff or powerchord. 'To Here Knows When', too, hardly qualifies as rock: the rhythm section is a dim, suppressed rumble, there's no riff or chord-sequence, just billowing parabolas of unfocused sound and a tantalising Erik Satie-ish melody that fades in and out of earshot. 'To Here Knows When' is MBV's most suicidal song – commercially, for sure (absurdly, it was released as a single), but also in the sense that the group as human entities are dissipated. As in abstract expressionism, the figure is obliterated.

MBV draw on the disorientating qualities of dance music production – the way hip hop, house and techno interfere with the ranking of sounds in the mix, allowing sounds to behave uncannily, psychedelically. On *Loveless*, they go beyond the ethereality of 'glide guitar' into full-blown alchemy (sampling their own feedback and playing it on a keyboard, so that there's even less sense that what you hear was generated by physical acts and fleshly creatures). And they abandon the naturalistic perspective of conventional rock production, which simulates the presence of a live band – bass here, guitar there, voice up front, the listener mastering the field of hearing. Instead, MBV are here there everywhere; their noise permeates, irradiates, and consumes you.

Consume is the word. On *Isn't Anything*, 'Feed Me With Your Kiss' reinvoked the Romantic poets' imagery of sexual vampirism, the regressive craving to devour and be devoured. It recalled Swinburne's 'Anactoria', with its imagery of 'amorous agonies' and of eating the beloved's body so that it is 'abolished and consumed'. MBV's music bridges the gap between the Romantic obsession with swooning and Zen's ecstasy-inducing breath-control techniques. MBV's guitar drone-swarm mingles with hyperventilating harmonies (male and female) that make the Valentines sound like they're expiring from love.

Sometimes, it's just too much; the Ecstasy-blitzed 'Blown A Wish' is like staring into the eyes of a lover whose pupils are so dilated they're like black holes pulling you to your doom. The jagged, aggressive edges of *Isn't Anything* are, on *Loveless*, smothered in soft-focus miasma; bliss turns entropic, suffocating. But that's the fascination: you're subsumed in a primal 'we' that has you gasping for air, aching for open space. MBV songs are tantric mantras (tantra being Zen sex magick, intercourse sustained at the brink of climax until a hallucinatory trance is induced), suffused with an apocalyptic, pre-orgasmic glow. This music is a smelting crucible of love in which every borderline and boundary (inside/outside, you/me, lover/beloved) is abolished. It's an incestuous inferno, a heavenly hell.

androgyny in the uk

My Bloody Valentine's 'presence', as ghostly and indistinct as it is, is definitely androgynous: it's hard to distinguish which songs are sung by Bilinda Butcher or Kevin Shields. But MBV's androgyny is radically different from the glam gender-bending of, say, the New York Dolls, Bowie, Manic Street Preachers or Suede – all of which attempted to appropriate feminine 'privileges' of narcissism and self-adornment while marginalising women as subject matter of, and subjects within, rock'n'roll. For all the *frisson* of their homoerotic lyrics, Suede's line-up restates the classic four-man composition of the rebel rock band, while Manic Street Preachers explicitly defined themselves against the MBV-like dreampop groups (who were notable for their routine integration of female musicians). In this light, the Manics' T-shirt slogan 'All Rock'n'Roll is Homosexual' really seems to be saying: 'Girls, keep out!'

By comparison, My Bloody Valentine's line-up is arguably a microcosm of a sexual utopia. While the drummer Colm O'Ciosig seems like a regular guy, the rest of the band runs the gamut of the sexual spectrum. Bassist Debbie Goodge plays the part of the tough woman or rock tomboy; her playing is the most aggressive element in MBV's sound. Singer and second guitarist Bilinda Butcher is more conventionally feminine, delicate and ethereal. Kevin Shields oscillates between dulcet-voiced androgyne and technology-obsessed boffin, a scientist probing the outer limits of sound.

But MBV's androgyny runs deeper than the internal sexual dynamics of the band. Bypassing the thrust and grind of phallic rock, MBV's music is the seething, smouldering incarnation of what Deleuze and Guattari call the 'Body without Organs' (BwO). The BwO is an ungendered flux of intensities, 'waves and vibrations' of pleasure and energy; its desire has no goal, target or object, just *buzzes*, intransitively. Deleuze and Guattari's notion owes something to Zen's 'Uncarved Block', a state of potency synonymous with infancy (when, psychoanalysis tells us, the child is androgynous). The Block is uncarved because it precedes contour, differentiation and (sexual) identity; it can only be recovered by learning 'the lesson of flowing'. Both neo-Freudian theorist Norman O. Brown and Jungian psychohistorian June Singer identify a longing to return to this androgynous un-body in a number of mystical creeds (Gnostics, Taoists, alchemy). These anarcho-mystics believed that, in heaven, we would be reborn as androgynes.

militant v. dormant

Thinkers who have sought to analyse and challenge the male/female dialectic underlying Western culture have often resorted to tabulating binary oppositions such as:

Male	*vs.*	*Female*
Mind	vs.	Body
Culture	vs.	Nature
Activity	vs.	Passivity
Intellect	vs.	Sentiment
History	vs.	Eternity

We could draw up our own little rock chart to compare and contrast, within a single gender, the attributes assigned to the Rebel Male and the Mother's Boy:

Rebel Male	*vs.*	*Mother's Boy / Soft male*
Erect	vs.	Limp
Tunnel Vision	vs.	Soft-focus, visionary
Amphetamine	vs.	Hallucinogens, marijuana, Ecstasy
Defined	vs.	Blurry
Manifesto	vs.	Mumbling
The open road	vs.	Sanctuary
Urban	vs.	Pastoral
Proto-fascist	vs.	Zen apathy
Combat rock	vs.	Slacker

The opposition between the combat rocker and the slacker, between warrior male and soft male, is the most polarised example of the split in rock between the Rebel and the Mother's Boy. Theweleit's *Male Fantasies* showed how Germany's professional soldiers feared the end of war: demobilisation felt like a fall into torpor and bourgeois mediocrity. For these proto-fascists, 'anything that is soft, pleasurable, or relaxing must be combated.... Relaxation seems tantamount to capitulation. To abandon the struggle is to risk "suffocation" – a feeling that comes from within.' At similarly *slack* moments in rock history, critics and bands have complained about the lack of antagonistic energy. In the early '70s, punk prophet Lester Bangs railed against 'sensitive' soft-rock singer-songwriters like James Taylor, while celebrating the insurgent 'raw power' of the Stooges; throughout the '80s, *NME* writer Steven Wells carried the banner for agit-pop (the Redskins, Chumbawumba) and poured scorn on 'miserabilists' like Morrissey; in the '90s, a new wave of militant bands (Consolidated, Rage Against the Machine) defined themselves against the 'Zen apathy' of the post-MBV dreampop bands and American slackers like Pavement and Mercury Rev. The subtext of all these calls for mobilisation is simple: rock had gotten too *girly*, too detumescent.

In the late '80s/early '90s, the polarisation increased to the point where everything interesting in rock happened at the extremes: rectitude *or* lassitude, hyper-motivation (Public Enemy, Henry Rollins) *or* complete unmotivation (Dinosaur Jr, PM Dawn), the fanatic's wired clarity of vision *or* the mystic and the mixed-up's dazed haze. The rant *or* the murmur.

One of the crucial differences that defines this split – militant v. dormant – is the question of sleep. If, as Norman O. Brown argues, 'sleep is uterine regression', then you might expect combat rock to resist such a sweet surrender of consciousness. Agit-punk guerrillas Nation of Ulysses make resisting 'sleep's supplicating arms' a central

plank of their *13-Point Program To Destroy America* (1991).
'Sleep is a coma, a death-like state, which people pull will-
ingly over themselves like a blanket', they declare in the
LP's sleevenote manifesto, before vowing: 'While society
sleeps, bound to this archaic ritual, we shall take over. . .'
Metallica, a band whose songs are riddled with militaristic imagery, recorded a song called 'Enter Sandman' (from
Metallica, 1991) which is all about the dread of sleep. In
the video, a small boy (so often, the archetypal metal protagonist) is terrified of taking his nightly plunge into the
dark waters of the unconscious, where he's plagued by
nightmares. The genre that Metallica pioneered, thrash
metal, is afflicted by 'alertia' (as Jon Selzer coined it) – a
condition of morbid wakefulness, and the antithesis of
oceanic rock's inertia. Stop-start tempo changes forestall
the bliss of forgetfulness in favour of the on-edge vigilance
of the survivalist; staccato riffs chop up the musical flow.

The bastard son of punk and metal, thrash is the ultimate anti-psychedelic music. Where the hippies were
pacifists, thrash metal is warlike music (even when they're
making war *against* war!). Where the non-combatants of
psychedelia believed in mellowing out in the countryside,
thrash is the music of technological overkill. Where Van
Morrison dreamt of laying down in the 'silence easy' of a
newfound Eden, thrash would find the peace and quiet
unsettling. Thrash would *make some fuckin' noise*, detonate
a homemade bomb, drive its Harley Davidson through the
bluebell knoll. Like the Futurists, testosterone would impel
these overgrown teen delinquents to desecrate 'the holy
green silence', deface the 'ineffable landscape' of the
Romantic imagination.

Another way of conceptualising the militant/dormant,
Rebel/Mother's Boy dichotomy is to see it in terms of the
work ethic v. the play(boy) ethos. For some, rock is a form
of muscular toil, hard physical labour. And then are those –
often decried as self-indulgent dilettantes – for whom rock

is play, a chance to make a mess. Psychedelia involved a shedding, on the part of young males, of the emotional armour that working life demanded. If these boys were to fight in Vietnam, they needed to be toughened up even more. Hippies embraced indolence and effeminacy as a way of declaring themselves unfit (and unwilling) to participate in a culture that on the one hand led to stress-induced heart attacks and on the other to an early grave in South-East Asia.

Laziness was subversive in the (idle) hands of the counterculture; work was to be replaced by 'play power'. The Soft Machine are classic examples of late '60s layabouts. Products of the permissive Simon Langton School in Canterbury (favoured by local artists and intellectuals), the Soft Machine bummed their way through the South of France and the Mediterranean. They celebrated and mocked their own ne'er-do-well lethargy in songs like 'Why Are We Sleeping?' and 'As Long As He Lies Perfectly Still'.

As solo artists, Kevin Ayers and Robert Wyatt continued to play the role of effete dandies. Ayers called one of his backing bands the Soporifics and wrote songs like 'Butterfly Dance' in which he declared that 'everything is play'. In 'Diminished But Not Finished', he renounces all ideologies in favour of an agnostic self-indulgence. His whole oeuvre is bathed in a sun-kissed insouciance; it seems to take place, as Dave Maready put it, in 'an endless summer on someone else's money circa 1970'. The pinnacle of his hermetic hedonism is 'Song From the Bottom Of a Well': for Ayers, the universe is just 'a comfortable bath'. He happily drowns himself in the womblike well, laughing at a world whose toil and turmoil seems absurd. Robert Wyatt's solo albums also courted infantile regression. But even after his conversion to militant Communism, Wyatt could still confess, 'I've always been one to shirk responsibilities if there was an opportunity' and 'my ideal state of life would be one of total inactivity. . . . I don't approve of these people charging about all the time'.

Another 'decadent' of the post-hippie era is Brian Eno, with his playful attitude to music-making, his solo albums with their cast of washed-up idlers, and his refusal of rock's delinquent/warrior postures. There's an invisible line that connects Ayers/Wyatt/Eno to the drowsy dreampop groups of the late '80s (MBV, A.R. Kane, whose 'The Madonna Is With Child' sees the protagonist wail to his mama that she promised they were gonna 'sleep forever') and beyond to the slacker groups of the '90s.

Then there's the glam-rock tradition that links Marc Bolan to stay-at-home Morrissey to Brett Anderson, fey and foppish singer of Suede. Speaking of the band's debut single 'The Drowners' (1992), with its languorous, swoony longing to be ravished and engulfed, Anderson declared: 'I'm interested in lying back and taking it. . . relinquishing control. And that's traditionally a female thing, isn't it?' Advocates of Anderson's brand of gender bending see it as a brave and valid attempt by men to rebel against masculinity, a gender fix that oppresses them as much as it does women. Suzanne Moore, however, has argued that male 'gender tourists' are merely (ab)using the male privilege to dabble in the 'Other'; they try on 'optional feminine subjectivities' for size, while evading the less desirable aspects of female existence that are not so easy to divest if you're a real woman.

What to make of the mother's boy? Is he truly androgynous? Are his passivity, his apparent acceptance and affirmation of castration, his womb-nostalgia, the marks of a female-identified masculinity, or has the 'soft male' simply taken the soft option? Are these dandies, slackers, playboys and would-be playthings merely a partial, unfulfilled version of what a true New Man should be? Above all, amongst all the 'Boys Keep Swinging' fun'n'games, the feminisation and effeminacy, where do women fit in?

lift up your skirt and speak

double allegiances:
the herstory of rock

Turning our attention from what rock'n'roll has made of women to what women have made of rock, it's immediately apparent that, whereas the prototypes and precursors of male rock rebellion are easy to locate, the ancestors for female rock rebellion are rather more elusive. Instead of clearly defined trajectories (e.g. the beats/Jim Morrison/ Iggy Pop/Nick Cave lineage), female rebellion is a kind of subterranean river that wells up unexpectedly from time to time, seemingly out of nowhere, then disappears below the surface again. Despite the recurrent media crazes for 'women in rock', the position of female artists has always been as precarious as in male-dominated movements like Surrealism, the beats, and the counterculture.

Jack Kerouac's *On the Road* wasn't just the Bible of the beats, but a founding text for the first wave of rock rebels. Women's position in the beat movement is captured in the title of a memoir by Joyce Johnson, briefly married to Kerouac: *Minor Characters*. In it, Johnson is herself an aspiring writer who longs to participate in Kerouac's wanderings. When she asked him why she couldn't join him on the road, Kerouac would always 'stop me by saying that what I really wanted were babies. That's what all women wanted and what I wanted too, even though I said I didn't.' Women were marginal yet indispensable to the beats, providing safe harbour, nurture and nourishment; beats were 'real men', it was often said, because they got women to bankroll their lazy lifestyle, rather than the usual vice versa. In *Off the Road*, Carolyn Cassady remembers her life with Neal Cassady; unlike Kerouac and Cassady's adventures in the great wide open, and their exuberant abandon, Carolyn's tale is of claustrophobia and abandonment. In one passage, she's been left alone with their child after Cassady's set off on another escapade with Kerouac. She dreams, sadly, of how, without the baby, 'I'd have been free. . . '

This idea of woman's proper role as home-maker/stay-at-home was further enshrined in the '60s counterculture, despite its assault on bourgeois conventionality. So the namesake heroine of the classic hippie movie *Alice's Restaurant* isn't an Alice In Wonderland-style psychedelic explorer, but a den-mother whose tender loving care and culinary labour sustains the commune. While her roustabout husband (who dreamed up the groovy idea of communal living in a church) gets drunk, and the wandering minstrel Arlo Guthrie comes and goes, Alice provides the fulcrum of stability for others' adventures. At one point in the movie, when she hears the refrain 'Alice'll cook us all something to eat' one time too many, she too runs away from home, telling Guthrie: 'I guess I'm the bitch that had too many pups. Couldn't take them all milking me.'

Such 'house mothers' really existed (Alice was based on a real person). The Jefferson Airplane's communal household on Fulton Street in San Francisco was maintained by a young woman called Sally Mann who provided cooking, cleaning and general nurturing. In return, 'she is paid nothing except the gratitude of the Airplane,' wrote *Rolling Stone* at the time. The great acid rock nomad Jimi Hendrix himself relied on the services of 'temporary wives'. He said: 'I only remember a city by its chicks. They take you around, they wash your socks, and try to make you feel nice when you're in town.' The den-mother tradition continues to this day in the Los Angeles metal scene, as documented in the Penelope Spheeris movie *The Decline of Western Civilization II*, where girls are still taking care of struggling bands, washing their clothes, driving them around, subsidising their drug habits. Some Guns N'Roses wannabes keep filofaxes full of phone numbers of girls at whose apartments they can crash, and go so far as to list the services available: which one has a car, which one has cable TV. The spirit of Kerouac and Cassady lives and breathes, eh?

The *Rolling Stone* profile of Sally Mann appeared in a 1969 issue devoted to groupies. Being a groupie was and is, of course, one way for women to get close to the action. The *Rolling Stone* special includes under the groupie rubric not just girls who specialised in sleeping with rock stars but also a number of clothing designers, photographers, rock writers, and other creative women. Despite the 'legitimate' nature of their contributions to the scene, these women are somehow deemed ancillary, hangers-on enjoying glory by association.

For the most part, women's medium for rebellion was limited, in the counterculture, to sexuality. Frank Zappa celebrated groupies as Freedom Fighters of the Sexual Revolution: 'It's good for the girls. Eventually most of them are going to get married to regular workers, office workers, factory workers, just regular guys. These guys are lucky to be getting girls. . . who have attained some level of sexual adventurousness. It's good for the whole country. These guys will be happier, they'll do their jobs better. . . .' In reality, we suspect that many groupies were frustrated artists themselves, just looking for any connection to the creative excitement. 'Really being a groupie is like borrowing a series of lives from people and thinking you can be them,' an 'anonymous groupie' told *Rolling Stone*. 'It's not something you can *do*. That's why groupie chicks are so miserable. It's a constant frustration, the groupie scene.' The motto for these 'sexually liberated' rock chicks might have been: if you can't beat 'em, fuck 'em.

Given the choices offered by rock culture – desexualised mother-figure or wild-and-free but wholly sexual libertine – it's hardly surprising that the early she-rebels of rock'n'roll had a conflicted relationship with femininity. Looking at

1) can-do
2) "feminine" rock   double allegiances   **233**
3) masked 4) anti-identity
     clichés

the scattered history of female rock rebellion, we can distinguish four strategies (although when it comes to the careers of specific artists, these strategies often overlap). The first is a straightforward can do approach, as in 'anything a man can do, a woman can do too'. This tradition runs from Suzi Quatro through Joan Jett to L7: hard-rock, punky attitude, women impersonating the toughness, independence and irreverence of the male rebel posture. These women 'succeed' to the extent to which they suppress any 'girly' tendencies. The tomboy approach seems unsatisfactory, however; it simply emulates male rebellion, including its significant component of misogyny, implicit in the stance of someone like Joan Jett, who wants to be one of the boys, accepted into the gang.

Another approach attempts to infuse rock with 'feminine' qualities; rather than imitate men, it tries to imagine a female strength that's different but equivalent. Examples include the passion and torment of Janis Joplin and Lydia Lunch, the dignity and social concern of Tracy Chapman and Natalie Merchant of 10,000 Maniacs, the defiant autonomy and political outspokenness of Sinead O'Connor and Queen Latifah. This affirmation of 'feminine' qualities consolidates female identity against the attacks of both straight society and rebel counterculture. But, even as it valorises the 'feminine', it runs the risk of confirming patriarchal notions of what femininity is (emotional, vulnerable, caring, maternal, etc.).

A related strategy celebrates female imagery and iconography, but in a more provisional, postmodern way. Femininity is not a fixed set of characteristics for these artists, but rather a wardrobe of masks and poses to be assumed. So figures like Kate Bush, Madonna, Siouxsie Sioux and Annie Lennox shift between a series of female archetypes in a strategy of investment and divestment: using clichés without being reduced to them (or so the argument runs). This 'dressing up' approach ransacks history and mythology for provisional identities that can be used as weapons; women turn stereotypes against the society that created them. Critics of this strategy would say that it also invites misunderstanding and condemns the practitioner to the 'inauthenticity' of masquerade, living life as a constant performance.

Finally, there is an aesthetic that concerns itself not with the consolidation of female subjectivity, but with the trauma of identity formation. Here, female gender is neither an essence nor a strategic series of personae, but a painful tension between the two. To be a woman is to be torn between the fact of biology and the fiction of femininity. This tension reflects the unresolvability of the nature v. culture debate. In rock, explorers of the agony and ecstasy of living with contradiction and irresolution include Patti Smith, Rickie Lee Jones, Throwing Muses, Mary Margaret O'Hara. These 'all fluxed up' singers are rebelling against identity itself, and so this is perhaps the most radical (but also most dangerous and self-confounding) form of female rebellion. It means a life based not around identity but *process*; at times blissfully liberating, this approach also works against effectiveness and action in a world that relies on stable identities and clearly articulated statements.

Of course, none of these women are cardboard cutouts, and many have straddled or shifted between categories at one point or another. Patti Smith started out as a 'tomboy' but eventually embraced a mystical exaltation of the 'feminine'; many of the 'living in flux' women also play with sexual personae, bridging the gap between decentred identity and the *strategic* schizophrenia of masquerade. When it comes to 'women in rock' nothing is very clear; confusion breeds confusion.

Looking at the work of female surrealists in *Subversive Intent: Gender, Politics, and the Avant-Garde*, Susan Rubin Suleiman focuses on the problems they had in inventing a set of their own images 'different from the image of the exposed female body, yet as empowering as that image is'. For women in rock, the equivalent problem is the need to find subjects that lend themselves to rock'n'roll treatment (with its premium on passion, confrontation, urgency and extremity of expression); subjects outside the old rock rebel narrative that has hitherto condemned women to marginal roles (as passengers on a motorbike, as the sanctuary at the end of the hero's odyssey, as the object of desire or dread). And female rockers are discovering that they have their own turmoil, their own demons, even their own version of the Dionysian fire.

These women have a complicated relationship to the canon of rock rebellion, similar to the 'double allegiance' that Suleiman detects in the work of experimental women artists: 'on the one hand, [allegiance] to the formal experiments and some of the cultural aspirations of the historical male avant-garde; on the other hand, to the feminist critique of dominant sexual ideologies, including those of the very same avant-gardes. . . .' A figure like Courtney Love can, therefore, admit that her band Hole were heavily influenced by the hardcore band Big Black, while dedicating herself to destroying the hardcore scene's machismo and misogyny that Big Black so epitomised. The question is whether it's possible to rival male rock's extremity of expression, while severing the music from the anti-woman impetus that so often underwrites its force.

one of the boys:
female machisma

'I just think I identify more with male musicians than female musicians because I tend to think of female musicians as. . . ah. . . females.'
Kate Bush, 1978

There's a terrible poignancy to Bush's tautological stumblings. The pioneers of female expression in rock, those who we now look back on as heroic precursors to today's female artists – Bush, Patti Smith, Chrissie Hynde – were venturing into uncharted territory, and pretty much the only models available to them were male. To make an impression at all, they had to imitate male rebels and define themselves against the 'limitations' of femininity.

When she was growing up, Patti Smith was shot by both sides in the cross-fire between traditional patriarchy and the male rebel tradition. She didn't want be 'daddy's little girl' – but the alternative was the misogyny of the Rolling Stones. She threw her lot in with the latter ('this was no mama's boy music. . . . Blind love for my father was the first thing I sacrificed to Mick Jagger'), but women's position in the scheme of '60s rebel rock was shaky at best. In bohemian culture, the 'feminine' signified domesticity, conformism, or an ideal of sanctuary and succour. For the most part, women's choices were limited to mistress or muse. Little wonder, then, given the Hobson's choice between different forms of subordination, that 'ever since I felt the need to choose, I'd choose male'.

Like other rebellious girls before and since, Smith was a tomboy. In a 1993 essay in *Details*, she remembered, 'All

mistress or muse?

through childhood I resisted the role of a confused skirt tagging the hero. Instead I was searching for someone crossing the gender boundaries, someone both to be and to be with. I never wanted to be Wendy – I was more like Peter Pan.' She wore pants instead of '50s frilly crinolines, hated using the ladies' room, tried to expunge every feminine mannerism that she'd acquired from her mother. In her search for heroes, she fastened on a handful of extraordinary women – Madame Curie, Joan of Arc, Audrey Hepburn. But most of her role models were male: Arthur Rimbaud, Brian Jones, John Coltrane, Keith Richards (she imitated his haircut), and above all Bob Dylan (she dressed like him, walked like him, copied his cool).

Like so many women who want to be where the countercultural action is, Smith at first could only imagine getting there via her sexuality. When she looked at the art world, the only women in the frame were models and lovers, and at one point she decided to become an artist's muse – as if she could see no way around Robert Graves's declaration, in *The White Goddess*, that 'Woman is not a poet; she is either a Muse or she is nothing'. In her early days as a struggling poet and musician, she did try being an artist's moll, supportive and nurturing. Of her relationship with Allen Lanier of Blue Oyster Cult, she recalled, in 1975, that 'I was really trying to be a woman for this guy.... You know, I always wanted to really learn about being a woman; because I never really considered the female within me.' At a 1977 Hammersmith Odeon show, she yelled out 'I'm a genuine starfucker! I ain't never gotta sell out because my old man is Allen Lanier and he makes the bread in our house!' Despite all this, despite the fact almost all of her influences and heroes were male, Patti Smith eventually formulated a feminised version of living-on-the-edge rock'n'roll with her freeform 'Babelogues' and her vision of herself as a female Messiah (more on this later). Eventually she seems to have buckled under the pressure of sustaining this androgynous persona, and hurtled to the opposite extreme, throwing herself wholeheartedly into motherhood and domesticity. Chrissie Hynde also grew up as an admirer of the male rebel tradition, and, not surprisingly, as a tomboy. She told *Rolling Stone* in 1981: 'I think the rebel in me started to rear its ugly head when they told me at a certain age to wear stockings and garter belts and all that stuff. Then when they told me in health class that I was gonna go through a major change and start having monthly upheavals in my life for the next twenty-five years, I thought, "Screw you. Leave me out."'

Moving to England in the mid '70s, Hynde made her name in the London music scene as a writer for *NME*, and her first piece (on Brian Eno) had her posing as a dominatrix. Cool-as-ice, the tough chick tomboy who gets to hang out with the rough guys: this was the persona with which Hynde muscled her way into the rock fraternity. Like Patti Smith, she tried to write a role for herself as a woman in the beat script. Chris Salewicz wrote in *NME* of the way Hynde seemed 'to take comfort in on-the-road terminology like "canteen" and "bedroll" and claims it was only recently she adjusted to sleeping in beds again after having slept on floors for so much of her recent life.'

Hynde's androgynous looks and cool attitude played a major role in her career. Before she formed the Pretenders, Malcolm McLaren had planned to make her the frontwoman for a band called the Love Boys, 'with Hynde's tomboy looks meant to be played to the androgynous hilt so that gender disorientation was to be the basic name of the game,' wrote Nick Kent. But Chrissie Hynde never fully took on the swagger and bravado of machismo. She admitted: 'There's nothing butch about me. So that's the big myth, you know – the "loudmouthed American". I *am* the loudmouthed American – no one can be meaner, no one can be more of a *cunt* than I am. But I don't *want* to be. It's a front, you know? I just do what I do to get what I have to get.' Her 'female machismo' stance was, she claimed, just a skin-deep strategy. Her great hero was Ray Davies of the Kinks, whose persona was fragile and sexually ambiguous rather than macho. In the early '80s, Hynde and Davies were briefly married, an amusing alliance of gender-benders (although gender-*denters* is closer to the mark). Whatever the truth about the way she felt inside or comported herself in everyday life, on record Hynde created one of the definitive tough girl personae in rock herstory. The Pretenders' music was a punked-up version of '60s Brit-beat (the Kinks, the Who, etc.); what made it striking was Hynde's lyrical and above all vocal contribution. Her voice – a slurred, sensual alloy of neediness and nastiness, vulnerability and viciousness – is one of the first, and best, examples of a female equivalent to the classic rock'n'roll snarl/swagger (as opposed to a female parody of it). On songs like 'The Wait' and 'Precious' (from the 1980 debut *Pretenders*), she lets rip a strafing stream of syllables that's a weird mix of speed-rap, jive-talk and baby-babble. It's punk-scat, all hiccoughs, vocal tics, gasps and feral growls, weirdly poised between love and hate, oral sensuality and staccato, stabbing aggression. On 'Stop Your Sobbing', Hynde's quavery, spasming reiteration of the title's plea seems to revel in the voluptuous possibilities of pain; her empathy and identification with the hurting man becomes eroticised, as though they're both licking each others' wounds. In 'Brass in Pocket' her self-pleasuring singing is pure sass, a feline narcissism, as she preens herself and prepares to conquer the attention of a potential lover, lingering languorously over lines like 'I'm special'. As with many of her songs, most of the lyrics are distended and slurred to the point of indecipherability.

But what made her a mildly controversial figure at the time was the aggression of songs like 'Precious', with its 'fuck-off' careening off the surface of the song like a ricochet, or the streetwise sarcasm of 'Tattooed Love Boys'. In the latter, the target of her derision isn't, however, the macho men themselves but middle-class girls who play with fire by romanticising subcultures like bikers, getting romantically involved, and getting the shit beaten out of them.

On *Pretenders II* (1981), there's a song that cracks the tough chick facade to reveal the precariousness of the she-rebel lifestyle. 'The Adulteress' was inspired by the divorce proceedings between Ray Davies and his wife, in which Hynde was officially named adulteress. Instead of her usual super-cool strut, Hynde appears here as a sad, self-mocking woman; where once, in 'Private Life', she derided notions of attachment and obligation as 'so wet', now she confronts the possibility of spinsterhood. Independence suddenly seems like insecurity. She imagines being a figure of gossip ('she's desperate now'), watching the outlaw status she once craved become unheroic and pathetic as she gets older. She never meant to be 'evil', a homewrecker, and the song trembles with the bewilderment of someone who didn't realise the limits on her until she ran straight into them.

in search of peter pan

Patti Smith and Chrissie Hynde emulated male rock rebels' toughness out of necessity: it seemed to be the only way to get what they wanted, to be free of the restrictions that trammelled women in pop. For Kate Bush, what she wanted to do was so antithetical to the representations and the representatives of womankind that she saw in pop, she could only define her music as male. In 1978, still a teenager, she declared: 'When I'm at the piano writing a song, I like to think I'm a man, not physically but in the areas that they explore. Rock'n'roll and punk. . . they're both really male music. . . . Every female you see at the piano is either Lynsey De Paul, Carole King. . . that lot. . . . That stuff is sweet and lyrical but it doesn't push it on you and most male music – not all of it but the good stuff – really lays it on you. It's like an interrogation. It really puts you against the wall and that's what I'd like to do. I'd like my music to intrude.'

Unlike Patti Smith or Chrissie Hynde, Bush's image was far from tomboyish; in cover art and videos, she pushed her femininity to the fore. But the tradition she aspired to – English progressive and art-rock – was as sparsely populated with female artists as the punky-bohemian lineage that inspired Smith and Hynde. Bush's heroes (and later mentors) were Pink Floyd and Peter Gabriel. Because she wanted to make 'serious' music like them, rather than the kind of 'girly'/girl-targeted music that no rock critic would ever take seriously, she had to imagine herself as male in order to *create*.

Perhaps that's why the figure of Peter Pan loomed so large in Kate Bush's imagination (as it did for Patti Smith). Peter Pan is best understood not as a boychild but as the genderless androgyne of prepubescence; his refusal to grow up is as much an evasion of adult sexuality and gender divisions as it is a clinging to childish wonder and playfulness. In pantomime, he's always played by actresses. In her history of gender-bending, *Vested Interests*, Marjorie Garber takes issue with the notion of Peter Pan as 'a kind of Wendy Unbound', a genderless creature 'who can have adventures, fight pirates, smoke pipes and cavort with redskins'. But the fact that Peter 'can do all kinds of things that Wendy, Victorian girlchild that she is, is forbidden' is precisely why a young woman like Bush would be fascinated by him. In J.M. Barrie's 'Afterthought' to the play, Wendy returns to the nursery only to be married off and become a mother herself; Peter remains forever a carefree child. Wendy's fate is everything that Bush wanted to avoid, while Peter is the incarnation of everything she aspired to.

On her first LP, *The Kick Inside* (1978), 'Kite' sees Bush yearning for Peter's aerial freedom, but her 'feet are heavy', tying her to the *terra firma* of common sense. On 'In Search of Peter Pan' (from *Lionheart*, 1978), Bush sings in the sad voice of a child whose vast imagination is already running into the brick wall of the reality principle. While the child's friend Dennis keeps a photo of his hero tucked under his pillow, Bush has 'a pin-up' of Peter Pan. Bush seems to hold very dear this image of the pre-sexual child who retains a sense of the 'game', of the infinite possibilities of play and imagination. At the end of the song, she recites the 'Wish Upon a Star' refrain from Disney's *Pinocchio*.

A decade later, Polly Harvey, singer/guitarist of the band PJ Harvey, grew up in a small English village, with much the same confusion about her sexual identity as Bush or Patti Smith. With no female playmates, just her beloved older brother and his friends, Harvey became a tomboy. 'I used to pee backwards, all the classic symptoms,' she says. 'We used to play armies, never any girly games. Then when I was at secondary school I used to get told off for going in the girls' toilets and not wearing a tie 'cause I looked so much like a boy. . . . I was devastated when I started growing breasts, it was horrible.'

Harvey's early horror of femininity wasn't symbolic, but pragmatic: wearing girls' clothes meant constriction of her boy-sterous body, restriction on the kinds of games she could play, being 'sugar and spice and all things nice'. 'I can remember when I was younger my mum really wanting me to wear dresses. And I'd wear them and then roll around in as much mud as I could possibly find, or I'd just sit in one position all day and look sulky until I was allowed to put my trousers back on again.'

Remarkably, given her emergence in the early '90s, after decades of 'women in rock' and the appearance in recent years of a host of powerful female performers, Harvey's heroes and influences are almost all male: Captain Beefheart, Tom Waits, William Burroughs, Nick Cave, the Pixies, Big Black's Steve Albini (who produced her second album *Rid of Me*). Like these classic male rebels and neo-beatniks, her art stems from the desire to escape domesticity. 'It's escape from claustrophobia, from suffocating, which you feel a lot in the country.... You do feel like you're suffocating and being strangled by your parents.' Like many of the rebels in the first section, she is fascinated by serial killers and people who live on the psychic edge.

Yet there's a deep ambivalence towards masculinity running through her work. On one hand, she aspires to the *neutrality* of the male rock'n'roller – his freedom to just *get on with it* without having to consider questions of gender. So she will declare: 'I hardly ever give a lot of thought, particularly when I'm involved with making music or writing, to whether I'm male or female. I feel neither one nor the other.' On the other hand, she's both envious of and repelled by machismo's swagger. Many of her songs see her impersonating and parodying the rebel's self-aggrandisement. In 'Man-Size', she plays the part of a leather-booted macho man whose tyrannical bluster seems largely a battle to 'get girl out of my head'. Following the logic of 'the best form of defence is attack', the character ends up torching this feminine alter-ego or anima-spirit. '50 Ft. Queenie' is the ultimate phallic woman, a well-endowed Amazon who proclaims herself 'king of the world'. Queenie's a titanic, tyrannical figure in the tradition of Jimi Hendrix's 'Voodoo Chile' or the swaggering Staggerlees of the blues (Muddy Waters et al. were a big influence on the Led Zep-like thunder of *Rid of Me*). In 'Me-Jane', Jane fights back against the breast-beating braggart Tarzan, yelling 'stop your fucking screaming'. Men, in Harvey's world, are both ludicrous and larger than life; they're bullies with an undeniable power and freedom, a 'birthright' that Polly wouldn't mind usurping. And who can blame her?

bad reputation

Of course, there have always been female artists who've barged their way right through the 'women in rock' problematic, with a kind of brazen 'can do' attitude. These women – Suzi Quatro, Joan Jett, L7 – have proved that it's true: a woman can play the role of tough reb[el] as convincingly as any man. But they've done so at [the ex]pense of bringing anything new, different, to the sto[ck rock] [po]sture. Dan Graham calls this stance *macha*, 'a si[mpler version of] the male "macho" principle'.

Suzi Quatro is the archetypal male [...]. As a teenager, she fronted one of the few [(if only)] all-girl garage punk bands, the Pleasure Se[ekers ... their] classic 1966 alcoholic anthem 'What A W[ay To ...]. [Th]e young Quatro inverts and caricatures th[e classic '60s pu]nk braggadocio and disregard for the op[posite sex]; she snarls that she'd choose a bottle of beer ove[r a boyfriend] any day of the week. Later, Quatro came un[der the tutel]age of British teenybop svengali Mickie Mos[t, and becam]e a big star in the UK with tough-but-catchy glam-[boogie] singles like 'Can the Can' and '48 Crash' (mostly penne[d] by the hit-factory team Nicky Chinn and Mike Chapman). Quatro's denim-clad, no-nonsense image showed she was one of the boys.

Quatro was little more than a novelty in the early '70s and never taken seriously – partly because of the modest ambition of her music, partly because her version of gender-bending (dressing down, de-glamorising herself) didn't register as impressively as the artifice and androgyny of male glam-rockers like Bolan and Bowie. But Quatro did inspire Joan Jett to pick up a guitar and eventually form the Runaways. This all-girl band, managed by the eccentric svengali Kim Fowley, never really made it, but did spawn solo careers for Jett and lead guitarist Lita Ford.

Joan Jett's songs and black-leather image was pure macha: a feisty, defiant espousal of the 'bad girl' role, over music that resurrected the stomping beat and hollered anthemic choruses of early '70s bubblegum-glam like the Sweet and Gary Glitter (whose 'I Love Rock'n'Roll' gave Jett her biggest hit). Joan Jett was paying homage to a music that was itself a homage (to '50s rock'n'roll). Jett's

stance was delinquent and proud of it (check album titles
like *Bad Reputation* and *Glorious Results of a Misspent
Youth*). Lita Ford re-emerged in the late '80s to score some
success as a heavy metal singer. In her videos, she oscillated between playing the alluring, vulnerable spandex-clad
siren, and the rampant lead guitarist wielding her axe like
a phallus. The contradictions of 'women in rock' weren't
overcome or glossed over, but were actually exposed by
these jump-cuts between passive and active, temptress and
tearaway.

Other women muscled their way into the men-only field
of heavy metal. Protégés of Motorhead, the all-female
Girlschool were an adequate, second-division metal band.
More striking were Heart, a mixed gender band fronted by
Ann and Nancy Wilson who were hugely successful in
America in the late '70s. If their mimicry of Led Zeppelin
was more feminine than most Zep-clones, it's because they
could draw on the precious, fey side of Robert Plant. While
they did convincing imitations of Zep's raunchy funk-rock
in songs like 'Rockin' Heaven Down' and 'Even It Up', they
could also 'legitimately' explore lacey, ornate zones of
mock-medievalism – as in 'Sylvan Song' or 'Dream Of the
Archer' – without being dismissed as wimpy.

The Wilson Sisters wrote a number of songs that imagined she-rebel heroines: the 'tailshaking filly' of 'Kick It
Out' who broke loose on the day she was born, the adven-
turess of 'Little Queen', and above all, 'Bébé Le Strange'
(title track of their 1980 album). Bébé was inspired by the
hordes of young female fans who'd written to the band
about the inspiration they'd drawn from Ann and Nancy.
Ann explained that 'Bébé Le Strange' was 'a kind of collective name for all the young people who have contacted us;
it's a name like Johnny B. Goode – it stands for much more
than a "feminist statement" about rock. It goes beyond
that!'

*

Like hard rock, the hardcore punk scene also demands that women act 'hard' if they want to be accepted. In Sonic Youth, Kim Gordon plays bass and shares singing/songwriting duties with Thurston Moore and Lee Ranaldo. Gordon has written eloquently in the *Village Voice* of the paradoxes that face a woman who wants to play a style of music that isn't 'feminine'. 'Before picking up a bass I was just another girl with a fantasy. What would it be like to be right under the pinnacle of energy, beneath two guys crossing their guitars, two thunderfoxes in the throes of self-love and male bonding?. . . . For my purposes, being obsessed with boys playing guitars, being as ordinary as possible, being a girl bass player is ideal, because the swirl of Sonic Youth music makes me forget about being a girl. I like being in a weak position and making it strong.'

At times, Gordon's 'cool chick', delinquent image is a bit like Joan Jett with hipper reference points and a degree in modern art; this cartoon-like quality is part and parcel of Sonic Youth's blankly ironic resurrection of rock rebel clichés. In their first phase of activity, Sonic Youth's aesthetic was marked by a dazed-and-confused, apolitical vagueness and an infatuation with delinquency. This eventually became self-parodic: witness the cover of their 1990 album *Goo*, which featured a Raymond Pettibon cartoon of a couple of teenage rebels. Lost in reverie, the girl remembers how she and her boyfriend murdered her parents and then ran wild on the freeway.

The scene from which Sonic Youth emerged, American post-hardcore, was notable for its flirtation with ambivalent or taboo material, its aspiration to psychosis. Given the general requirement that Sonic Youth songs be in some sense 'at the outer limits of human experience', Gordon's songs have been obliged to offer cloudy, ambivalent images of female desire and identity. In 'Secret Girl' (from 1986's *Evol*), she's a disembodied, barely-there, ghostly non-presence: she describes herself as a boy who enjoys 'invisibility', but perhaps, in some oblique, subconscious way, she's

referring to the invisibility of the tomboy in rock, the girl
who can only be accepted by concealing herself under a
veneer of cool, and 'passing' for male. On *Daydream Nation*
(1988), Gordon's characters are either passive or out-of-
control. In 'The Sprawl', she's a voracious but vacant teen-
girl who always wants 'more more more'. 'Eliminator Jr' is
a delirious sexual fantasy in which Gordon alternates
between violent gasps, like she's been winded by a body-
blow, and visions of male strangers 'coming right through
me'. According to Sonic Youth biographer Alec Foege, the
song is an 'impressionistic account' of the infamous 'preppy
murder' of 1988 in which Robert Chambers strangled his
girlfriend (during what *he* claimed was rough sex).

Later, Gordon's songs get more feminist. In 'Kool Thing'
(from *Goo*) she delivers rap payback, trivialising such icons
of black male rage as Public Enemy by treating them as
sexual objects – turning the Black Panther into a sex kit-
ten. Mid-song, she goes head to head with Chuck D, asking
him where girls fit into their revolutionary campaign
against white corporate America, and parodies Public
Enemy's *Fear of A Black Planet* as a 'fear of a female planet';
Chuck D's riposte is an incoherent stammer. 1992's *Dirty*
offered explicit agit-prop, in the shape of 'Youth Against
Fascism' and 'Swimsuit Issue' (in the latter, Gordon
declares her support for Anita Hill). By this point, Gordon
had settled into a godmotherly role *vis-à-vis* a new generation of female bands like L7 and Hole (she produced Hole's
debut LP) and the burgeoning Riot Grrrl movement.

L7 are the ultimate descendants of the tomboy tradition.
This all-female band manages to combine overt feminism
with an austere hard-rock from which every trace of the
'feminine' has been expunged. Their sound is a straight-
down-the-line punk-metal that fuses the pace of the
Ramones with the ponderousness of Sabbath. From their
uninflected, affectless vocals (which take the pursuit of cool
to the point of zombie-like autism), to their playing
(stripped-down, no frills) L7 seem so concerned to avoid

anything that smacks of feminine decorativeness or soft-
ness, they come over as almost a caricature of hard rock.
'Fast and Frightening', for instance, celebrates a female
anti-heroine who's 'got so much clit', she doesn't need to
have balls. On 1992's *Bricks Are Heavy*, 'This Ain't
Pleasure' sums up L7's muscular work ethic approach to
rock'n'roll: no pain, no gain. The music, lyrics and image all
exude an aura of sullen, baleful, but very self-contained
toughness: there's none of the abandonment or depredation
of an Iggy Pop or Johnny Rotten. L7's music glowers,
simmers, but keeps its rage inside, never explodes, never
kicks out the jams.

What is unusual about L7 is their overt political awareness and alignment with feminism, which extends to
playing Pro-Choice benefits. 'Pretend We're Dead' lambasts
the dormant slacker nation and urges them to wake up and
get involved in politics with the cheerleader-like chorus
'c'mon, c'mon, c'mon'. 'Wargasm' probes the links between
masculinism, militarism and masturbation – the Gulf War
as cable TV porn-fest. In 'Everglade' a tough chick talks
back to a rough boy, having been trampled in the mosh-pit.
A sort of politically-correct version of the Runaways, L7
show that trying to be as hard as the boys is just a dead
end. Surely women have more to offer rock than the same
old hardened, repressed armature of cool? Are L7's notorious antics – like the incident at the 1992 Reading Festival
when singer/guitarist Donita Sparks pulled her tampon out
of her vagina and hurled it into the crowd – really that
much of an improvement on heavy metal's ritual feats of
misbehaviour?

open your heart:
confession and catharsis from janis joplin
to courtney love

Like the machismo that it mimics, the macha stance is all
about hiding feelings behind the mask of cool. At the opposite extreme from the tough rock chick is the female tradition of confessional singer-songwriters, whose soul-baring
turns suffering into an affirmation: a kind of strength-
through-vulnerability. For a particular breed of female
singer-songwriters, personal candour and political concern
are different sides of the same coin. It's not so much that
they adhere to the credo 'the personal is political', but that
they believe wrongs can be righted in both private and public realms, if only the truth can be uttered – if the tissue of
lies is torn apart and an 'authentic' reality unveiled.

   The notion of authenticity is a survivor of the previous
half-century, the era of Marxism and psychoanalysis.
These two human sciences were confident that oppression
and repression could be defeated by demystification and
the talking cure; that the shining light of reason could
penetrate the veil of ideology and the murk of neurosis.
Postmodern thought has undermined the idea that 'the
truth' can be grasped in language. But the notion of
authenticity continues to thrive in mainstream culture.
From the neo-soul testifying of pop singers like Michael
Bolton and Mariah Carey to talk shows like Oprah
Winfrey's, we live in a culture of confession, where to
speak your pain and passion is considered the first step
towards emotional health. The confessional singer-songwriters in this chapter lie somewhere between the blues,
soul and folk traditions of 'telling it like it is' and the self-
realisation therapy advocated by women's magazines and

counselling shows.

Although some popular singer-songwriters have recently tried to reclaim the torch-song and country traditions (k.d. Lang, Sinead O'Connor), most are grounded in folk. Folk's subject matter has always been divided equally between heartbreak and hardship. Female folk-singers have often adopted the persona of the earth mother, a sadly wise, gently chiding observer of men's folly. The folk voice is less sexual than blues and jazz; its plaintiveness lends itself to songs of personal and political woe. Sometimes the two intertwine, as in Sandy Denny's version of the traditional song 'The Banks of the Nile' (from *Fotheringay*, 1970) – the lament of a woman whose lover has been drafted to fight in Egypt. She vows to cut off her hair and join the army to be by his side, but he tells her that she's too delicate and that the Equatorial sun will bronze her rosy English complexion. So Denny is left behind to mourn the way that wars rob us of our sweethearts.

Generally, though, singers tend to separate personal and political anguish. Sinead O'Connor's songs, for instance, alternate between bare-bones confession and righteous truth-telling, but rarely connect the two. Her debut album, *The Lion and the Cobra* (1987), was a tentative, adolescent affair, packed with autobiographical songs about heartbreak, bitterness and the struggle for emotional autonomy, often couched in mythological imagery. The Stud Brothers wrote of O'Connor's 'rigorous autobiography': 'It's as if, in recording her own experiences, she's stopped living in order to become a more legitimate chronicler of her past.' Such self-contemplation isn't (entirely) a form of narcissistic self-preoccupation, but a means of finding how you got here, how to get out, where to go next.

In the interval between the debut and its 1990 sequel *I Do Not Want What I Haven't Got*, O'Connor seemed to have decided she was a controversial figure whose duty it was to speak out against oppression – on behalf of an audience she didn't, at that point, yet command. Ranging from politically enraged songs like 'Black Boys on Mopeds' to graphic sexual confessions like 'Jump in the River', the album seems governed by O'Connor's conviction that putting her own emotional house in order and setting the world to rights were inextricably intertwined facets of the same quest for truth. The title, *I Do Not Want What I Haven't Got*, with its Zen-scented aura of New Age affirmation therapy, was only the beginning. 'Feel So Different' even begins with an Alcoholics Anonymous-style pledge of self-acceptance. 'The Emperor's New Clothes' is a unilateral declaration of (emotional) independence, in which personal politics are phrased in the jargon of the body politic: 'I will have my own policies'. Sinead wants to be the Queen of Truth. But unlike the male rebel dream of sovereignty, her vision emphasises the monarch's *duty*, not self-indulgence.

As soon as she became famous with her version of Prince's torch song 'Nothing Compares 2 U', she seized the opportunity to make waves, refusing to allow the American national anthem to be played at one of her shows, and reaching a climax in 1992 with the infamous *Saturday Night Live* incident in which she ripped up the Pope's picture with the words 'Fight the real enemy'. What underlay this compulsive, exhibitionistic need to speak out? O'Connor rejected her Catholic upbringing but admits to having internalised its guilt. Caught in an unliveable place between the anti-woman, anti-sexuality indoctrination of Catholicism and her own desire to be godly, she describes herself as a Christian who hates the Church.

But O'Connor's compulsion to utter the unspoken, unspeakable truth, to *come clean*, has an even deeper auto-biographical origin. Shortly after the *Saturday Night Live* incident, she revealed that she had suffered abuse as a child at the hands of her mother (whose mental distur-bance O'Connor blamed on Catholicism). In her anguish, the young Sinead made a pact with God. 'I didn't know if I was going to be able to stay alive, and I asked God to help me, [promising that] I'd work for him. . . . He gave me my voice, and I have to use my voice in every way, not just singing. . . . I've only ever had one thing to say, and I've created the circumstances where I can say it. That's why I ripped up the picture.' Setting herself up as a sort of fusion of the Virgin Mary and Christ, O'Connor imagines a Christianity that is all-forgiving, feminised, maternal – rather than based on the suppression/sublimation of female sexuality. (Hence the title of her 1994 album *Universal Mother*.)

O'Connor's 'Holy Mother' posture is a monstrously amplified version of protest folk's earth mother stance, the gently reproaching voice of a wronged, outraged nature. From Joan Baez and Buffy St Marie to Tracy Chapman and Natalie Merchant, it's an enduring persona. More subtle is the approach of a singer like Suzanne Vega, who prefers to imagine the worldview of the victims of oppression through vignettes rather than overt proselytising or protest. In 'Luka' (from 1987's *Solitude Standing*), Vega plays the role of an abused child. The idea is that a first-person account can communicate the horror more vividly than a blunt attempt to grapple with the issue (as is the case with 10,000 Maniacs' matronly 'What's the Matter Here', also about sexual abuse). In fact, 'Luka' is surprisingly similar to the small, ghostly, blood-drained characters populating many of Vega's other songs – 'Neighborhood Girls', 'Tom's Diner' – meek and weak figures on the periphery of mainstream existence.

Vega's song-stories fuse the registers of personal and political, combine social commentary with a sense of idiosyncratic personal space. 'Bad Wisdom' (from 1992's *99.9° F*) finds an oblique angle on what might otherwise be too heavy. The focus is another young child, a girl, who seems to have been abused, leaving her body with 'strange information' which traps her between innocence and adulthood. 'Bad Wisdom' is presented almost as traditional folk, with very sparse musical accompaniment, but it's closer to a docu-drama than a protest song. Vega doesn't bemoan the girl's lack of support systems or saviours, but lets the girl sing sweetly of having 'fallen through the crack', where neither her mother nor her friends can reach her.

dear diary

Sinead O'Connor's Christian take on confessional song-writing is a return to the guilt-wracked origins of the diaristic impulse: in the sixteenth century, clergymen kept journals in order to attest to the purity of their lives. When confessional poetry emerged in the 1950s and '60s, it had a similar soul-cleansing role, albeit geared towards mental hygiene rather than spiritual spotlessness. The genre's most popular female exponents – Sylvia Plath and Anne Sexton – distilled the mess of their inner lives into intense but carefully-crafted verse. Yet many critics were disconcerted by their work, finding it too raw, too unmediated for their delicate sensibilities. Reviewer Charles Gullans wrote of Sexton: 'I feel that I have, without right or desire, been made a third party to her conversations with her psychiatrist.' (In fact, Sexton was originally encouraged to write by her therapist.) 'For the author, one might feel pity, if she could not control herself,' Gullans concluded. Years later, in 1988, Octavio Paz would display a similar queasiness in his critique of the artist Frida Kahlo, whose work mostly consisted of anguished self-portraits: 'I feel that I am before a complaint, not before a work of art.' In these statements, a squeamishness about female desire and suffering is thinly disguised by a tenuous distinction between visceral expression in art, and art that is deemed little more than viscera, blood and guts smeared on the page. The subtext of their objections seems to be: why can't those damn women keep it in?

Rock, of course, has always had a tendency to conflate the singer's person with the personae in the songs: rock literati like Elvis Costello and Lou Reed, who see their songs as mini-novels populated by characters, are waging a losing battle. Autobiography has never been a problem for rock, which rides roughshod over questions of detachment and transfiguration. (Perhaps that's why Anne Sexton made a stab at combining poetry and rock with her band Anne Sexton and Her Kind.) Rock can never be too raw.

Joni Mitchell was one of the first female artists to wear the label of 'confessional songwriter'. In *Written in My Soul*, a book of interviews by Bill Flanagan, she quotes Nietzsche's image of 'penitents of the spirit' who 'write in their own blood'. Describing the soul-stripping that went into the making of her 1971 album, *Blue*, Mitchell said: 'You wouldn't want to go around like that [i.e. totally naked]. To survive in the world you've got to have defences... And at that time in my life they just went.... In order to make that album we had to lock the doors in the studio. . . . When the guy from the union came to the studio to take his dues I couldn't look at him, I'd burst into tears. I was so thin-skinned. Just all nerve endings.' Mitchell seems to be saying that she's literally (in the) raw in these songs on *Blue*, naked and bleeding. Taken to its logical end, the ethos of authenticity leads to the idea of a one-on-one conversation between singer and listener, confidences whispered directly into your ear. In the same interview, Mitchell admits that she finds being onstage too remote: 'let me be on a pedestal that is not *separating* so much.'

Later in her career, Mitchell tried to write in a more detached fashion, an obliqueness that was matched by a musical shift from the bare-bones arrangements of *Blue* to the fluid, numinous soundscapes of albums like *The Hissing of Summer Lawns*. But, she complains, with these albums she was criticised for changing 'I' to 'you'. 'Dylan sang a lot of personal things saying "you". As a male that's better....' But Mitchell's critics could not accept this distancing effect from a woman. She explained this phenomenon by comparing the relationship between singer and listener to that between friends: 'If a person you met when they were vulnerable suddenly got strong it would threaten you, because you have to re-adjust your role. . . your friend is [no longer] someone you protect or comfort. . . Sometimes somebody's strength makes another person weak.' Here, Mitchell hints that her new detachment as a writer interfered with the enjoyment of (male) critics who secretly relished her portrayal of emotional frailty, because it allowed them to entertain fantasies of coming to her rescue. Herein lies the danger of the confessional idiom, which so often slots woman into the stereotype of victim, vulnerable, defenceless. Then again, is it better to reflect a woman's life in all its complexities and conflicts, than to feel obliged to put across a 'positive' image of omnicompetence that only sets up more unobtainable goals?

In 1994, Liz Phair's *Exile in Guyville* became the first album by a female artist to top the Pazz & Jop chart (*Village Voice*'s annual poll of America's top critics) since Joni Mitchell's *Court and Spark* in 1974. *Exile in Guyville* updates the confessional idiom: Phair's voice is confidential, colloquial, right-in-your-ear, but instead of earnest post-hippie authenticity Phair lives with a more provisional, '90s sense of identity. In the hilarious, unnerving 'Flower', she's a lecherous dominatrix who gleefully objectifies a cute boy, disregarding his personality in favour of his prick, which she imagines 'slamming, ramming, in me'. Yet in 'Fuck and Run' she's the sexual victim, seduced and abandoned, who wonders aloud 'whatever happened to "a boyfriend?"', i.e. someone who'd stick around the morning after. These oscillations between rapacity and pathos, nasty and needy, established Phair's reputation as a thoroughly post-modern, thoroughly mixed-up rock chick – riven with contradictions, capable of strength and weakness in different contexts.

'Johnny Sunshine' inscribes these polarities into the song's structure, juxtaposing Phair's two voices: low, husky and rock'n'roll v. high, girly and 'non-rock'. Phair sings of a footloose lover taking to the road in an affectless, ultra-kool monotone over a rockin' *motorik* stomp; but this exhilaratingly propulsive narrative is counterpointed, and undercut, by a second, 'feminine' voice that speaks not of abandon but of being abandoned. Then a hymnal coda, an echo of the Stones' 'You Can't Always Get What You Want', gently accuses: 'you left me nothing'. Phair's critical *succès d'estime* is based on the way she manages to inhabit garageland rock'n'roll yet inflect it with a confessional vulnerability. More specifically, she has feminised an alternative rock tradition usually associated with men: the geeky songsmith à la Elvis Costello or Paul Westerberg of the Replacements.

emotional nudism

'Writing may be a revelation of character, it may even be a form of madness, but for the one who writes, it can equally be a way of staying sane. . . . It is a truism to say that writing something very nasty can be a way of keeping nice.'
Jacqueline Rose, *The Haunting Of Sylvia Plath*

The myth of confessional music or poetry as the *truth*, pure and unmediated, is, of course, just that: myth. Confession is a narrative; even in our most private journals, we interpret, select, frame our lives like a painting. In rock, the Dear Diary approach to songwriting is a hardy perennial. In recent years, it's even undergone something of a revival, with the vogue for alternative singer-songwriters (Julianna Hatfield, Barbara Manning, Liz Phair, etc.). For some, though, the song-as-journal approach is too self-composed, too straightforward; these women take the pursuit of authenticity to exhibitionist extremes, resulting in a sort of emotional nudism.

Notions of 'catharsis' and 'getting my demons out' have long been clichés in rock parlance. With the music of Lydia Lunch and her progeny (Hole, Babes In Toyland) these metaphors are returned to their original vividness. Compared to the measured confidences of confessional songwriting, Lydia Lunch's work is closer to the 'Confess!' of exorcism; what was once used *against* witches and 'possessed' teenage girls by patriarchal authority, is now used by their modern day equivalent, wild female rockers – as a tool of self-expression, therapy, rebellion.

From her early days at the forefront of the late '70s New York No Wave scene in bands like Teenage Jesus and the Jerks and 8-Eyed Spy, through collaborations with Foetus, Rowland Howard, Thurston Moore, and a plethora of solo albums and spoken word projects, Lunch has gotten under the listener's skin by pulling back her own skin to reveal the morbid processes within. Her work invites and confounds voyeurism. The title of her retrospective *Hysterie* captured these ambiguities by playing both on the idea of hysteria (the female psychosomatic 'disorder' turned into a spectacle by nineteenth-century psychiatrist Jean-Martin Charcot for the edification/entertainment of male physicians) and the notion of writing the secret history (or herstory) of a woman's life. Exploding the decorous format of autobiography, Lunch's work is an archaeology of self-knowledge, excavating through the strata to uncover the primal wound that compels her to be an artist (like Sinead O'Connor, Lunch suffered sexual abuse as a child). In a 1988 interview with *Melody Maker*, she said: 'I'm here to explain and document what goes on in my life knowing that other women have gone through the same thing. I'm not finding solutions to the problem, I'm not saying there is a solution, I'm merely *underlining* the problem so everyone can see it as obviously as I do.'

Lunch's work is a kind of *assault course* of therapy: getting it out of her system by imposing it on the audience. Her early music was highly disciplined and tightly channelled; she wanted Teenage Jesus and the Jerks to be 'a very rigid regiment of almost military precision', rather than 'a spontaneous combustion'. In songs of this period, she explores the dynamics of victim and victimiser – most explicitly in 'In the Closet', where she compares herself to Manson victim Sharon Tate and complains of being unable to express herself or 'enunciate'.

Bloodletting, an ancient healing practice, becomes a central metaphor in Lunch's work. Blood is pain made visible, a transgression of the boundaries between inner and outer, private and public. In 'I Woke Up Dreaming', she describes her lover as 'my razor'; 'Baby Doll' pleads with her mother for permission to 'bleed just once'. *Queen of Siam*, Lunch's 1980 solo album, teems with imagery of bodies dissolving into streams of blood and tears: this is negative *jouissance*, agony-as-ecstasy, pain libidinised. In 'Tied and Twist', she intones nursery-rhyme imagery of drowning in 'a million tears'. 'Knives in the Drain' is a horrific sexual metaphor that plays on the analogous images of wound and vagina, weapon and phallus: Lunch is 'split and unbled'. On this same album, she also harks back to a tradition of female catharsis – the torch song genre – by covering Billie Holiday's 'Gloomy Sunday'.

As the '80s progressed, Lunch's work would divide between the allegorical (the burnt-out psychic wasteland of *Honeymoon in Red*, the apocalyptic visions of *Stinkfist*) and full-on, assaultive autobiography (spoken-word albums like *The Uncensored Lydia Lunch* and *Oral Fixation*). Where other female singers wanting to express the extremities of pain or rapture have bypassed language for non-verbal expression (Patti Smith, Yoko Ono, Diamanda Galas), Lunch's solo vocal performances remain coherent and decipherable, even at her highest pitch of rapid-fire rage. Her insights and anguish are too important to be garbled into glossolalia; instead she sprays the audience with logorrhoea, machine-gun style. For her harrowing harangues, Lunch adopts the persona of the bitch, the shrew, the harridan: patriarchy's great fear, the woman who *will not shut up*.

In an interview in the book *Angry Women*, Lunch

describes herself as the raging voice of the silenced, suffering majority of women: 'I'm only using my own example for the benefit of all who suffer the same multiple frustrations: fear, horror, anger, hatred. . . And the stories aren't just personal – often they're very political.' 'Daddy Dearest' (from *Oral Fixation*) takes the form of a letter to the father who abused her. The graphic, unsparing details, coming from a girl of six or seven, only three and a half feet tall, are devastating. She recounts how he regularly tried to burn off a freckle on her ass; vividly describes his invasion of her body, with particular attention to the way the stench of his breath – Bourbon, nicotine, onion – mingled with the smell of her own violated 'baby pussy'. With a degree of restrained vitriol redolent of Sylvia Plath's famous poem 'Daddy', Lunch finally exposes her father for his crime of imposing his 'stink and filth' upon her sweet innocence, for derailing the natural development of her life.

In the title monologue, 'Oral Fixation', she confesses that she's frustrated by the compulsive nature of her art. She says she's locked into a cycle of self-abuse (drinking, drugging) and abusiveness (bitching, whining), and she wants out. But for the moment, her abuse (of us!) is the first step towards healing: not so much a talking-cure as a shrieking-cure. In a 1986 interview with *Sounds*, she wondered aloud about her affliction: 'I don't know why I have to slit my guts and hope somebody will stick their filthy, stupid head inside and take one small breath and grasp what the fuck it's like to exist in someone else's shoes.'

Lunch isn't always the victim in her songs. In her 'Black Romeo' monologue, Lunch plays the part of the torturer. It's the tale of a couple, a man and woman, who are driven by boredom and desperation to kill their pet cat. As so often in the Romantic imagination, murder becomes the zenith of a desire that spirals upwards implacably, until violence offers the only hope of release. Thinking about life, Lunch's alter ego realises that both she and her lover are voraciously hungry for 'MORE'; the only way to satisfy him is for her to gift him with another creature's life.

The description of the cat-killing is horribly graphic, a little like the Rodney King video – blow after blow. Finally, her shoes are dripping with blood but there's 'no more naggin'' from Black Romeo. She identifies with both the torturer and the victim: the nagging black cat sounds suspiciously similar to her description of herself as a whining nag in other monologues, or to her mimicry of an imaginary, disgruntled, male audience member who complains that he didn't pay good money to be harangued by a woman 'on the rag'. Aside from echoing the case of Myra Hindley and Ian Brady, the 'Moors Murderers' who sealed their love for each other by killing children, 'Black Romeo' also seems to be a story of displaced and externalised self-hatred: the black cat standing in for the dark side of the woman that she has to stamp down.

On 'Oral Fixation' itself, Lunch moves away from the intensely personal to a wider, political frame, with a coruscating, impressionistic view of the battle of the sexes. She takes on the voice of masculinity, exaggerates and parodies, singling out in particular the Outlaw/Rebel – very familiar to her through associations with the likes of Nick Cave and Clint Ruin. The neo-Nazi with his 'nightstick dick', the Clint Eastwood-style gunslinger/vigilante, cult leaders Jim Jones and Charles Manson, the Dionysian rebel Jim Morrison, serial killers like Ted Bundy, mass assassins – all occupy different positions on the same spectrum of death-worshipping masculinism. Her diatribe recalls Gore Vidal's notion of M3, the Miller-Mailer-Manson Man: the American frontier spirit frustrated and perverted into a 'death-machine' drive to the End of the Night. As her derision gets ever more acrid, she parodies the excuses spouted by the sociopath, who pleads exemption because he *can't control himself*. Where Lunch's 'lack of control' takes the form of verbal diarrhoea, the inability to stop speaking her hurt and humiliation, with the Macho Man it's an inability to deny his 'nature', to stop hurting and humiliating others. The implacable onrush of her monologue parallels the uncontrollable *necro-logue* of the lowly male specimens she examines under her microscope.

vomit (he)art

Lydia Lunch is the godmother of the '90s 'angry women' like Courtney Love of Hole and Kat Bjelland of Babes In Toyland. While they owe a great deal to Lunch's taboo-breaking aesthetic and ferocity of expression, musically Hole and Babes In Toyland take their cues from male-dominated American hardcore. On Black Flag's *Damaged* and *My War*, singer Henry Rollins wallowed in a mire of humiliation and self-loathing. Black Flag paved the way for grunge's castration blues, the flailing sound of failed masculinity. As a female grunge band, Hole were doubly 'castrated', misfits within grunge's subculture of maladjusted male misfits. Another big influence on Courtney Love was Big Black, which might seem odd, given their misogynist streak; Love says she responded to a male pathos concealed beneath Big Black's vindictiveness. In a way, Hole reclaim abjection as a terrain of damaged subjectivity of which women have an insider's knowledge. It's as if Hole say: hardcore and grunge boys profess to be outsiders, therefore women, as ultimate outsiders, are surely the truest punks.

On Hole's 1991 debut LP, *Pretty on the Inside*, Courtney Love proclaimed her outsider status forcefully with the opening song, 'Teenage Whore'. 'Teenage Whore' turns the lowliest member of rock society, the groupie, into the ultimate (anti) heroine. Love rasps out an unclassifiable alloy of growling defiance and retching disgust, while Hole's tortuous music grinds out her humiliation and hatred with a creakiness that betrays how long this howl has been lurking in the back of the throat.

Hole's name – evocative of a wound, and of the vagina –

brings to mind the linguistic proximity of 'vulva' and 'vulna' (the Latin for wound and the etymological root of 'vulnerable'). Love's performance is a striptease that removes too many layers to be titillating, exposing a subcutaneous realm of female horror that makes men flinch and recoil. 'Cut it open,' Love howls in 'Berry'. Speculum becomes spectacle, the invisible interior is displayed; as with Lydia Lunch, it's as though one of Charcot's female patients has taken charge of her own theatre of hysteria and transformed the humiliation of being an exhibit into an empowering exhibitionism. (Courtney Love had, in fact, worked as a stripper at various points in her life.)

At the time of *Pretty on the Inside*, Courtney Love's image (which she shared with her friend and ally Kat Bjelland) was what she called the 'kinder-whore look': heavy eye make-up and lipstick combined with little girl dresses, like a child's attempt at grown-up seductiveness, or a grotesque parody of the pre-pubescent cuteness that's been destroyed by sexual maturation (a post-punk 'Baby Jane'). Sometimes the dresses were ripped, making the look even more disconcerting, as if she were the victim of sexual assault. This juxtaposition of an image of (violated) innocence with songs that graphically explored adult female sexuality was in part an attempt to rub audiences' faces in the virgin/whore dichotomy. But also, Love says, it was 'a way of saying "something's wrong" – I'm big-boned, I shouldn't be wearing that dress, I'm a grown woman!'

In 'Babydoll', the infantilisation is imposed rather than assumed; she is literally belittled by men, feels herself 'withering' and finally disappearing altogether. Love's alter ego here embodies sex ('her pants undone') but there's nothing sexy about the song, since her own desire plays no part. She's a passive toy, drained of energy by vampiric figures whose bulk overwhelms her. Sapped, she is reduced to an object of desire, worthy of only the most insultingly diminutive label: 'Babydoll'. Love takes the word between her teeth and shreds it.

On the back-sleeve of *Pretty on the Inside*, a painting by then-bassist Jill Emery picks up the theme of fractured self-image. It's reminiscent of Willem De Kooning's 'Women' paintings, with their contorted female images, but infused with the empathy of Frida Kahlo's anguished self-portraits. A woman stares at herself in a hand-mirror. Her body is distorted: the torso is emaciated, the ribcage exposed, but the arms are muscular, unnaturally large. Her knuckles are grazed and bleeding, and tears mar her cheek like hard stones. A valentine heart lies exposed on her chest, fringed with arrows, and miniature, dismembered arms jut out of the side of her head. But the most significant element of the picture is the hand-mirror, whose reverse-side, facing the viewer, depicts an eye as unblinking as the woman's own, as she contemplates herself. What she sees is like an anorexic who looks in the mirror and finds obesity. She sees beauty nowhere, inside or out, just mess. *Pretty on the Inside* is all about the gulf between the unreachable ideal and the dis-graceful real. The phrase 'pretty on the inside' has traditionally been offered by mothers as consolation to plain girls worried about their looks. Hole aim to bring out the full meaning of the idea that beauty is only skin-deep by exposing the unpretty truth of the body's interior.

If Babes In Toyland share many of Hole's themes and traits, it's because singer Kat Bjelland and Love were close friends and collaborators: first in a band called Sugar Baby Doll and later in an early incarnation of Babes. Like Love, Bjelland engages in close combat with the stereotypes that corner and cage her. On the debut album *Spanking Machine* (1990), 'Swamp Pussy' has the same jerky voodoo-beat as the Cramps' psychobilly, but turns the sniggering sleazy misogyny of Cramps' songs like 'What's Inside A Girl?' and 'Smell of Female' into flaming fury. It's as though abjection has come alive, taken monstrous form, and threatens to devour man. 'Swamp Pussy' is the Cramps turned inside out. As with Hole, it's as though

Bjelland is teetering precariously on the edge of the abyss of female biology; women's proximity to bodily processes is both a source of dark power and a threat to identity. In 'Handsome and Gretel' (*Fontanelle*, 1992) the good little girl turns out to be a bad little girl with a 'crotch that talks'.

For Babes In Toyland, emotional nudism becomes open-heart surgery; catharsis is a volcanic eruption of vile fluids, as in the song title 'Vomit Heart'. Here, Bjelland roars 'pull my head apart', as though only dismemberment can uncover the truth of her being. While the title vaguely evokes bulimia, these lyrics suggest another 'female perversion' – self-cutting, or its less drastic mind's eye equivalent, morbid fantasies of self-mutilation. Such fantasies can function as a way of venting overwhelming feelings of self-loathing: the body is punished, even obliterated, because of the trouble it brings its owner.

A similar projection of self-hatred takes place in 'Pearl' (from *Fontanelle*), with its image of a blackbird screeching inside Bjelland's mind. 'It's like guilt, like a conscience thing, like something that's annoying you and you just want to pacify it all the time. . . ,' Bjelland told *Melody Maker*. 'It's like I'm tired of the blackbird screaming in my head.' She's often resorted to imagery of illness and bodily dysfunction, describing her mind as 'ulceric', like 'an ulcer, and our music is like Pepto-Bismol [an antacid]. . . like, really pink and nice, except it tastes like shit! But it makes you feel better.'

The title of *Fontanelle* takes this physical imagery to the point of self-parody (as do the images of raw, bloody meat on the inner sleeve). The word fontanelle can mean a bodily hollow or pit, or a space between the bones of a baby or foetal skull. It evokes the idea of *trepanation*, a prehistoric practice in which a hole was made in the skull in order to allow the demons responsible for mental illness or delirium to escape. The idea that women have a problem releasing and directing their anger has a long pedigree. The poet

Emily Dickinson saw herself as a 'loaded gun', and as 'Vesuvius at home', waiting to erupt; Kristin Hersh of Throwing Muses sang of having 'a gun in my head'. When comparing the angry women bands of the '90s with their masculine counterparts, it's now almost a truism to argue that male rage is explosive and female rage is implosive. Where male punk bands, from the Stooges onwards, project their aggression outwards like a projectile, with many of these female bands, anger backfires, becomes self-consuming.

Anger has always been considered unbecoming in a woman. The poet Adrienne Rich remembers that as a child, her temper was perceived as 'a dark, wicked blotch in me, not a response to events in the outer world. My childhood anger was often alluded to as a "tantrum", by which I understood the adult world to mean some kind of possession, as by a devil.' In a *Rolling Stone* interview, Yoko Ono recalled feeling like a ghost while she was in college, sitting around striking matches to watch them burn: 'I thought maybe there was something in me that was going to go crazy, like a pyromaniac. See, I was writing poetry and music and painting, and none of that satisfied me. . . . I felt that I was a misfit in every medium.' She feared that her own energies would turn in on herself instead of taking the form of rebellion.

Marianne Faithfull, partner to that other leading icon of the '60s, Mick Jagger, had similar fears of being consumed by her own rage, but instead of releasing it in art chose to damp down the fires with drugs. 'Drugs kept me from being a terrorist,' she declared in an interview with Stones' chronicler A.E. Hotchner. 'By that I mean there came a point where I think I felt that either I was going to explode out into something, into actual acts of violence in some way, or I was going to have to implode to contain it. And I decided to keep it in. . . . But that destructiveness could easily have gone the other way. If I had fallen in with Ulrike Meinhof, for example, I can see I would have readily joined my terrorism to hers and exploded in violence against society.' Instead of becoming a firebrand, Faithfull became one of the most famous burnt-out casualties of the '60s; on albums from *Broken English* (1979) to *Blazing Away* (1990), the once dulcet-toned folk maiden sang extinguished torch songs in a voice like cinders.

Rock – the culture of the angry young man – has only recently, and reluctantly, become a home for female belligerence. Nonetheless, with its premium on authenticity and rawness, rock is the ideal medium for this kind of catharsis. Singers like Courtney Love and Kat Bjelland build a burning bridge between rock's roots in the testifying traditions of gospel and blues and contemporary self-realisation discourse, with its notions of opening up, getting in touch with your anger, 'owning' your negative feelings. One minute Bjelland talks of being primarily influenced by gospel, soul and blues singers, the next she's describing songs like 'Fork Down Throat' as 'scream therapy – if you let it all out, you feel better.' The angry young woman: missing link between the blues and bulimia?

let it bleed

'For all these years, I felt like all these different people at a dinner party. When you've got the virgin and the whore sitting next to each other. . . they're likely to judge each other harshly. But it's never about good girl and bad girl. . . You can't have your body without your shadow.'
Tori Amos, 1992

Another soul-baring singer hit the scene at around the same time as Courtney Love and Kat Bjelland. But although her songs are just as candid, Tori Amos is seldom bracketed with the angry young women. She's seen more as a successor to the Joni Mitchell confessional singer-songwriter tradition. While Amos's subject matter is arguably as unsettling as Hole's or Babes', its musical setting – post-Kate Bush art-pop – is too decorous and 'feminine' to be sanctioned by alternative tastemakers. Despite its fragrant form, Amos's music really is like an emotional striptease, a delicate balance between seduction and confrontation.

Her debut album, *Little Earthquakes* (1992), is autobiographical, about the tensions between her religious background and her sexually rebellious spirit, and her struggle to find her own voice. Amos was a child piano prodigy with a preacher for a dad. In concert, she tells anecdotes about her disapproving family (like her saintly grandmother) and her own precocious sexual awakening. At the age of six, Jim Morrison and Robert Plant convinced her that the Devil had all the best riffs; her version of Led Zep's 'Whole Lotta Love' is hilarious, half mocking the song's penile dementia, half still a little in awe and in lust.

In a way, she's taken on the persona of the '60s male rebel and feminised it, rewriting the classic dynamic of breaking loose from domesticity and sexual repression as the story of the Prodigal Daughter. The whole album is based around the idea of *the talking cure*, of finding one's voice (one song is called 'Silent All These Years'), and turning suffering into a story. At the same time, like Lydia Lunch, she knows that her outpourings fit all too well the stereotype of the woman who 'talks too much': in one song she mimics a man's opinion of her (she can 'never shut up'). Her songs combine Christian imagery (crucifixion, guilt, confession) and the psychobabble of West Coast therapy.

'Me and A Gun' is her ultimate confessional, a plea for absolution for a crime that blames the victim instead of the perpetrator. An a cappella account of being raped, the song is almost unbearably harrowing, not because the lyrics are unsparingly graphic, but precisely because the anguish is held in check by the driest kind of humour (she describes some of the absurd thoughts that go through one's head at such moments of extremity). In a way, the song rebuts in advance those critics who have accused Amos of exploiting her sexuality (she alludes to the fact that she was wearing a sexy outfit, implicitly challenging the notion that she was 'asking for it'). Amos clearly feels that she has a right to explore her own desires, dress comfortably and display as much of her psyche and body as she wants without having to feel 'responsible'. The damage done to her by being safe and repressed, she seems to be saying, may be more damaging ultimately than taking one's chances in the world. Her religious background would tell her that being raped was the punishment for a lifestyle that was improper, unfeminine; she refuses both the stifling security of purdah, and the notion that rape is the natural and inevitable risk a woman runs for sexual freedom.

What is most conservative about Amos, and perhaps why she's been accused of *using her sexuality*, is the surface attractiveness of her music: highly ornamented AOR, centred around her piano rather than guitar riffs, deceptively light on the ears. Just as Kate Bush was underrated because of the prettiness of her music and image, and because she rose to fame at the same time as more confrontational singers like Siouxsie Sioux, so Tori Amos looks tame next to Courtney Love. At times, she does come over as the cute girl performing for Daddy's attention, too inculcated in 'feminine wiles' to be considered a real she-rebel. At the same time, subversion is contextual: with her softcore feminism, Amos should perhaps be valued as an ally of the angry women bands – someone who's opened up a second front on AOR territory.

Certainly, Amos's ideas about speaking-the-truth, tussling with the traumas that shaped her, are couched in almost identical language to Lunch, Love et al. She's described her art as an attempt to 'be open because I've been so closed in the past. The self is an endless vat of soup. That minestrone does not stop.' After a nervous breakdown and the rape, she describes a process of working through her feelings of victimisation: 'It's about freeing the attacker in yourself, tearing away all the layers.'

As with the other cathartic performers, blood is Amos's supreme metaphor for confession. 'People are afraid of what they might find if they try to analyze themselves too much,' she's said, 'but you have to crawl into the wound to discover what your fears are. Once the bleeding starts, the cleansing can begin.' 'Precious Things' imagines painful memories dissipating by haemorrhage: 'let them bleed'. For Amos, Babes and Lunch bloodletting is like a form of speech: it offers physical and mental relief, gives volcanic vent to the festering negativity that's pent-up inside the body that's been silenced for so long.

angel with a broken wing

Contemporary female artists like Courtney Love and PJ Harvey play havoc with several traditional rock themes – not just authenticity and confession, but also the rebel fantasy of living on the edge. Where male artists who walk a high-wire over the abyss of self-destruction tend to present a spectacle of mastery, female performers who flirt with disaster tend to elicit different responses: a morbid mixture of voyeurism, pity and sadistic delight at the possibility that she might fall. The male artist who *plays with madness* – from Artaud and Van Gogh to Iggy Pop and Nick Cave – is impressive, a voyager into the dark underworld or outer-worlds of consciousness; female artists who appear to put their sanity in jeopardy, on the other hand, run the risk of being dismissed as 'merely' mad.

Even so, the late '80s and early '90s saw rock culture take a sudden interest in female subjectivity. Just as '60s rock admired and envied black experience for the intensity and authenticity endowed by a history of suffering, so recent rock has begun to regard women as the ultimate outsider. Having exhausted male experience, rock sensed that female angst and anger offered a whole new frontier, ripe for colonisation. Wildly different singers and performers – Bjork Gudmundsdottir of the Sugarcubes, Sinead O'Connor, Kristin Hersh of Throwing Muses, Mary Margaret O'Hara, Alison Shaw of Cranes, Polly Harvey – became the focus of what we call the Betty Blue Syndrome: the seemingly unbalanced woman whose intensity elicits, from (male) fans and critics, both envious awe and protective feelings.

It's an appealing fantasy for men who long for a girl they can save and heal: they can write themselves into the script as a knight in shining armour coming to the girl's emotional rescue. The woman's artistic powers are inextricably linked, in his imagination, with her lack of control over herself; often, it seems that she can't help herself, that her creativity comes to her from an external realm. And to make it even easier, some female artists describe their creative process in just such terms, as though they were a conduit for the otherworldly or the unconscious.

Many of the most recent singers pegged with the Betty Blue Syndrome possess an ethereal image – glamorous but gauzy, soft-focus and desexualised. It's a look designed to provoke awe and tenderness rather than lust. Being 'ethereal' is a good compromise between the desire to be glamorous and an aversion to being ogled – it de-emphasises the body, while still evoking a more abstract, mythical femininity. Being otherworldly implies being out of reach, shaking off mundane definitions and demands. Unfortunately, the mystic child-woman image tends to invite a more sophisticated male gaze – one that rhapsodises rather than drools – but just as surely turns the chanteuse into an object of fantasy.

When she was in the Sugarcubes, Bjork was rapturously characterised as a sprite-like enigma, to the point where the band members themselves began to complain of the music press's infantilisation of her. A few years later, the Sundays' Harriet Wheeler and Curve's Toni Halliday became the new ethereal darlings. Revealingly, one critic defined Curve's songs as being about 'a loss of innocence. . .

or rather, its forcible removal'. Alison Shaw, singer of
Cranes, also became the focus of a weird mix of voyeurism
and empathy. Framed in her band's ominous techno-goth
soundscapes, Shaw's disturbed and disturbing voice – a
sort of kindergarten version of avant-diva Diamanda
Galas's glossolalia – triggered much speculation about the
traumas that shaped it. Typical metaphors usually involve
padded cells or nine-year-old girls locked in attics.

In many ways, this cult of the ethereal/damaged girl
singer is just an updated version of the worship of the torch
singer as an 'angel with a broken wing'. Witness, for
instance, the sleevenotes for the Billie Holiday box set *The
Legacy*, in which journalist Michael Brooks recalls meeting
the forty-year-old singer when he was a young man: 'All I
wanted to do was reach out and take this woman in my
arms, in the way a parent does with a small child who has
been subjected and broken by the cruelties of life for the
first time. For a very brief moment I became an adult and
maybe a part of me has been trying to recapture the purity
of that emotion ever since.'

Perhaps such framing by male fantasy is inevitable, given
the paradox (and it applies to male 'tortured artists' as
much as to female) that the strongest artistic expression is
often born of weakness, incompleteness and incapability.
The archetypal example of this paradox is probably the life
and work of Janis Joplin, who still divides opinion. For
some, Joplin remains one of the most forceful artists of the
'60s, a trailblazer of untrammelled female expression. For
others, she's the ultimate self-destructive woman, whose
overwhelming aura was powerlessness, not artistic power.
Her male counterparts, Jim Morrison and Jimi Hendrix,
still sell one million and three million albums respectively
every year. Janis sells a meagre 50,000. Janis's music may
not have endured (how many of her songs can you name?),
but her image sure has: dishevelled, wasted, wrecked,
wracked with neediness. For many, she exemplifies the

second-class status of women in the counterculture (whose jagged contradictions eventually broke her). Some even argue that the girl groups and singers of the early '60s – the Shangri-La's, the Ronettes, Lesley Gore's 'You Don't Own Me' – offered better role models for women; this, despite the fact that these girl singers had little or no creative control over the spectacle of elegance or autonomy they presented, and were basically puppets of the male-run pop production line.

Joplin's self-destructive impulses, the basically suicidal trajectory of her lifestyle, does not have the same charismatic, Dionysian aura of other, 'too fast to live, too young to die' figures from the '60s like Brian Jones or Hendrix, since debauchery and delirium have always seemed less acceptable in a woman than a man. Jim Morrison could lay waste to his looks and his dignity, abandon personal hygiene to the point of stinking like a bum, but, even bloated and bearded, he still had the aura of a seer. Joplin's mythos is altogether shabbier.

Perhaps Joplin's problem was that the break she was making with acceptable female conduct was more drastic than anything her male counterparts attempted. They, after all, could draw on a tradition of adventurism: from the myth of the Prodigal Son to the idea that 'boys will be boys', bad behaviour is, if not exactly sanctioned, seen as a logical extension of masculinity. Male delinquency is regarded as a misdirected expression of energies that could be properly channelled (into sport, warfare, the cut and thrust of free enterprise).

Joplin did have one 'wild woman' ancestor, from the same era and milieu as the black blues singers that inspired the male rebels of the '60s. 'Empress of the Blues' in the 1920s, Bessie Smith had a shamanic aura to rival Robert Johnson's. In the notes to Smith's *Complete Recordings*, New Orleans guitarist Danny Barker writes of her effect on an audience in terms of 'mass hypnotism'. Like Joplin, she lived hard and fast, and died relatively young (in a car crash in 1937). Also like Joplin, Smith's songs alternated between grievous heartbreak and aggressive sexuality; her temper was ferocious, and she gave as good as she got when it came to the rotten men in her life (she's even said to have shot at her husband after one of his cheating spells).

Above all, Smith's appetite – for love, booze, experience – was voracious, all-consuming. In 'I Want Every Bit of It', she sings of wanting everything or 'none at all', while 'Young Woman's Blues' is a formidable declaration of independence for its era: refusing to marry or settle down, she declares that she'll never be 'done running around'. Although she did marry, she had affairs with both men and women, and generally fought to circumnavigate most of the restrictions placed on women in her day. Janis Joplin so identified with the undomesticated, streetwise aspects of Smith's persona that she paid for half of Smith's tombstone. And, according to her biographer Myra Friedman, towards the end of her career Joplin developed an alter-ego persona, Pearl, which was partly modelled on Bessie Smith and her rough'n'tumble life.

For some, Joplin's life and work testifies to a female rebellion that, while constricted by the gender constraints of the era, still counts as a tremendous breakthrough and a triumph. In an essay for the CD retrospective *Janis*, Ellen Willis argued that the problem Janis faced was that 'the male-dominated counterculture defined freedom for women almost exclusively in sexual terms. As a result, women endowed the idea of sexual liberation with immense symbolic importance; it became charged with all the secret energy of an as yet suppressed larger rebellion. Yet sexual freedom itself was largely defined as availability to male desire, and so for a woman to express her rebellion in that limited way was at the same time a form of submission. Whether or not Janis understood that, her dual persona – lusty hedonist and suffering victim – suggested that she felt it.'

'Janis's lyrics may have been mired in female masochism,' argues Myra Friedman in her Joplin biography *Buried Alive*, but 'her performances bespoke an inspired liberation of the female spirit that roared right up to the stars.' But for today's listener, this impression of Joplin may be hard to resurrect. On *Cheap Thrills*, her 1968 album with Big Brother and the Holding Company, Joplin sounds like a cross between Aretha Franklin and a brawling, bawling drunk. The agonised, haemorrhaging grain of her voice is like a dry heave, retching and wretched. Her vocal contortions suggest the white-singer-in-blackface overstatement of a Joe Cocker or Robert Plant. But where Plant amplified the sexual braggadocio of the blues into phallocratic tyranny, Joplin revels in neediness and pathos. She doesn't seem to be in control of her passion, but controlled by it. In reality, Joplin's singing, with its apparently improvised hollers and moans, was a carefully constructed simulacrum of spontaneity: according to Friedman, the singer planned every last throe and spasm of passion, plotting a precise place for each shriek and wail on her records.

While Joplin's music has the achey craving of gospel, in her life, faith was replaced by secular surrogates – the 'cheap thrills' of sex, drink, drugs – that exacted a terrible price. Joplin's revolt against her prim, middle-class upbringing in Port Arthur, Texas, rivals that of any of the bad boys of the '60s. While her family listened to Mozart, she found herself going to the wrong side of town to listen to blues, 'the devil's music'. Joplin always wanted to be one of the guys, and she succeeded. But outside of her outlaw gang, she was a pariah. Rampant sexuality cuts different ways for men and women; to boast of insatiability was a mark of heroic non-conformism for male rebels, but for women it was a taint: the female equivalent of stud is. . . *nymphomaniac*.

Joplin was maddeningly frustrated by this double bind. Her friend Jack Smith said of her frenzies: 'It became some phenomenal energy thing that had to be sated and [a] tension that she couldn't release.... It reminded me of some later Van Gogh self-portraits, like Vincent in flames!' Another friend says that after taking Seconal, 'she'd walk the streets at night and try to get run over and run into buildings with her head'. In an essay written shortly after Joplin's death, Ellen Willis argued that the singer was, just like Jimi Hendrix and Jim Morrison, engaged in a heroic 'war against limits'; like Jimi and Jim, Janis should be considered 'not so much a victim as a casualty'. Joplin's description of her hunger for experience anticipates Lydia Lunch's 'oral fixation': she told *Rolling Stone*'s David Dalton that on her arrival in San Francisco she 'wanted to smoke dope, take dope, lick dope, suck dope, fuck dope, anything I could lay my hands on I wanted to do it'. She was sexually omnivorous, sleeping with men and women. Myra Friedman attributes Joplin's problems to the lack of a 'cohesive' ego, so that instead of a stable identity, she was 'spewing, splattering, splaying all over, without a centre to hold' — even her most sympathetic biographer seems to have regarded her as a sort of amorphous amoeba of constant craving! Like the cat-killers in Lydia Lunch's 'Black Romeo', Joplin wanted MORE, MORE, MORE.

woman unbound:
hysterics, witches and mystics

Tomboy rockers mimic the toughness of the macho rebel; soul-baring singers try to transform vulnerability into a kind of strength. Other female artists have looked to the past for models of female power, fastening on mythological figures (the witch) or mystical archetypes (Mother Nature, the Moon, the Sea) as a glamorous launching pad for re-invention of the self. But invoking such imagery is a hazardous strategy: it runs the risk of consolidating stereotypes (the cliché of woman as irrational, supernatural) or lapsing into essentialism (woman as biologically linked to nature).

The two ultimate images of women as irrational and insubordinate beings are the hysteric and the witch. In fact, for centuries they've been seen as a kind of proof of the scary, secret nature of women: what women would be like if they weren't kept under strict control. Earlier we imagined Lydia Lunch as one of Dr Charcot's hysterics who'd managed to take control of the proceedings and present her own delirium as a spectacle. Catherine Clément has argued that 'an audience, ready to satisfy its fantastic desire, is necessary for the spectacular side of sorcery and hysteria. It is, above all, an audience of men: inquisitors, magistrates, doctors.' To what extent does this analogy apply to the way Janis Joplin 'made a spectacle' of herself?

Hysteria is a loaded and highly problematic concept to introduce into a discussion of female creativity, even as a metaphor. The term comes from the Greek word for uterus, *husterikos*. For centuries, psychosomatic and mental disorders in women were attributed to a 'wandering womb'. In other instances, such delirium was perceived as the mark of possession by demons. Freud noted the parallels between the symptoms of his female patients (paralysis, blindness, logorrhea, speaking in tongues) and the fevered discourse and antic contortions of the women who were tried as witches. He wrote to a friend: 'Why do the confessions extracted by torture have so much similarity to my patients' narratives during psychological treatment?'

In the Middle Ages and the nineteenth century alike, women grew up in conditions of extreme sexual repression. Hysteria was one form of 'revolt': the force of desire, prevented from expressing itself either in action or language, reasserted itself in psychosomatic symptoms or eruptions of glossolalia. The body 'spoke', disgracing its owner and disconcerting everyone else. In the pre-modern era, it was religious authority that dealt with these wild women; in the late nineteenth century, medicine stepped into the breach. Freud envisioned psychoanalysis as a science of what had hitherto been religion's province (i.e. the irrational). Like the exorcists, psychoanalysis 'interrogated' the murky, turbulent realm of the 'feminine'. Nabokov was closer to the mark than he imagined when he sneeringly dismissed Freud as 'the witchdoctor of Vienna'.

In a sense, hysteria is the very stuff of pop, both on the part of performers and fans: *Webster's Dictionary* defines it as a 'psychoneurosis marked by emotional excitability and disturbances of the psychic, sensory, vasomotor, and visceral function', and, more colloquially, as 'unmanageable fear or emotional excess'. Pop has always been about the *too much*, the melodramatic amplification of passion or pain. But hysteria has been explicitly reclaimed by a handful of female artists who are far from innocent of its origins in patriarchal science. Lydia Lunch entitled a retrospective of her work *Hysterie*, and her performances sometimes simulate the torrential outpourings of the hysterical discourse. Diamanda Galas has spent time in mental hospitals, as performer and patient; she has aligned herself with the persecuted and demonised women of the past, including those proto-hysterics, witches; she has described schizophrenia as an ultimate 'form of freedom from *permission*'. These women have reimagined hysteria's out-of-controlness as being *beyond* Control, as a revolt against the censorship of the Super Ego. At the same time, both Lunch and Galas are supremely in control as artists: they 'own' their delirium. Galas has taken self-control and subjugation of the body to the point of having her tubes tied: no wandering womb for her. She regards childbirth as barbaric and primitive, and sees sterility as an essential part of becoming a shaman: 'every witch has cats – you never hear of a witch having children!' As a modern-day sorceress, she has declared war on the eternal enemy of witches, the Roman Catholic church, becoming a militant AIDS protester and participating in a protest at St Patrick's Cathedral in New York against Cardinal O'Connor's homophobia.

With both Lunch and Galas, hysteria only works as an analogy. Lunch's is really a strategic, self-willed delirium, as much a case of verbal terrorism as involuntary discharge. Galas seems to have found a way to channel her negative energies into 'a pointed, focused message – like a gun'. In some ways, there's a parallel between this reclamation of hysteria – a patriarchal term which has historically been used to oppress women – and Madonna's use of stereotypical imagery. Madonna and Janis Joplin reimagined the whore as a sexual rebel; Lunch and Galas resurrect the witch as a terrorist against patriarchy. In both cases, this strategic re-investment is fraught with dangers. Galas's gun can backfire, providing ammunition for those who would dismiss her as deranged.

Psychoanalyst Monique David-Menard argues that 'the hysteric has no body'; some kind of trauma has prevented her from developing a sense of her body's integrity or its erogenous potential, and the blocked sexuality resurfaces in symptoms. Elaborating on this theory, Ned Lukacher adds: 'For some reason, the sexualisation of her body smells so bad, is so disgusting, that [the hysteric] would rather not have a body at all.' There are obvious connections here with the voluptuous imagery of abjection, the eroticisation of disgust, the mutilated and broken bodies, that figure so strongly in Lydia Lunch's work.

Lunch differs from the 'true hysteric' in that she knows exactly what caused her problems: sexual abuse. She has said, 'It's quite brutal to realize at the age of six that one is no longer a *child*. You feel that something has snapped that will never return to you. . . . until. . . you return the power to yourself that has been stolen by that other person – and that's very difficult, and takes a long time to master.' Lunch is like Catherine Clément's hysteric who 'relives the past, bearing witness to a lost childhood that survives in suffering' – except that she's fully conscious and in charge of this re-membering (reconstructing the dismembered body that flaunts itself so graphically and gorily in her early songs).

Diamanda Galas reclaims for women what had hitherto been the mark of the male visionary artist: feminine subjectivity. Writers like Baudelaire and Artaud (both of whom Galas admires and whose texts she has set to music) have been hailed for their 'feminine writing' (*écriture féminine*), their daring descents into the 'dark continent' of the unconscious. In *Feminine Endings*, musicologist Susan McClary analyses how 'the very qualities regarded as evidence of superior imagination – even of genius – in each period of music are, when enacted on stage, often projected onto madwomen.' The madwoman sections of certain classical symphonies are where the composer feels free to break with conventional musical structures in order to gesture at the *beyond*, the irrational: avant-garde composition has progressed by colonising the hysterical experience. McClary hails Diamanda Galas because she 'defies and dispenses with the conventional framing devices that have aesthetized previous portrayals of women and madness.'

It could be argued that the hysterical uproar of

Dionysian rock is good art, but bad politics: in its convulsions and spastic frenzy, all limits are transcended, but nothing constructive can endure from that frenzy. In this, hysteria resembles the urban riot's explosion of pre-political rage; both hysteria and riot allow the oppressed/repressed to get it out of their systems, but not to overthrow the System. Yet Lydia Lunch and Diamanda Galas bring out the latent political dimensions of hysteria.

chicks on broomsticks

According to one strain of feminist thought, throughout history witches were dissidents against patriarchy who refused their allotted place in society (silence and subservience, housekeeping and childbreeding), and were therefore persecuted and exterminated. Any eccentric or rebellious woman was at risk from accusations of being a witch, scapegoated for causing all kinds of ills. Catherine Clément, like Freud, sees a link between the witch and the hysteric: both were in revolt against domesticity, both were seen by their persecutors as the incarnation of nature's terrifying wildness. But while the hysteric is alienated from nature and from herself, the witch harnesses and controls the primal forces, making them the source of her magical power. The witch symbolises the paganism that Christianity suppressed, or co-opted by channelling and sublimating goddess-worship into the Cult of the Virgin Mary. Where the Virgin is passive, selfless, the archetypal 'female eunuch', the witch is potent, sexually voracious and terrifying.

Female artists have often aligned themselves with witches: prominent examples include the poets Emily Dickinson and Elizabeth Barrett Browning and the surrealist painter Leonora Carrington, who incorporated pagan imagery in her paintings (like the white horse from a Celtic witch-legend, the Saga of Rhiannon). At times,

Carrington's flirtation with the irrational erased the border between art and life: in the late '30s, she suffered a mental breakdown when what she called her 'sub-personas' invaded and possessed her. For Carrington, schizophrenia was the logical outcome of her revolt against fixity of form and identity: 'We have to escape from the existential habit of existing in a certain shape, as I did when I was mad.'

As frequently as female artists have imagined themselves as modern-day witches, male critics have likened powerful, perturbing female creativity to sorcery. Edward James pictured Carrington brewing her paintings 'in a cauldron at the stroke of midnight'. Writing about Patti Smith in 1978, Paul Rambali claimed, 'In the dark ages she'd have been burned at the stake. Now she's a rock and roll witch.' The witch is a female equivalent of the Dionysian shaman that has served as prototype for a lineage of male rock rebels (Jim Morrison/Hendrix/Nick Cave etc.). With her magical powers, her transcendence/transgression of social norms, her flight-y independence, the witch is a model for rock she-rebels.

Rock's most famous witch-song is Fleetwood Mac's FM-radio perennial 'Rhiannon (Will You Ever Win)' (1975), written and sung by Stevie Nicks. Its heroine is the Welsh witch from the same Celtic saga that inspired Carrington. 'It's just about a lady who's a goddess of steeds and a maker of birds,' explained Nicks. Rhiannon is a mysterious figure who can take flight at will. Nicks sings the song as a warning to Rhiannon's male admirers, who can never pin her down, own or know her, because she rides the winds, always eluding their grasp. Rhiannon is a proto-feminist free spirit who doesn't so much refuse as evade and elude male sexual conquest: hence the taunting chorus 'will you ever win?'. 'Rhiannon' helped seal Stevie Nicks's image as an ethereal nymph, with her gauzy clothes and head full of mythopoeic fancy and superstitious lore.

With her self-professed 'deep love of the mystical' and fascination with English history and Celtic lore, Nicks is something like the American equivalent to Kate Bush. Throughout her career, Kate Bush has delved into mythology, history, and literature, trying on costumes and personae (Peter Pan, Cathy from *Wuthering Heights*, Houdini's wife, Molly Bloom from *Ulysses*) that allow her to imagine a wilder life. On her 1985 album *The Hounds of Love*, a song-cycle called 'The Ninth Wave' is an elaborate allegory of Bush's feelings of estrangement from primordial, natural energy. In one of the suite's songs, 'Waking the Witch', Bush plays the part of a girl who's being punished for trying to 'fly' outside the prescribed roles for women. The prosecutor's voice – a deep *Exorcist* growl – suggests that it's really the Forces of Righteousness that are satanic, not the bewildered girl-child who is eventually drowned like a bird with a stone round its leg.

Kate Bush's exploration of female archetypes and iconography is mirrored by Siouxsie Sioux's succession of image-changes: in retrospect, the art-rocker and the art-punk were much closer than anyone imagined at the time. During the most visible and influential period of her career – from late '70s shock-rock infamy to chart success in the '80s – Siouxsie's look fused the dominatrix, the vampire and the Halloween witch into a singular form of style terrorism. She inspired a generation of British girls to adopt the Gothic look (sepulchral clothes, pointy Cleopatra-style eye make-up, angular, jet-black hair, deathly-white make-up).

1981's *Juju* was the first album on which Siouxsie explicitly invoked pagan and occult imagery, with songs like 'Spellbound', 'Halloween' and 'Voodoo Dolly'. 'Spellbound' imagines a child being swept up into a 'rag doll dance' by a sinister, primal energy force that erupts through the nursery walls like demonic laughter. This primordial energy is regressive and untamed: Siouxsie instructs the children to throw their parents down the stairs if they forget to say their prayers. In true Bahktinian carnival style, the social order has been turned upside down, infants govern their elders, and all structure has dis-

solved in a Dionysian whirl – a pandemonium unleashed
by the witch's malign spell.

Diamanda Galas's image is also midway between sorceress and vampire. In the babbling, bubbling glossolalia of
her daemonic-diva vocal style, Galas invokes the ungodly
elemental forces that are subjugated and silenced by
Judaeo-Christian patriarchy. Like the witch, she conjures
up the hidden but everpresent, always insurgent realm of
the unconscious. Galas explicitly aligns herself with the
traditions of paganism. She believes that, since the ancient
Greeks, woman's voice has always been 'a vehicle for transmission of occult knowledge or power. It's always been tied
to witches and the shamanistic experience.'

Appropriately, her vocal style has elicited comparisons
to exorcism, talking-in-tongues and hysteria: all techniques
in which 'daemonic' female desire makes itself present.
Galas, however, is perfectly happy with even the most negative connotations of sorcery: 'When a witch is about to be
burned on a ladder in flames, who can she call upon? I call
that person "Satan," although other people may have other
names, and it's the same entity that schizophrenics call
upon to create an essential freedom they need.' Whatever
people call her, she is proud to wear the badge of the outsider: 'So you say, "Yes, I am the Antichrist, I *am* Legba, I
am all these things you are afraid of."'

ooze out and away

Other female artists have aligned themselves with nature,
but they conceive of it not as chaotic and malign but as a
benign power. Their songs brim with oceanic feelings and
cosmic-consciousness, similar to the Gaia-worshipping
espoused by psychedelia's mother's boys. But where the
male mystics imagine being enveloped by the (m)other,
their female equivalents *identify* with Mother Nature. In
the process, they run the risk of essentialism – the notion

that woman is innately closer to nature, instinct, intuition, and therefore outside civilisation, reason, language.

Some feminists have gladly embraced this identification of woman-as-nature, despite its hazards, precisely because it's a way of valorising feminine attributes, and because it provides a stable base for a positive female identity. In this vein, Hélène Cixous's 1975 essay 'Sorties' uses the ocean as a metaphor for female subjectivity; unlike the masculine trait of fortifying the self against invasion, female consciousness oozes out beyond the self to embrace the world. Women feel more connected to nature and the cosmos, according to Cixous, since they are part of a continuum, an 'endless body, without "end"'. Where masculine sexuality 'gravitate[s] around the penis', feminine sexuality is polymorphous. 'Her libido is cosmic, just as her unconscious is worldwide: her writing also can only go on and on, without ever inscribing or distinguishing contours. . . .'

This 'cosmic libido' or oceanic sensibility is intimately connected with écriture féminine, writing that privileges flux and fluidity. Cixous's ideal 'feminine' artist is able to access language's hidden interior (the semiotic realm of pre-verbal utterance – babytalk, glossolalia – which language shapes into decipherable patterns). S/he 'has never ceased to hear what-comes-before language reverberating' beneath the orderly syntax of regular discourse.

Cixous's idea of the sea as mother is ancient, echoing the creation myths of the earliest human civilisations. Phoenician, Vedic and Egyptian cosmologies all begin with a watery chaos out of which earthly reality takes shape. In *A Natural History of the Senses*, Diane Ackerman recalls the sensation of scuba-diving in the Bahamas. 'I became aware of two things for the first time: that we carry the ocean within us; that our veins mirror the tides. As a human woman, with ovaries where eggs lie like roe, entering the smooth, undulating womb of the ocean from which our ancestors evolved millennia ago, I was so moved my eyes teared underwater, and I mixed my saltiness with the ocean's.... Home was everywhere.'

Sandy Denny, folk-rock's greatest 'earth mother' singer, felt the same mystical adoration for the sea. In 'One Way Donkey Ride' (*Rendezvous*, 1977), she feels the ocean of love singing in her veins. On 'The Sea' (from *Fotheringay*, 1970), Denny is an 'Ocean Gypsy' (to borrow a title from another British folk-rock group, Renaissance) – a female wanderer who identifies with the sea because both of them follow their wayward impulses wherever they like in defiance of male expectations. She warns of 'the coming of the sea', a flood tide creeping under the doors of London homes, demolishing every citizen's (psychic) defences. Like the heroine of the Byrds' 'She Don't Care About Time', Denny's alter ego is indifferent to timetables and schedules; she lives Everywhere and Everywhen. (There's a similar Zen-tinged mysticism in Yoko Ono's 'Don't Count the Waves', where the sea confounds the Western male response to the natural world – measuring it with a view to mastering and exploiting it. Ono's wordless voice, adrift in a maze of chimes and reverberations, offers the 'correct' response – awe-struck surrender.) In Denny's 'The Sea' and 'One Way Donkey Ride', the ocean represents death, which she doesn't fear, but welcomes as the end of separateness, a return to cosmic communion. Throughout her songs, she identifies with the Moon, the Ocean, and Eternity, which for Carl Jung were feminine archetypes that inhabited humanity's collective unconscious.

Stevie Nicks is another folk-rock maiden with a thing about the Moon and the Ocean. Prefigured in songs like 'Crystal' and 'Silver Springs', the oceanic imagery really blossoms in 'Sara' (from the 1979 Fleetwood Mac album *Tusk*). The shimmering soundscape created by Lindsey Buckingham is an aural analogue of what Nicks yearns for in the chorus: 'drowning in the sea of love'. Cradled in susurrating waves of scintillating acoustic guitars and clouds of breathy backing vocals, Nicks siphons nectar from her throat, tracing the melody's elliptical, uncanny path through the ebb-and-flow of sound. The song is a strange, unfathomable reverie that could be about an emotional (if not literal) *ménage à trois* between Nicks, her best friend Sara, and Sara's male lover. In the end, the song's real statement is mystical: Nicks is in love with love, with its oceanic power to dissolve boundaries.

Psychedelia's oceanic feelings of 'intimate immensity' are a sublimated longing for 'womb-space', for a time when the infant and mother together made up the entire universe. Could it be that the female mystics in this chapter are also indulging in a symbolic form of incestuous union? For the most part, these female artists appear to identify with this Ur-Mother (Nature, the Sea) as a model of benign omnipotence and grandeur; it seems to play the same role in the female imagination as fantasies of kingliness or self-deification do for the male.

But there are a handful of female artists whose work has undeniably regressive, pre-Oedipal qualities. Most notable is Liz Fraser of Cocteau Twins, a band whose music positively luxuriates in those 'semiotic' elements that are connotative of the lost maternal body. First and most important is Fraser's singing: a garbled phoneme soup (imagine Welsh sung backwards, through a sieve) that's mostly indecipherable but always sounds rich in wholly private, non-verbalisable meaning. Fraser revels in the oral voluptuousness of utterance. Her titles and lyrics are full of assonance, alliteration and echolalia: 'Kookaburra', 'Quisquose', 'The Itchy Glowbo Blow'. When she sings, it sounds like babytalk *and* lullaby (an early EP was actually called 'Lullabies'); Fraser plays both infant and mother, duetting with herself in an endless serenade.

Musically, Cocteau Twins recreate in sound this self-suckling paradise. Their music plays up all the chromatic, synaesthetic elements that distinguish the regressive rock, 'perfumed fog' tradition from Hendrix to Can to Brian Eno to My Bloody Valentine: lustrous guitar textures (effects-laden and heavily studio-processed), cascades of gauzy sound that seem to swathe the listener like atomised droplets of fragrance. Iridescence and deliquescence are the Cocteaus' watchwords, as signalled by titles like 'The Spangle Maker', 'Pearly Dewdrops Drops', 'In the Gold Dust Rush'. Cocteau Twins' music transports us back to the gilded realm of the infant-mother dyad, when all the baby can perceive is a dazzling chaos of sensory stimuli.

Finally, the titles and scant shards of intelligible lyric all confirm the incestuous longings that underlie this music. The titles run the gamut of psychedelia's obsessions: motherhood and infancy ('When Mama Was Moth', 'Suckling the Mender'), the lost state of grace ('In Our Angelhood'), the bower-of-bliss (*Bluebell Knoll*, 'Lazy Calm'), the sea and the moon (*Echoes in a Shallow Bay*, 'Sea, Swallow Me', 'Ooze Out and Away, Onehow' – the last two from *The Moon and the Melodies*). Even their love songs are *infantile*; the Cocteaus' version of amorous desire is oral rather than genital – the lover's body as a limitless plenitude of 'exquisite stuff' (as 'Iceblink Luck' puts it), a toddler's wonderland of confectionery and ice cream, mother's milk and honey-pie. Hence kissed-out titles like 'Sugar Hiccup' and 'Spooning Good Singing Gum'.

Hugo Largo were another band often described as oceanic. This New York quartet were responsible for some of the most uncompromisingly 'feminine' sounding music of the last decade, despite the fact that three of the four band members were male. Singer/lyricist Mimi Goese came from a performance art background; the male musicians – Tim Sommer, Adam Peacock, Hahn Rowe – had played in avant-garde and hardcore bands, but became disenchanted with the assaultive, sado-masochist nature of the noise aesthetic. So Hugo Largo's sound was based around the absence of a drum beat and guitar riffs. The result was a totally different interpretation of the word 'rock'; not phallic insistence, but a gentle, cradling motion. Goese's meandering vocal lines, the soft pulsations of Peacock and Sommer's twin basses, and Rowe's striations of violin, all undulate around an implied rhythmic vertebrae.

The oceanic quality of their music was mirrored lyrically only once, in 'Blue Blanket', a song that never made it on to their two albums. Amidst the tidal sway of violin and bass, singer Mimi Goese's voice undulates; if it were a surface, the listener would be dipping and swooning into its folds. 'Everyone looks beautiful,' Mimi sings, 'under the water': transfigured, made graceful, unburdened by gravity. Sea and sleep are united in a lovely image – the 'Blue Blanket' – that recalls Diane Ackerman's poignant feeling that, underwater, 'home was everywhere'. It's heaven, down there.

who's that girl?:
masquerade and mastery

'The only thing you can do if you are trapped in a reflection is to invert the image.'
Juliet Mitchell, *Psychoanalysis & Feminism*

Confessional singer-songwriters find strength in absolute honesty; mystics, witches and hysterics look to female power that lies beyond culture in the wildness of Nature. But there's another tradition in female pop that works within culture rather than seeking to transcend or escape it. Instead of stripping away layers to reveal an authentic self, it plays with cultural representations of femininity. For artists like Siouxsie Sioux, Madonna, Annie Lennox, Kate Bush and Grace Jones, masquerade becomes a way of provoking and confounding the male gaze. The traditionally feminine 'trivial pursuit' of fashion and self-adornment is reclaimed as a *reinvention of the self*. Women have long been accused of being superficial, fickle, depthless, mendacious; masquerade turns these negative stereotypes into a weapon. These artists refuse to be tied down to any one identity.

Feminist thought has hotly debated the possibilities and dangers of such a strategic use of masquerade. Some have criticised the dominant strain of feminism for its 'essentialist' belief in the intrinsic, biological attributes of femaleness. Following postmodern theory's assault on the very notion of fixed, centred identity, critics have mooted the possibility of a feminism that assumes a more fluid, mutable notion of gender. This more playful approach in turn paved the way for an ironic use of archetypal/stereotypical feminine imagery.

Teresa de Lauretis, a feminist film theorist, describes the sea change in feminist thought as the emergence of 'the concept of a multiple, shifting, often self-contradictory identity... an identity that one... insists on as a strategy.' De Lauretis makes a crucial distinction between 'those two terms *mask* and *masquerade*, which reappear conspicuously and are both meant, worn as they are, as weapons of survival. But the former is there to represent a burden, imposed, constraining the expression of one's real identity; the latter is flaunted, or, if not, at least put on like a new dress which, even when required, does give some pleasure to the wearer.' In pop terms, it's the difference between Janis Joplin's messy revolt against the 'mask' of conventional femininity, and Madonna's supremely self-controlled deployment of 'masques' as a strategy of self-empowerment.

De Lauretis's distinction between the burden of mask and the freedom of masquerade figures in two Suzanne Vega songs on her 1992 album *99.9°F*. In 'Private Goes Public' Vega suggests that 'face is the place' where interiority goes public. The face is both something that betrays its owner (as in the involuntary grimace or blush) and something you can hide behind, a shield or veil. She vacillates between dropping her defences and joining the hurly burly of social intercourse, or preserving the private space of her inner life. And in 'As Girls Go', it's a man, a transvestite, who enjoys the liberating possibilities of masquerade. The song questions the fictive nature of femininity, since this person is 'more girl' than any 'real' girl.

Discussing Joan Riviere's essay, 'Womanliness as a Masquerade', Marjorie Garber points out that 'the woman constructed by culture is... according to Riviere, already an impersonation. Womanliness *is* mimicry, is *masquerade*.' Pop culture theorist Lawrence Grossberg has formulated the ostensibly paradoxical notion of an *authentic inauthenticity* to explain the strategies of self-created icons like Madonna. Instead of the fraudulent posture of honesty

(Grossberg's witty term is 'inauthentic authenticity', e.g. Bruce Springsteen, Tracy Chapman) this approach accepts the constructed nature of the performer's persona. 'Although [authentic inauthenticity] seems to celebrate the absence of any center or identity, it actually locates that absence as a new center. That is, it celebrates the fragmentary, the contradictory, the temporary.' The fictive nature of sexual identity offers an existential freedom: a figure like Madonna or RuPaul 'can deconstruct gender at the moment of celebrating it (and celebrate it precisely because one can deconstruct it).' But, the traditional feminist might interject in exasperation, isn't this having one's cake and eating it too? The delusion that one can play with fire and not get burned?

Rock has always oscillated between privileging unvarnished truth and espousing a reinvention of the self through glamour. Punk aggravated this confusion, drawing as it did on both the traditions of social realism and protest music, and on glam rock. Poly Styrene and her band X-Ray Spex explored one side of punk; their songs were an anguished response to a world in which media brainwashing and social conditioning made authenticity impossible. 'Art-I-Ficial' (from *Germfree Adolescents*, 1978) is a tirade against constructed prettified femininity; Styrene howls that the 'mask's not me'. 'Identity' rails against a world where rebellion is turned into a marketable off-the-peg persona in the blinking of an eye. Although she ached for some kind of authentic self, Poly Styrene nevertheless took inauthenticity as her identity: her name and songs like 'I Am A Cliché' flaunt her fabricated nature.

That other great female punk, Siouxsie Sioux, had a less conflicted relationship with artifice. In many ways, she's a female Bowie: her career has consisted of an endless succession of costume changes and sexual personae. (In fact, as a bored teenager in suburban London, she hung out with 'Bowie boys', style-obsessed, sexually ambiguous young men.) Of all the punks, Siouxsie and the Banshees were most indebted to glam rock (they even covered T.Rex's '20th Century Boy'), and along with the equally Bowie-obsessed Bauhaus (who covered 'Ziggy Stardust'), they inspired Goth, the post-punk offshoot that abandoned politics for magick and mystique.

At roughly the same time as Siouxsie the glam-terrorist was 'playing the alien' on *Top of the Pops*, Kate Bush was also exploring a multitude of identities. Bush was never as hip as Siouxsie, because her roots weren't Bowie and Bolan but early '70s art-rock (the outlandish theatricality of Peter Gabriel in early Genesis, Pink Floyd's conceptualism). In her videos and live performances, Bush changed costumes to accompany the different characters in her songs: the temptress of 'Babooshka', the romantic heroine in 'Wuthering Heights', the mad inventor's loyal son in 'Cloudbusting', the bride seeking vengeance in 'Wedding List', the VietCong soldier of 'Pull Out the Pin'. Bush has said: 'When I perform, I'm definitely someone else. She's a lot stronger and I wouldn't be as daring as her.'

A closer parallel to Siouxsie's forbidding *sangfroid* vocals and hard-edged androgyny is Grace Jones. After early cult stardom as a disco diva, Jones recorded *Warm Leatherette* (1980) and *Nightclubbing* (1981). On these albums, the camp artifice inherent in disco (with its Tin Pan Alley/showbiz ancestry and its links to gay club culture) is developed into a full-blown postmodern theatre of role-play. Indeed, her live performance, elaborately staged and with multiple costume changes, was called *One Man Show*, punning on both her androgynous looks and on the fact that there was no single, no real, Grace Jones. Interiority is abolished in favour of impenetrable but mesmerising facades.

On record too, each song sees Jones playing a different character, especially when they're cover versions of songs made famous by other singers. In 'Love Is the Drug' she takes on Bryan Ferry's persona of the lounge lizard cruising the singles bars looking for another fix. In Smokey Robinson's 'The Hunter Gets Captured by the Game', the gender reversal is complicated: as diva-dominatrix, Jones is playing the role of a man who is himself the victim of reversed roles and turned tables. 'Walking in the Rain' seems more 'autobiographical': Jones wanders listlessly, a member of a third sex (she feels like a woman and looks like a man), and thus an exile on Main Street. But 'Demolition Man' (a song written for her by Sting) is pure metamorphosis: here Jones is a demon-lover death-machine wreaking havoc wherever (s)he goes. Like Iggy's A-bomb kid in 'Search and Destroy', Jones is 'a walking nightmare', a disaster waiting to happen, with a deadly magnetic allure that draws victims to her like moths to flame.

More than an artist expressing herself, the Grace Jones of *Warm Leatherette* and *Nightclubbing* is the focus for, and figment of, a team of specialists: her designer/mentor Jean-Paul Goude, producers Chris Blackwell and Alex Sadkin, and a troupe of expert musicians like the dub-funk rhythm section Sly & Robbie. On the two albums, Jones only co-wrote three songs and wrote one other ('Feel Up', in which she's a thirty-two-year-old seducing a teenage Jamaican rude boy) – not unusual in disco. An obvious parallel is with Donna Summer, protégé of producer Giorgio Moroder and songwriter Pete Bellote. Summer also played a series of characters: pornotopian siren from the age of the orgasmatron ('I Feel Love'), hooker ('Bad Girls'), torch-singer ('Macarthur Park'), ordinary working girl as fairy tale princess (the concept album *Once Upon A Time*). After seizing control of her career and becoming a born-again Christian, she unveiled the 'real' Donna Summer with her cover version of the New Age-y 'State of Independence'. Clearly, she felt that her former image – a weird mix of Ice Queen and Porn-Dream – was both an unliberating role model for women and an oppressive mask for herself.

Grace Jones's career raises a host of questions about masquerade as strategy: is she agent or actor (inserted in a screenplay scripted by others)? Her cover version of Joy Division's 'She's Lost Control' assumes a special irony in this light. The contradictions were deliberately heightened with her one-off *Slave to the Rhythm* project (1985), masterminded by ZTT, the label who had previously stagemanaged the sensational phenomenon of Frankie Goes To Hollywood. The *Slave to the Rhythm* album was tantamount to an essay on the constructed nature of pop stardom. To what extent was Jones alienated from the production of her image as an alien, dominated even as she came across as a dominatrix?

So much of Jones's aesthetic seems bound up with the eroticisation of alienation: witness the fetishistic sex of 'Warm Leatherette', her version of the Daniel Miller song inspired by J.G. Ballard's ideas about the eroticism of carcrashes, or the disconnected femme fatale of 'Private Life' (written by Chrissie Hynde) who scorns a man for his wimpy notions of attachment and intimacy, and boasts 'I'm very superficial'. Writing about *Nightclubbing*, Ian Penman celebrated Jones for the way she'd 'turned the commodity into a body, rather than the usual vice versa'. Years later, Penman's paradox was literalised and folded into a sort of pretzel of contradictions, with Jones's appearance in an ad campaign for a motor car. Working from Jones's androgyne-as-automaton aura, the commercials played havoc with the metaphors of woman-as-car and car-as-woman, and left you wondering who was selling whom.

Apart from Madonna, the singer who has most successfully brought masquerade into the mainstream is Annie Lennox. In Eurythmics, Lennox certainly made a concerted bid to be taken seriously as a female Bowie. (In 1993, she penned a poem/paean to Bowie for an *Arena* special on the middle-aged glam rocker.) Around the time of *Sweet Dreams (Are Made of This)* (1983), Lennox's image – a short, sharp shock of inorganic orange hair, virulent red lipstick, a streamlined and hard edged physique, big-shouldered men's suits – was a perfect blend of Bowie's 'Thin

White Duke' and Grace Jones's glacial androgyne. In the song 'Sweet Dreams', she plays the dominatrix, her voice oozing cold wisdom when it comes to men's wiles: some want to abuse, some 'want to be abused'. Like Madonna, Lennox aimed to set herself up as a human question mark, a bewitching but baffling enigma; like Madonna, she wrote a song called 'Who's That Girl?'. For the video, Lennox tried to resurrect the cross-dressing confusion of Bowie's 'Boys Keep Swinging' by playing both the male and female parts in the love triangle that is the video's mystery story.

Ideas of glamour as reinvention of the self were in the air: it was the height of New Pop, the UK movement that refloated glam rock ideas as an alternative to the various dead-ends trailing from the still-warm corpse of punk. ABC's strings, schmaltz and gold lamé suits, Adam Ant's procession of heroic archetypes, Boy George's gender-bending: Eurythmics cannily plugged into this new pop Zeitgeist in which the subversive possibilities of artifice were being reappraised. 'Who's That Girl?' casually incorporated a buzz-phrase of the day, 'the language of love': bands like ABC, with their *The Lexicon of Love* LP, and Scritti Politti, with their Barthes-influenced deconstruction of 'the lover's discourse', had trailblazed a strategy of ironic deployment of romantic clichés, which were simultaneously celebrated and unravelled.

As their career developed, Annie Lennox ran through a plethora of derivative poses: the white Aretha Franklin demanding 'Respect' on 'Sisters Are Doin' It For Themselves' (with the real Franklin relegated to backing vocals), the sassy soul mama who gives her faithless biker boyfriend a dressing down on 'Would I Lie To You?', the Tin Pan Alley showgirl of 'There Must Be An Angel', the commanding Piaf-like chanteuse of her 1992 solo album *Diva*.

One song stands out amongst all this corn, though: 'I Need A Man' (from 1987's *Savage*) is Lennox's one truly confounding (im)posture. Over an immaculate simulation of the discofied raunch purveyed by the Stones in the mid

'70s, Lennox plays Jagger's swagger to the hilt, parodying his own caricature of low-down blues rapacity. In the song, the female protagonist treats men like men treat women: as object, prey, plaything. Her contempt is as obvious as her lust, her repetition of the word 'baby' beautifully belittling. In the video, Lennox is so vamped up and caked in make-up she could be a male transvestite, echoing the Stones' own cross-dressing escapades in the promo for 'Have You Seen Your Mother, Baby, Standing in the Shadow?'. 'I Need A Man' is a Moebius strip of gender confusion: is Lennox playing a man in drag who's impersonating a man-eating vamp, or a 'real' female vamp, or what? Annie Lennox's more feminine personae often have an air of drag about them. For Marjorie Garber, drag puts 'in question the "naturalness" of gender roles through the discourse of clothing and body parts'. The question is: what is communicated when a female artist like Lennox or Madonna goes into drag in order to play feminine roles? How can the questioning of clichés and stereotypes be distinguished from mere conformist perpetuation of those stereotypes?

me, myself, i: autonomy & control

As well as being a videogenic masque-wearer, Annie Lennox has some renown as a strong role model for women. We should probably admit that we don't find representations of 'strength' in pop particularly compelling. The autonomy of figures like Lennox and Joan Armatrading has the reek of mental hygiene and health-and-efficiency. As Simon Frith and Angela McRobbie wrote of the soft-core feminism of Helen Reddy's 'I Am Woman': 'What you hear is the voice of an idealised consumer, if the commodity for consumption in this instance is a packaged version of women's liberation.' The posture of tyrannical, marauding omnipotence is pure rock'n'roll; benign self-empowerment isn't.

Yet the 'strong woman' seems to resonate for a lot of pop fans. It's particularly true in black music, and with artists who are highly influenced by soul's ethos of pride and dignity. Lennox is an obvious example: it's no coincidence that her most forthright feminist statement, 'Sisters Are Doin' It For Themselves', was couched in soul's bluster. Throughout her career, Lennox has blown hot and cold, oscillating between the frosty hauteur of her Euro-androgyne persona and a warmer, R&B sass.

Another decidedly cool customer is the black British singer-songwriter Joan Armatrading. Her songs and image project a self-contained, self-sufficient resilience, as in 'Willow' (from 1977's *Show Some Emotion*), where she quietly boasts of being 'shelter in a storm' for those weaker than herself, or in the absolutely Armatrading-definitive 'Me, Myself, I', the title track of her 1980 album. The melody's staccato metre starkly underlines the assertive (but not aggressive) stance of the lyrics; sure, she wants a boyfriend, but only one day a week. The other six, she cherishes quality time with herself. In typical Armatrading fashion, she denies being a narcissist; it's simply that she 'don't want company'. Although she's been nicknamed Joan Armour-plating by mocking DJs and critics, her songbook actually contains far more tender than tough songs. But even in her romantic songs, she valorises self-possession over abandon, obsession, dependency: 'More Than One Kind of Love' argues that friendships are more enduring and valuable than passion, and vows that she'll never lose her 'sense of self'.

In the late '80s, Janet Jackson became a superstar with the immaculately designed soft-core feminism of *Control* (1986). There is some doubt as to what extent this was a *spectacle* of control: Susan McClary points out that when Jackson first joined up with her producers Jimmy Jam and Terry Lewis, they'd already finished the music for the song 'Control' and just slotted her (and lyrics about her life) into it. She argues that 'the mix throughout highlights the powerful beats, such that Jackson constantly seems thrown off balance by them'. But although her state-of-art sound was the creation of her producers, it does seem that Ms Jackson (as she insisted on being addressed in one song) had seized control of her hitherto undistinguished career, simply by choosing to work with Jam and Lewis. The lyrics certainly give the impression of a young woman coming into her own.

'Control' is Jackson's manifesto for the modern girl who calls her own shots, in love as well as business. Jam and Lewis fashion a stuttering, staccato electro-funk that's the perfect vehicle for her self-assertion. 'Nasty' is even more pugnacious: it's an '80s cyber-funk version of 'Respect', in which Jackson puts the rude boys firmly in their place. Much of the rest of *Control*, however, is more traditionally feminine and alluring. After this splendid album, Jackson over-reached herself with the hubris of *Janet Jackson's Rhythm Nation 1814*. Shifting from personal politics to pontifications on the parlous state of the American body politic, she sang unwieldy, pompous songs like 'State of the World'. By 1993's *Janet*, Jackson clearly felt she had nothing more to prove, and abandoned both the feisty self-assertion and the high-minded idealism of her adolescent phase for 'adult' sexuality – svelte, seductive, utterly traditional.

In the sexual politics of hip hop culture, respect is a major issue for female artists, given gangsta rap's imagery of ho's and gold-diggers, backstabbers and ballbreakers. For Queen Latifah, the onus is on women to respect themselves and thus earn respect. Women who act like 'bitches', Latifah told *Ear* magazine, 'have no respect for themselves and it shows, so the guys don't have any respect for them, either. The rappers don't treat their mothers and sisters like that. None of them would come up to me and say "Latifah, b-i-t-c-h."' Queen Latifah cultivated a persona that exudes dignity and self-composure; instead of using the 'royal we', she talks about herself in the third person: 'On earlier records I'd drop a line about South Africa or drugs, but "The Evil that Men Do" is dedicated to what makes Latifah mad about what's going on in the world and in the environment and about how people don't do anything to cure or change it.' For some, Latifah's aura of self-discipline and sagacity doesn't have the magnetic, mesmerising allure of more 'unsound', male rappers. Latifah's version of sovereignty is closer to benign despotism than gangsta rappers' tyranny and terrorism (although she did entitle an early song 'Wrath of My Madness'). She's too dignified, too much of a positive role model to be baaad.

Far more powerful (as art) than Latifah and Monie Love's unthreatening self-empowerment in their collaboration 'Ladies First' are those female rappers who take on the bitch role with all its vengeful viciousness – like the foul-mouthed Roxanne Shanté, whose 'Fatal Attraction' threatens to castrate a man who won't leave his wife for her. Shanté started her career with 'Roxanne's Revenge', a caustic response to U.T.F.O.'s 'Roxanne, Roxanne'; speaking up for the fictional 'bitch' dissed in U.T.F.O's song, Shanté inaugurated a clamorous spate of answer and counter-riposte records. Then there's Salt-n-Pepa's debut LP *Hot, Cool & Vicious* (1986), whose songs confounded attempts by right-on critics to label them as proto-feminist rap. What to make of the unsisterly malice of 'I'll Take Your Man', or the vindictive glower of 'It's Alright'? These songs suggested that Salt-n-Pepa's stance was almost an exact mirror-image of male rappers' gladiatorial aggression and deadly rivalry. And while 'Tramp' dissed men as sleazy, faithless dogs, the fact that it was a reworking of Carla Thomas and Otis Redding's classic duet/duel 'Tramp' highlighted the traditionalism of Salt-n-Pepa's sexual politics: the song was squarely in the longstanding soul tradition of women forthrightly demanding reciprocal treatment from their men, but only *within* the terms of conventional gender relations (e.g. Aretha Franklin's 'Do Right Woman – Do Right Man'). On later albums, Salt-n-Pepa ranged from 'Let's Talk About Sex' (1990's *Blacks' Magic*), in which they came over as positivity-peddling youth counsellors, to the predatorial lechery of 'Shoop' (1993's *Very Necessary*). In this song, Salt-n-Pepa pull off an ideological coup, deftly managing to objectify men yet simultaneously celebrating male sexual aggression and hardness: 'If looks could kill, you'd be an Uzi'.

cool as ice

The Ice Queen is perhaps the closest rock equivalent to female rap's super-bitch attitude. Ice is the opposite of all that women are supposed to be: warm, flowing, giving, receptive. Like Lady Macbeth, the Ice Queen has unsexed herself, dammed up her lachrymal and lactation ducts. She offers cold, not comfort. Her hard surfaces can't be penetrated. She is an island, an iceberg.

Grace Slick is rock's original Ice Queen. In 'White Rabbit' and 'Somebody to Love', the most famous songs she wrote and sang for Jefferson Airplane, Slick's baleful, declamatory singing conjures the impression of someone who's above it all, looking down on man's folly and passing judgment. Her piercing voice seems to go through you like a lance. Slick's aura was forbidding. In a 1974 interview for Katherine Orloff's book *Rock'n'Roll Woman*, Slick discussed her image: 'Sometimes I like to look peculiar.... I dressed like Hitler once.... I think [the press] see me as being a little icy, sort of rowdy, a little bit sarcastic. That's pretty much the way I am.'

Over on the East Coast, Nico took the Ice Queen persona even further. On *The Velvet Underground and Nico* (1967), her Teutonic hauteur fits perfectly with the Velvets' speed-freak cool. Like Jefferson Airplane, the Velvets went straight from folk-rock to whiter-than-white noise, bypassing R&B's body-heat. On her solo albums, Nico goes even deeper into a wasteland of arid, ascetic, Aryan sound. *Chelsea Girl* (1967) offers delicate, mournful folk, but one song, 'It Was A Pleasure Then', looks ahead to the desolate, wintry soundscapes of *The Marble Index* (1969), one of the most harrowing and death-fixated albums in rock history.

On *The Marble Index*, Nico is singing religious music for nihilists. Her collaborator, ex-Velvet John Cale, constructs a shimmering, reverberant ice palace for her out of harmonium, celesta and other non-rock textures. The Ice Queen's autonomy becomes autism ('No One Is There'). She fetishises disconnection as a safeguard against the thawing warmth of messy intimacy. Nico longs to be beyond desire, to reach the numbed stillness of entropy (heat-death). She dreams of a sort of negative nirvana; to lie in state at Time's 'undead end', immaculate and inorganic. 'Nibelungen' describes a world drained of affect, bleached of colour; again, she longs to be 'asleep'. While it may be a reductive interpretation to regard *The Marble Index* as the ultimate heroin album, its hunger for narcosis, its frigid expanses, recalls William Burroughs's description of the junkie's quest for a metabolic 'Absolute Zero'. The only way to erase doubt and kill pain completely is to enter a *living death*.

Desertshore (1971), the sequel to *The Marble Index*, saw Nico once again working in collaboration with Cale. The title and songs like 'Janitor of Lunacy' suggest that Nico felt herself stranded, incapable of taking the plunge into oceanic feelings, banished to a bleak and lifeless zone on the periphery of the 'real world'. Nothing can shatter Nico's splendid ice-olation; she longs for someone to 'erase my empty pages'. On 'Mutterlien', a hymn adrift in an ambient Antarctic, Cale's reverbed piano makes sound shiver and shudder, like the throes of hypothermia.

If Nico felt herself stranded in the desert, then Siouxsie Sioux's renunciation of oceanic feelings was a means to power. The first Banshees album, *The Scream* (1978), contains some of the most unfluid, fleshless rock music ever created, stringent and staccato. 'Metal Postcard (Mittageisen)' fetishises the inhuman perfection of metal, which Siouxsie declares will 'rule in my master scheme'.

'Jigsaw Feeling' explores sensations of alienation from the body: the imagery of fractured organs and limbs, the sense of a disassembled bodily identity, resembles the hysterical un-body that figures in Lydia Lunch's songs. In 'Jigsaw Feeling', the Ice Queen cracks up: Siouxsie oscillates between 'feeling total' and being 'split in two'. It is only her dazzling, frozen exteriority that keeps the psychotic interior contained. Later in her career, songs like 'Christine' and 'Eve White/Eve Black' dramatise the schizophrenic's struggle not to 'shatter kaleidoscope-style'.

'Regal Zone' (from 1979's *Join Hands*) is the ultimate ice statement: Siouxsie stands 'alone in a Regal Zone', erect and intimidating. Similarly, Siouxsie's early image – S/M dominatrix clothes, peek-a-boo bras that exposed the breast but were far from titillating – invited the voyeuristic gaze only to punish it. Her image, her *sangfroid* vocals, her commanding demeanour all signify 'Look, Don't Touch'. Siouxsie doesn't want to be made of *fleisch* (that evocative German word that means both flesh and meat), she wants to be made of metal or ice, impenetrable, invulnerable.

This desire to be obelisk or basilisk (the mythological cold-blooded reptile whose glance was lethal) had a sinister side. Siouxsie wasn't just the first woman to take on glam rock's androgyny; in the early days of the Banshees, she also followed through glam's flirtation with fascism, to the point of wearing a swastika. For most punks, the swastika was a shock tactic or cheap nihilism, but for Siouxsie, fascism's fascination seems to have run a little deeper. In a 1985 interview with *Blitz*, she recalled that 'when I was fifteen or sixteen I used to go out of my way to have very unattractive hairstyles, very short, geometrically very ugly, cropped and very frightening to the opposite sex... I think I always knew the way I wanted to live... was completely as a fascist. I mean, I call myself a fascist personally, I like everything my own way.'

Monumentalism – the desire to be as imposing as a statue – is proto-fascist because it's a flight from the liquidity of female biology, of nature. Like the Futurists, Siouxsie's aesthetic fetishised stark contours and severance; in 'Desert Kisses' (from 1980's *Kaleidoscope*) she even wrote a song of outright hydrophobia, where 'tidal fingers' hold her in their 'deadly grip'. Although she gradually distanced herself from the Banshees' early flirtation with fascism, Sioux continued to take on magisterial and forbidding female archetypes, like the dominatrix and the witch. On 'Arabian Knights' (from *Juju*, 1981), she updates Grace Slick's posture of the stern matriarch who passes judgment on men's wicked ways, excoriating Islam's patriarchal enslavement of women behind the veils of purdah, where they're reduced to the role of 'baby machines'. In 'Monitor' she's an imperious dominatrix, commanding her plaything to 'sit back and enjoy'.

As her career developed, Siouxsie found her way to more 'feminine' images of power. At the same time – surely no coincidence – her lyrics ooze moisture. With *A Kiss in the Dreamhouse* (1982), the Ice Queen melts; proto-fascist rigour softens into luxuriant, languorous decadence. From the ornamented Klimt-inspired cover image to the heady haze of neo-psychedelic sound, the album was all lush sensuality and blissful blur. The opening 'Cascade' has Siouxsie enswirled in droplets of fragrant sound, 'like liquid falling'. In 'Green Fingers', Siouxsie's even able to imagine women's proximity to nature as a magical source of strength, not vulnerability. Supernaturalism rather than anti-naturalism becomes the new model for the Banshees, as the earthly lore of the witch supersedes the glacial terrorism of the Ice Queen. With its Rites-of-Pan flute, 'Green Fingers' recalls the psychedelic classic 'The Garden of Earthly Delights' by the United States of America, in which Dorothy Moskowitz sings ominously of 'venomous blossoms' and 'omnivorous orchids' that lurk within a girl's eyes; love is a Venus fly-trap whose nectar lures man to a sticky end.

Siouxsie revels in similar imagery of deadly voluptuousness in 'Melt', where sex is blissful bondage, 'tiny deaths' that leave the man 'beheaded'. 'Slowdive' imagines swimming and swooning in carnal confusion, taking the plunge into the uncontrol of desire, bathing in flesh. 'She's A Carnival' offers a less sinister vision of the psychic fragmentation that once threatened Siouxsie. She celebrates the idea of the self as a benignly chaotic polyphony of unruly desires and clamorous voices. Fascism fears the mob, but in 'She's a Carnival' Siouxsie imagines mingling and merging with a festive multitude, in the spirit of Dionysus. Where once Siouxsie's musical alter egos were sharply etched against the landscape, now she spins in a 'dizzy haze', and her forbidding glare is replaced by a smile like 'Mardi Gras'.

On the next album, *Hyaena* (1984), 'Swimming Horses' is outright oceanic rock, a song inspired by seahorses. Still, Siouxsie's interest in gender bending (women should be strong, men should be as weak as the incapacitated, 'melting man' of 'Melt') persists: Siouxsie was struck by the fact that it's the male of the seahorse species that gives birth. She clearly likes the idea of women being freed of the burden of fecundity. By 1991's *Superstition*, Siouxsie completed her trajectory from the vampire woman of her Goth goddess prime, to the vamp of 'Kiss Them For Me'. Here, she modelled herself on '40s movie idols like Rita Hayworth, who played strong and sometimes sinister female roles.

Punk revolted against the pseudo-liberation of the post-hippie '70s by espousing uptightness, fetishism and the unnatural. The early London punk scene had much in common with Warhol's Factory: lots of drag queens and gender bending, massive ingestion of amphetamines (which suppressed sexual desire and replaced it with narcissistic exhibitionism). A continuum runs from the Velvet Underground and Pop Art, through glam rock's decadence, ambisexuality and fascistic flirtations, to punk's style terrorism. If Siouxsie was punk's Nico, then someone like Jordan (who modelled Vivienne Westwood's clothes in McLaren's boutique, Sex) was its Edie Sedgwick: a face, a scenester. Jordan enjoyed the power she got from wearing confrontational clothes: 'Punk wasn't necessarily a sexual thing. . . . People were scared out of their wits of me.'

For Siouxsie and the punkettes, hauteur + couture + sex = rebellion. Female style terrorists like Jordan and Sue Catwoman, with their blend of vamp and dominatrix, were crucial to punk's shock value. At a punk party in early 1976, with the fledgling Pistols about to play one of their first gigs, Malcolm McLaren was excited by the presence of a rock journalist, and begged Jordan to do something outrageous to get them publicity. According to Jon Savage's *England's Dreaming*, he said: 'Take your clothes off, girl.' Jordan agreed to do it only if it could be incorporated into the band's performance. The photographs of Johnny Rotten ripping her clothes off were 'used everywhere'. Get your tits out, lass – for the revolution!

un-typical girls:
post-punk demystification

Siouxsie extended punk's reinvention of the self into a fancy-dress parade of fantastical personae; she used mystique as a form of terrorism. Another strand of punk – the demystification contingent – developed in the opposite direction. Struggling to expose the ideological underpinnings of society, these bands directed their energy towards dismantling conventional constructions of femininity and masculinity. All-male agit-prop bands like Gang of Four and Scritti Politti and all-female and mixed-gender bands like the Slits, the Au Pairs, the Raincoats, and Delta 5, rallied behind two key notions: that 'the personal is political', and that 'radical content warrants and demands radical forms'. Together they formed an 'anti-rockist' movement that was opposed to the traditionalism of content and form that characterised both mainstream rock (with its heterosexism) and teenybopper chartpop (with its reliance on romantic illusions).

Brutal demystification was always at the heart of punk. Love and sexuality didn't go unscathed; songs like the Buzzcocks' masturbation anthem 'Orgasm Addict' or ATV's ode to impotence, 'Love Lies Limp', tried to deal with desire in a way that shunned the romantic roleplay of the trad love song in the belief that the truth, however unsightly and bathetic, was at least authentic.

Poly Styrene of X-Ray Spex was obsessed with the fragility of authentic identity in the face of media conditioning. On *Germfree Adolescents* (1978), Styrene's X-Ray vision reveals the tissue of lies, the cat's cradle of puppetstrings that lurks behind the facades of consumer capitalism.

'Identity' is a desperate protest against media manipulation of desire; Poly Styrene unleashes a foghorn bellow that's simultaneously a Munch-like howl of inner emptiness and a roar of refusal. In 'I Am A Cliché' and 'I Am A Poseur' she assumes the brainwashed zombie persona with a vengeance à la Sex Pistols' 'Pretty Vacant', reflecting back at society its own nightmare of 'what's gone wrong with our children?' But when punk's embrace and flaunting of inauthenticity became a cliché itself, the tangle of contradictions brought Styrene to the verge of a breakdown. On tour, Styrene hallucinated a mysterious energy force pulsing outside her hotel window. Interpreting this as a bad omen, she quit music and began a quest for some kind of stable and authentic 'ground of being', eventually finding it in Hare Krishna.

amazons in the kitchen

Those other archetypal female punk rockers, the Slits, were also strung out on the tensions between revolt against the emptiness of consumer society and the longing for a holistic, grounded way of life. Their aesthetic veered from demystification to mysticism (an exaltation of Mother Nature and natural rhythm). The Slits' initial focus was on demystifying the means of musical production, and their earliest recordings (released belatedly as an untitled 1980 album) offer an artless, atrocious racket. The acoustic primitivism of 'Once Upon A Time in A Living Room', and its title, suggest the song wasn't just recorded live but composed spontaneously. Many bands, before and after, have covered the same ground, where ambition far exceeds ability: lo-fi, fuzz-overload, unsyncopated rhythms, nursery rhyme melodies. Some commentators regard the Slits' early songs as far more excitingly subversive in their refusal of expertise than the more musicianly fare on the Slits' 1979 debut *Cut*. But listening now, the sense of liberation and glee, of unskilled upstarts seizing the moment, is hard to recapture.

The pseudo-tribal percussion of 'Bongos on the Lawn' does, however, look ahead to *Cut*, the Slits' masterwork. On the cover, the band appear as modern primitives, naked except for loincloths and smeared head to foot in mud. Posed in front of a classic English cottage with roses clambering up the white wall, the Slits stare defiantly, proud Amazons. On the back, they lurk in a bush, faces daubed with warpaint. In the spirit of this abrasive demystification of the female form, songs like 'Spend Spend Spend' offered a simultaneously sarcastic and poignant exposé of the living death of mass culture.

Such schematic social critique could easily have made the Slits into female equivalents of the Clash (with their songs about tower block alienation and feeling 'Lost in the Supermarket'). But the Slits' music, a dreamlike dub-inflected punky reggae, conveyed a much more evocative and melancholy sense of atomised individuals numbed out on the cultural methadone of pop culture. The spooky 'FM' describes radio transmissions as 'frequent mutilation', serving sinister forces who want you to feel inadequate and scared. Singer Ari Up keeps wondering 'what's feeding my screams', hinting that media counselling shows create problems, fuel anxiety (particularly for women), in order to keep them hooked.

Very much part of the 1979/1980 post-punk mindset which saw pop culture as a web of lies, the Slits also laid into gender stereotypes and conventional sexuality with a gleeful exuberance. After 'Newtown', with its desolate parade of shopaholics and romance-junkies adrift in a haze of cheap dreams, 'Ping Pong Affair' sees Ari going through emotional cold turkey – measuring out the evenings of slow withdrawal from her boyfriend with smoking and masturbation. 'Love und Romance' caricatures sentimentality and fidelity: snug and smug with her fiancé, Ari gloats 'who wants to be free?!'

The Slits' anthem, though, is the baleful 'Typical Girls'. Here, they distance themselves from conventional femininity with a series of put-downs that, if they came from a male voice, would sound misogynist. The Slits define themselves as the antithesis of the non-rebel girls who are dupes of media brainwashing, their heads befogged with anxieties about appearance and hygiene. The crux of the song hints at a sinister conspiracy: the typical girl is an invention, a 'marketing ploy' sold to young women. The reward for conformism and self-castration is to get a 'typical boy'. *Who needs it?*

Like the Slits, the Raincoats' initial impetus was an assertion of the right of untrained incompetents to make music. For some, their early anti-musical rumpus was their most subversive moment. In this view, it's the moment of empowerment – the squall and the gall of it – that counts: a spectacle of liberation that has been repeatedly re-enacted in the fanzine/post-post-punk underground, with diminishing returns. There's a theory that the untutored are more free when it comes to making unprecedented, out-there music than everyone apart from the most advanced virtuosos (as with the cult affection/awe for '60s teengirl garage band the Shaggs, who were trying to play pop, but sounded like they came from Mars). In his sleevenotes for the live album *The Kitchen Tapes* (1983), Greil Marcus takes this line: 'No one – not even, you had to think, the Raincoats themselves – could have replicated five minutes of an early Raincoats show. Early recordings... did not seem to have subjects; they seemed to *be* in the way that other music was *about*... The records did not sound like statements... they sounded like events, one-time incidents, that, as in life, resulted from the band's inability to exactly follow its intentions.' Marcus mourns the Raincoats' shift from 'disorderly naturalism' to 'something of a career'.

Separated from the giddy cultural context of the late '70s – when everyone from Scritti Politti to the Pop Group was deconstructing rock's syntax – the Raincoats' music seems, to retrospective ears, to have actually improved with the acquisition of rudimentary technique. Without a smattering of skill it's doubtful that they would have been capable of making the strikingly 'feminine'-sounding post-rock of 1981's neglected mistress-piece *Odyshape*. The first album, *The Raincoats* (1979), bends and buckles rock form but doesn't break it. This ragged, homespun folk-punk, with its elastic rhythms, reedy vocals and rickety structures, is midway between the do-it-yourself spontaneism of the early live performances and *Odyshape*'s loosely knit soundscapes. *The Raincoats* exhilarates because the band's sheer will-to-self-expression galvanises their tenuous technique.

Lyrically, demystification is the Raincoats' thing. Like the Gang of Four's anti-romantic song 'Love Like Anthrax', Raincoats' songs 'Black and White' and 'In Love' (from the *Adventures Close To Home* EP) are attempts at a 'truthful' representation of the romantic experience: all the classic symptoms of falling in love (loss of appetite, hallucinating the beloved's face wherever you go) are unsettlingly re-presented in terms of dysfunction, delusion, delirium. The implication is: who would WANT to be in love if this malady and constant haunting are the consequences? All this is woven into the musical fabric of 'In Love', with its agitated tempo and stammering, clamorous harmonies.

In a 1981 interview, violinist/vocalist Vicki Aspinall explained why the Raincoats were drawn to non-rock'n'roll subject matter: 'There have been areas which are supposed to be traditional female areas, to do with emotion, the house and the domestic sphere. . . [Unlike other female rockers] we haven't avoided it altogether, but just tried to write about it in a way that's true to ourselves.' The Raincoats pulled the wool from under rock's heroic postures by dealing with banal, unromantic domains of female experience, like motherhood ('Baby Song') or being followed by a stalker ('Life on the Line'). 'Shouting Out Loud', the opening track on *Odyshape*, defines a woman as 'a man with fears'. Where combat rock like the Clash turns oppression into a self-glamorising drama of Us against Them, the Raincoats focus on more routine forms of immiseration, like the passive aggressive husband of 'No Looking' who punishes his wife with silence and avoids eye contact.

The Slits and the Raincoats' trajectory took them through demystification of the feminine towards a more affirmative politics of the body and a return to a less alienated, more 'natural' way of life. And this shift to an investment in nature was matched by an almost mystical belief in 'natural rhythm': the undulating grooves of reggae, funk and African music were seen as less forced, less masculine than rock. The Slits' 'In the Beginning There Was Rhythm' makes rhythm a cosmological principle. Over a punk-funk riff and a dub-spacious mix, Ari Up babbles a speed-rap paean to 'natcherel riddim', the force that governs everything from sex to the cycles of the seasons. Like their freeform funkateer allies the Pop Group (who appeared on the other side of the 'In the Beginning' 7-inch), the Slits imagined themselves at the forefront of a revival of tribal consciousness, the recovery of a more authentic lifestyle. They took from Rastafarianism not just bass-heavy rhythms but the idea of a spiritual (not literal) migration back to the Motherland, an escape from the alienation of 'Babylon' (Western consumer capitalism).

The Raincoats' stab at what was then sometimes unkindly referred to as 'brown rice funk', 'Animal Rhapsody' (from the live cassette *The Kitchen Tapes,* 1983), also had a nouveau hippie, green-conscious vibe. Over a loose and limber shuffling groove, the Raincoats chant phrases like 'get to know your body/get to know your mind' – giving off a pungent whiff of holistic therapy. The joy of unfettered sexuality and natural harmony has seldom seemed less enticing. As with a lot of the demystification bands (see also the Au Pairs' *Sense and Sensuality*), the Raincoats' discovery of desire and the pleasures of the body couldn't escape being rendered dull and worthy by the programmatic nature of their politics.

play that agit-funky music, white girl

The post-punk vanguard seized on funk not just as a signifier for health and natural living, but as the basis for a new
kind of militancy. With bands like Gang of Four and the Au
Pairs, crude funk riffing didn't signify fun or grooviness,
but struggle, determination, defiance. Their songs give life
to the slogan 'the personal is the political' by revealing the
scripted nature of interpersonal relations, their socially
programmed inauthenticity. Songs like the Au Pairs' 'Come
Again' or Delta 5's 'You' may use the first person singular,
but they're not confessional. Instead, they're dramatisa-
tions of situations that expose the gap between what the
protagonists believe and the underlying ideological structures that determine their feelings, thoughts, actions.

'Come Again' (from the Au Pairs' 1981 debut LP *Playing
With A Different Sex*) treats sex as performance (as both a
struggle to achieve quotas of enjoyment and as a role-play-
ing game). Its cruel poignancy is that the characters,
played in duet form by Lesley Woods and Paul Foad, are a
'progressive' couple who are attempting to make sex more
reciprocal and mutually satisfactory, only to find themselves entrapped in another set of expectations. As the
aspiring New Man struggles earnestly and anxiously to
pleasure his partner by digital stimulation, the woman
realises, with dawning despair, that despite his sincere
attempts to do the right thing, he's still trying to get a
result out of her, to perform. And so, instead of liberation,
she's just found 'a new way to fake'. A song about friction in
every sense of the word, 'Come Again' is supremely discom-
forting; the Au Pairs' riffs and voices nag and chafe.
Writing at the time, Greil Marcus pinpointed the 'acrid'
quality of Woods's voice: 'precisely the sound pop music has
not prepared us to hear from a woman'.

A big influence on the agit-funk bands was neo-Marxist
Antonio Gramsci's idea of hegemonic 'common sense', i.e.
the way that the ruling ideology presents itself as somehow

natural and ordained. The Au Pairs' 'It's Obvious' attacks the notion that men and women are 'equal but different', not by unravelling the notion, but by parroting it in a tone of withering sarcasm, as though sheer reiteration alone could expose its fatuity.

Like the Au Pairs, Delta 5 were a British, early '80s agit-funk band with a mixed-gender line-up and songs that dramatised the tensions of personal politics. The band wrote love songs stripped of romantic frippery that revealed relationships as struggles for control and autonomy. 'Mind Your Own Business', for instance, recalls Matt Groening's 'Jeff and Akbar' cartoons, where the fez-wearing lovers oscillate between gooey sentiment and venomous recrimination. In the song, one character is always demanding access and involvement, while the other firmly fences off borders/fends off boarders. 'You' is a gleeful diatribe against a negligent partner who is forever forgetting to call or rebuffing sexual advances. Neither Julz Sale's triumphant accusations ('I found out about... YOU!!!') nor the band's crisp, assertive funk relent for a second.

Such defiance took on a more positive aura with other punk-funk bands who seized on the Funkadelic idea of dancing your way out of constrictions (free your mind and your ass will follow, etc.), and created a kind of motivational disco. Maximum Joy's 'Stretch', with its 'say yes!' chant, was like affirmation therapy turned into a dancefloor workout, while New York's mostly female avant-funksters the Bush Tetras wrote songs like 'Stand Up and Fight' that were crash-courses in assertiveness training. With its jerky quasi-funk riffs and staccato chants, the Bush Tetras' music bristled like a porcupine: this was urban survivalist music, a struggle to stake out personal space in an overcrowded environment full of 'Too Many Creeps'.

Post-punk demystification is one of the great phases of 'women in rock': there had never been such concerted involvement of women in bands, as players and ideologues.

At the same time, much of the music of the Au Pairs, Delta 5, et al. has not aged all that well, nor have those bands endured as influences or reference points. They seem inextricably bound to a particular historical phase in the dispersal of punk. The post-punk vanguard, which included these mostly female bands as well as Scritti Politti, the Pop Group, etc., responded to the 'death of punk' (its co-optation and mass-marketing) by pursuing purity. This meant self-consciously distancing themselves from conventional rock'n'roll structures (anti-rockism); attempting to circumvent the major label record industry by establishing an independent infrastructure of labels, distribution and shops; and practising rigorous *questioning* – vaguely redolent of Maoist self-criticism tribunals – at every level of activity from inter-band politics to lyrics to stage presentation, in order to expunge reactionary ideas.

Inevitably, this quest for purity bled into a puritanical suspicion of fun, glamour, pleasure. The contradiction over which the agit-pop project ultimately foundered is that, even though the goal was to liberate the affairs of the body'n'soul from the distorting effects of conditioning and ideology, the resulting erotic politics often didn't feel very liberating or sexy. In their determination to expose the political nature of what goes on in the bedroom (love-as-contract), the demystification bands only showed half the story: they suppressed the psychoanalytical, irrational dimensions of sexuality and gender. Consciousness-raising too often meant suppressing the unconscious, shackling it even more tightly under the regime of the conscience. Ultimately, attempts to avoid being *controlled* (by others' coercion, by one's own compulsive urges or trained traits) spilled over into an oppressive self-control.

Although the demystification bands made what Greil Marcus calls a 'dance of affirmation that things are not as they seem', there was little left after this process of stringent deconstruction to affirm. Attacking sugary notions of femininity kind of took the spice out of life, since they didn't really replace them with anything except a kind of unisex earnestness. Historically, the movement was poised on the cusp of the shift from radical feminism (which had aimed to abolish gender differences), to the cultural feminism that prevails to this day (which accepts the existence of gender difference but tries to valorise female attributes).

The Raincoats' career followed this trajectory pretty closely: they started out aiming to de-naturalise notions of femininity and masculinity, and accordingly came over a bit grey and worthy; later they celebrated nature and the body with affirmative dance music and 'lifestyle politics'. Finally, in the late '80s, two members of the band regrouped as the pop band Dorothy, and this time they were in synch with the latest 'post-feminist' ideas about using traditional feminine imagery as a strategy of empowerment. They dressed like glamorous '40s film stars, wore lots of make-up, and made glossy, opulent music reminiscent of Diana Ross.

More in the next chapter on this shift: from anti-glam demystification to glammed-up deconstruction, from unisex to *vive la différence*. . .

what a drag:
post-feminism and pop

'*Deliberately assumed and foregrounded, femininity as a mask,
for a man, is a take-it-or-leave-it proposition; for a woman, a
similar flaunting of the feminine is a take-it-*and-*leave-it*
possibility. *To put on femininity with a vengeance suggests the
power of taking it off.*'
Mary Russo, 'Female Grotesques'

When the demystification movement petered out in the
early '80s, some of its leading lights entered into a more
complicated and precarious strategy of subversion: pop
deconstruction, otherwise known as New Pop. For instance,
Scritti Politti abandoned the neo-Marxist ideology and
abrasive anti-pop texture of songs like 'Hegemony', and
embraced the seductive gloss of funk, soul and reggae.
Where once their grubby, collaged artwork included details
of their recording costs (in order to demystify their means
of production), the new Scritti covers paid ironic homage to
deluxe commodities like Chanel perfume. And where the
demystification bands had stripped away the veil of false
consciousness in the vague hope of finding the truth, Scritti
now celebrated the idea that there is no truth, only language. Scritti's idea was to inhabit pop's discourse – the
lore of love, the allure of glamour – and unsettle its terms
from within, *deconstruct* it.

The New Pop movement of the early '80s was not a golden age for 'women in rock'. Forceful females like Leslie
Woods of the Au Pairs were supplanted by figures like the
backing singers in the Human League – ordinary girls who
were hired after singer Phil Oakey met them in a disco.

Along with Annie Lennox, Clare Grogan of Altered Images was one of the few women to take up New Pop ideas. Altered Images went from the post-punk demystification of their debut single, 'Dead Pop Stars', to the ironically cutesy image and fizzy pop of 'Happy Birthday' and 'I Could Be Happy' (which veered uncomfortably close to infantilism), before Grogan abruptly 'matured' with the (still ironic) glamourpuss persona of such heavy-breathing disco hits as 'Bring Me Closer'. Grogan's succession of altered images and her tongue-in-cheek knowingness made her a prophetess of what would later be dubbed post-feminism.

The term post-feminism began to circulate in the mid '80s as one of those buzzwords that vaguely moot a new Zeitgeist. Susan Faludi saw it as part of the backlash against feminism: 'Just when record numbers of younger women were supporting feminist goals. . . . the media declared the advent of a younger "post-feminist generation" that supposedly reviled the women's movement.' But this buzzword has also been used in another way – to gesture at a new wave of feminism that doesn't necessarily jettison old style feminist agendas (equal pay, child care, abortion rights, etc.), but does tend to focus more on media representation as a battleground. We use this controversial term neither as a slur nor as a compliment, but as a tag for a particular sensibility: a more distant, ironical take on feminism practised by younger women.

Post-feminism bears a relation to feminism similar to that of post-modernism to modernism: playful where its predecessor was sober, flaunting an ironic and provisional sense of identity where the earlier -isms believed in an authentic self. Both the post- formations alarmed and offended traditionalists who insisted that their respective -isms could hardly be over because their job had never been completed. Perhaps the best way to conceive of post-feminism/post-modernism is as the next phase of feminism/ modernism, not its repudiation and supercession. Each takes the ideas of its predecessor for granted, but questions some assumptions and orthodoxies, and points out new possibilities.

Practically, the 'post' seems to signify the possibility of reclaiming some of the stereotypical aspects of femininity that feminism had trashed. French thinker Luce Irigaray was pondering these possibilities back in the '70s: 'One must assume the feminine role deliberately. Which means already to convert a form of subordination into an affirmation, and thus to begin to thwart it....' In other words, it may be possible to turn what is out of one's control into something one 'owns' and consciously deploys.

Minorities have espoused this strategy – homosexuals turning pejoratives like 'queer' and 'dyke' into badges of pride, gangsta rappers transforming 'nigga' into a fraternal greeting. This subversion of language, literally upturning meaning by the affirmation of negative, exclusionary terms, could, argues Irigaray, 'jam the theoretical machinery'. It is a defiant assertion of difference, a rejection of the liberal fantasy of integration and assimilation: we don't want to be just like you. Just as gangsta rap disconcerts white liberals and black radicals alike by exaggerating the most negative stereotypes of black delinquency, so post-feminist artists have played with stereotypes like the vamp and the whore. In both cases, it's a double-edged strategy, fraught with potential misunderstandings.

Madonna is, of course, the public figure who's given these ideas the widest exposure (and *exposure* is the operative word). But her 'authentic inauthenticity' originates not so much from post-modern concepts circulating in the air as from gay culture. The camp aesthetic and drag have always revelled in the fictive nature of gender, the fact that femininity is located not in the essence of the person but in accoutrements: make-up, wigs, high-heels, glamorous clothes. Just as Siouxsie Sioux drew on the masquerading spirit of the ambisexual Bowie Boys she hung out with, Madonna is a reverent disciple, absorbing gay culture's ideas and then mass-marketing them.

The song/video, 'Vogue' (1990), has many claims to being the ultimate Madonna statement. Not only is it a classic example of her adroitness at hijacking subcultural ideas (the black gay cult of vogueing) and mainstreaming them for mass consumption, the song is also virtually a Madonna manifesto. 'Vogue' preaches a secular gospel of self-reinvention and empowerment through mastery of surfaces: it's the punk idea of 'anyone can do it', adapted for the Reagan-Bush era. Through concerted beautification and glamorisation, anyone can look like a member of the ruling class.

The vogueing subculture was brilliantly documented in Jennie Livingston's film *Paris Is Burning* (released in 1990 but shot in 1987). It's a poignant peep into the lives of black and Hispanic drag queens and transsexuals who live for the 'balls' in which they strut their extravagantly dressed-up stuff and compete in a number of categories. The winners are those who most immaculately achieve the Look: jet-set supermodel glamour, preppy, military, B-boy etc.

The scene is extremely hierarchical. Voguers belong to 'houses' (as in the House Of Ninja, the Royal House of Saint Laurent), which provide both a surrogate family (each is presided over by a House Mother) and a way of structuring competition. Houses are a black gay counterpart to street gangs. Vogueing has its own version of rap, a vicious form of verbal combat known as 'shading', which involves criticising a rival's dress, coiffure, make-up or etiquette. Even the dancing – vogueing – is a form of sublimated rivalry, 'like taking knives to each other, but in the form of dance', as one voguer puts it. Like gangsta rap, vogueing is a caricature of capitalism's war of all-against-all.

Livingston's documentary is sympathetic to the voguers, at least partially going along with the notion that their symbolic appropriation of the high life constitutes a triumph. But it's as easy to come away with the impression that the voguers are victims, not victors. Doubly marginalised – not just black, but gay – the voguers imitate the values and imagery of a straight world from which they are utterly excluded. One of the most touching characters in the film, a soft-spoken, willowy Hispanic teenager who's called Venus Xtravaganza, declares that his/her dream is to be 'a spoiled rich white girl – they get what they want whenever they want it, and they don't have to really struggle with finances, nice things, nice clothes.' Many of the voguers fantasise about becoming a successful model, then branching out into movies or singing, eventually marrying a rich white man and adopting children.

The voguers' fantasies are so conventional, so colonised, as to verge on a parody of straight values. They want to possess the opulence of the millionaire, or better still the rich man's wife. Their ideas of what it is to be female are as reactionary as they come – being a real woman means knowing the arts of seduction, having everything but not having to pay for it, passivity, conspicuous consumption, vanity. Vogueing is a perfect example of Jean Baudrillard's concept of 'hyper-conformism': the feedback loop that occurs when real people simulate the media's representations.

Vogue is probably the most alienated subculture in the world. And beneath its glittering surfaces lurks the grim reality of poverty and danger (many voguers turn to prostitution to pay for clothes and make-up). Even in its supreme state of triumph – on the dancefloor at the balls – when the voguer 'possesses' the dream, the alienation is there, writ large in the contorted postures of the vogueing style. The dance (as in Madonna's video for 'Vogue') involves shifting rapidly between a series of stop-frame, frozen poses, like stills from a fashion shoot. The kineticism of dance is replaced by a sequence of tableaux of petrified elegance. Vogueing is the pure triumph of voyeurism over transcendence.

Madonna's co-optation of the subculture only doubled the tragic dimension to vogueing: at least their fantasies of prestige, alienated as they were, had belonged to them;

now they were sold to the world as a titillating freak show. The lyrics to 'Vogue' suggest that Madonna felt she was paying tribute even as she ripped them off, that she found the vogue ethos not just inspirational, but analogous to her own struggle. 'Vogue' could be interpreted as Madonna fessing up that she too is nothing but a *female impersonator*.

The key moment in the song is when Madonna, exhorting the whole world to discover the joys of posing, declares: 'there's nothing to it'. This is a blatant lie: in the video, Madonna appears in a myriad of poses, styled as the classic beauties of Hollywood, and each tableau must have required hours of make-up, styling, lighting, tinting and processing in the editing room. And we know the amount of energy, money and risk required for the real-life voguers to achieve the look. Then again, to take a Baudrillardian slant, maybe this 'nothing' is what is subversive about vogueing: the idea that behind the shimmering surface of make-up and masquerade, there is no authentic identity. 'Femininity' is deconstructed, revealed to be an array of attachments, additions and subtractions. In this view, 'Vogue' is a dizzy, confounding moment in which the apparently reactionary and ultra-conformist becomes revolutionary: meaning implodes, turns evanescent.

As a musical-visual *tour de force*, 'Vogue' is irresistible, in a very literal sense: even the most hostile Madonna-watchers find it impossible to resist its spell-binding seduction. But, this rare instance aside, we find little in the way of liberation in Madonna's work precisely because it seems so much like work. In Bataille's terms, Madonna's self-serving makes her servile rather than sovereign. There's a grim, aerobic, almost Protestant strenuousness to the Madonna spectacle, and while her reward is obviously the narcissistic enjoyment of her own image, it's hard to see what the payback is for the audience. Eminent musicologist Susan McClary has stoutly defended Madonna's songs and divined all manner of radicalism in their key changes and structure; for us, it's all too apparent that Madonna is a mediatician not a musician, that in most of her music, for all its burnished state-of-art production, there's a lack of real grain and swing. While her songs are often coercive in conjunction with the visuals, more often than not the music is totally flat on its own. An image-fascist, Madonna is the perfect MTV-age star, privileging eye over ear.

Madonna has been criticised for being a control freak, and while that critique often conceals a traditional fear of the powerful woman, it may also be an intuition that there is something fundamentally unliberating and anti-musical about an artist who exudes an aura of excessive self-control. McClary argues that 'Madonna is best understood as head of a corporation that produces images of her self-representation, rather than as the spontaneous, "authentic" artist of rock mythology.' And like all self-employed people, Madonna is exploiting herself, her own resources: she is both boss and employee, imperialist and colony. Is this the best, or the worst, of all worlds?

there's a riot going on:
grrrls against boy-rock

'Punks are not girls, if it comes to the crunch we'll have no options but to fight back.'
Seminal punk fanzine *Sniffin' Glue*, 1977

'Death to all fucker punk boys who refuse to acknowledge the girl punk revolution.'
Riot Grrrl, 1992

The Situationists believed that all that was required for a revolution was a federation of teenage gangs: male adolescent delinquency and vandalism was an instinctive, inarticulate revolt against 'the spectacle' and 'the commodity' (the two alienated forms of leisure via which consumer capitalism exerted its thrall). In the early '90s, a movement emerged with a female take on the same idea. Riot Grrrl radicalised the teenage pen-pal and fanzine network in which girls had used teenybop idols as a pretext to write about their own desires and fantasies. In rough-and-ready xeroxed 'zines with titles like *Girl Germs* and *Malefice*, Riot Grrrls discuss their feelings of alienation from a boy-dominated hardcore punk scene in which they're marginalised; they decry the media's promotion of unattainable ideals of perfect femininity; they write moving confessional accounts of their experiences of harassment and sexual abuse.

Initially based largely in Olympia, Washington, and in Washington, DC, Riot Grrrl quickly came to the attention of the media, and was sucked into a spiralling vortex of coverage. By early '93, many of the Riot Grrrls felt the scene had been mediatised out of existence, misrepresented and trivialised; some refused to use the term to describe themselves, because it had so rapidly become a freefloating signifier circulating through media hyperspace. But by then, Riot Grrrl had achieved its own momentum – just as punk rock had in 1977 – and had spawned copycat movements in other cities and other countries like the UK.

Riot Grrrl draws on strategies, ideas and values from all three phases of feminism-in-rock. There's a strong element of post-punk demystification: a fierce questioning of conventional ideas of femininity, a concerted rejection of traditional rockist ideas of 'cool' and mystique, a forthright challenge to the notion that technical virtuosity is a prerequisite for creative endeavour. Riot Grrrls preach empowerment through forming bands and producing fanzines – it's the old punk DIY ethos of 'anyone can do it', but with a feminist twist (they're rejecting masculine notions of expertise and mastery).

Riot Grrrl also has some separatist qualities. Its aim is to carve out a space for young women where they're free to express themselves without being overshadowed or scrutinised by boys. While not all the Riot Grrrl bands, gigs and conventions are women-only, they often have restrictions – like demarcating the area at the front of the stage as a female zone where girls can mosh without getting mashed up by brawny boy-punks. At the most basic, pragmatic level, they demand equal access to the music. As well as these practical reasons for separatism, there's also a strong lesbian element to Riot Grrrl, and historical links with the gay punk homocore/queercore movement, who are allies and fellow victims of exclusion.

Finally, there's a post-feminist strand running through Riot Grrrl ideology. While a lot of Riot Grrrls refuse to align themselves with feminism, many have mothers who were involved in the first and second waves of the feminist movement. It's as though feminism is almost taken for granted. Some Grrrl performers follow 'godmother' figures like Courtney Love and Kim Gordon in their playful but confrontational reclamation of stereotypes and feminine glamour. The classic example is the way, early on, some daubed slogans and words with lipstick on their bodies – like 'SLUT'. Bikini Kill singer Kathleen Hanna explained the tactic: 'When you take off your shirt [onstage] the guys think "Oh, what a slut" and it's really funny because they think that and then they look at you and it says it.' Some go even further in embracing the stereotype, exploding the double standard that calls a promiscuous woman 'loose' and a promiscuous boy a 'stud'. A *Hungry Girl* contributor writes: 'SLUT. Yeah, I'm a slut. My body belongs to me. I sleep with who I want. . . I'm not your property.'

Such defiant *détournement* of stereotypes and conventional imagery figures strongly in Riot Grrrl fanzines. The 'zines are dotted with conflicting images of women: porn models, Victorian beauties, happy housewives from advertisements, pretty little girls from children's books. These illustrate articles ranging from emotive accounts of rape and incest, to sophisticated political critiques, to cooking recipes, poems and David Letterman-like lists ('Top 10 Reasons It's Cool to Hang Out with Yourself and NOT Have A Boy'). But the Grrrl-zines' biggest preoccupation is with the need to break down 'boy-rock', the homosocial camaraderie of the alternative and hardcore music scenes, which shun(t)s girls (to the sidelines). Although manifestos are not something that women have historically favoured as a means of expression, Riot Grrrls have seized on the format. The 'zines are full of declarations of intent and definitions of the Riot Grrrl project. 'Riot Grrrl Is. . . . Because we will never meet the hierarchical BOY standards of talented, or cool or smart. They are created to keep us out, and if we ever meet them they will change, or we will become tokens.'

One of the sharpest and most keenly felt themes running through Riot Grrrl literature is the rejection of *cool*. 'For the most part, cool attributes have been claimed by our society as "male",' wrote one Riot Grrrl. 'This means that the only way a person brought up GIRL (and thus the opposite of what is cool) can be "truly" cool is to assimilate into male culture via toughness.' Since being cool means 'repressing our supposedly feminine qualities like niceness and telling people how we feel', the anonymous polemicist urges Grrrls to turn dorkiness into a new cool, in order to 'confuse and disrupt the whole process... Being a dork is about. . . demystifying yourself, not fitting yourself into james dean pictureland.' In a sense, Riot Grrrls are rebelling against rebellion, or at least against the ossified notion of the *cool rebel* who doesn't care – inscrutable, affect-less, solipsistic.

Perhaps the most striking thing about Riot Grrrl rhetoric is its very insistence on the word *girl* rather than woman. Carol Gilligan and Lyn Mikel Brown have argued that the onset of puberty has a calamitous effect on girls' confidence and self-image, an opinion that's echoed in Grrrl-zines with proclamations like: 'Clinical studies show being a teenage girl fights self-esteem better than most other leading factors.' Riot Grrrls often seem nostalgic for the invincible tomboy of prepubescence, whose sense of possibility has yet to be withered by being sexualised. Hence cutesy 'zine titles like *Crumbly Lil Bunny* and bandnames like Bratmobile. The latter's album title *Pottymouth* summons up images of tiny she-devils refusing to behave like 'sugar and spice and all things nice'.

At the same time, Riot Grrrls seem to reject the tomboy rocker approach. While often regarding figures like Joan Jett or Kim Gordon as illustrious prototypes, they find the strategy of wanting to be 'one of the guys' ultimately unsatisfactory. Gordon has talked of how she 'always idolized male guitar players. It was exciting to be in the middle of it but also feel like a voyeur. There were isolated female musicians, but there was never any bonding or anything.' By contrast, Kathleen Hanna sees this as a half-measure. 'What other [female] bands do is go, "It's not important that I'm a girl, it's just important that I want to rock." And that's cool. But that's more of an assimilationist thing. It's like they just want to be allowed to join the world as it is; whereas I'm into revolution and radicalism and changing the whole structure. What I'm into is making the world different for me to live in.' So Riot Grrrls attempt to create a supportive environment in which girls can have a go. In Grrrl bands, it's men who are the tokens, like Billy Boredom, the guitarist in Bikini Kill.

What about the *music*?, you might well ask. Despite their 'pro-girl' ethos, Riot Grrrl hasn't questioned the gender-orientation of music qua music, and there's been only lipservice acknowledgment of bands like the Raincoats or Throwing Muses who've attempted to interrogate the phallocentric forms of rock itself. From a rock critical perspective, most Riot Grrrl bands seem to be engaged in a reinvention of the wheel: they sound like very traditional hardcore or late '70s punk bands. They may criticise tomboy rockers, but musically they *sound* like tomboys, throwing rather straightforward punky tantrums. Partly, this stems from the nature of the subjects and emotions they deal in – rage, defiance, self-hatred, the struggle to *speak*. The other reason this music sounds simplistic and retrograde is that the DIY ideology agitates against acquiring musical technique (which can only help when it comes to inscribing gender difference into sound). There's also a rather puritanical elevation of content over form, message over music, that stems from the proselytising, 'inspirational' nature of the movement.

But a rock critical perspective – one that evaluates the music in terms of innovation, formal excellence, etc. – is highly inappropriate when it comes to Riot Grrrl. These women are not necessarily *interested* in making a contribution to rock history or the evolution of the form. Riot Grrrl is foremost about *process*, not product; it's about the empowerment that comes from 'getting up and doing it', and the inspiration audience members draw from witnessing this spectacle of self-liberation. Following traditional fanzine thinking, Riot Grrrl ideologues tend to believe that the proliferation of DIY culture is a good thing in itself: the more bands, the more 'zines, the merrier. Making your own entertainment, however flimsy or derivative, is infinitely superior to consuming someone else's work, however excellent or innovative.

Riot Grrrl has historical links with the British late '80s movement of 'shambling' bands (also known as the 'cutie' scene for its cult of innocence), and with a similar US milieu based around the Olympia, Washington label, K Records. The shamblers and K went beyond do-it-yourself, making a veritable cult of incompetence. It's no longer enough that 'anyone can do it', but that the music must *sound* like 'anyone can do it'. Sloppy, out-of-synch, lo-fi: all these things signify authenticity. The amateur ethos (do it for love not money) has become a wilful amateurish-ness, a deliberate, concerted refusal to acquire skill, even accidentally. Beat Happening, founders of K, never rehearse, only play together onstage or when recording; the natural acquisition of technique has been consciously retarded, frozen. It's a kind of musical anorexia, a deliberate arresting of development in order to preserve innocence and stave off the professionalism that's associated with the corrupt rock biz.

Riot Grrrl brings an extra feminist element to this demystification of music-making in that it rejects 'boy' notions of excellence and expertise. So it's ironic that much of Riot-rock sounds like English punk circa 1978, US garage circa 1966 – some of the most masculinist rock ever. Bikini Kill's self-titled 1992 debut sounds like Poly Styrene yelling over muffled buzzsaw ramamalama punk that could be a bootleg of the nascent UK Subs in rehearsal. By sheer will and chutzpah, Kathleen Hanna's pulmonary bellow carries along her cohorts in her wake: she's a worthy successor to Styrene, rather than a mere imitator. In a different context, you could imagine her rivalling the unbridled aggression of an Iggy Pop or Johnny Rotten. But the Stooges and the Pistols were, contrary to oft-held belief, shit-hot bands, within their chosen rigid parameters.

So it's Hanna's voice and lyrics that grip the imagination: the spirit is wild, but the musical flesh is puny. 'Feels Blind' deals with what is sometimes known as 'female masochism', but is really, the song suggests, a case of women who are so hungry for affection and attention that they 'eat your hate like love'. 'Suck My Left One' is about sex as terrorism: it's at once a horrific tale of incest and a turning of tables, a reclamation of a woman's right to be sexually ferocious. Mother tells her to be a 'polite girl', even as her father and the boys in her life abuse her. But if she expresses her own physical desires, she's a threat, as the chorus/title's command/demand makes clear. Hanna practically gnashes her teeth as she sings it, again matching the feral abandon of Iggy Pop.

Ironically, the exhortation 'riot, girls!' is one of the challenges Iggy threw at a crazed audience during the gig documented on the Stooges' live album *Metallic K.O.* A comparison between Bikini Kill and the Stooges reveals some of the differences between male and female rebellion. Iggy turned self-mutilation and reciprocal abuse between audience and singer into a grisly theatre; Bikini Kill sing about unsolicited, real-life abuse over which they have no control. Iggy, following Jim Morrison, envisioned incest as the ultimate symbol of transgression/transcendence in his Oedipal fantasy 'Sister Midnight'; for the Riot Grrrls, incest isn't a metaphor but an omnipresent threat. It haunts their imagination as a symbol of patriarchal domination.

Released in 1993, Bikini Kill's second album saw them linking up with their UK allies Huggy Bear: BK's side is titled *Yeah Yeah Yeah*. 1977 punk took the viciousness of '60s garage punk and redirected its misogynistic aggression against society; Riot Grrrls return to punk's source, the war of the sexes, only this time it's the girls who are shouting down the boys. A number of the songs are accusatory, addressed to the classic punk 'you', but here, for once, it's a nameless male adversary who gets his comeuppance. On 'White Boy', Hanna is a whining mall-brat spouting misandry rather than misogyny. 'Don't Need You' uncannily echoes all those '60s punk classics with titles like 'Don't Need You No More': 'Us punk rock whores don't need you' could almost be a parody of the studly postures of garageland's Mick Jagger wannabes. But there's also an anthem of affirmation, 'Rebel Girl', which hails the female anti-heroine as 'the queen of my world' and hints at lesbian desire with lines like 'in her kiss I taste the revolution'. It's an anthem of sorority after decades of rock'n'roll's blood-brother imagery (think of the Stooges' 'TV Eye', with Iggy's final hoarse hollers of 'brothahs!').

If Bikini Kill are sonic traditionalists by choice, there's no limit to Huggy Bear's ambition. Unfortunately, there are myriad limits to this mixed-gender band's ability. Their would-be experimentalism is crippled by a fanatical, almost doctrinaire rejection of the notion of 'virtuosity'. Huggy Bear believe that incompetence is the righteous route to avant-gardism: if you don't know the rules, you can't obey them. Their records, and those of their allies in the 'Huggy Nation' (Blood Sausage, the Furbelows, Linus, Limpstud) sometimes recall the spontaneism of early Scritti Politti and ATV (prime movers in late '70s DIY/demystification), or even the Dadaist sound-collages of Faust. But a wilful shoddiness holds them back from being anything more than a retread of avant-garde pathways.

The title of Huggy Bear's 1993 single, 'Her Jazz', is perhaps a claim that women are instinctively avant-garde and improvisatory, that their very nature revolts against structure. Unfortunately, this contention is somewhat belied by the low-level, rabblerousing rumpus of the music, with its call-to-arms slogans: 'This is happening without your permission. . . her jazz signals our time now.' A rejection of everyone from the political establishment to the record business to the rock critical hierarchy, 'Her Jazz' aspired to be an epoch-defining, line-drawing, Year Zero kind of single, like 'Anarchy in the UK' – you're either with us or against us. On their half of the Bikini Kill link-up, *Our Troubled Youth*, Huggy Bear's music remains surprisingly modest and retro-fixated: at best it recalls the '60s punk revivalism of the Pastels or Suzi Quatro's all-girl garage band the Pleasure Seekers.

Convulsing the British music press into pro- and anti-camps, despite their refusal to allow interviews, Huggy Bear became mediatised very rapidly. And you have to wonder – using the expression in full awareness of its connotations – if they weren't 'asking for it'. Talk of 'revolution' is as irresistible to the media as it is to those who spout it. Revolutionary rhetoric and manifesto mongering will always be one of the great adolescent highs: it imparts a sort of erection of the soul, it's cheaper than amphetamine (although arguably just as bad for your emotional development), and it always draws a crowd.

By taking on this masculinist discourse of violent overthrow, polarisation, and BIG SHOCK, Huggy Bear condemned themselves to the lineage of masterplan bands, from the Pistols through Sigue Sigue Sputnik to Manic Street Preachers: a lineage that has delivered less and less musically with each turnover. Unless the revolutionary sales patter is grounded in an equivalent radicalisation of rock form, history's verdict will be, quite fairly: 'all mouth and no trousers'. Situationist-inspired slogans like 'Rubbing the Impossible to Burst' are all very well, but it's music that conjures a mind's eye vision of utopia. Nonetheless, Riot Grrrl has jolted open a space in which such revolutionary music might be created. Consciously inscribing gender difference into sound could be one way of opening up a whole new frontier for rock.

body's in trouble

Rock'n'roll is the sound of adolescence. The hormonal turbulence of the adolescent body has always fuelled its hyperactivity, either as simple lustful urgency, or sublimated as *insurgency* (combat rock's causes and crusades). In the '50s and '60s, it was the flaunting of the body that made rock'n'roll both subversive and authentic. But by the mid-'70s, frank-and-free sexuality was no big deal. Punk looked elsewhere for its shock effects; it rejected the idea that sex was liberating, disfigured the body, used pornographic imagery as a weapon rather than a source of gratification. By the '80s, the body was the commonplace of pop, omnipresent and normative: nothing could be more conformist than the continual exhortations to 'set your body free'. Progressive bands attacked the carnal realm by fetishising the body's destruction (Nick Cave, Big Black), or they soared above it (REM, Hüsker Dü).

It was as if radical rock culture instinctively grasped the fact that the body, once the instrument of rebellion, had been co-opted. In the '80s, mainstream culture exhorted us to maximise the body's capacity for health, youthful vigour, sexual pleasure. Against this ethos of self-realisation, the likes of Morrissey exposed the hidden truth of adolescence: awkwardness, sexual incapacity, neurasthenia, emasculation. But even though Morrissey (and his successors like Brett Anderson of Suede) rebelled against the traditional phallic model of rebellion, his flirtation with being feminised is just a new twist on the old business of boys misbehavin'. Rampant or ravished, virile or vulnerable, the adolescent male body has continued to occupy the centre stage of rock's imagination: boys keep swingin', to the exclusion of female experience.

Perhaps not for much longer. The last half-decade has seen the rise of women artists who explore a specifically female experience of adolescence, in which the body figures as the source of desire, embarrassment and anxiety, and as an object of disgust and self-directed aggression. Where rock once aimed to liberate sexuality, these women want to liberate themselves from being sexualised, from the pressure to meet quotas of health and beauty. This can mean exposing bodily imperfection, or emotionally distancing themselves from the physical side of life. Sometimes these artists explicitly draw on teenage girls' fumbling, pre-political attempts to evade adult sexuality altogether: the 'female perversions' of anorexia and self-cutting.

The context that has warranted such a revolt is the subject of Naomi Wolf's *The Beauty Myth*. Wolf argues that women's entry into the workforce in the decades following the Second World War was concurrent with the rise of the cosmetics industry – and that this was no coincidence. Since women's sense of self-worth no longer revolved around keeping the home spotless, advertisers looked for another way of stoking female anxiety, and turned to personal appearance.

Of course, women have always spent time and money, even risked their health, in order to conform to the standards of the day. In the Middle Ages, they plucked out eyelashes and shaved the hairline to get that sexy, 'high forehead' look. In other centuries, women inserted themselves into constricting garments to attain an hourglass figure, starved themselves or gobbled amphetamine-based diet pills. But in the late twentieth century, anxiety about appearance and body-shape has been whipped to a feverish pitch, and methods of self-improvement have been invented at a prodigious rate in order to capitalise on that anxiety.

For Wolf, the beauty cult is nothing less than a patriarchal conspiracy to distract young women from feminist politics, by making them believe their problems can be solved and their dreams realised if they can just reach that perfect body weight, that ideal facial profile. The beauty cult is perhaps the most extreme example of a general trend in Western society in which therapeutic solutions, rather than political involvement, are promoted as the key to a better life. From TV counselling shows to women's (and increasingly men's) magazines, it's suggested that *you have the power* to change your life, to maximise your potential for health, fitness, pleasure. The focus, and onus, for improving life falls on the individual, not society.

For women, the body increasingly becomes a site of intractable conflict. Sexual development doesn't bring empowerment but vulnerability. It's a cruel double bind: look good and you 'invite' sexual harassment; fail to meet prescribed standards of physical perfection, and you're prey to imposed feelings of worthlessness. Body-related problems are a major obsession of the Riot Grrrl 'zines, ranging from the grievous (anorexia, harassment, rape, incest) to the apparently 'normal' (anxieties about food, appearance). Allusions to perfection appear often in these fanzines, skewered with sarcasm. In issue #7 of *Riot Grrrl*, Erika grapples with her ambivalence: 'i hate mirrors. i really do. i can't stand my reflection, my face. i know i'm not ugly. not that i can see it, i just know.' Yet she can't help feeling inadequate, fixating on her looks: 'i used to have fantasies about taking a razor and shaving off my face and when it grew back it would be perfect. no flaws, no points of interest whatsoever.' But while some Grrrls fantasise about invisibility, others resort to turning their bodies into billboards, scrawling slogans on their arms and legs. Female artists flit between these extremes – the desire to disappear and strategic exhibitionism – as they struggle with body-trouble.

the body trap

The songs and singing of Canadian singer-songwriter Mary Margaret O'Hara oscillate between elegance and awkwardness. In 'Body's in Trouble' (from *Miss America*, 1988) the gait of her voice is out of synch with the music's easy glide: the body impedes and intervenes. 'Body's in Trouble' is the perfect expression – in its title, and in O'Hara's amazing vocal performance – of the body betraying its owner, of body language belying the decorous appearances that are maintained in spoken language. This body has a mind of its own.

In an interview, O'Hara complained that 'my body moves terribly weird. . . . We got fired, our old band, we lost jobs 'cause of the way I moved. People said I was sick, one lady got her money back, yelling, another said I belonged in a padded cell.' At the same time, the body is where the music is *born*. O'Hara describes finding it impossible to lip-synch during the making of the 'Body's In Trouble' video: 'I could *not* do it. It was the worst. I always move when I'm singing, so every take came out different, because all the sounds shoot out on different pulses, so even the result is counter to the correct time signatures. . . I couldn't match it up, and dance, and be filmed at the same time.'

In her essay 'Female Grotesques', Mary Russo recalls a dreaded admonition from her childhood: 'She is making a spectacle of herself.' She writes, 'Making a spectacle out of oneself seemed a specifically feminine danger. The danger was of exposure. Men, I learned somewhat later in life, 'expose themselves,' but that operation was quite deliberate and circumscribed. For a woman, making a spectacle of herself had more to do with a kind of inadvertency and loss of boundaries.' Dread of embarrassing oneself leads to a life of 'silence, withdrawal and invisibility', although it can also be conquered and diverted into 'the bold affirmations of feminine performance, imposture, and masquerade'.

The first strategy – minimising the risk of embarrassment by becoming minimal, unobtrusive, body-less – figures in songs by Suzanne Vega and by Hugo Largo. In 'Undertow' (from her 1985 eponymous debut), Vega longs to escape the body's cage. She imagines stripping her lover down to his skeleton, and finding a mutual freedom in pure ethereality. But she is defeated by her own insistent, fleshly needs. 'Hunger makes me weak', she croons: her body won't allow her to fade into sleek invisibility. This whole album is riddled with ascetic and anorectic imagery. In 'Straight Lines', the narrator tries to become 'streamlined'. Adornment – flowers, her long hair – are stripped down to 'Straight Lines'. She takes a fetishistic pleasure in the sensation of 'cold metal' against her skin; the music is skeletal and staccato, and every syllable is crisply articulated. The metaphor of streamlining extends itself to her emotional life, as she sheds her lovers, although they continue to haunt her dreams. Eventually, she reaches her goal, cutting 'through the circles' of her previous life and attaining a minimal self, free of attachments, alone. Her desire to transcend female, bodily reality has left her unfettered but isolated.

Vega's female characters are frequently bloodless and ghostly; hers is a postmodern version of folk, acoustic music for disconnected individuals who inhabit urban interiors. Her heroines are alienated from nature and the body. In 'Blood Makes Noise' on *99.9°F* (1992), a girl can't hear a doctor's questions for the sound of her own blood in her ears. In 'Small Blue Thing', she's able to look down 'objectively' on her fragility and pathos, to see herself as an object. Throughout Vega's work, the body is what holds her spirit back; hence her desire to reduce herself, to fly above or flee the human frame in all its vulnerable singularity.

In Hugo Largo's 'Turtle Song' (from *Mettle*, 1989), Mimi Goese remembers the excitement of childhood, when the world was full of wonder and possibilities unbounded by the body. She yearns for the freedom of the prepubescent girl, before the stringent restrictions of appropriate feminine behaviour outlawed tomboy pursuits like playing in the mud. Like Vega yearning to be sleek, Goese remembers envying the swiftness of the cheetah, who has no fat to weigh down its bones. Her reverie spills over into anguish at the impossibility of metamorphosis: if only she could be outside herself, 'thinking someone else's thoughts', and not trapped and howling from inside the 'well' of fixed identity. The body, instead of the source of fleetfooted animal power, is a pit which contains and imprisons consciousness. Like Vega's, Goese's lyrics reveal a desire to exist as pure spirit. The longing to metamorphosise probably partially accounts for so many female songwriters' interest in mythology, the supernatural, and children's fantasies. From Kate Bush's 'In Search of Peter Pan' to Stevie Nicks's witch-heroine 'Rhiannon', the idea of fleeing the fixity of bodily identity resonates deeply for women.

Perhaps the ultimate expression of a female desire to be invisible is A.C. Marias's enigmatic single 'One of Our Girls Has Gone Missing' (1989). The band's singer-songwriter Angela Conway described her work as 'music to disappear to'. 'One of Our Girls Has Gone Missing' is a cryptic story of a woman whose rebellion takes the form of going absent-without-leave. Conventional 'political' women's music assumes that women's liberation lies in being upfront, making demands, speaking out. A.C. Marias belongs to a different tradition of female subversion, in which woman is elusive, unfathomably *other*. Conway believed that 'One of Our Girls' is 'very assertive, it's saying enough's enough. Disappearance can be quite a powerful thing. To be not present can be more powerful than actually being present and proclaiming your identity as "woman".'

If some female artists dream of escaping the cage of the body, others stage a kind of prison riot, a carnal insurrection. The songs of PJ Harvey dramatise the conflicts of possessing a body, of desiring and being desired, in a way that's sexually charged but not exactly sexy. Polly Harvey has perfected a kind of self-exposure, in lyrics and self-presentation, that uniquely combines seduction and threat, intimacy and estrangement. On her debut album *Dry* (1992), the cover is a close-up of her mouth, smeared with lipstick and contorted in an expression that is poised exactly midway between pucker and tight-lipped defiance. On the back, there's a photograph of Harvey reclining in the bath: her naked breasts are visible, but her expression suggests self-possession and serenity rather than availability. Around the time of the album's release, she also appeared topless on the cover of the *NME*: her back is turned to the camera, but the outline of her breast is visible. The shot perfectly captures the ambivalence of her persona, at once candid and veiled, seductive but autonomous.

Harvey has admitted: 'I have a complex about my body. I don't feel comfortable with how I look at all... I think I like to turn it on myself and make myself feel more ridiculous as a way of dealing with it.' She adds: 'I like to humiliate myself and make the listener feel uncomfortable. [Combining the two] would be the ideal package.' There's an echo here of Lydia Lunch-style eroticisation of disgust, of embarrassment and the blush as a kind of rapture.

In an interview with *Siren*, Harvey declared: 'I think these songs feel really uncomfortable.... It's like tripping yourself up and falling over all the time, it just makes you uncomfortable.' The body is almost invariably a source of discomfort and conflict in her songs. In 'Dress', her body is 'a heavy-loaded fruit tree', overflowing the garment's tight confines. Herky-jerky music underlines the dilemma that faces Harvey as she considers the tensions involved in dressing in a feminine way. (At the time, she favoured a no-nonsense, tomboyish, rock'n'roll look.) The gown holds out the promise of pleasure in its sensual folds, but it's also constricting – limiting her movements and carrying with it all kinds of implications and possible consequences. In the video, Harvey is clad in a frilly '50s gown – the kind that a teenager might wear to a school prom. As she lies down on the ground, the male members of the band quickly enclose her in cardboard, framing and immobilising her as the perfect image of girlhood. In the song, Harvey longs to throw caution to the winds and follow impulse, but is stopped in her tracks. Like a mantra, she repeats the chorus 'if you put it on'. This is the song's crux: everything pivots around the decision to wear the dress. Put it on, and she might attract a really cute boy; but she might also 'provoke' other kinds of unwelcome attention. It will determine other people's impression of 'what kind of girl' she is.

In 'Plants and Rags', the body again appears as a cumbersome object, a dead weight impeding her free movement, as she repeats a sinister line about slipping herself 'into a body bag'. 'Sheela-Na-Gig' turns around the gap between woman as ethereal icon and the fleshy reality of female physiology. The sheela-na-gig is a startling image, if you've ever seen one – it's a Celtic fertility icon, a statue of a bulky, squatting woman pulling apart her vagina for all to see. In the verses, Harvey flaunts her 'child-bearing hips', only to be rebuffed by the chorus, where she plays the part of the contemptuous or scandalised male: 'You exhibitionist!' While icons of the Female Absolute from sheela-na-gig to the Virgin Mary are idealised, flesh-and-blood women with their periods and smells are deemed dirty.

On PJ Harvey's second album *Rid of Me* (1993), the female body asserts itself with even more ferocity. The music is strenuous, visceral: the way Harvey gouges out her riffs, the deliberateness with which she hacks out rhythm chords, never lets you forget that a flesh-and-blood human is wrestling with an instrument, a thing; that the noise comes from her body. The songs incarnate love as close combat, often sounding like nothing so much as Led Zeppelin. The title track 'Rid of Me' is a *Fatal Attraction* scenario, where a woman turns her 'lack' into a voracious threat. The song ricochets violently between revenge fantasies (Harvey's menacing growl) and the desperate neediness of the backing chorus, 'lick my legs' (sung by drummer Rob Ellis in an excruciating, humiliated falsetto).

In the song 'Dry', Harvey sounds plaintive and parched as she offers the ultimate ego-puncturing riposte to a man: 'You leave me dry.' 'Hook' and 'Yuri G' have Harvey's voice filtered through an amplifier, so that she sounds bound-and-gagged, suffocated; she can't 'see' or 'feel'. Harvey has talked of the implosive nature of female rage, the way it festers if it's not vented. 'It's only occasionally that I'll let it out and shout at someone.... That's why you get ill, that's why your shoulders hurt, that's why you bite the skin off your nails, off your lips, because there's all this aggression you just turn in on yourself all the time.'

Along with this vandalistic assault on the jail cell of her own body, Harvey also imagines escaping corporeal existence altogether. One of her obsessions is flying: as a sculpture student, she made a 'whole series of flying objects hanging from the ceiling based on the Icarus theme'. In the *Siren* interview, she declared: 'I'd love to be able to fly. You get a sense of freedom and are able to look down on things instead of being on the same level.' Like the Icarus rockers in the first section, Harvey seemingly longs to escape the abjection of biological identity and soar into a realm of limitlessness. But in her music, the female body continually asserts itself, to the distress but also the *jouissance* of its owner.

physical graffiti

The body can sometimes function as a kind of text or canvas on which the alienated woman projects her inner turmoil. Louise Kaplan used the term 'female perversion' to describe morbidly obsessive and cathartic rituals like anorexia and 'delicate self-cutting'. Such self-cutting is quite different from the theatrics of Iggy Pop (who swan-dived on to broken glass and smashed his teeth on the mic) or Sid Vicious (who gashed his wrists onstage). For these male rock rebels, self-mutilation is a form of aesthetic terrorism. As with real terrorists, it symbolises their messianic zeal, their willingness to sacrifice themselves for an idea and for an effect, their desire to *épater la bourgeoisie*. But teenage girls and grown women have been inflicting ritual damage on themselves for years, without an audience. In some ways, delicate self-cutting parallels Robert Bly's ideas about male rites of initiation and ritual wounding. For women, though, such mutilation is furtive; it's less about marking the passage to adulthood and more a way of marking out the borders of their unruly bodies, a way of achieving a precarious sense of self. As the self-cutting heroine of Katherine Harrison's novel, *Exposure*, puts it: 'I longed for a wound that showed. . . . As if to break the terrible numbness, I was always calling myself back into my body, reminding myself that I was here.'

Kristin Hersh of Throwing Muses even wrote a song called 'Delicate Cutters'. She discussed the syndrome: 'It mainly affects women – they cut themselves, sometimes they write words in their skin. They mutilate themselves as a release, it releases blood, and as a sign to the world – you're looking at my outside and this is what's inside.' According to Kaplan, 'the delicate self-cutter thinks of her skin as a container for the dangerous body substances and organs and all the unsupportable arousals emanating from inside her body' – not unlike the soldier males in the first section. Self-cutting originates in the 'need to define and protect the boundaries of their bodies'. At the same time, blood is invested with *jouissance*, harks back to pre-Oedipal bliss – Kaplan calls it 'mother-blood'.

In 'Delicate Cutters' (an acoustic ballad from the 1986 album *Throwing Muses)*, Kristin Hersh's voice sounds utterly broken as she makes a mysterious journey into a labyrinth of chambers which seems to represent her own body-and-soul – closed off to the world, its entrances heavily guarded. The walls are both trapping her and *are* her. The song is a ballet of avoidance and confrontation. She smashes her head through a window and enters a room full of delicate self-cutters; eventually she makes it to another room, crowded with 'innocent children'. For Hersh, the song dramatised her adolescent struggle to abandon heavily fortified psychic defences and, she said, let 'the world into the inside'. It's an allegory of the tortuous process of emerging from the masochistic morass of adolescence and learning to open up, connect. In a 1988 interview with *Melody Maker*, she remembered that 'when I was seventeen I was a skinny little girl... I cut myself to see what my blood looked like. I'm sure I wasn't the first person to do it, but where does that impulse come from?' Even after she became pregnant at the age of nineteen, she still felt 'about twelve years old... very anti-body...I couldn't figure out why our spirits were supposed to have bodies.' Another of Kaplan's female perversions, anorexia, which Hersh suffered from, inspired the song 'America (She Can't Say No)'.

Kat Bjelland of Babes In Toyland has hinted at personal experience of self-cutting: 'Before I made music, I used to walk around in silence for days, or do obnoxious things to myself.' The titles 'Vomit Heart' and 'Fork Down Throat' suggest anorexia/bulimia as a metaphor for the purging of unacceptable emotions. Like self-cutting, anorexia can be an attempt by the adolescent girl to subjugate a body whose sexual maturation feels like loss-of-control: the anorexic revolts against being enslaved by biological rhythms and falling prey to the sexual gaze of men. Noelle Caskey argues that 'the anorexic grows up viewing her body as a reflected image of the desires of others. It is not *herself*; it is something exterior and foreign, and at the same time more relevant to others than to herself.'

Anorexia is a concerted struggle to arrest one's own development and retain the independence of the prepubescent tomboy. The anorexic monitors her intake of calories, pukes after every meal and guzzles laxatives in order to remain in a virginal state; determined self-starvation results in shrinking breasts and halts the menstrual cycle. A precursor of modern anorexia is the syndrome *anorexia religiosa*, in which high-minded young women like Saint Catherine of Siena exempted themselves from a corrupt world via self-starving and mortification of the flesh. Fasting, of course, is one method holy men and ascetic mystics have used to induce ecstatic effects. According to Hilde Bruch, 'being hungry has the same effect as a drug, and you feel outside your body. You are truly beside yourself.'

Anorexics are often drug fiends, literally: diet pills have long been a source of amphetamine for speed-freaks unable to score. It's interesting that young women who are revolting against female biology should turn to speed, arguably the ultimate masculinist, megalomaniac drug, promoting a sense of self-definition and separation from the environment. As well as killing appetite, speed can also dampen sexual drive, replacing it with autistic self-sufficiency. Speed-freak rebels often suffer from feelings of sexual squeamishness similar to those of teen-girl anorexics: think of Johnny Rotten's dismissal of intercourse as a boring 'squelch session'.

slaves to the rhythm

'I never inserted anything that large into my body, I'm not gonna pass something that large. . . . Besides, [if] I can't live in my body, how can anything else grow there?'
Lydia Lunch on childbirth

If rock has always been in revolt against the reality-principle (which dictates that you simply can't have it ALL), female rockers' relationship with the reality of their biology has often been fraught and ambivalent. The idea of reproductive potential – that something can grow inside of them – is often perceived as a threat. Who wants to be reduced to being an incubator? In a poem written when she was sixteen and pregnant, Patti Smith describes feelings of cumbersome abjection: 'Bloated. Pregnant. I crawl through the sand like a lame dog – like a crab – pull my fat baby belly to the sea – pure edge – pull my hair out by the roots – roll and drag and claw like a bitch – like a bitch – like a bitch.' (Ultimately, she gave her baby up for adoption and fled to bohemia.) In a 1975 interview, Smith spoke of how she 'always felt there was something good to get out of my body, but I was constipated in a way. But even though I was a really homely kid and creepy, I was a happy child, because I had this feeling that I was going to go beyond my body physically.'

Another punk icon, Siouxsie Sioux, also combined female ferocity with an ambivalent attitude to female biology. 'We Hunger' (from 1984's *Hyaena*) imagines pregnancy in terms of the appalling rapacity of the insect world. Vampiric imagery of leeches sucking a body dry suggest a horror of suckling. Pregnancy is parasitic infestation, a loss of independence and, ultimately, identity to a devouring Other: 'Eat me, feed me'. We've seen how Siouxsie's aesthetic fits with Vorticist and proto-fascist Wyndham Lewis's dictate: 'good art must have no inside'. Her aspiration towards the glacial exteriority of the objet d'art was a shunning of the moist, pulsating fecundity of organic life.

Modern-day punk Courtney Love is less able than Siouxsie to distance herself from the abject. In 'Loaded', pregnancy is a degeneration to bovine ignominy, 'suckmilk' oozing from her 'sweet cream udder'. She feels like meat, ready to be slit open and exposed. 'Mrs Jones' is a horrific account of an abortion, full of stink and viral infection: a revolt against the animalism of human existence that rivals the Sex Pistols' 'Bodies'. (Another mostly female band, the Breeders, expressed similar revulsion for reproduction: the band's name comes from gay slang for heterosexuals, the title of their debut album *Pod* (1990) refers to the uterus, and the song 'Hellbound' was the schlocky, B-movie horror story of 'an abortion that lived'.)

But Courtney Love also manages to imagine the ickiness of female biology as a source of power. In 'Pretty on the

Inside', she balefully warns that there's 'no power like my ugly'. Like Diamanda Galas, Love at times wields the abject interior of the female body as a kind of weapon. And having been an early supporter of Riot Grrrl, she criticised the movement for its fixation on the prepubescent tomboy as the ultimate proto-feminist rebel. In *Melody Maker*, she pointed out the almost anorectic streak running through Riot Grrrl ideology: 'GIRL is not menstruating, GIRL is non-orgasmic, GIRL is naive, cute, bratty, un-threatening in her clumsiness and incompetence... I have always called myself a girl, but I am going to stop now.'

On their 1992 LP *Binge and Purge*, the Lunachicks combine teen-delinquent grrrl-power and a gleeful revelling in (rather than repulsion from) the messy murk of female bodiliness. 'Plugg' is fuelled by a 'throbbing pelvis' totally different to the one that underwrites male rock: it's a song about menstrual pain, as boisterous and kick-ass as any hormonally charged punk rock ditty in the male canon. The title track, 'Binge and Purge', mocks the 'good girls' who try to conform to cheerleader standards of sterile cleanliness by revealing the true goo concealed beneath the pom-poms (periods, bulimia). The song is punctuated by sounds of vomiting: instead of the rock brotherhood's circle jerk, these she-rebels find sisterly unity in the 'circle purge'.

From the high-spirited taboo-busting of the Lunachicks to the raging revulsion of Hole, female bands are making rock'n'roll confront a reality it has always excluded: female adolescent experience, with its sense of sexual development as loss of control. These groups reimagine the teenage girl's 'perverse' strategies of rebellion as counterparts to male forms of delinquency.

Early female rock rebels tried to transcend biological fate, wanting adventure instead of domesticity, or looking for a way out of the very categories which structure gender as either/or: Patti Smith, by identifying with the tradition of male Romanticism; Kate Bush, by withdrawing into mythopoeic fantasy. More recent female rockers – Throwing Muses, Hole, PJ Harvey – have staged their revolt on the battleground of their own bodies.

As such, these artists fulfil Hélène Cixous's dream, expressed in her essay 'Laugh of the Medusa', that 'Woman must write herself', draw on her singular bodily experiences in order to create a new kind of language, a way of thinking and speaking that's less linear and cut-and-dry than masculine discourse. American feminist Adrienne Rich has come to similar conclusions. She makes a useful distinction between biological essentialism and using biology as a strategy: 'Patriarchal thought has limited female biology to its own narrow specifications. The feminist vision has recoiled from female biology for these reasons; it will, I believe, come to view our physicality as a resource, rather than a destiny.'

adventures close to home:
domesticity's tender trap

'Houses are really bodies. We connect ourselves with walls, roofs, and objects just as we hang on to our livers, skeletons, flesh and bloodstream.'
Leonora Carrington, *The Hearing Trumpet*

'I remember being a psychology student and reading that one thing that determines whether or not a woman gets institutionalized is whether her house is clean or not. And I thought, Aw, right! Then I get my own house and I can't even sit down if the bed isn't made and I thought, Wow, what are we all trying to clean here? Where is the mess? It's not in the bedroom!'
Kristin Hersh of Throwing Muses

The home has long been a highly charged symbol for women. It's traditionally female territory: simultaneously a source of power and imprisonment, a place where woman reigns and is reined in. In the '50s, peace and plenty resulted in the explosive growth of suburbia. This had massive effects on gender relations: on one hand, the misogynistic discourse of mom-ism; on the other, the emergence of feminism, in response to the cult of domesticity, with its hidden underside of female misery, isolation and powerlessness. The clean house became analogous to having a clean soul. Where spic-and-span spotlessness had once indicated a striving for social respectability, it became the symbol for female self-worth. In response, Betty Friedan's *The Feminine Mystique* (1963) challenged the reduction of women to homemakers and child-breeders.
Domesticity has never been a sexy subject for rock'n'roll;

the home is the last place you'd look for action. For female rockers, this devaluation of the domestic can pose problems; women's adventures often take place in *the great indoors*, as opposed to the external spaces – the wild streets, the desert wilderness – that are the backdrop to male rock adventurism. This indoors is literal (the bedroom) and figurative (the imagination). Ann Powers writes of female songwriters like Tori Amos and Tanita Tikaram as 'unicorn keepers' in the tradition of Kate Bush, Stevie Nicks and Sandy Denny. 'Scholars never study the doodles in their daughters' notebooks; if they did, they'd find traces of the Brontës and old Norse myths, of drawing-room scandals and lovelorn suicides. Kept inside, women invented a wilderness.' Imagination becomes a refuge: girls become gypsies in inner space, rather than exiles on Main Street.

It's hardly surprising, then, that the home has figured as a powerful but conflicted metaphor of female identity for many women artists. Kate Bush's 'Get Out of My House' (from 1982's *The Dreaming*) is one of the most striking examples. Over vaguely tribal percussion, Bush flits between a schizophrenic array of alter egos. The main voice seems to feel immense solidarity with her house, and defiantly declares that no stranger will 'enter me', as she busily scrubs away stains and nurses painful memories. But another voice interjects, stuttering with shrill panic, that the house is a container for 'm-m-my mess' and 'm-m-madness'. Invaders must be fended off: this closely guarded dwelling, this 'I', is all she has. A man tries to woo his way into the inner sanctum, but Bush refuses his entreaties, escaping deeper into inner space, a mythopoeic world of fantasy in which she finds freedom through metamorphosis (she turns into a braying mule, believe it or not). Only in the imaginary can Bush find a way to transcend the conflicts of gender, the binary opposition between armoured selfhood and self-dissolution.

Bizarrely, the title 'Get Out of My House' recurred nearly ten years later as a line in 'Teenage Whore', on Hole's

Pretty on the Inside. This song could be taken as a dialogue between a daughter and her mother, and with others who have placed the protagonist in the position of bad girl/outsider. Controlling who enters her 'house' (i.e. body) is one of the teenagers' few avenues of power – even if it means allowing herself to be abused. Courtney Love walks a tightrope between control and degradation: does her choking howl signify shame, demoralisation, or accusation? Her body has become the battlefield for a struggle of ownership.

The Lunachicks present a different kind of mother-daughter confrontation in 'Mom' (from *Binge and Purge*, 1992). Here, they lambast an obsessional housewife who can't leave her house until the place is perfectly clean. The song's manic, escalating tempo simulates the neurotic frenzy of this would-be supermom who will never find peace in her domestic prison – but also evokes the desperation of a daughter who wants to make a break for it before she turns into her mother. Singer Theo Kogan advises her to step outside and 'smell the air', but mom doesn't heed her. In the end, Kogan realises the situation is futile and bids farewell to Mom and home.

Several years before the female grunge bands, though, Kristin Hersh was grappling with what she's described as 'the agoraphobia versus claustrophobia dilemma: the problem of what a home is, when do you leave it, how are you going to make yourself a home. The problem is that where there's security, there's also entrapment.' The first Throwing Muses album is full of imagery of being hemmed-in or smothered by domestic intimacy. In 'Vicky's Box', home is a place 'where the heart lies': the word 'lies' is full of foreboding ambiguity, suggesting the domestic interior as a space of self-deception, entropy and wasted potential. The home is a space of pristine surfaces and restrictive role-play: women's 'proper place' is the last place that a woman can be herself.

By 1988's *House Tornado*, Hersh had a couple of years experience of being a mother and housewife under her apron belt, and as the LP's title suggests, she'd become obsessed with the idea that domesticity could be the setting for extremes of experience just as much as rock's wide open spaces. 'The idea of the savage housewife is intensely appealing,' she declared in an interview. 'I spent all my time in the past writing about my bloody teenage years and now I'm thinking I have to settle down, to become thirty-five years old. But I'm twenty and there's so much violence in a house, so much of a dynamic.'

In the opening song, 'Colder', Hersh plays the part of a housewife who's become part of the furniture, her activities so mechanical that she can't separate herself from the objects she's surrounded by. It's a very different take on Erik Satie's proto-ambient dream of *furniture music*, music that takes 'the sounds of the environment into considera-tion'. The song sounds subdued but restless; mundane tasks have dulled the imagination and blocked creativity, but haven't instilled peace of mind. 'If I did the same thing five hundred times could you see it in the dark?', worries Hersh. The image brings to mind the time-lapse cinema of *Koyaanisqatsi*, where everyday human activities are sped up into a blur, so that routine solidifies before your eyes, takes on a sculptural quality. Numbed by repetition, the housewife feels her life-spirit getting colder and dimmer, until she's just an object herself: she feels like she's 'an alarm clock'.

This identification with inanimate things runs through a number of women's songs – an expression of feelings of powerlessness and anonymity. Possibly it's related to a syndrome Julia Kristeva calls the 'trimming of anguish', in which one copes with overwhelming feelings of dread by projecting them on to a phobic object. Hersh often resorts to such identification with the inanimate or abject. In 'Hate My Way', it's her pillow and her kitchen that 'scream'.

On *House Tornado*, 'Marriage Tree' features another housewife who's been transformed into an automaton by the thoughtless and thankless tasks that make up her daily grind. At the end of the song, there's a hint of long-ings to give up the ghost and be taken care of, or to escape altogether, to 'take to open roads'. The deceptively poppy 'Juno' conceals a haunting melancholy: there are 'many places to go', but not for the narrator. It's a kind of jubilant salute to the housewife, or to the women who got left behind when the beatniks went 'on the road'. The most devastating song on *House Tornado* is 'Walking in the Dark', despite its sharp, bright piano, which is evenly pitched between buoyancy and fidgety foreboding. This housewife is captive, caught in a tender trap, 'tangled in my family's hair'. Again, there are hints of pregnant poten-tial, a rich and teeming dreamlife denied an outlet. Hersh could be talking to herself, or to the women who are forced to live behind masks, hiding their glow but pulsing with unlived life.

happy house

One of punk's many targets was the bland braindeath of suburban life. Female punks had even more reason to dread settling down than the boys. With songs like 'Suburban Relapse' and 'Happy House', Siouxsie Sioux was doubtless exorcising the feelings of entrapment she endured as an arty, angsty adolescent growing up in the bourgeois London suburb of Bromley. In 'Suburban Relapse' (from *The Scream*, 1978), the narrator is a house-wife whose 'string snapped' while engaged in the dreary business of doing the dishes. Mad, she throws consumer durables at her neighbours, exposes herself in public. The song could perhaps be seen as a belated riposte to the Rolling Stones' 'Mother's Little Helper', which sneered at depressed housewives who rely on tranquillisers to get them through the day. But it's unclear whether Siouxsie identifies with the woman who is revolting against routine (there but for the grace of God go I), or whether she scorns her with the standard punk arrogance of the 'elect' who've managed, by sheer dint of will, to pull themselves out of the mire of mediocrity.

'Happy House', from 1980's *Kaleidsocope*, makes a disconcerting parallel between home-sweet-home and the asylum. Both are containers for wildness, places where impossible desires are caged and fester. The song presents a scene of domestic non-bliss in which silence is enforced. Siouxsie slyly suggests that there's room inside for anyone prepared to 'say "I do"': the commitment of marriage is equated with being committed to the loony-bin.

At roughly the same time, a singer from a previous generation of female rebels, Marianne Faithfull, had a hit with a song about the anguish of a housewife. 'The Ballad of Lucy Jordan' was written by a man, Shel Silverstein, but Faithfull's harrowing version is definitive. An unfulfilled thirty-seven-year-old suburban wife who's full of unrequited dreams, Lucy Jordan is overpowered by her fantasies (of a legion of lovers, of riding through Paris in a sportscar). None of them will ever come true, because as she sings her song, she is preparing to kill herself. Living to and through her husband and kids, circumscribed on every side, reduced to a robot tending flowers and sprucing up the house, she's already dead inside. She climbs up on the roof, and when the mysterious, derisive laughter she hears in her head grows to a fever pitch, hurls herself off. If only Lucy Jordan could simply have floated away above the rooftops, like the housewife-turned-Icarus in Talking Heads' 'And She Was'.

On *Cut* (1979), the Slits provide something of a cross-section exposé of urban alienation via a woman's point of view. 'Spend Spend Spend' is a brilliant, heartbreaking glimpse into the life of a woman whose compulsive consumerism is an attempt to fill her emptiness. Over a brittle, bleak, punk-reggae soundscape, Ari Up's wavering voice sings of escaping her desolate nest in a tower block and consoling herself with impulse purchases. Even the language of her inner life has been colonised by advertising: shopping, she says, offers 'a new improved remedy' for her angst.

Years later, TV talk shows – always on the look-out for new problems in need of solving through counselling and self-help – discovered the 'shopaholic'. Susan Faludi sees shopping as a diversion of women's energies away from politics and feminism: 'the 80's culture stifled women's political speech and then redirected self-expression to the shopping mall. The passive consumer was reissued as an ersatz feminist, exercising her "right" to buy products, making her own "choices" at the checkout counter.' Faludi points out that studies indicate that 'the more confident and independent women became, the less they liked to shop.' Cable TV's home shopping networks completed women's isolation: now there's no need to even leave the house in order to satisfy the addiction. Some order thousands of dollars worth of goods by phone, then cancel the order before it's shipped out: pure purchase of the moment.

After the dispirited 'Spend Spend Spend', the Slits hurl themselves into the manic glee of 'Shoplifting', in which shopping is reimagined as female *delinquency*. In fact, Louise Kaplan includes compulsive shoplifting as a female perversion. It's certainly a major leisure activity of teenage girls whose desires exceed their finances. The Slits, however, aren't mall-brats but squat-punk survivalists, and they're only stealing what they need: food. Their jubilant, uproarious yowl – 'We pay FUCK-ALL!' – suggests that petty larceny is also a sort of purchase of the moment – in this case, getting something for nothing is empowering, not enslaving.

These songs hint that, if 'the poverty of everyday life' is the major form of oppression in late twentieth century Western society (as the Situationists argued), then women are on the cutting edge when it comes to experience of boredom and alienation.

all fluxed up:
rebels against structure

Traditional treatments of 'women in rock' have tended to
look for strong role models, applauding those who've succeeded against the odds in a male-dominated industry.
Forthright statements are valued over the 'weakness' of
contradiction and ambivalence. The accent has been on
empowerment and improvement (self and social).

Yet some of the most powerful music by women originates in confusion rather than certainty. These artists
have worked from within the problematic of (female) identity. Their aesthetic has been based not in subjectivity, but
in what Julia Kristeva calls a *subject-in-process*. Identity is
seen as open space rather than structure, full of the clamour and turmoil of divided impulses and contradictory
desires. So this torn subjectivity is expressed through language that's fractured and frayed, that oscillates between
incoherence and visionary lucidity.

Flux can be liberating, a welcome release from the rigidity of identity. But the experience of being decentred can
also be terrifying and incapacitating. There's a fuzzy line
between being fluxed up and fucked up, between the subject-in-process and the schizophrenic. Some psychoanalytic
theorists regard schizophrenia as a language problem.
Learning language is how the infant becomes an 'I'; as it
relinquishes its symbiotic relationship with the mother, the
child acquires the ability to speak and express its desires,
to function in society. Detachment from the maternal is the
foundation of language, which is perhaps why, for some
women, language – particularly in its most rigorous, logical

and judicial sense – feels alien and alienating. Fluxed-up singers from Patti Smith to Mary Margaret O'Hara have rejected this 'man-made language', and tried to create a more *musical* form of poetic utterance. Poetic language subverts common sense language by putting in jeopardy the subject/verb/object structure that constitutes the individual as 'I'. But opening the 'I' to a mob of unruly desires and dreads is risky. The poet flirts with ego-loss and derangement, walks a tightrope over the abyss of unreason. For those whose sense of identity is shaky at best, the experience of being a multitude rather than a single, solid self can be shattering. Often, the choice for female artists is between presenting a strong, unified front (suppressing confusion and doubt in order to cut an impressive figure in the male-dominated power structure), or exploring their inner turmoil in their work (running the risk of being dismissed as inarticulate or hysterical or mad). Nonetheless, this second approach makes for some of the most powerful and radical art, for those who look to be challenged rather than comforted.

'Rimbaud writes this letter and he says. . . in the future when women get away from their long servitude to men. . . they're going to have new music, new sensations, new horrors, new spurts. . .'
Patti Smith

In some ways, Patti Smith is the ultimate female rock rebel. All the contradictions of 'women in rock' percolate inside her work. She started as a tomboy/female beatnik who totally identified with the male Romantic tradition; at the pinnacle of her creativity, she was engaged in a radical feminisation of rock form, and imagined herself as a kind of female Messiah; after all this, she abandoned rock'n'roll for the most standard-issue female existence, being a mother and home-maker.

Patti Smith's first rock'n'roll efforts involved taking

classics of rebel masculinity and giving them a female twist: her first single was a cover of 'Hey Joe' (replacing the wife-murderer of the original with a female terrorist, Patti Hearst), while her debut album *Horses* (1975) kicked off with a cover of Them's 'Gloria'. This proto-punk classic of male lust, covered by a legion of garage bands in the '60s, becomes in Smith's treatment an anthem of lesbian desire.

Merely emulating the toughness and swaggering insolence of male rebellion wasn't enough for Smith, though. Instead, she tried to imagine a female Dionysian spirit, a wildness that was equal but different to male presentations of freedom. Although her band was all male, and steeped in rock tradition, she saw their music as radically feminine. In a 1978 interview, she declared: 'We don't have a fixed set or formula. We're not like a male band either, in that the male process of ecstacy in performance is starting here' – Smith mimed jerking at the base of an imaginary giant phallus – 'and building and building until the big spurt at the end. We're a feminine band, we'll go so far and peak and then we'll start again and peak, over and over. It's like ocean.'

The contradiction – being overwhelmingly inspired by male artists and rock'n'rollers, yet aspiring to create a 'feminine' music – was not as insuperable as it might initially appear. The Romantic tradition that Smith looked to consisted of male artists who believed they were in touch with the feminine within. From Rimbaud to Jim Morrison, these artists had set a premium on flow, flux, the chaos of the unconscious. By identifying with these male avant-gardists and Romantics, Smith found a way to reclaim women's own wildness.

Patti Smith's most successful attempts to create a non-phallic rock, organised around endless crescendos rather than the tension/explosion structure of male rock, took the form of long pieces like 'Land' and 'Radio Ethiopia'. Like 'The End' on the Doors' debut, 'Land' is the climax and centrepiece of *Horses*. It's a classic example of the Velvet

Underground's minimal-is-maximal approach – simplistic rock'n'roll repetition accumulating into an overwhelming gush and rush of sound. The piece is truly 'like ocean', wave after wave of noise crashing like breakers, then remounting their assault. Smith is carried along on their crest like a surfer, her delivery veering from classic rock'n'roll urgency ('Go Johnny go') to a giddy stream of mythological imagery.

Lyrically, 'Land' is awesomely ambitious, attempting both to return to the primordial source of rock'n'roll and to push forward to a new spiritual realm. This tension is inscribed in the sound, which is simultaneously garage rock'n'roll primitivism at its most basic (the riff and beat are so simple they're almost inane), and a reaching out towards abstract expressionist blur. Namechecking the dance crazes of the '50s and early '60s – the Watusi, the Mashed Potato, the Alligator – Smith harks back to the primal dervish-whirling delirium of rock'n'roll. In *Shadow Dancing in the USA*, Michael Ventura sees rock'n'roll as a radical invasion of sexuality and the body into Christian culture, 'a gash in the nature of Western things'. Because of Elvis Presley, 'the voodoo rite of possession. . . became the standard of American performance in rock'n'roll'. Smith returns to the non-sense and glossolalia of Little Richard's awopbopaloobop, and gives it a Joycean spin: her singing is pure rock'n'roll holler *and* the invocatory babble of a prophetess.

Ironically, although Smith is the visionary, the principal protagonist of her vision in the song 'Land' is 'Johnny'. He is the archetypal rock'n'roll bad boy, clad in leather and carrying a switchblade. But the real subject of the song is not 'The Wild One' (the Brando/Dean rebel) but a nameless wildness, imagined as a stampede of horses. Horses have long figured for adolescent girls as a symbol of potency and independence. In Smith's vision, horses become the image of elemental power, natural grace, and unbridled freedom – a tempest she can ride. The horses have the same function

for her that surfing has for some male rock adventurers –
indeed, when she stares at the waves they seem to her like
a horde of Arabian stallions.

In 'Land', Smith vacillates between taking control and
losing control, identifying with the rebel male prototype
and imagining his blissful dissipation into a grander wildness. Johnny becomes a rock'n'roll suicide: he uses the
knife not as a phallic weapon, but to open his throat, slash-
ing through his vocal chords. Bleeding, he merges with the
raging sea. The heart of the song comes when Smith looks
into Johnny's hair as it becomes a stairway to heaven, envisioned as 'the sea of possibilities'. The figure of the rebel, in
all his solipsistic grandeur, dissolves – sundered by desires
that exceed the human frame. Similarly the rock'n'roll form
of 'Land' haemorrhages into a freeform flux; the pell-mell
stampede ebbs into lagoons of eerie sound fringed with
murmured Smith vocals.

If 'Land' has both the rock hero and rock form surrender-
ing to an inundation of chaos, 'Radio Ethiopia' (the title
track of the 1976 follow-up) is a total insurrection against
structure. There's only the loosest of rhythmic vertebrae,
and even that departs halfway through, leaving unmoored
percussion and clustered clouds of cymbal-spray. The guitars quickly abandon the semblance of riffs, dissolve into
gouts of freeform noise and graffiti-like scrawls of endless
soloing. Patti Smith goes beyond emulating a rock'n'roll
shaman like Jim Morrison, with his clear diction and bombastic gravity; she sounds like the genuine article, a
shaman from the Amazon, tripping madly on hallucinogenic tree-bark. She gnashes and drools, chokes and gasps
strangulated incantations. The closest to this voodoo delirium that any male singer has gotten is Iggy Pop's howls at
the climax of 'TV Eye' and Tim Buckley's *Starsailor*.

Patti Smith had a name for the gushing gibberish she
unleashed in songs like 'Land' and 'Radio Ethiopia':
Babelogue. The Babelogue is the opposite of a monologue or
soliloquy, forms that are centred and self-aggrandising

(despite the doubt and anguish that often inspires them). In her babble-ogues, Smith was attempting to recover the primal speech that existed before our fall into language (the Biblical collapse of the Tower of Babel). Clearly articulated language seems too inadequate for the expression of emotion, too stiff to suit the speed and complexity of feeling. Rock'n'roll and soul have always flirted with incoherence, subjecting words to the stress of passion, encouraging language to approach the condition of music, and at the furthest instance leaping outside meaning into the pure emotion of falsetto, growl or roar. In 'Radio Ethiopia', Smith makes this momentary breakdown of meaning into the entire body of the song.

On 'Land', 'Radio Ethiopia', and other songs, Smith is in revolt against syntax and diction. In a 1976 interview with *Melody Maker*, Smith attempted to explain her and the band's hostility to structure, which had led to criticisms of technical incompetence: 'I, unfortunately, was very rebellious at school. I wouldn't learn my grammar. . . . No one explained to me that I could transfer it into something celestial. . . . Some people are rebels and wear leather jackets and slice up people. We are different rebels. We wouldn't learn our grammar and we wouldn't learn our chord structures. We just wanted to be free.'

In the sleevenotes to *Radio Ethiopia*, Smith invokes the freedom 'to defy the social order and break the slow kill of monotony. . . . The anarchy that exudes from the pores of her guitar are the cries of the people wailing in the rushes.' Smith envisions herself as both the music's charismatic centre, as the ringleader of chaos, and as a figure who vaporises in the topsy-turvy tumult she's instigated, because she is the conduit of other's desires. Smith managed to reconcile this tension – between being the focus of attention and dissolving in flux – with her fantasy of being a self-sacrificing star. On the title track of her third album *Easter* (1978) she imagines herself as a female Messiah resurrecting the spirit: her music's fluidity irrigates the arid and sterile Wasteland that rock culture has become. One character in her play *Cowboy Mouth* (written with Sam Shepard) declared: 'The rock'n'roll star in his highest state of grace will be the new saviour.' Patti Smith tried to be the first female saviour-shaman in rock history.

Still, Smith remained torn between her allegiance to the heroic figures of the male rebel tradition and her desire to unleash a female wildness that obliterates figuration altogether. Nowhere is this more apparent than on 'Rock'n'Roll Nigger' (*Easter*). The nigger here is a woman (the title obviously inspired by Yoko Ono's 'Woman is the Nigger of the World'). 'Rock 'N' Roll Nigger' is Smith announcing that female rebellion is the new frontier. In some latent fashion, the song is saying: if hipsters have always wanted to be White Negros, and woman is the nigger of the world, then why can't female rebellion be the model for all future rebels?

But in a rambling rant halfway through the song, Smith namechecks male innovators (Hendrix, Jesus, Jackson Pollock) as 'niggers', as though she's casted around for female archetypes of rebellion and come up empty-handed. The sleevenotes declare that 'any man who extends beyond the classic form is a nigger'. This resembles the arguments of theorists like Hélène Cixous, who claim that male avant-gardists like Joyce and Mallarmé were somehow engaged in *écriture féminine*; they were able to rupture the strictures of patriarchal thought and syntax because they had special access to the 'dark continent' of femininity. Certainly, these *poètes maudits* and their rock'n'roll descendants (Morrison, Iggy, Tom Verlaine) were Smith's models. Apart from the black sheep that is 'Rock'n'Roll Nigger''s original focus (Smith herself), Woman appears in this song only in the form of 'the infinite sea'.

The female archetypes that she sometimes invokes – in 'Poppies', she names Sheba, Salome and Venus – are as much impediments as empowering. They are double-edged visions of femininity often used against women. Venus, she yells, is 'eclipsing my way'. Smith gets inside the 'feminine' words, stretching their meanings even as she confronts them: 'Every woman is a vessel, is evasive, is aquatic'. But even as she acknowledges and embraces her 'feminine' heritage, she can't help but be swayed by the impressive male rebels who have helped create images of women which make them niggers in this world. She quotes André Breton's *Nadja* on the jacket of *Radio Ethiopia*: 'beauty will be convulsive or not at all'. Yet the Surrealists perpetrated much misogyny – Breton himself described the drive for women's independence after World War One as 'bourgeois' – and female Surrealists were largely marginalised within the movement. One of the best, Leonora Carrington, suffered the indignity of having her canvases used as grounds by her lover Max Ernst: he literally painted her out of the picture.

Patti Smith has talked about how the few women she saw in art were artists' models, so it's no wonder she preferred the male archetype. At the same time, she had no doubt that her creativity came from being in touch with the same realm of 'feminine' flux (the unconscious) from which the Surrealists and earlier Romantic artists had siphoned. She gestured at this space of flux and mutability, of pulsations that dissolved form and hierarchy in her sleevenotes for *Easter*: 'layer after layer. wall after wall. there is always more. there is always more after'. Smith's womblike imagery – 'a space warm and glowing. infinite yet dense' – corresponds to what Kristeva calls the chora, a kind of internal memory of the lost bliss of infancy that each individual carries around within.

Artists and poets draw on the chora's flux in order to loosen up the desiccated nature of commonsensical communication, and to dissolve the rigour of conceptual thought. Patti Smith's double bind was that she admired the psychic surfers (the male rebels who could 'play with madness', skimming its turbulent surface without drowning in it); at the same time, she worshipped 'the infinite sea'. And because she lacked a prototype for a female Dionysian spirit, she was out there on her own.

the boho dance

In the '70s, while Patti Smith was Godmother of New York punk, Joni Mitchell was Queen of Southern California soft rock; but for artists supposedly so far apart, they had a surprising amount in common. Both had worshipped Dylan and shared beat's premium on flux. Musically and lyrically, Mitchell's songs grew progressively more elliptical as she moved away from her folky beginnings. On albums like *Court and Spark* (1974) and *The Hissing of Summer Lawns* (1975) her voice glides and swoons, pirouettes and weaves. For rock fans, Mitchell's fluttery, quavering folky-jazzy voice can seem too feminine for (dis)comfort. Her hostility to fixed, easily legible meanings is expressed not in Patti Smith's babble but in prolix gush. Like many confessional songwriters, Mitchell crams each line with too many words. Lord knows, this is not a particularly female sin, but one of which many post-Dylan songwriters are guilty. Think of Elvis Costello and Squeeze: over-diligent wordsmiths, craftsmen who burnish and adorn their songs with an excess of lyrical and musical ornamentation. But whereas these male songwriters' verbosity seems the result of overweening cockiness, with Mitchell, it's as though millions of thoughts and overflowing feelings are stuffed into a forever wandering structure and threaten to overflow the fabric of the song.

On *The Hissing of Summer Lawns*, the music is as diffuse as her lyrics, an ambient folk-jazz devoid of solos. Mitchell's voice is mixed high, so that it doesn't seem to intersect with the music, but glides over it. The result is like poems set to music, music that is itself more like sound paintings than rock, full of chiaroscuro shading and watercolour nuances (one song is called 'Shadows and Light').

Like Mitchell's singing, the sound is all fleetness and airy
iridescence: the lyrics slip between the cinematic details of
the outside world and the meandering flux of inner space
(her head is 'full of quandary').

Mitchell is open to the mundane epiphanies that disrupt
habit-governed everyday life, alive to *satori* and serendi-
pity. But for all its somersaults and swerves, her voice is
self-possessed – there's none of the violent uncontrol of
Patti Smith's Babelogues. Mitchell's voice is the incarnation of her whole persona: elegant, graceful, a little
detached and above-it-all. The ballerina and the bird seem
to be her role models. In search of serenity and symmetry,
there's nothing remotely Dionysian about Joni.

In the most crucial song on *The Hissing of Summer
Lawns*, Mitchell kisses goodbye the 'old romance' of 'The
Boho Dance', the glamour of artists living in poverty – the
whole 'White Negro' fantasy of walking on the wild side.
'The Boho Dance' is a put-down of a slumming male
bohemian who has dared to sneer at her for no longer being
street-credible. Mitchell says that she never really felt at
home on the streets. In 'Women and Pop: A Series of Lost
Encounters', Hilary Little and Gina Rumsey write: 'It's no
accident that what most of us find we lack is *street* credibil-
ity'. For women, the streets are not the unproblematic zone
of adventure they are for boys, but a threatening terrain,
pregnant with the threat of harassment and rape. While
adolescent boys hang out, maraud aimlessly, girls more
often explore 'the great indoors', sharing fantasies together
or writing diaries alone. Joni Mitchell's oblique songs are
the grown-up version of the diaristic impulse: it's as though
she's introjected the beatnik's nomadic spirit, and roams
through her own thoughts.

If Joni Mitchell has an obvious successor, it's Rickie Lee
Jones. Her career and songs bring out even more clearly
the problematic relationship women have to 'The Boho
Dance'. Jones started out as a female beatnik. She ran

away from home at the age of fourteen to live the hep-cat life in Los Angeles. Her music and singing incarnate beat ideals like flux and fluidity, wanderlust and wonderlust, and her songs are situated in a mythical, post-modern fantasy of bohemia, sort of Coolsville meets Alice In Wonderland.

For women, a wanderer's life can be even more alluring than it is for men. Women have even stronger reasons for wanting to escape domesticity, since the home is where they are supposed to end up. As they grow up, young women are usually expected to do more household chores, help cook and supervise siblings. But even as it beckons as an escape route from self-denying drudgery, bohemianism is fraught with dangers for women: as Mitchell put it, the streets are not their (natural) habitat. Often, the best they can hope for is to be the male rebel's girl.

Where her eponymous 1979 debut was a largely unproblematic evocation of the bohemian dream, 1981's *Pirates* sees Jones losing her cool, starting to crack. In 'We Belong Together' (from *Pirates*), Jones is seduced by the rebel postures of her beau (one minute he's Brando, the next James Dean). Unfortunately, the only female role model she can envision for herself is Natalie Wood (Dean's girlfriend in *Rebel Without A Cause*). This gratuitous allusion to such a minor figure in the annals of rebel iconography suggests that Jones felt like an outsider even amongst The Outsiders. In 'Pirates (So Long Lonely Avenue)', her lowlife buddies thrive on 'the edge of living on the run', but Jones can't sustain the pace or maintain her balance. In 'A Lucky Guy', Jones finds it hard to be as blasé and uncaring as her man, and blows her cool by telling him she loves him. Being cool means being detached, unemotional, and she can't carry it through: she gets too attached, and he makes a break for it.

Rickie Lee Jones's music is steeped in jazz, mirroring an ideal for living based around improvisation and 'living in the now'. Her singing constantly aspires to scat's grace-in-flux. Her words – even cold on the page, a freeform stream of consciousness, riddled with oblique images and abrupt swerves of thought – are further twisted and slurred by semiotic excess. Rickie Lee Jones's voice incarnates her ambivalent relationship to the hipster fantasy: it's the sound of nervousness aspiring to languor, an outsider who wants to belong, to get in the groove.

If much of the debut album conforms a little too closely to smoky, beret-clad clichés of 'hep', *Pirates* has her singing in the midst of an unprecedented sound-web of ambient/cinematic post-jazz. In particular, 'Traces of the Western Slopes' is an unmoored drift with no fixed metre, teeming with spectral echoes of American hipster musics past and present. Always melodic, but never a melody, the song is all flow, but uneven, a groove that fluctuates, staving off resolution. Lyrically, it's unfathomable, an intertextual polyphony of panoramic details, internal reveries, unwelcome memories, wholly private associations. If it's about anything, it's about the West as the holy grail of all beatniks and adventurers, the promised land and lost frontier which in reality is a hinterland of lonely drifters and washed-up wanderers. The schizoid structure of 'Traces of the Western Slopes' seems to connect with Jones's biographical circumstances: drug abuse, doomed affairs with unreliable boho males, something close to a breakdown, and what seems like a loss of faith in the whole bohemian fantasy.

On subsequent albums, Jones seems more 'centred', and, perhaps because of this, a less compelling artist. Flux remains her watchword, and there's still a hostility to easy legibility. On *The Magazine* (1984), 'Gravity' has lots of wordless singing, while on 'Runaround', her phrasing slides into overrun and choked lines. One suite of songs is named 'Rorschachs', after the inkblots used by psychoanalysts to encourage free association by their patients: it's as though Jones wants you to read anything you like into her work (not an uncommon stance on the part of songwriters).

The Rorschach allusion suggests that Rickie Lee Jones

might agree with the notion of art as therapy, of the subject-in-process staving off mental rigidity with infusions of poetry and music. But in her post-*Pirates* work, the dizziness, polyphony and kaleidophrenic imagery have been banished, doubtless for the sake of sanity. By the time of her 1991 album, *Pop Pop*, Jones was constricting herself within the classic proportions of the torch song: her readings of jazz standards were decorous and polite compared to the exorbitant unravelling she wreaked on 'My Funny Valentine' on 1983's *Girl at Her Volcano*. By the end of the '80s, Jones's volcano was dwindling into dormancy. And with her cover of Bowie's 'Rebel Rebel' on 1993's *Traffic from Paradise*, Jones sent a love letter/fond farewell to the 'hot tramp', wild child of her distant past.

fraught flux

Roughly contemporary with Rickie Lee Jones's post-modern jazz-pop, but on the other side of the Atlantic, the Raincoats were forging a fragmented post-punk sound. Earlier, we dealt with the Raincoats in terms of their lyrical content (their demystification of love and sexuality, their exploration of un-rock'n'roll areas of female experience). Yet their most radical innovations were formal: where Rickie Lee Jones, Joni Mitchell and Patti Smith all relied on male musicians to realise their ideas, the Raincoats were an all-female collective, self-consciously struggling to create an explicitly 'feminine' sound. And they succeeded: the sorely neglected second album, *Odyshape* (1981), is one of the great lost moments of women-in-rock, its possibilities never really followed up.

Writing about the Raincoats' 1979 eponymous debut in *Melody Maker*, Vivienne Goldman declared: 'It's taken me twenty-seven years of listening to music to hear a woman's rock album.' Antecedents like the all-girl pop-metal band the Runaways were 'surrogate men' defined by 'male puppeteers'. But the Raincoats' non-hierarchical, communal set-up, their shying away from solos and macho grandstanding, marked 'a conscious change from the topdog/underdog pattern set up by the patriarchal structure. . . they're each so mindful of not out-voicing the other Raincoats that half the time they don't finish what they're saying.'

Looking for non-phallocentric models for pop, the Raincoats inevitably drew on reggae, African music, and folk: cultures where participation is valued over expertise, where there's no specialised class of musicians set above 'non-musicians', and everybody has a go. (This obviously connected to post-punk concerns like do-it-yourself.) The Raincoats favoured poly-rhythmic percussion (as opposed to the phallic insistence of rock's backbeat). Poly is the essential prefix: poly-rhythmic, poly-ethnic, poly-vocal. So 'No One's Little Girl' (from *The Kitchen Tapes*, 1983) is a shambolic fusion of cultures (Celtic violin meets reggae), no steady beat, and a roundelay of untutored, artless voices.

The sound on *Odyshape* is a tapestry of ethnic, British folk, and post-punk threads; instead of jamming together ferociously (the male approach to improvisation), the Raincoats almost *knit* together. On a song like 'Family Tree', there's no backbeat, only an implied but absent rhythmic pivot, around which the instruments undulate and weave. The instruments on 'Only Loved At Night', 'go their own way'. The gamelan percussion is decorative, the dub reggae deep bass drops out of the mix for long spells, the guitar is agitated. Yet the song is not a mess: a musical conversation is taking place, a mood and a sense of movement is created – but in a way that departs from any accepted rock notion of propulsion.

Along with their musical self-effacement (the fear of 'out-voicing each other'), Raincoats' lyrics are tentative, faltering. Many of their songs are polylogues (that 'poly-' prefix again!), a hesitant call and response within a single, confused mind. In 'Odyshape', there are continuous conversations taking place in the background, while the foreground vocal seems to be experiencing a kind of panic attack. The song is structured around jittery fits of embarrassment (the woman is 'walking sad' and 'looking bad') that ebb and then resurge, like a blush that can't be mastered. Meanwhile, an elastic rhythm section relaxes and tenses up in synch with the spasms of self-consciousness. Tentative emotions – embarrassment, awkwardness – that are foreign to the rock repertoire oblige the Raincoats to come up with whole new structures for music.

Sometimes the Raincoats depart so far from rock rhythms that they're hard to respond to as pleasurable: the unsteady, rubbery tempos of 'Baby Song' are just too fitful, too eccentric (literally out-of-the-groove). But again, this discomfort is appropriate for the confessional nature of the lyrics. The Raincoats' words are broken shards of emotion, jutting feelings, a fretful vacillation between agitated options. If flux is at the heart of the Raincoats' aesthetic, it's not blissful or mystical as it was for Patti Smith, but fraught.

Later in the '80s, another mostly female group captured in sound the dance of a mind in disarray. On the debut album *Throwing Muses*, songs are forever changing tempo and mood, as though subject to sudden wind changes. Kristin Hersh seems to pack several songs into one, jump-cutting from plangent folk balladry to visceral folk-punk tempest. 'I guess you just have to think of a collage,' she once suggested. There's a sense of immediacy in Throwing Muses' songs, of thought catching fire. Passion does not conform to the regular proportions of rock's epic form, with punctual explosions and the guarantee of eventual resolution, but comes in waves, mirroring the perverse, self-confounding trajectories of anguished thought. Yet this music indisputably *rocks*. To a new female rhythm, as much the creation of male drummer David Narcizo, with his strange martial metres, as of bassist Lesley Langston and the twin rhythm guitars of Hersh and Tanya Donnelly.

On the first LP, songs like 'Call Me' and 'Soul Soldier' intersperse poignantly melodic lulls with oppressive thickets of viscous, visceral guitar; song structures twist and turn in synch with Hersh's tangled, tumultuous train of thought. She makes her inner life into an adventure, an assault course. 'Vicky's Box' embodies claustrophobia even as Hersh sings about it; the rubbery bass and web of guitars subtly modulate to create a sense of paralysis, while Narcizo's military percussion nails the lid down. The gnarled guitar of 'Soul Soldier' is so suffocating (Hersh sings of lovers who 'couldn't breathe'), and the treadmill rhythm so arrested, like a wheel churning helplessly in the mud, that when the song slips free and glides into a poignant melody, the listener is tempted to gulp for air. This brief, gentle moment is an oasis, an island in the mindstorm.

Although wary of the 'women in rock' fix, with the risk it brings of being treated as novelty, Hersh told *Melody Maker* in 1989: 'We can be aggressive but people aren't used to female aggression, they're only used to male aggression which, in music, takes the form of these *yang* elements, the BOOM BOOM BOOM, straight ahead, or melodies that don't. . . fly up much. And a lot of female music seems to be based on strings of subtleties, like Liz Fraser [of Cocteau Twins], Salem 66, the Raincoats. . . Yin elements.' It's this female aggression that warps, corrodes, buckles and fractures the structures of rock.

the schizo-logue

'[Poetry is] like letting a lot of wild animals out in the arena,
but enclosing them in a cage, and you could let some extraordinary
animals out if you have the right cage.'
Anne Sexton

There are plenty of precedents for Muses-style fragmentation (of form and perspective) in women's writing of the twentieth century. Aside from Virginia Woolf, one classic example is Doris Lessing's novel *The Golden Notebook* (1962). It presents the portrait (or rather multiple portraits) of Anna, a woman trying to hold her life together. The only way she can document its many strands is to keep four different notebook diaries, each dealing with a different facet of her existence. As Lessing writes in the introduction, 'She keeps four, and not one because, as she recognises, she has to separate things off from each other, out of fear of chaos, formlessness – of breakdown.' Anna herself writes at one point: 'I've reached the stage where I look at people and say – he or she, they are whole at all because they've chosen to block off at this stage or that. People stay sane by blocking off, by limiting themselves.' At the other extreme, she finds people who *don't* block themselves off: 'Sometimes I meet people, and it seems to me the fact they are cracked across, they're split, means they are keeping themselves open for something.' To Lessing and Anna, accepting multiplicity and chaos seems to be a more realistic way of dealing with the fractured nature of women's lives. Perhaps, for some, it's the only way.

Both Lessing's schizo-confessional and Sexton's 'wild beasts in a cage' metaphor fit Throwing Muses, who more than any other band make rock'n'roll literally *crack up*. Hersh's personae change almost as rapidly as the jagged tempos. 'Hate My Way' starts with a military, stop-start beat, over which Hersh's bloodcurdling, staccato voice makes a grisly list of potential personalities, models of deformed and damaged subjectivity, that she could be if she wanted: the smack addict, who has severed contact with society; the lover, who fears mortality; the Holocaust victim, whose fears are real and warranted; and the neurotic whose nameless dread is projected on to a phobic substance (sweat) in order to diminish anguish. Hersh contemplates all these ways of focusing her primal aggression and fear, and then declares: 'No, I hate my way.' It's as though, instead of projecting her fear and loathing on to a scape-goat or bogeyman, she's consumed by her own hatred. It turns back on her, or drifts over the landscape, fleetingly fastening on images that seem to echo her own wounded state.

Hersh identifies with victims or abject things – slugs, TV, a boy entwined with his crashed bike, a girl with a mutilated hand – her voice taking on tones of passivity or pain as appropriate. But she also identifies with aggressors and violators. She can see herself in mass murderer Oliver Huberty *and* in child-murder victims; Huberty carried a gun, Hersh has a gun in her head. Her negativity could go either way, vent itself as aggression or self-annihilation. Throwing Muses' music, in its self-confounding, simmering rage, is the FEMALE GUN: anger that isn't projected or exploded (like a projectile), but that backfires, eats away at itself like acid.

Many Throwing Muses' songs feature shaky narrators who don't just despise themselves but seem in danger of losing hold on identity altogether. In 'Vicky's Box', Hersh can only love 'pieces of things' she hates. On 'Snailhead' (from 1987's *Chains Changed* EP), she seems close to dis-solving in the maelstrom of sound and accelerating tempos. She is the 'Snailhead', her mind a torpid, intractable morass. Panicky and full of self-doubt, her voice speeds faster and faster in an attempt to hurtle beyond her wracked state and rise above words. Words can't cut through the slimy muck inside her 'Snailhead'.

Finally, in 'Devil's Roof' (from 1989's *Hunkpapa*), Hersh makes her schizophrenic imagery explicit, declaring right at the start: 'I have two heads'. One is bodily and one is ethereal, but she knows they are bound together. After years of writing songs about characters with a tenuous sense of self, Hersh herself admitted, in a 1991 interview with *Melody Maker*, that she suffers from bipolarity (a newfangled term for manic depression). On the album that was released around the time of Hersh's coming clean about her condition, *The Real Ramona*, the opening track, 'Counting Backwards', took its title from a technique used by Hersh's husband in which he counts her down into a hypnotic state and then converses with her personae (which she described in the interview as 'Good Kristin' and 'Bad Kristin'). In some ways, all this problematises her work, since it invites fans and critics to hem in the songs with literal interpretations; a song then becomes the document of a specific individual with a specific mental disorder, rather than a cracked mirror in which the listener can recognise a heightened version of their own inner conflicts. Then again, why should the fact that Hersh is the 'real thing' – after decades, centuries of artists feigning or aspiring to madness – diminish her art?

not be alright

'I seem to keep getting in the way of what's being said.'
Mary Margaret O'Hara, 1989

Mary Margaret O'Hara offers a slightly more blissful account of fraught flux. On her brilliant debut *Miss America* (1988), O'Hara connects the pre-punk legacy of troubled AOR (Joni Mitchell, John Martyn) with the vocal schizophrenia of post-punk singers like Kristin Hersh and Mimi Goese of Hugo Largo. Scatty/scattered/scat is the thread. The unsaid and unsayable come shuddering and twitching through the words in curves, hiccups, blurts and tics. She – the voice, the body-in-trouble – is noise, interference, a medium that will not subordinate itself to the message.

In songs like 'A Year in Song', 'Not Be Alright', 'Body's in Trouble', O'Hara is a decentred diva, a woman in three or more minds. In everyday life, she's profoundly suspicious of judgmental language and the categorical utterance. 'I wouldn't want to say I'm anything, and I wouldn't wanna say anyone else is anything. Don't know enough to say, to judge.' Her gift and impediment, blessing and curse, is an inability *not* to see all sides of everything. She has the delightful plight of possessing a dazzled intelligence, too enraptured by possibilities to take the plunge of deciding on anything. Nietzsche said that there has to be a 'will to stupidity' within any belief: that mental closure is essential if you want to act or make any imprint on the world. Mary Margaret O'Hara says: 'Soon as something gets said, I feel that you leave out so many thoughts, by saying, "*This is this*".'

O'Hara's titles and lyrics are a maze of intransitive verbs ('To Cry About', 'My Friends Have'), abstractions ('joy is the aim'), reversals, and indefinites, all conjuring the impression of irreconcilable feelings, jangling nerves, people out of synch with each other, with themselves. (Another 'kooky' Canadian singer-songwriter, Jane Siberry, has talked of how, as a child, she heard a stylus skipping on a scratched record: she was astonished because it was the first time she'd heard anything that sounded like the inside of her head.) O'Hara's voice catches in her throat, then sweeps upwards in an effortless swooning arc. But despite her hostility to plainspeaking, O'Hara only flirts with babble. She believes firmly in working with language: 'When I was younger I did a lot of stuff that was gibberish, just vocal noise. Feelings can come across in abstract stuff if you really work at it, and aren't just jumping around to get away. But I think I can do all that within words. Words can lead people in, and then you take it further.'

O'Hara's singing, although seldom non-verbal, sometimes induces a feeling in the listener akin to dyslexia, as you struggle to decipher the lyrics through the stuttering syntax and slurred delivery. In 'Year in Song', she stammers in a gush and rush of rapture, cries out that she isn't 'ready to go under', then dissolves into ecstatic onomatopoeia. Her voice bubbles, physically *overflows* the text.

Where 'Year in Song' is about the bliss of self-forgetting, 'Not Be Alright' is about the painful side of incoherence. The singer is struggling to keep hold of herself, not to fall apart. Half-sentences jut out at ungainly angles, like a spool of tape caught in the mechanism. O'Hara can't get in the groove. The music – jarring, jerky funk – sounds like disintegration just barely held in check.

'Not Be Alright' is the evocation of a breakdown, of a state of dis-grace. O'Hara stumbles into technical language as if striving to build herself a solid base on which to stand: 'to seek to ensure'. The song seems to be about the inability to relax, just experience things, shed self-consciousness and connect with the world: 'it just will not "just be"'. The ultimate expression of this terminal anxiety is insomnia, and by the end O'Hara is worrying that if she falls asleep, she'll never wake up. It's as though she's trying to fight off falling into the morass (of sleep, of despair) with language, but her words fracture under the stress. The lyrics aren't utterances so much as nervous tics, vocal/mental spasms that are purely neurotic, in so far as neurosis is an attempt to assuage anxiety and fend off the Void by ritual actions. O'Hara gestured at the nature of this terrifying threat to identity when she described waking up in the middle of the night and 'there's no sense of *anything*, just that you're this blob, and you're gonna go further into this feeling if you don't come out of it right this minute.'

O'Hara's most graceful and pleasing songs are those couched in conventional genres like the jazz-tinged torch song ('Keeping You In Mind') or the country ballad ('Dear Darling'). These idioms are associated with women (their most famous exponents being Billie Holiday and Patsy Cline, respectively), and are traditional formats for women to vent their angst. It's only when singing in these styles that O'Hara is able to *finish her sentences*: it's as though the structure and symmetry of the torch song and country ballad allow O'Hara to hold herself together, to stave off the breakdown of 'Not Be Alright' and adhere to syntax.

But her most radical and rewarding songs lie somewhere between the classical perfection of 'Keeping You in Mind' and the lurching arhythmia of 'Not Be Alright'; songs like 'Body's in Trouble', 'A Year in Song' and 'To Cry About', where traditional structures are in the process of succumbing to the flux, but haven't wholly disintegrated.

little voices

'It seems to me that there's an eye that's absorbing my life, assimilating the information and sending it back in symbols, characters and information. . . . I like to think [the music] comes from another place.'
Rickie Lee Jones, 1990

'I don't take any credit for the music. . . . I don't feel like I had much to do with it at all except to do the wracking work of experiencing the emotion that made me get there. That was horrible stuff. But I don't feel responsible for the beauty that came out of it. . . . I do feel something's working through me.'
Kristin Hersh, 1986

As these quotes suggest, many of the all-fluxed-up artists have trouble taking credit for what they've created, or seeing themselves as in control of their art. They tend to perceive their creativity not as within but as coming from outside – another realm that they have access to, or a force that speaks through them. Is this passive self-image a matter of conditioning? This notion of 'woman as vessel' seems to echo centuries of misogynist thinking which regards women as receptacles for carrying babies – from Aeschylus' 485 BC play, *The Oresteia* (where the mother is judged not to be a parent, but 'just a nurse to the seed'), to the American Pro-Life movement, which would give a foetus more rights than its mother.

There is a more positive interpretation of this creative

self-effacement, one that connects with the post-structuralist idea of 'the death of the author'. Abandoning the notion of the artist as a godlike figure who is wholly original and self-sufficient, these post-structuralist critics argue that we don't speak language, but rather that *language speaks us*; that poetry occurs at the point of friction between the impersonal system of language and the individual's unconscious desires. What's called 'genius' is just an ability to go with the flow, a willingness to be flooded with visions. So Kristin Hersh will say, modestly, 'I feel I'm not exceptional in that maybe other people just have a hard time listening to their voices.'

Perhaps this metaphor of hearing voices relates to the traditional rock cliché of 'getting my demons out', art as exorcism. In a 1985 *Melody Maker* interview, Kate Bush declared: 'There are always so many voices telling me what to do. . . . I don't want to disappoint the little voices that have been so good to me.' Of course, male artists have traditionally been happy to have it both ways; by invoking the muse, they can accept the freeing notion of outside inspiration while also accepting the credit for artistic genius. Women rarely mention their spouses or lovers as muses, but stick to spectral, otherworldly imagery which they seem unable to pin down or govern. So Mary Margaret O'Hara will say: 'The best times are when you feel it's not you that did it, it just came to you out of nowhere, a gift.' And Jane Siberry talks of tuning in to the collective consciousness: 'I look at what I'm writing and I'm feeling more and more like an antenna. And this takes the pressure off me, I don't feel so stressed about what I'm writing.'

Sheila Chandra, a singer who explores the modal, drone-based links between ethnic music and folk-rock, has written of experiencing an epiphanic possession she calls 'the zen kiss': 'It's as if an outside influence has entered me, sound is channelled through my body.' Writing songs, she sometimes enters 'a dream state. . . . like tapping into a collective unconscious, or even into the personality of a song that actually exists before I write it'. Her music is atavistic and mystic (she called one album *Weaving My Ancestors' Voices*) but also post-modern. In the series of tracks entitled 'Speaking In Tongues', she leaps between Dadaist-style onomatopoeia and snippets from advertising jingles; Chandra sees her percussive vocal music as 'post-sampling compositions', but what's interesting is that both the 'collective unconscious' and the 'human sampler' metaphors serve to erase her own creative role, make her merely a conduit for outside forces.

For Jones, Siberry, Chandra and the rest, these 'voices' or external forces seem to be a useful way to conceptualise the creative process, which otherwise might seem overwhelming. It allows them partially to disown their own dark emotions (unlike psycho-babbling TV talk shows and women's magazines, with their exhortations to 'own your pain'). But there's a slightly disturbing division between interior life and public self, an inability to connect the inner turmoil with everyday, practical existence. Then again, maybe it's this sense of chaos that makes them such arresting artists. More problematic is the fact that a lot of these metaphors fit all too well with certain stereotypes of women (as irrational, uncontrolled, more prey to madness than men). Hearing voices is close to schizophrenia – too close for comfort?

One theorist who has explicitly linked female creativity with the irrational is Hélène Cixous. Her notion of *écriture féminine* is founded on the belief that women (and a handful of male geniuses) can access the unconscious. For Cixous, women's revolutionary contribution, as writers, is to irrigate the arid schematics of male language with the flux of the unconscious, which is like a water table beneath the desiccated, desert surface of male discourse. Cixous envisions female writing as the unleashing of an unruly inner plurality of desires and disgusts. Of course to babble is to run the risk of being marginalised, written out of history altogether. And in rock, it's true: the great female babblers of rock history – Yoko Ono, Patti Smith, Kristin Hersh – have not quite made it into the canon of rebellion. Cixous claims that the Voice of female writing comes from 'a time before law, before the Symbolic took one's breath away and reappropriated it into language'. Poetry liberates breath from the strictures of language. Patti Smith's Babelogue or Liz Fraser's gibberish are grown-up reversions to baby-talk: the pure expression of demand or distress, without words.

dyslexic divas

Wordless singing has always been the last resort of a desire or despair that can't be communicated through language. Usually, such non-verbal singing has surfaced as outbursts or breakdowns in a song, points at which inexpressible longing suddenly asserts itself at the libretto's expense: Van Morrison's scat-soul 'inarticulate speech of the heart', Iggy's bestial howl at the climax of the Stooges' 'TV Eye'. But a number of female singers have made 'speaking in tongues' the substance of their art – most notably art-pop sirens Liz Fraser (Cocteau Twins) and Lisa Gerrard (Dead Can Dance), and avant-garde divas Yoko Ono and Diamanda Galas.

Like Mary Margaret O'Hara, Liz Fraser and Lisa Gerrard are reluctant to stand on a soapbox: their rebellion against diction goes hand in hand with a refusal to dictate. Notoriously frustrating as interviewees, they will not have their utterances broken down, set into a context, analysed (though of course some critics get around their non-cooperation). Fraser and Gerrard don't conceptualise this reluctance in feminist terms (e.g. subversion of the 'oppressors' language'); they have a seemingly instinctive, gut aversion to the WORD.

In fact, Lisa Gerrard says that she was dyslexic as a

child, and has always been troubled by words. 'I always had an instinct that there's something I want to express through syllables which fit what the music suggests. I don't need an identity within the music as a spokesman. I don't have anything to say intelligently about this world at all, I'm in a very confused state, and I want to embrace life as opposed to resolve it.' In songs like 'Mesmerism' and 'Flowers of the Sea', Gerrard searches for what Baudelaire, in *Spleen and Ideal*, called 'the speech of flowers and other voiceless things', unleashing a wavering, consonant-free warble that recalls Middle Eastern muezzin wails or the Bulgarian women folk singers on albums like *Le Mystère des Voix Bulgares*.

Other female vocalists – Bjork (solo and with the Sugarcubes), Sinead O'Connor, Rickie Lee Jones – resort to wordless singing periodically, giving their music an intense fluidity. The Sugarcubes' 'Birthday' (*Life's Too Good*, 1987) is a marvellous, unfathomable tale about a child-woman and her fantasy world, with Bjork intoning her secrets in a furtive, elf-sprite whisper amidst stealthy jazz-punk weirdness. At the chorus, Bjork unleashes a monstrous starburst gush of ecstasy/agony, a mix of orgasm, birth-pang, hiccup and mystic wonder that seems to explode in the listener's head. Bjork sings the insatiability of the child who hasn't learned to curb its voracious desire, to settle for less: her voice devours everything around her, it's as big as the sky. Her glossolalia is not a collapse in meaning so much as an excess of meaning, a blast of profundity too intense to be contained in the fabric of language.

Kate Bush's 'The Sensual World' (title track of her 1989 album) traces this strain of 'feminine speech' back to the place where it was most notoriously colonised by a man: Molly Bloom's meandering soliloquy at the close of James Joyce's *Ulysses*. Bush originally intended to use lines straight from *Ulysses*, but couldn't get permission, and so recreated the spirit in her own words. Her voice dancing amidst a forest of Celtic or Arabic textures (uillean pipes, fiddle, bouzouki), Bush takes Molly Bloom's non-verbal, 'Mmmmm' for her chorus, revelling in the sensuousness of sound without syntax, affirming her sense of connection with Nature. *The Sensual World* LP is Bush's most explicitly female-identified statement: it features songs like 'This Woman's Work' and 'Rocket's Tail' (in the latter, she employed the all-female vocal group Trio Bulgarka, whose Bulgarian folk singing makes the experiences of everyday domestic life sound transcendental). In sharp contrast to her earlier yearning to follow in the footsteps of male role models, Bush here declares once and for all her investment in the feminine. In a 1989 *Melody Maker* interview, she said 'The Sensual World' was 'very much a chance for me to express myself as a female in a female way and I found that original piece [Molly Bloom's speech] very female talking. . . '

the scream

Other women have taken non-verbal singing even further, reaching extremes that parallel Arthur Janov's Primal Scream Therapy. The two premier exponents of this approach are Yoko Ono and Diamanda Galas. Equipped with formidable technique (both are from avant-classical backgrounds), Ono and Galas turned an Edvard Munch-like scream into an 'opera of the deluge' (Céline).

Galas uses her operatic training to uncage an infernal menagerie of voices. On *The Litanies of Satan* (1982), her libretto is a Charles Baudelaire poem. Galas vocalises abjection – the realm of 'maternal horror' that the Romantic poets like Baudelaire, Rimbaud and Lautréamont explored – as a hideously voluptuous babble. On the album's second side, the 'solo scream' composition 'Wild Women With Steak Knives' finds Galas as the embodiment of patriarchy's nightmare, the marauding, avenging *vagina-dentata*. In *Angry Women*, she says: 'I considered "Wild Women with

Steak Knives" the homicidal love song of a schizophrenic woman – that was the first work I did with 5 microphones, working with different personalities and using varied vocabularies and languages. . . speaking in tongues. . . and the training of the vocal chords to yield an ubervoice, a superhuman instrument that's not about being a singer but about being a channel through which the Absolute can manifest. . . .'

On her three-album 'plague mass' project, *Masque of the Red Death*, Galas speaks for the abject themselves, those segregated from society as unclean, the victims of AIDS, and in particular her brother, who died in 1986. Inflicting dreadful violence on passages from the Old Testament, gospel songs, and French symbolist poetry, Galas plays the role of both oppressor and oppressed. Her gamut of split-personae – cackling crones, afflicted lepers, cajoling child-women, hectoring hierarchs, professional mourners – requires a dizzying array of vocal techniques (gospel, opera, Dadaist sound-poetry) and a battery of distorting studio effects. Animating abjection, giving it voice, Galas incarnates the maelstrom – the abyss into which male artists from Edgar Allan Poe to Iggy Pop made 'heroic' descents.

But Galas's virulent virtuosity and 'intravenal song' were actually anticipated a decade earlier in the work of Yoko Ono. On her early solo albums *Yoko Ono/Plastic Ono Band* (1970) and *Fly* (1971), Ono uses her voice as a freeform jazz instrument, emitting a torrent of throttled phonemes and ectoplasmic ululations. On 'Mindholes' and 'O Wind (Body Is the Scar of Your Mind)', Ono's banshee shrieks and gibbering prayer-wails float through a soundscape of Indian tabla percussion and unhinged guitar scrapings, filtered through echo and reverb that predates dub reggae; the resultant weirdness rivals contemporaneous avant-rockers like Can, Faust and Tim Buckley. 'Why' pre-empts John Lydon's punk-muezzin vocals on Public image's 'Death Disco' by nearly a decade; Ono retches up gusts of grief-stricken incomprehension over a rockabilly-meets-funk rhythm, spraying out her pain like a machine gun, while freeform trumpeter Ornette Coleman squawks in the background. 'Why Not' is even more extreme: Ono's voice bubbles in her throat somewhere between death-rattle and baby-talk. The whole song consists entirely of the chokings and contorted vowels that Mary Margaret O'Hara might interject after a beautifully sung line. Like Patti Smith on 'Radio Ethiopia', Ono sounds like a Native American shaman tripping on DMT, or a voodoo dancer at the height of possession.

The music Ono extracts from her male players is astonishing. (John Lennon believed he never played wilder guitar than on these records, and he was right.) Tracks like 'Touch Me' are based on the same 'feminine' principles as the music of Can and early '70s Miles Davis: trance-inducing rhythm-loops combined with infinite refractions of modal improvisation, clusters of sound-debris, random fractures. 'Mind Train' typically combines discontinuity and groove, as Ono freaks out over a regular-as-clockwork locomotive rhythm. 'The Path' is a dub-wise soundscape full of heavy breathing that could be mounting fear or ascending orgasm. In the sleevenotes for *London Jam* (the first disc of her retrospective set *Onobox*) she talks about creating 'a "New Music", a fusion of avant-garde-jazz-rock and East and West'. Like Davis, Can, Buckley and others, she seems to have been striving for a One World Music; her glossolalia was an attempt to cut through language and return to the pre-Babel universal tongue.

Elsewhere in the *Onobox* booklet, she writes: 'What I was trying to attain was a sound that almost doesn't come out. Before I speak, I stutter in my mind, and then my cultured self tries to correct that stutter into a clean sentence. . . and I wanted to deal with those sounds of people's fears and stuttering. . . and of darkness, like a child's fear that someone is behind him but he can't speak or communicate this.' Actually, she's describing a performance she organised in a 1961 concert at Carnegie Recital Hall, back in her pre-Lennon days as a Fluxus artist and musician in her own right (she jammed with minimal-is-maximalists and drone theorists like John Cage, David Tudor and La Monte Young). Nonetheless, the quote fits perfectly with her vocal terrorism on the *London Jam* tracks. After this merciless avant-gardism, Ono decided on a more listener-friendly approach. Instead of recording improvisatory jam sessions that were totally spontaneous and unrehearsed, she wrote songs with messages and recorded them with session musicians. The results were overtly political, didactic songs couched in slick, glossy music whose lack of edge undermined Ono's militancy. From outspoken statements of feminist pride ('Warrior Woman', 'Angry Young Woman'), to heavy-handed satire ('Men, Men, Men', which reverses sexism and belittles men as stud puppets whose lips are for kissing, not expressing stupid opinions), Ono assumed the persona of a female sage, alternately patient and peeved about male power tantrums. Where before her voice sounded *mad* (both enraged and insane), now she presented herself as a representative of sanity and of a sensible female wisdom denied by patriarchy.

Only 'Woman Power', a 1973 song that anticipates '80s rap and industrial music with its dry, angular beat and fearsome rock riffs, has music to match its militancy. Over funk-metal machine music like some mutant mix of Kraftwerk and Led Zeppelin, Ono declares herself President. But even this megalomanic tirade can't compare with the dementia of the 1970-71 music, where Ono was a one woman chorus of Furies.

The poignant choice Ono felt she had to make – between being a dignified, assertive spokeswoman who deals with issues in clear language, or a bawling, babbling hysteric breaking the barriers of sound with her pre-verbal anguish and anger – is one many female artists face. In the event, what Ono lost in artistic intensity, she never gained in political influence: nobody was listening. But this dilemma

– whether to speak suffering or to speak *about* suffering, to *voice* or to *verbalise* – remains a profound one for female artists. Is it better to sacrifice aesthetic power for the sake of political explicitness, or to opt for purity of artistic expression, at the expense of being understood?

The first two sections of this book documented the warring sides of rock's soul: the punk v. the hippie, the warrior v. the soft male. These antagonistic impulses define rock'n'roll as we know it. They can be traced back to a fundamental conflict in the male psyche – between the impulse to break the umbilical cord and a desire to return to the womb, between matricide and incest. Rock has never resolved this punk/hippie, rebellion/grace dialectic; its history has been a violent oscillation between either extreme.

In some sense, though, rock 'knows' that the Dionysian rebel tradition in rock is played out, that pure masculinity has little left to say. Which is why, just when it seemed safe simply to *be* in a band, male or female, gender flared up again as an issue. Having exhausted the psychosexual dynamic of male rebellion, rock culture is confronting the possibility that the only new frontier is the specifically female experience that has hitherto been left out of the script. In the punk v. hippie dialectic, Woman alternately represents what's being run from and what's being run to; she's always object, never subject.

For decades, rock'n'roll was based on the 'White Negro' syndrome, an emulation of black machismo, flamboyance, passion and self-aggrandisement. From '60s blues to punks identifying with Rastafarian reggae to suburban mall-brats mimicking the psychopathic cool of gangsta rap, white kids have long identified with black male rebellion. But in recent years, alternative rock has begun to replace racial envy with gender tourism. This sensibility-shift has been signposted by the epoch-defining boy-rock bands of the day,

Nirvana (who wore dresses in the video for 'In Bloom') and Suede (whose Brett Anderson has talked of taking on feminine passivity and embracing an unmanly 'relinquishing' of control). Furthermore, both these bands have aligned themselves with a trend that writer Ann Powers dubbed 'Queer Straight': Kurt Cobain described himself as 'gay in spirit' after the band climaxed a TV appearance with same-sex kissing, while Brett Anderson declared himself 'a bisexual man who's never had a homosexual experience'. (Another can-of-worms that deserves its own book...)

Such gestures of allegiance to femininity (and repudiation of trad masculinity) are the climax to a snowballing process that began in the late '80s. On the one hand, a mounting interest in new female artists; on the other, an investment in 'the feminine' as a new terrain of consciousness. Self-consciously female bands and those that longed for a piece of the gyno-action made 'women-in-rock' a sort of perpetual novelty.

Will it last, this strange venture into alternative subjectivities? Or will it become normalised at some point? The previous big wave of 'women in rock' (the post-punk demystification bands of the late '70s and early '80s) petered out, and a new Dark Ages for gender began. Neither New Pop nor the American guitar-traditionalism that followed as a counter-reaction did much to challenge conventional gender roles or representations.

In the late '80s, a new breed of striking female performers emerged, either in mixed gender bands (Sonic Youth, Throwing Muses, the Sugarcubes, My Bloody Valentine, Pixies/Breeders, etc.) or as solo artists (e.g. the 'kooky' singer-songwriter school that includes Mary Margaret O'Hara and Jane Siberry). After five years in which women's involvement in bands had gradually become run-of-the-mill (not just as singers, but as bassists, drummers and guitarists) it was something of a surprise when the presence of women in rock became an issue again in 1992, with the rise of self-consciously female bands (Hole, L7 et al.) and the Riot Grrrl movement.

Why is it still such an issue? Partly because rock discourse needs big issues to sustain itself. The women-in-rock question provided a sorely needed injection of animation and animosity at just the point at which rock culture seemed to be flagging. It's also partly a reaction against the masculinism of grunge. And finally, it's a grass-roots gust of impatience with the perennial marginalisation of women, as if to say, 'sure, things are improving – but not fast enough'.

If there's a problem with the new surge of female activity in rock, it's that innovations have remained mostly at the level of content (lyrics, self-presentation, ideology and rhetoric expressed in interviews), rather than formal advances. Where are the great female sonic wizards? Even the most striking and powerful of the new female artists are musical traditionalists, bringing new kinds of subject matter and subjectivity to masculine formats. Women have seized rock'n'roll and usurped it for their own expressive purposes, but we've yet to see a radical feminisation of rock form in itself.

Female artists have, self-consciously or instinctively, attempted such a project at various points in the past: Yoko Ono, Patti Smith, the Raincoats, Throwing Muses. But as impressive as their achievements have been, they're strangely isolated – landmarks on the rock landscape that no one visits, least of all women. Unlike the male trailblazers who stretched the rock form – Hendrix, Can, Eno – these female innovators have had few, if any, progeny: their legacy is pregnant with possibility, but neglected. It's ironic, for instance, that PJ Harvey only listened to Patti Smith after she'd heard innumerable comparisons between herself and Smith. While the *idea* of Patti Smith, the fact that she existed, has been inspirational to many, virtually no one has followed up her most radically form-dissolving work.

In this cultural moment of extreme gender-consciousness, it seems that female artists are more interested in communicating and telling stories than in taking on that rather masculine scientific obsession with breaking the barriers of sound. Which is fair enough. But after this invigorating and necessary period of hyper-awareness, female artists will almost surely back away from such self-consciousness and allow gender to become a sort of sub-text, one that informs everything, but subtly. For such artists, gender would be less a prison (whose bars have to be rattled loudly), and more like, say, living over the San Andreas fault: a persistent source of friction that – every so often, when the jagged edges of the tectonic plates snag – sends violent tremors through the strata of rock. Always there at the back of the mind, always threatening to shake things up when they get too settled.

notes
bibliography
index

notes

40 'England is obscene': Julian Temple interviewed in *NME*, October 27, 1979.

40 Vivienne Westwood in *Melody Maker*, June 30, 1979.

41 Fred Vermorel quoted in *NME*, date unknown.

CHAPTER 4: BORN TO RUN

43 Robert Bly interview appears in Keith Thompson, 173-9.

44 Densmore, 306.

44 Jim Morrison quoted in Densmore, 310.

47 Kurt Cobain quote from Geffen press release for *Nevermind*, 1991.

48-9 Julian Barnes on Prince Charles, *The New Yorker*, July 20, 1992

49 'I believe all those things': Morrissey quoted in *Melody Maker* booklet 'The Smiths', 1990.

49 'state of dissatisfaction': interview with Reynolds, reprinted in *Blissed Out*, 22.

50 Saville, 70.

50 Hodson, 187.

50 Dylan on Donald White quoted in Turner, 65.

52-3 Frith, 'Beggar's Banquet' in Marcus, ed., *Stranded*, 34.

54 Iggy Pop interview in *NME*, March 24, 1979.

57 Willis, 57.

57 Carroll and Noble, 422.

60 'an excessive susceptibility': Harold Bloom on Byron, quoted in Paglia, 354.

60 'Driving is the American Sublime': Paglia, 358.

61 Bangs, 154.

63 Morgan, 51.

63 'perpetually repeated hijacking': Virilio, 101.

CHAPTER: 5: BROTHERS IN ARMS

67 John Clellon Holmes quoted in Joyce Johnson, 83.

68 Joe Strummer in booklet for *The Clash on Broadway* CD box set (Columbia Records, 1991).

73 Paul Simenon quoted in *Clash on Broadway* booklet.

74 Gaines, 168.

75-6 Sergei Nechaev in Morgan, 73.

76 Manic Street Preachers interview with Reynolds, printed in *Melody Maker*, July 20, 1991.

76 These Animal Men interview in *Melody Maker*, July 9, 1994.

77 Campbell, 353.

84 Theweleit, *Male Fantasies* Volume 1, 284.

CHAPTER 6: FLIRTING WITH THE VOID

85 'evolutionary revulsion from slime': Paglia, 11-12.

86 Paglia on 'The Ancient Mariner', 325.

86 Collins and Pierce, 117.

89 Theweleit, *Male Fantasies* Volume 2, 42-3.

95 Theweleit, *Male Fantasies* Volume 1, 410.

98 'my own apathy and spinelessness': Cobain quoted in Geffen press release for *Nevermind*, 1991.

98-9 Henry Rollins interview in *Details*, January 1993.

100 'shame about being human': interview in *NME*, April 3, 1982.

100-1 'playing in your own pooh-pooh': interview in *Melody Maker*, February 25, 1978.

101 'pictures of Mark Mothersbaugh': interview in *NME*, December 9, 1978.

101 'like a horrible maggot': interview in *NME*, July 14, 1979.

CHAPTER 7: WARGASM

102 Wyndham Lewis quoted in Jameson, 97.

102 Boccioni in Appollonio, 15.

102-3 F.T. Marinetti in Appollonio, 22-4.

107 Lemmy Kilmister interview in *Lime Lizard*, August 1992.

108 Iggy Pop interview in *NME*, February 2, 1980.

108 Mailer, 345-7.

109 'black-out'/'bloody miasma'/'empty space': Theweleit, *Male Fantasies* Volume 2, 271-8.

109 'embrace of burning grenades': ibid, 184.

110 'compulsive soldiers': ibid, 398.

110 Ron Asheton interview in *Motorbooty* #5.

111 Nietzche, *Beyond Good and Evil*, 74.

111 Iggy Pop interview in *NME*, March 24, 1979.

112 '[it's about] keeping us tight':

Vivien Johnson, 114.

112 'million volt socket': ibid, 185.

114 Frith, 'Only Dancing' in McRobbie, ed., *Zoot Suits and Second-Hand Dresses*, 133.

114 Bowie interview in *Arena*, Spring/Summer issue,1993.

115 Stephen Davis, 102.

115 'Futurist Manifesto of Lust' in Appollonio, 71-2.

CHAPTER 8: I AM THE KING

118 Didion, 21.

118-9 'a pure expression of joy': Morrison in Densmore, 310.

119 Tosches from introduction to Dalton, *Mojo Rising*.

120 Bataille, 'The Practice of Joy Before Death,' 239.

121-2 Mary Gaitskill on Axl Rose in *Details*, July 1992.

123 Bataille on sovereignty, throughout *The Accursed Share*, Volumes 1-3.

124 Farren, 59.

125 'lived right now. . . acte gratuit': Stevens, 105.

127 Bly, 104.

128 'cultivated a self-exaltation': Norman Cohn, 151.

128 'total emancipation of the individual': ibid, 286.

132 Ossie Davis in Cleaver, 60.

132 'we shall have our manhood': ibid, 61.

133 'torrents of blood': ibid, 210.

133 'across the naked abyss': ibid, 206.

133 'Let. . . your love seize my soul': ibid, 207.

133 'sacred womb': ibid, 208.

133 'before we could come up': ibid, 206.

133-4 'It is a hollow, cruel mockery. . . Muhammed Ali': ibid, 92.

134 LL Cool J interview in *Details*, November 1992.

135 'I always loved boxing': Miles Davis, 174.

135 Tate, 86-7.

136 Murray: 148.

137 Marcus, *Mystery Train*, 76.

139 Sly Stone interview with *Rolling Stone*, November 1971.

139 Bobby Womack interview in *NME*, October 6, 1984.

139 Warshow quoted in 'The Price of

Fame' by Barney Hoskyns in *NME*, August 14, 1982.

CHAPTER 9: MY WAY

141-2 Mailer, 339.

142 Timothy Maliqualim Simone quoted in Stanley, xxvii.

142 Mailer, 345-6.

143 Paul Rothchild quoted in Dalton, *Mojo Rising*, 59.

143 'Eternity is God': Nuttall, 151.

143-4 John Clellon Holmes in Stevens, 106.

144 Vaneigem, 18-19.

144 Ulrike Meinhof quoted in Vague, 49.

144 'Romantics, Symbolists, Dada': Nuttall, 127.

145 'Manson represents': *Rolling Stone*, June 1970.

145 Siouxsie Sioux quoted in Savage, 241.

149-50 Dialogue from *Slacker* reprinted in Linklater, 85.

150 Nymphs interview with Reynolds, printed in *Melody Maker*, February 15, 1992.

151 'extols child torture...John Wayne Gacy': Parfrey, 117.

151-2 'the most refreshing art' and 'Aesthetic Terrorists': ibid, 123.

152 'I don't find everyone who kills': ibid, 125.

152 'he fucked and tortured... insightful individual to make music': ibid, 125-7.

152 Suleiman, *Subversive Intent*, 68.

PART TWO

CHAPTER 1: FROM REBELLION TO GRACE

158 F.T. Marinetti, 'Geometric and Mechanical Splendour and the Numerical Sensibility' in Appollonio, 154.

CHAPTER 2: BACK TO EDEN

163 Incredible String Band interview in *Melody Maker*, September 30, 1967.

164 Paglia, 187-8.

168 'unalterable homelessness': M. Mark in Marcus, ed. *Stranded*, 15.

169 'an ancient land': ibid, 12.

170 Nick Kent on Syd Barrett in *NME*, April 13, 1974.

172 Nick Mason quoted in Schaffner,

146.

174   Alex Paterson from *Melody Maker*, March 10, 1990.

174   Fraser Clark quoted in Rucker et al., 142-3.

175   Paul Oldfield, *Melody Maker*, March 10, 1990.

175-6   John Moore, 29-31.

CHAPTER 3: STARSAILING

182   Christian Wolff in Cage, 54.

183   Cage, 163.

183   Sri Chimnoy in Berendt, 209-10.

184   Shapiro and Glebbeek, 148-9.

186   Lee Underwood and Tim Buckley in *Downbeat*, June 16, 1977.

186   'return to the mother's womb': Ferenczi, 18.

186   'partial substitute for the sea': ibid, 54.

187   Wilhelm Reich quoted in Theweleit, *Male Fantasies* Volume 1, 374.

188   'How can we verbalize': Kristeva, 'Motherhood According to Giovanni Bellini,' 239.

189   François de Sales in James, 18 [note].

CHAPTER 4: FLOW MOTION

191   '[Repetition] gives you power': Bussy et al., 17-18.

191   'the healing powers of music': interview with Reynolds, printed in *Melody Maker*, July 15, 1989.

192   'bass tone': Bussy et al., 16.

192   'acoustic landscape painter': ibid, 29.

192   'planetary rhythms. . . parallels of colour and tones': ibid, 35.

195   Karoli interview with Reynolds, printed in *Melody Maker*, July 15, 1989.

199   'comparable to a weed': Deleuze and Guattari, 12.

199   'the fabric of the rhizome': ibid, 25.

199   'continuous self-vibrating region': ibid, 22.

199   Czukay quoted in Bussy et al., 70.

200   'the child, the mad, noise': Deleuze and Guattari, 344.

201   'the becoming-child of the musician': ibid, 350.

201-2   'Critics can't stand these records': Eno in Tamm, 54-6.

202   'system of syllable rhythm': ibid, 81.

203   'increasing hysteria and exoticism': sleevenotes of *Thursday Afternoon*.

204   G. Roheim quoted in Brown, *Love's Body*, 57.

204   Mark Peel quoted in Tamm, 143.

204   'As soon as we become motionless': Bachelard, 184.

204   'The exterior spectacle': ibid, 192.

204   'neither in the desert': ibid, 206.

204-5   'look at the past': Eno quoted in Tamm, 86.

205   Roger Caillois in Cioran, *Anathemas and Admirations*, 209.

205   Stephen Demorest and Lester Bangs in Tamm, 106.

206   Brian Eno quoted in Tamm, 90.

CHAPTER 5: SOFT BOYS

211   Jimi Hendrix quotes from *Spin*, April 1991.

214   Kristeva, *Black Sun*, 12.

215   Morrissey interview in *Q*, September 1992.

215   'If, as a small child. . . my need's greater!': Morrissey interview in *Spin*, November 1992.

216-7   Hopey Glass on Elvis in *The Wire*, September 1992.

218   Ackerman, 289.

218   Daphne and Charles Maurer quoted in Ackerman, 289.

219   Eno quotes from *Details*, July 1992.

222   Deleuze and Guattari, 149-66.

224   Theweleit, *Male Fantasies* Volume 1, 389.

224   Brown, *Love's Body*, 45.

225   'the holy green silence': from F.T. Marinetti's 'Destruction of Syntax', in Appollonio, 95.

226   Maready on Kevin Ayers in *Chemical Imbalance*, Vol 2 #3.

226   'I've always been one': Robert Wyatt interview in *Melody Maker*, March 15, 1980.

226   'my ideal state of life': Wyatt interview in *Melody Maker*, June 14, 1975.

227   Brett Anderson interviewed by Reynolds, printed in *Melody Maker*, June 19, 1993.

PART THREE

CHAPTER 1: DOUBLE ALLEGIANCES

230   Joyce Johnson, 142.

231 Cassady, 77.
231-2 Quotes on Sally Mann and from Jimi Hendrix, Frank Zappa and anonymous groupie from *Rolling Stone*, February 15, 1969.
234-5 'the exposed female body': Suleiman, *Subversive Intent*, 26.
235 '[allegiance] to the formal experiments': ibid, 163.

CHAPTER 2: ONE OF THE BOYS
236 'Blind love for my father': Patti Smith interviewed in *Honey*, February 1977.
236 'ever since I felt the need': ibid.
236-7 Smith in *Details*, July 1993.
237 Graves, 446.
237 'I was really trying to be a woman': Smith interview in *NME*, April 12, 1975.
237 'I'm a genuine starfucker!': Smith interview in *NME*, January 22, 1977.
238 'I think the rebel in me': Hynde interview in *Rolling Stone*, November 26, 1981.
238 Chris Salewicz interview with Hynde in *NME*, October 18, 1980.
238 Nick Kent in *NME*, March 17, 1979.
238 'loudmouthed American': Hynde interview in *Rolling Stone*, May 29, 1980.
240-1 Kate Bush interview in *Melody Maker*, June 3, 1978.
241 Garber, 168.
242-3 PJ Harvey interviewed by Press, printed in *Spin*, August 1993.
244 Graham, 119.
245 Ann Wilson quoted in Garr, 210.
246 Kim Gordon in the *Village Voice Rock & Roll Quarterly*, Fall 1988.
247 Foege, 252.

CHAPTER 3: OPEN YOUR HEART
250 Stud Brothers interview with Sinead O'Connor in *Melody Maker*, December 12, 1987.
251-2 O'Connor's 'pact with God' in *Melody Maker* news, October 31, 1992.
253 Charles Gullans's review reprinted in McClatchy, 131.
253 Paz, 244.
254 'penitents of the spirit': Joni Mitchell interviewed in

Flanagan, 222.
254 'To survive in the world': ibid, 242.
254 'let me be on a pedestal': ibid, 235.
254-5 'Dylan sang. . . another person weak': ibid, 243-4.
257 Lydia Lunch interview in *Melody Maker*, April 9, 1988.
259 Lunch interviewed in *Angry Women*, Juno and Vale, 107.
259 Lunch interview in *Sounds*, June 7, 1986.
262 'something's wrong': Courtney Love interview with Press, 1993, unpublished.
264 Kat Bjelland quotes from interview in *Melody Maker*, September 19, 1992.
265 Rich, 46.
265 Yoko Ono quoted in Hopkins, 18.
265-6 Marianne Faithfull quoted in Hotchner, 232.
266 Bjelland interview with Reynolds, printed in *New York Times*, February 9, 1992.
268 Tori Amos interview in *Melody Maker*, November 16, 1991.
270-1 Curve feature in *Melody Maker*, March 16, 1991.
271 Sales statistics for Janis, Jimi and Jim from *The Independent on Sunday*, March 20, 1994.
274 'female masochism': Friedman, xxviii.
274-5 'It became some phenomenal energy thing': ibid, 30.
275 'she'd walk the streets': ibid, 39.
275 Willis, 67.
275 'wanted to smoke dope': Friedman, 48.
275 'spewing, splattering': ibid, 63.

CHAPTER 4: WOMAN UNBOUND
276 Clément in Cixous and Clément, *Newly Born Woman*, 10.
277 Freud's letter to his friend Fleiss, ibid, 12.
278 'freedom from *permission*': Diamanda Galas in Juno and Vale, 8.
278 'every witch has cats': ibid, 13.
278 'a pointed, focused message': ibid, 8.
278-9 Ned Lukatcher in introduction to David-Menard.
279 Lydia Lunch in Juno and Vale, 107.

279   Clément in Cixous and Clément, 5.

279   'evidence of superior imagination': McClary, 101.

279   'conventional framing devices': ibid, 111.

281   Leonora Carrington interview in *The Observer Magazine*, date unknown.

281   Paul Rambali in Patti Smith feature, *NME*, September 16, 1978.

281   Stevie Nicks interview in *NME*, January 19, 1980.

283   'a vehicle for transmission': Galas in Juno and Vale, 10-11.

283   'When a witch. . . I am the Antichrist': ibid, 19.

284   Cixous quotes all from *Newly Born Woman*, 87-8.

284-5   Ackerman, 20.

CHAPTER 5: WHO'S THAT GIRL?

290   'multiple, shifting, self-contradictory': de Lauretis, 9.

290   'mask and masquerade': ibid, 17.

290   Garber, 355.

291   Grossberg, 227-8.

292   Kruse, 455.

294   Ian Penman in *NME* Christmas Issue, 1981.

296   Garber, 151.

296   Frith and McRobbie's 'Rock and Sexuality' in Frith and Goodwin, 385.

297-8   McClary, 207 (note).

302   Siouxsie interview in *Blitz*, November 1985.

305   'Punk wasn't necessarily a sexual thing': Savage, 187.

305   'Take your clothes off, girl': ibid, 148.

CHAPTER 6: UN-TYPICAL GIRLS

310   Raincoats interview in *Melody Maker*, September 26, 1981.

312   Marcus, *In the Fascist Bathroom*, 191.

314   ibid, 190.

CHAPTER 7: WHAT A DRAG

317   Faludi, xix.

318   Irigaray, *The Sex Which Is Not One*, 76-8.

322   McClary, 149.

CHAPTER 8: THERE'S A RIOT GOING ON

325   Kathleen Hanna quoted in *Melody Maker*, October 10, 1992.

325   'Riot Grrrl Is...': *Fantastic Fanzine* #2.

325-6   'cool attributes have been claimed': *Riot Grrrl* #7.

326   'Clinical studies show': *Fantastic Fanzine* #2.

326-7   Kim Gordon and Kathleen Hanna quoted in *LA Weekly*, July 10-16, 1992.

CHAPTER 9: BODY'S IN TROUBLE

335   'my body moves': O'Hara interview in *Melody Maker*, November 26, 1988.

335   'I could *not* do it': O'Hara interview with Reynolds, printed in *Melody Maker*, March 11, 1989.

335   Russo, 213.

337   A.C. Marias interview with Reynolds, printed in *Melody Maker*, February 17, 1990.

338   'I have a complex': PJ Harvey interview with Press, printed in *Spin*, August 1993.

340   'That's why you get ill': ibid.

341   Harrison, 114.

341   Kristin Hersh quote from interview with Press, August 1986.

341   Kaplan, 381-2.

342   'when I was seventeen': Hersh interview in *Melody Maker*, March 19, 1988.

342   Kat Bjelland interview with Reynolds, printed in the *New York Times*, February 9, 1992.

342   Caskey, 184.

343   Hilde Bruch quoted in Caskey, ibid.

343-4   'Bloated. Pregnant.': Patti Smith interview in *Honey*, February 1977.

344   'always felt there was something good': Smith interview in *NME*, April 12, 1975.

345   Courtney Love 'Viewpoint' on letters page, *Melody Maker*, April 3, 1993.

346   Cixous in Marks and de Courtivron, 245.

346   Rich, 39.

CHAPTER 10: ADVENTURES CLOSE TO HOME

348   Ann Powers in the *Village Voice*, May 12, 1992.

349   'agoraphobia versus claustrophobia': Hersh interview with Reynolds, reprinted in *Blissed Out*, 33.

350   'the savage housewife': Hersh interview in *Melody Maker*, March 19, 1988.

350   Erik Satie quoted in Cage, 76.

353   'the eighties culture stifled': Faludi, 71.

353   'the more confident': ibid, 174.

CHAPTER 11: ALL FLUXED UP

356   Smith interview in *NME*, September 16, 1978.

357   Ventura, 152-6.

359   Smith interview in *Melody Maker*, May 22, 1976.

363   Little and Rumsey, 242.

366-7 Raincoats interview in *Melody Maker*, December 1, 1979.

368   'think of a collage': Hersh interview with Press, August 1986.

369   'We can be aggressive': Hersh interview in *Melody Maker*, January 28, 1989.

370   'She keeps four': Lessing, vii.

370   'I've reached the stage': ibid, 469.

370   'Sometimes I meet people': 473.

371-2 Hersh interview in *Melody Maker*, January 26, 1991.

373   'I wouldn't want to say': O'Hara interview with Reynolds, printed in *Melody Maker*, March 11, 1989.

373   'When I was younger': interview with *Melody Maker*, November 26, 1988.

374   'there's no sense of anything': O'Hara interview with Reynolds in *Melody Maker*, March 11, 1989.

376   Hersh interview with Press, August 1986.

376   Bush interview in *Melody Maker*, August 24, 1985.

376   O'Hara interview with Reynolds, *Melody Maker*, March 11, 1989.

376   Jane Siberry interview in *Lime Lizard*, September 1993.

376-7 Sheila Chandra quotes from liner notes to *The Zen Kiss* (Real World, 1994).

378   Cixous in Marks and de Courtivron, 93.

379   Lisa Gerrard interview with Press, printed in *Only Music*, Spring 1987.

380   Bush interview in *Melody Maker*, October 21, 1989.

380-1 Galas quoted in Juno and Vale, 8.

AFTERWORD

386   Brett Anderson in *Melody Maker*, December 12, 1992.

bibliography

ACKERMAN, DIANE. *A Natural History of the Senses*. New York: Random House, 1990.
APPOLLONIO, UMBRO, ed. *Futurist Manifestos*. London: Thames and Hudson, 1973.
BACHELARD, GASTON. *The Poetics of Space*, trans. Maria Jolas. Boston: Beacon Press, 1969.
BANGS, LESTER. *Psychotic Reactions and Carburetor Dung: The Work of a Legendary Critic*, ed. Greil Marcus. London: William Heinemann Ltd., 1988.
BATAILLE, GEORGES. *The Accursed Share* Volumes 1 – 3, ed. Robert Hurley. New York: Zone Books, 1991.
———— 'The Practice of Joy Before Death'. In Bataille, *Visions of Excess: Selected Writings 1927-1939*. Manchester: Manchester University Press, 1985.
BERENDT, JOACHIM-ERNST. *Nada Brahma: The World is Sound: Music and the Landscape of Consciousness*, trans. Helmut Bredigkeit. London: East West Publications, 1988.
BLACK, JOEL. *The Aesthetics of Murder: A Study in Romantic Literature and Contemporary Culture*. Baltimore: Johns Hopkins University Press, 1991.
BLY, ROBERT. *Iron John*. New York: Vintage Books, 1992.
BROWN, LYNN MIKEL AND CAROL GILLIGAN. *Meeting at the Crossroads: Women's Psychology and Girls' Development*. Cambridge, Mass: Harvard University Press, 1992.
BROWN, NORMAN O. *Life Against Death: The Psychoanalytical Meaning of History*. London: Sphere Books, 1968.
———— *Love's Body*. New York: Random House, 1966.
BURCHILL, JULIE, AND TONY PARSONS. *The Boy Looked at Johnny: The Obituary of Rock and Roll*. London: Pluto Press, 1978.
BURROUGHS, WILLIAM. *The Naked Lunch*. New York: Grove Press, 1959.
BUSSY, PASCAL, AND ANDY HALL. *The Can Book*. Harrow: SAF Publishing, 1989.
CAGE, JOHN. *Silence: Lectures and Writings*. Middletown: Wesleyan University Press, 1979.
CAMERON, DEBORAH, AND ELIZABETH FRAZER. *The Lust to Kill: A Feminist Investigation of Sexual Murder*. Cambridge: Polity Press, 1987.
CAMPBELL, JOSEPH. *Hero with A Thousand Faces*. London: Paladin, 1988.
CAMUS, ALBERT. 'The Rebel'. In *The Rebel: An Essay on Man in Revolt*. New York: Vintage Books, 1956.
CARROLL, PETER N., AND DAVID W. NOBLE. *The Free and the Unfree: A New History of the United States*. Harmondsworth: Penguin Books, 1977.
CASKEY, NOELLE. 'Interpreting Anorexia Nervosa'. In Suleiman, ed., *The Female Body in Western Culture*.
CASSADY, CAROLYN. *Off the Road: My Years with Cassady, Kerouac and Ginsberg*. New York: Morrow Books, 1990.
CHADWICK, WHITNEY. *Women Artists and the Surrealist Movement*. New York: Thames and Hudson, 1985.
CIORAN, E.M. *Anathemas and Admirations*, trans. Richard Howard. New York: Arcade Publishing, 1991.
———— *The Temptation to Exist*, trans. Richard Howard. London: Quartet Books, 1987.

CIXOUS, HÉLÈNE. 'The Laugh of the Medusa'. In Marks and de Courtivron, eds., *New French Feminisms*.

CIXOUS, HÉLÈNE, AND CATHÉRINE CLÉMENT. *The Newly Born Woman*, trans. Betsy Wing. Minneapolis: University of Minnesota Press, 1986.

CLEAVER, ELDRIDGE. *Soul on Ice*. New York: Dell Publishing, 1968.

COHN, NIK. *Ball the Wall: Nik Cohn in the Age of Rock*. London: Picador, 1989.

———— *Awopbopaloobop Alopbambboom: Pop from the Beginning*. London: Paladin, 1969.

———— *King Death*. New York: Harcourt Brace Jovanovich, 1975.

COHN, NORMAN. *The Pursuit of the Millennium*. London: Paladin, 1984.

COLLINS, MARGERY L., AND CHRISTINE PIERCE. 'Holes and Slime in Sartre'. In Carol Gould and Marx Wartofsky, eds, *Woman and Philosophy*. New York: G.P. Putnam's Sons, 1976.

DALTON, DAVID. *Mojo Rising: Jim Morrison, The Last Holy Fool*. New York: St. Martin's Press, 1991.

———— , DAVID FELTON AND ROBIN GREEN. *Mindfuckers: A Source Book on the Rise of Acid Fascism in America*. San Francisco: Straight Arrow Press, 1972.

DAVID-MENARD, MONIQUE. *Hysteria from Freud to Lacan: Body and Language in Psychoanalysis*. Ithaca, NY: Cornell University Press, 1989.

DAVIS, MILES (with QUINCY TROUPE). *Miles: The Autobiography*. New York: Simon and Schuster, 1989.

DAVIS, STEVEN. *Hammer of the Gods: The Led Zeppelin Saga*. New York: Ballantine Books, 1985.

DE LANDA, MANUEL. 'Non-Organic Life'. In *Zone: Incorporations*. New York: Zone Books, 1992.

DE LAURETIS, TERESA, ed. *Feminist Studies / Critical Studies*. Bloomington: Indiana University Press, 1986.

DELEUZE, GILLES, AND FELIX GUATTARI. *A Thousand Plateaus: Capitalism and Schizophrenia*, trans. Brian Massumi. Minneapolis: University of Minnesota Press, 1987.

DENSMORE, JOHN. *Riders on the Storm: My Life with Jim Morrison and the Doors*. New York: Delacorte Press, 1990.

DIDION, JOAN. *The White Album*. London: Weidenfeld & Nicolson, 1979.

EHRENREICH, BARBARA. *The Hearts of Men: American Dreams and the Flight from Commitment*. New York: Anchor Press, 1983.

FALUDI, SUSAN. *Backlash: The Undeclared War Against American Women*. New York: Crown Books, 1991.

FARREN, MICK. *The Black Leather Jacket*. New York: Abbeville Press, 1985.

FERENCZI, SANDOR. *Thalassa: A Theory of Genitality*. London: Karnac Books, 1989.

FLANAGAN, BILL. *Written in My Soul*. Chicago: Contemporary Books, 1986.

FOEGE, ALEC. *Confusion Is Next: The Sonic Youth Story*. New York: St. Martin's Press. 1994.

FRIEDMAN, MYRA. *Buried Alive: The Biography of Janis Joplin*. New York: Harmony Books, 1992.

FRITH, SIMON, AND ANDREW GOODWIN, eds. *On Record: Rock, Pop and the Written Word*. London: Routledge, 1990.

———— 'Only Dancing: David Bowie Flirts with the Issues'. In McRobbie, ed., *Zoot Suits and Second-Hand Dresses*.

———— , AND ANGELA McROBBIE. 'Rock and Sexuality.' In *On Record*.

———— 'Beggar's Banquet.' In Marcus, ed., *Stranded*.

GAAR, GILLIAN G. *She's A Rebel: The History of Women in Rock & Roll*. Seattle: Seal Press, 1992.

GAINES, DONNA. *Teenage Wasteland: Suburbia's Dead End Kids*. New York: Pantheon Books, 1990.

GARBER, MARJORIE. *Vested Interests: Cross Dressing and Cultural Anxiety*. London: Routledge, 1992.

GLEBBEEK, CAESAR, AND HARRY SHAPIRO. *Jimi Hendrix: Electric Gypsy*. New York: St. Martin's Press, 1990.

GLEICK, JAMES. *Chaos: Making A New Science*. London: Sphere Books, 1988.

GRAHAM, DAN. *Rock My Religion: Writing and Art Projects 1965 – 1990*, ed. Brian Wallis. Cambridge, Mass: MIT Press, 1993.

GRAVES, ROBERT. *The White Goddess*. London: Faber & Faber, 1961.

GRINSPOON, LESTER, AND PETER HEDBLOM. *The Speed Culture: Amphetamine Use and Abuse in America*. Cambridge, Mass: Harvard University Press, 1975.

GROSSBERG, LAWRENCE. *We Gotta Get Out of This Place: Popular Conservatism and Postmodern Culture*. London: Routledge, 1992.

HARRISON, KATHERINE. *Exposure*. London: Fourth Estate, 1993.

HARAWAY, DONNA. *Simians, Cyborgs, and Women: The Reinvention of Nature*. London: Routledge, 1991.

HODSON, PAUL. 'Bob Dylan's Stories About Men'. In Thomson and Gutman, eds, *The Dylan Companion*.

HOPKINS, JERRY. *Yoko Ono*. New York: Macmillan, 1986.

HOTCHNER, A.E. *The Rolling Stones and the Death of the Sixties*. New York: Simon and Schuster, 1990.

HUYSSEN, ANDREAS. 'Mass Culture as Woman: Modernism's Other'. In Tanya Modleski, ed., *Studies in Entertainment: Critical Approaches to Mass Culture*. Birmingham: Indiana University Press, 1986.

IRIGARAY, LUCE. *Marine Lover of Friedrich Nietzsche*. New York: Columbia University Press, 1991.

———— *The Sex Which Is Not One*. Ithaca, NY: Cornell University Press, 1985.

JAMES, WILLIAM. *The Varieties of Religious Experience*. Cambridge, Mass: Harvard University Press, 1985.

JAMESON, FREDERIC. *Fables of Aggression: Wyndham Lewis, The Modernist as Fascist*. Berkeley: University of California Press, 1979.

JARDINE, ALICE A. *Gynesis: Configurations of Woman and Modernity*. Ithaca, NY: Cornell University Press, 1985.

JOHNSON, JOYCE. *Minor Characters: A Young Woman's Coming of Age in the Beat Generation*. New York: Washington Square Press, 1983.

JOHNSON, VIVIEN. *Radio Birdman*. Rosanna, Australia: Sheldon Booth, 1990.

JONES, DYLAN. *Jim Morrison: Dark Star*. London: Bloomsbury Publishing, 1990.

JUNO, ANDREA, AND V. VALE, eds. *Angry Women*. San Francisco: Re-Search Publications, 1991.

KAPLAN, LOUISE J. *Female Perversions: The Temptations of Emma Bovary*. New York: Doubleday, 1991.

KEROUAC, JACK. *On the Road*. Harmondsworth: Penguin Books, 1972.

KESEY, KEN. *One Flew Over the Cuckoo's Nest*. London: Picador, 1973.

KING, FRANCIS. *The Magical World of Aleister Crowley*. London: Weidenfeld & Nicolson, 1977.

KRISTEVA, JULIA. 'Giotto's Joy.' In *Desire in Language: A Semiotic Approach to Literature and Art*, ed. Leon S. Roudiez. New York: Columbia University Press, 1980.

———— *The Kristeva Reader*, ed. Toril Moi. Oxford: Basil Blackwell, 1986.

———— 'Motherhood According to Bellini.' In *Desire in Language*.

———— *Powers of Horror: An Essay on Abjection*, trans. Leon S. Roudiez. New York: Columbia University Press, 1982.

———— *Tales of Love*, trans. Leon S. Roudiez. New York: Columbia University Press, 1987.

KRUSE, HOLLY. 'In Search of Kate Bush'. In Frith and Goodwin, eds. *On Record*.

LAING, DAVE. *One Chord Wonders*. Milton Keynes: Open University Press, 1985.

LECHTE, JOHN. *Julia Kristeva*. London: Routledge, 1990.

LEM, STANISLAW. *Solaris*. San Diego: Harcourt Brace Jovanovich, 1987.

LESSING, DORIS. *The Golden Notebook*. New York: Bantam Books, 1981.

LINKLATER, RICHARD. *Slacker*. New York: St. Martin's Press, 1992.

LITTLE, HILARY, AND GINA RUMSEY. 'Women and Pop: A Series of Lost Encounters'. In McRobbie, ed. *Zoot Suits and Second-Hand Dresses*.

LYDENBERG, ROBIN. *Word Cultures: Radical Theory and Practice in William Burroughs' Fiction*. Chicago: University of Illinois Press, 1987.

LYOTARD, JEAN-FRANÇOIS. *The Lyotard Reader*, ed. Andrew Benjamin. Oxford: Basil Blackwell, 1989.

MAILER, NORMAN. 'The White Negro'. In *Advertisements for Myself*. Cambridge, Mass: Harvard University Press, 1992.

MARCUS, GREIL. *In the Fascist Bathroom: Writings on Punk 1977-1992*. London: Viking/Penguin,1993.

——— *Mystery Train: Images of America in Rock'N'Roll Music*. London: Omnibus Press, 1977.

———, ed., *Stranded: Rock and Roll for a Desert Island*. New York: Alfred A. Knopf, 1979.

MARK, M. 'It's Too Late to Stop Now'. In Marcus, ed., *Stranded*.

MARKS, ELAINE, AND ISABELLE DE COURTIVRON, eds. *New French Feminisms*. New York: Schocken Books, 1981.

MCCLARY, SUSAN. *Feminine Endings: Music, Gender and Sexuality*. Minneapolis: University of Minnesota Press, 1991.

MCCLATCHY, J.D., ed. *Anne Sexton: The Artist and Her Critics*. Bloomington and London: Indiana University Press, 1978.

MCROBBIE, ANGELA ed. *Zoot Suits and Second-Hand Dresses: An Anthology of Fashion and Music*. Basingstoke: Macmillan Education Ltd., 1989.

———, AND SIMON FRITH. 'Rock and Sexuality'. In Frith and Goodwin, *On Record*.

MOORE, JOHN. *Anarchy & Ecstasy: Visions of Halcyon Days*. London: Aporia Press, 1988.

MOORE, SUZANNE. 'Getting A Bit of the Other: The Pimps of Postmodernism'. In *Looking for Trouble: On Shopping, Gender and the Cinema*. London: Serpent's Tail, 1991.

MORGAN, ROBIN. *The Demon Lover: The Sexuality of Terrorism*. London: Mandarin Books, 1990.

MURRAY, CHARLES SHAAR. *Crosstown Traffic: Jimi Hendrix and Post-War Pop*. London: Faber & Faber, 1989.

NIETZSCHE, FRIEDRICH. *The Birth of Tragedy and the Genealogy of Morals*, trans. Francis Golfing. New York: Anchor Press, 1956.

——— *Beyond Good and Evil: Prelude to a Philosophy of the Future*, trans. R.J. Hollingdale. Harmondsworth: Penguin, 1973.

NUTTALL, JEFF. *Bomb Culture*. London: Paladin, 1970.

ORLOFF, KATHERINE. *Rock'N'Roll Woman*. Los Angeles: Nash Publishing, 1974.

OSBORNE, JOHN. *Look Back in Anger*. London: Faber & Faber, 1957.

PAGLIA, CAMILLE. *Sexual Personae: Art and Decadence from Nefertiti to Emily Dickinson*. New Haven: Yale University Press, 1990.

PARFREY, ADAM, ed. *Apocalypse Culture. First Edition*. New York: Amok Press, 1987.

PAZ, OCTAVIO. *Essays on Mexican Art*. New York: Harcourt Brace & Co., 1993.

REYNOLDS, SIMON. *Blissed Out: The Raptures of Rock*. London: Serpent's Tail, 1990.

RICH, ADRIENNE. *Of Woman Born: Motherhood as Experience and Institution*. London: Virago, 1986.

ROCKWELL, JOHN. *All American Music: Composition in the Late 20th Century*. New York: Vintage Books, 1983.

ROSE, JACQUELINE. *The Haunting of Sylvia Plath*. London: Virago, 1992.

RUCKER, RUDY, R.U. SIRIUS, AND QUEEN MU, eds. *Mondo 2000: A User's Guide to the New Edge*. New York: HarperCollins, 1992.

RUSSELL, CHARLES. *Poets, Prophets and Revolutionaries*. Oxford: Oxford University Press, 1985.

RUSSO, MARY. 'Female Grotesques: Carnival and Theory'. In de Lauretis, Teresa, ed.,

Feminist Studies / Critical Studies.

SAVAGE, JON. *England's Dreaming: Sex Pistols and Punk Rock*. London: Faber & Faber, 1991.

SAVILLE, PHILIP. 'Bob Dylan in the Madhouse'. In Thomson and Gutman, eds, *The Dylan Companion.*

SCHAFFNER, MICHAEL. *Saucerful of Secrets: The Pink Floyd Odyssey*. New York: Harmony Books, 1991.

SEXTON, ANNE. *The Selected Poems*. London: Virago, 1988.

SHAPIRO, HARRY. *Waiting for the Man: The Story of Drugs and Popular Music*. New York: William Morrow & Co., 1988.

———, AND CAESAR GLEBBEEK. *Jimi Hendrix: Electric Gypsy*. New York: St. Martin's Press, 1990.

SINGER, JUNE. *Androgyny: Toward A New Theory of Sexuality*. New York: Anchor Press, 1976.

STANLEY, LAWRENCE A., ed. *Rap: The Lyrics*. London: Penguin Books, 1992.

STEVENS, JAY. *Storming Heaven: LSD and the American Dream*. London: Heinemann, 1988.

SUGARMAN, DANNY. *Appetite for Destruction: The Days of Guns and Roses*. New York: St. Martin's Press, 1991.

SULEIMAN, SUSAN RUBIN, ed. *The Female Body in Western Culture*. Cambridge, Mass: Harvard University Press, 1986.

——— *Subversive Intent: Gender, Politics, and the Avant-Garde*. Cambridge, Mass: Harvard University Press, 1990.

TAMM, ERIC. *Brian Eno: His Music and the Vertical Color of Sound*. Boston: Faber & Faber, 1989.

TART, CHARLES T. *Altered States of Consciousness*. New York: HarperCollins, 1990.

TATE, GREG. *Flyboy in the Buttermilk: Essays on Contemporary America*. New York: Simon and Schuster, 1992.

THEWELEIT, KLAUS. *Male Fantasies, Volume 1: Women, Floods, Bodies, History*, trans. Stephen Conway. Minneapolis: University of Minnesota Press, 1987.

——— *Male Fantasies, Volume 2: Male Bodies: Psychoanalyzing the White Terror*, trans. Erica Carter and Chris Turner. Minneapolis: University of Minnesota Press, 1989.

THOMPSON, HUNTER. *Hell's Angels*. New York: Ballantine Books, 1966.

THOMPSON, KEITH. 'What Men Really Want: An Interview with Robert Bly'. In Franklin Abbott, ed., *New Men, New Minds*. Freedom, CA: The Crossing Press, 1987.

TOSCHES, NICK. Foreword to Dalton, *Mojo Rising.*

——— 'The Sea's Endless, Awful Rhythm'. In Marcus, ed., *Stranded.*

TURNER, GIL. 'Bob Dylan – A New Voice Singing New Songs'. In Thomson and Gutman, eds, *The Dylan Companion.*

VAGUE, TOM. *Televisionairies: The Red Army Faction Story, 1963 – 1993*. Edinburgh: AK Press, 1994.

VANEIGEM, RAOUL. *The Revolution of Everyday Life*. London: Rebel Press, 1983.

VENTURA, MICHAEL. *Shadow Dancing in the U.S.A.* New York: St. Martin's Press, 1985.

VIRILIO, PAUL. *The Aesthetics of Disappearance*. New York: Semiotexte, 1991.

WILLIS, ELLEN. *Beginning to See the Light: Pieces of a Decade*. New York: Alfred A. Knopf, 1981.

WOLF, NAOMI. *The Beauty Myth*. New York: Anchor Books, 1992.

WOLFE, TOM. *The Electric Kool-Aid Acid Test*. New York: Bantam, 1981.

index

11. 7.96 ✓ roommis 15.25 (12.76) 65262